Which One Will You Feed?

Child Crime in Canada

Mike Kostelny, Ph.D.

Student Manual

Ordering Information:

For orders and inquiries, please contact:
1-888-404-1388
www.goldtouchpress.com
book.orders@goldtouchpress.com

Printed in the United States of America

A Dedicatory Prayer

O Lord, our God! I dedicate this work to the memory of a lost child inside the soul of this troubled youth who at 15 years of age tried his very best to kill me on Wednesday 26th September 2018 at 3:33 a.m. (in the wee hours before my 65th Birthday).

"Lost" was the sense of any individual accountability, the sense of any personal responsibility, any social morality, or even the genuine sense of good-feeling or caring between members of the human family! All that remains to date is the cold unyielding lack of any meaningful remorse or culpability or sense of shame for one's horrific actions, for what was done to me, without rhyme, without reason, but without doubt done with a hell-bent intent to end my life as quickly as possible.

Yes, there was malice in the maniacal manner in which this youth sought to take my life, wholly unprovoked; but deeper still is the faint cry, the hollow echo of a wounded child crying to be heard; a child suppressed, oppressed, neglected by a social network whose loving care towards him has long since grown stone-cold, callused, and unfeeling. Little wonder that there is no remorse, no psychological regret, no meaningful moral feeling left in the empty shell of this child. One who has lost his way, his mind, his soul, his inner well-being, his sense of what's right, what's wrong, his normal innate sense of what's the best thing to do. All is lost! What remains is painfully obvious to all rational beings to see: The sad product of a (once) little boy still lost and unloved but left to wallow in his own mire. A child not in control of himself, a prodigal son who still needs to 'come unto himself'. [Luke 15:17]

O Lord, our God, our Dear Heavenly Father: All that remains is Thy Miracle of Forgiveness! That this turbulent youth may find Thy Peace and come to know Thee, our Creator, our God, the God of this Universe! That this lost Youth may find the 'Path Home' again, from 'The Human Jungle' that has refused to love him, back to 'That Place of Perfect Rest', where Thou dwells.

O Merciful God, forgive this boy, my assailant, solely on the grounds that he knew not what he did. [Luke 23:34]

In the Name of Jesus, who loves all Mankind perfectly, even this youth, one of his lost sheep, I pray. Amen.

Dedicatory Theme

"A Thing Called *Character*!"

You are the fellow that has to decide
Whether you'll do it or toss it aside.
You are the fellow who makes up your mind
Whether you'll lead or will linger behind
Whether you'll try for the goal that's afar
Or just be contented to stay where you are.
Take it or leave it. Here's something to do!
Just think it over — It's all up to you!

Anon

****

William Shakespeare's Insight:

Now, as fond fathers,
Having bound up the threat'ning twigs of birch,
Only to stick it in their children's sight
For terror, not to use, in time the rod
Becomes more mocked than feared; so our decrees,
Dead to infliction, to themselves are dead,
And Liberty plucks Justice by the nose;
The baby beats the nurse, and quite athwart
Goes all decorum.

Measure for Measure (I, iii, 24-32)

Acknowledgements

Above all, as a Christian believer, I am truly thankful to my Heavenly Father for sparing my life on that fateful night of twenty-two knife stab wounds.

As the Police in charge of the "aggravated assault" investigation openly proclaimed to me the day following my attack: I had more than one angel (perhaps a Battalion of Angels) protecting me from harm's way, from the ultimate fate of being killed. They used such language as: Grace of God. And you're alive by a miracle.

I am so grateful to the Edmonton Police Service (EPS) for all their many efforts on that fateful night: (Eight police cars travelling at speeds unheard of in order to improve my chance of survival).

Of course, I am grateful to ETS (Edmonton Transit Service) Control Centre for radioing in a Police and Ambulance Emergency to my rescue as they watched *live* as my assailant knifed me twenty-two times.

I am so grateful to the Edmonton Ambulance Service who rushed me to the University of Alberta Trauma Unit as fast as possible with a Police escort at break-neck speed. I do know that the wheels were not always touching the ground, especially as we would hit a small dip or bump in the road, we would go sailing for quite a way. It seemed to me so surreal! But I thank Heaven for these Angels of Mercy.

I am also very thankful to the University of Alberta Hospital Trauma Staff and Unit who did their very best with the most advanced technology to put 'Humpty-Dumpty' back together again. Although I joked that Julius Caesar would have survived had he been rushed to this self-same Unit, I realize full-well that every member of that team worked professionally and quickly to ensure my best chance of survival.

I am grateful to the many nurses and medical assistants, doctors, and physicians, who all worked tirelessly all hours of the day or night to ensure that my many bandages and wounds were all properly tended to, with the best medical supplies available (whether in Edmonton or wherever I had to travel).

Of course, I am very grateful to all the prayers and well-wishes of my mother, Lillian, my family and friends; church members, and co-workers; City personnel as well as even total strangers who took the time to let me know that they are praying for me for a speedy and safe recovery.

And last but not least I am grateful to my fiancée, Victoria, who was (and is!) so supportive of me even though she still lives on the other side of the planet, in East Ukraine (still under daily attacks from the Russian Regime since March 2014). When she heard of my assault, she told me that the little hairs at the back of her neck *all* stood up! I knew exactly what she meant. So hard to believe that such madness can occur in a Peace-loving Country like Canada, she would exclaim! And somehow, I think I know exactly how incredible such an occurrence must seem to all those unfamiliar with Child Crime in Canada.

A Note of Explanation

This particular work is not only an Exposé on Child Crime in Canada but also purports to present a possible way to assist in Prison Reform. The intent not only is to provide an alternative to the mere social theory of Prison Reform, but to demonstrate (through storytelling) true character conversions; to show, in other words, that it is possible for a leopard to lose its spots; that it is possible for a 'cruel Caligula'-type personality to become a 'compassionate Casper' persona! It's not fairy-tale fantasy, but real-life everyday occurrences.

1.   In this work, I have a created a layout in the traditional sense of a V (five) Act Play: consisting of Acts I, II, III, IV & V! Each Act has at least two or three 'Scenes': Scene i; Scene ii; Scene iii; and so on. Under each 'Scene' there are capital letters and/or numerical chapter headings: (For instance, Act I, Scene i: 1,2,3,4...; or: Act II, Scene ii: A: 1,2, 3, ...).

The point in adopting this rather novel approach to storytelling is to imply that this story (which I believe needs to be told!) is *live* like a live theatre production that involves a Five-Act Play.

2.   All scriptural citations are from the Authorized KJV (King James Version) of the Bible.

3.   All quotes cited in this work are taken from the Author's *Great Quotes* series (Volume I and Volume II), unless otherwise stated. Please check out these quotes in the Author's books aforestated, if interested. At the time of this writing, these (two volumes of) Quote Books are in the process of being rewritten; hence, their page numbering is not available.

But if the reader so desires, he may purchase these Quote Books (from the publisher at: Y Mountain Press, at: book@byu.edu, Attn: Kent Minson) and via the "Author Indexing" can discover the quotes so desired. Or, as many publishers who refuse to publish quote books have told me: These quotes can typically be found via the internet, and/or Google search. (Happy hunting!)

4.   Because I am a University Professor (*Emeritus*) and have provided this book as a 'workbook' to help the youth of our planet to better understand the problem of youth (or 'child') crime in Canada and elsewhere, I hereby present the following **DISCLAIMER**:

N.B. (*Nota Bene*)
"*All* tunes/songs/video clips/links/quotes/etc., are herein provided to assist in Group Therapy Sessions, or privately, for individual study (to assist in learning) and for educational purposes *only*."

5.   The seventeen quotes (in quote marks) under "Food For Thought" classified as: "Rules for Raising Delinquent Children" were borrowed from a 1960s FBI citation (and are considered in the public domain).

6.   The other quotes noted as "Meditations" in "Rules for Repentance", and in "Rules for Raising a Happy Home" are taken from anonymous (unknown) sources and are deemed to be in the public domain.

7.   The seventeen points of: "How to Obtain Revelation [From On High]" are taken from various authors as indicated.

8.   The seventeen "Uplifting Insights" are taken from *Desiderata* (Latin for 'Things Desired'), a poem compiled by Max Ehrmann (in 1927) but currently in the public domain (since 2009, according to *Wikipeida*).

9.   All photos were taken by the Author and all "drawings" are Used By Permission of the Artist, Jaye Benoit (who has sold the right of the copyright to the Author).

10.   All citations from William Shakespeare's works are deemed to be in the public domain.

11.   All quotes from Adolf Hitler (unless otherwise indicated) are from his own book, *Mein Kampf* (written in 1923, but published in 1929). In 2016, the copyright of *Mein Kampf*

expired (according to *Wikipedia*) and is therefore in the public domain. [This work follows the 1943 Ralph Manheím translation, which is in the public domain.]

12.   To lessen the possibilities of litigation, I have altered (substituted) the actual true names of persons involved (where indicated) by stating the following: [FAKE Name], as in the 10E POV Section for instance.

13.   With respect to all references (opinions, added comments, etc.) made towards 'The Child' assailant (who tried to kill me), a brief citation from the actual Court Documents in his final Trial (dated 26 April 2019) will be made to (legally) substantiate that what the Author is stating is in fact accurate and correct.

The legal CDs (Court Documents) or portions thereof from which these brief notations are made will remain in the Author's custody and are not available to be disclosed (except as very brief citations in this book) to the General Public at large (as required by Canadian Child Crime Laws). The name 'B.B.' [FAKE name] will be inserted in all citations in this book that refer to the Assailant (in order to protect his identity).

The CDs referenced will involve: **CD I** (The Youth PreSentence Report of the Assailant; [aka: YPR]); **CD II** (Miscellaneous references to include: The list of the Assailant's current and prior charges [aka, the Author's Victim Impact Statement [VIS], Legal Commentary on the Youth PreSentence Report [LCYPR], The Peace Officer's Report [POR], and a legal document forbidding communication or contact between the Assailant and the Author [No Contact Document, or NCD]); **CD III** (The Psychiatric Report of the Assailant [PRA]); and **CD IV** (The Educational History of the Assailant [EHA]).

Contents

Foreword

This book is not a story about racism. This is not a story of a black (or, dark coloured) skin people versus white (or, light-coloured) skin people. Instead, this account is the age-old story as clear as night versus day, of the Powers of Darkness versus the Powers of Light! Of the Evil Forces versus those of The Good; of negative character traits versus those that are positive.

This story is not selective: it is indeed everyone's story. The story that bears telling and re-telling throughout the Epochs of Time. The story of you and me, of death and life. It is eternal. It is a never-ending struggle of hate overcome by love, as simple and plain as that children's tale: *How the Sun won the contest with the Wind.* Recall that simple challenge?

The Wind told the Sun that it could force an old man wearing a heavy winter coat to take it off, simply by blowing the coat off the man through a mighty gale! But the more the wind blew, the tighter the elderly man wrapped his protective coat around himself. Then, when it was the Sun's turn: The Sun simply used gentle kindness and extreme warmth until gradually the traveller voluntarily took his heavy coat off, which he would not do despite the unfeeling ferocity of the (wicked) Wind.

Preface

If

If you can keep your head when all about you
   Are losing theirs and blaming it on you,
If you can trust yourself when all men doubt you,
   But make allowance for their doubting too;
If you can wait and not be tired by waiting,
   Or being lied about, don't deal in lies,
Or being hated, don't give way to hating,
   And yet don't look too good, nor talk too wise:

If you can dream—and not make dreams your master;
   If you can think—and not make thoughts your aim;
If you can meet with Triumph and Disaster
   And treat those two impostors just the same;
If you can bear to hear the truth you've spoken
   Twisted by knaves to make a trap for fools,
Or watch the things you gave your life to, broken,
   And stoop and build 'em up with worn-out tools:

If you can make one heap of all your winnings
   And risk it on one turn of pitch-and-toss,
And lose, and start again at your beginnings
   And never breathe a word about your loss;
If you can force your heart and nerve and sinew
   To serve your turn long after they are gone,
And so hold on when there is nothing in you
   Except the Will which says to them: 'Hold on!'

If you can talk with crowds and keep your virtue,
   Or walk with Kings—nor lose the common touch,
If neither foes nor loving friends can hurt you,
   If all men count with you, but none too much;
If you can fill the unforgiving minute
   With sixty seconds' worth of distance run,
Yours is the Earth and everything that's in it,
   And—which is more—you'll be a Man, my son!

Rudyard Kipling (1865-1936)

[Rudyard Kipling wrote this poem "IF" in 1910; hence, "IF" is in the public domain (See *Wikipedia*, "IF").]

Which One Will You Feed?

All drawings by Jaye Benoit
(Used by Permission)

Introduction to Section One

As can be ascertained by a quick review of this particular volume, the attempt has been made to attract a young audience, or readership of young, yet inquisitive minds, the budding generation intent on solving problems long outstanding; but issues that simply will not go away. How ironic that a bus driver should write a proposal to the Youth of this World: to provide a social platform for discussion, and (as is the hope) to eventually discuss the pathway to a brighter future. For in simple terms, the future of this rising generation is only as bright as their faith. For with faith in God, all things are possible.

Such is the simple straightforward thrust of this work, the beginning of something wonderful, perhaps, the genesis of a brave New World, one in which we (as a Society) may dare to think for ourselves (even to dare to think outside the box), to dare to solve the insolvable: (an) "Impossible Dream".

In this work, I have introduced music videos (as a Theme), to set the mood (as it were) for the seventeen POVs (Points of View). I have also set aside blank spaces (as in a work-book Edition) for indications where remarks may be made to the preceding section, comments by the reader as to where they stand, as a group (or individual) therapy exercise. When this book is being used as a Group Therapy manual, the participant(s) may choose to respond to each individual section with whatever comments, thoughts, or impressions may come to mind. In a sense, this work is similar to the earlier psychological self-analysis used in interpreting ink blots on a sheet of paper (or other such psychological stimulants).

As to the seventeen negative and seventeen positive character traits, these specific qualities were not chosen at random but as part of a Linguistic Philosophy of word meanings (Semantics). More historically, they originally pertain to what used to be called: Faculty Psychology (back in the day of Immanuel Kant, and even later in the day of William James, two great philosophers).

Today, I have over-hauled this once antiquated form of thinking with a more detailed and self-introspective psychological analysis. I have termed it: Molecular Behavioural Psychology.

Let me explain what I mean: Let us say that a certain youth has a problem with unbridled anger: a real anger management issue (that is out of control). He tends to fly off the handle with the slightest provocation, to become not merely hostile, but often quite violent over seemingly minor or inconsequential matters. He demands that everything go his way (or the highway) regardless of the feelings, concerns, or rights of others. (Ever meet such a person? I bet you have! It's an all-too-common occurrence, isn't it?)

In this rather typical case of a 'rebel without a cause', I have formulated approximately thirty sub-categories (thirty-one so far, to be exact) all interconnected (or intertwined, as it were) with the state of mind commonly referred to: as that of a 'mad hatter': The patient who wishes to overcome, to control, and to manage his propensity to anger (as a temper tantrum).

This individual would ask himself specifically (for each of these thirty-one sub-categories) whether he thinks this or that subcategory applies to his 'anger management' issue. Spaces are provided for the participant to state examples or comments related to the major (General) Theme of: 'Anger' (or other *molecular behavioural* component to his psyche).

It has been said today: that 'Your emotions can kill you!' One of the most common negative emotions is: Anger. The heart, blood vessels, blood circulation, internal organs, are all negatively impacted by continual feelings of anger exemplified in rage, and other stressed-out factors of the human condition. In this work, Analytical Cognitive Philosophy and (Molecular) Behavioral Psychology have come together to form an in-depth introspective form of group (and/or self) therapy.

As the participant goes through these constructive steps of internal recognition, then the pathway is presented for that person seeking to overcome a particular negative trait, to proceed to develop positive character traits through a process simply called: *conversion*. For as is commonly understood in human psychology: the best way to overcome a negative trait is to replace it with a positive one. Bad habits when erased can create a vacuum that if not converted (into better or good habits) can develop into even worse habits. Therefore, the best way to permanently overcome a bad habit is to infuse or replace it with a good habit. Simple truth. Simple psychology.

In the *AA*'s (*Alcoholics Anonymous*) handbook, there are typically twelve steps to spiritual growth (necessary to overcome the physical addiction to alcohol, and other drugs). Even to develop a spiritual rapport with Higher Powers, there are (at least) Twelve Steps (see, for instance: *The Twelve Steps: A Spiritual Journey*, which is 'a working guide for healing' put out in 1988 by RPI Publishing Inc.). So, likewise (albeit in a much more detailed manner) there are numerous steps to overcoming the negative self (as outlined in this book) to develop a more positive, even a spiritual human being, a truly moral person, upright in every way humanly possible!

The point of the blank spaces in this book is to allow the participant to reflect and to think about his own personal character make-up. Not all negative traits would refer to the one individual, nor all the positive traits, nor would all the sub-categories or each major character trait. But there should be enough of an array of choices, and dispositions, that would cover many, if not most, of the varying facets of human psychology

In a future (2nd or 3rd) Edition of this work, the many sub-categories will be detailed with explanations (just as the major categories are for this fledging First Edition). The response from the public at large (through the e-book Edition of this work) may suffice to spearhead, or project a general understanding into (the concept of) what the 'molecular' ('major') category is comprised of.

Similar to the physical 'molecule' (which is composed of: electrons, protons, neutrons, photons, sub-atomic particles, quarks, and so on), so the psychological components of the *major* categories of a character (or personality) trait is comprised of sub-categories. In this new 'scientific' analysis of human psychology, a first step for resolving minor personality disorders, and errant behaviour (via Semantics) can be finally visualized.

In subsequent years of practicum and experimentation, new developments will likely be achieved. But as they say: "The march of a thousand miles begins with the first step!".

As this new form of revolutionizing human behaviour takes hold on society, possible reformation and even conversion can be a dream come true.

 Youth Feedback:
____

____

____

DISCLAIMER: N.B. (*Nota Bene*)
All tunes/songs/video clips/links/quotes/etc. are herein provided to assist in Group Therapy Sessions, or privately, for individual study (to assist in learning) and for educational purposes *only*.

[#1: U-Tube Reference]
Johnny Cash - The Ballad of Ira Hayes
https://www.youtube.com/watch?v=oEwSwQtSmDQ

The Ballad of Ira Hayes

Then Ira started drinking hard
Jail was often his home
They let him raise the flag and lower it
Like you'd throw a dog a bone
He died drunk early one morning
Alone in the land he fought to save
Two inches of water and a lonely ditch
Was a grave for Ira Hayes

Johnny Cash

Section One:
The Problem Stated

ACT I:
Prologue

"Before God and the bus driver we are all equal."
German Proverb

The Background Story:
The Aggravated Assault on My Life

Preamble

For legal reasons, I am not permitted to release the name of the fifteen-year-old Métis boy who tried to kill me, until he is dead (i.e., for the remainder of his life), according to Canadian Child Crime laws. Neither the public at large, nor my own family members, nor my fellow workers (with ETS, Edmonton Transit Service) are permitted to know of this troubled boy's identity even though this certain knowledge could potentially prevent a future 'assault' from re-occurring. Again, as I say, this policy is the law with respect to Child Crime in Canada.

The name I will attribute to my child assailant is therefore a fictitious name; but one that sends a strong message, in effect, a warning, a wake-up call not only to this 'child wanna-be killer', but to the Justice System in this Country to declare boldly a title appropriate for this child's own behaviour! [As based upon and mediated not only by the in-depth Psychiatric Report of his mental health, but also as clearly reflected by his extensive and highly disturbing criminal record to date!]. This deeply troubling criminal record will be 100% expunged upon the child's 18th birthday, whereby he is no longer legally 'a child', but becomes 'an adult' (for legal purposes) in Canada.

To wit, the name wherewith this 'child' shall be known within the annuals or records of this book is: "Billy Bundy" (or "B.B.", for short). Now there is a calculated logic to this appellation, this 'name tag' to my assailant: "Billy" can refer to "Billy Jack", a hero among the Native peoples, according to modern Folklore, as there are at least five (5) movies made in the *Billy Jack* Series (as I recall): he is the underdog for the down and out, the down-trodden and the oppressed, a sort of hero for lost causes, a David who would fight the Goliaths of this world.

The flip side of the title 'Billy Jack' is the dark or negative connotation, such as: 'Billy the Kid', a psychopathic killer of the Wild West who reportedly killed one man on average for every year of his life by the time he turned twenty-one years old (although only eight confirmed kills are officially recorded). But this legend is not just folklore: Billy the kid, was no *'kid'* in the sense of a harmless 'child' (just as the 'child' who tried to kill me was no harmless *'kid'*). Billy the Kid was a cold-blooded murderer. Oh, but in the days of the wild, wild West (when Billy the Kid lived) it was a rather grey area, to be called a 'murderer', as many people lived by the Law of the Wild West, by their gun, or six-shooter. For he who drew last, lost. And he who drew first, and fired the deadly shot was styled a type of 'hero', a top gun, a gunslinger in the sense of a famous outlaw, or gangster of the West.

Nor is the newly attributed surname, 'Bundy', to be taken too far: For 'Bundy' can refer to: Ted Bundy, the world-renown classic psychopath in American criminal history; or 'Bundy' can refer to: 'Al Bundy', the comic hero in the TV soap opera series, *Love and Marriage*. The reason my (child) assailant cannot in good faith be attributed to a Ted Bundy, is that he lacks the intelligence, ironically. Ted Bundy was a lady charmer with an above-average IQ (Intelligence Quotient): He had completed a degree in Psychology and was on his way to completing a Law Degree in Utah when he was arrested for the murder of four young females; one of the last victims: a twelve-year old girl. Later, thirty-two women were confirmed or, 'attributed', to his list of murders (with many more unsubstantiated at the time of his death).

Billy Bundy, (or "BB", as I will typically call him) has an IQ of 60 (well below average). Unlike 'Al Bundy' (the comical spoof of the typical hen-pecked husband), BB has virtually no sense of humour.

Only days before attempting to kill me, BB apparently had assaulted his own mother (as recorded in the Court Documents of his Trial 26th April 2019, as follows: On or about September 22 [2018], "B.B." assaulted "Roda" [FAKE Name, BB's mother] ... No complaint was filed as Roda [FAKE name] did not want to file a complaint". CD II, LCYPR, p. 6.); and he had badly bruised and beaten his own grandfather, a man partially disabled, in a walker. (Also, to cite Court Document III: "[BB's] grandfather reported [BB] has threatened to kill him on multiple occasions... He stated at times this has escalated to the point where he fears for his life. His grandfather also reported [BB] has, in the past, carried knives, sharpened screwdrivers, and a claw hammer. As a result, his grandfather secures all knives in the home, but [BB] continues to be found with weapons in his possession", p. 13. Furthermore, "The ACFS Child Intervention Services Review indicates that on September 22, 2018, [BB's] grandfather called ACFS requesting [BB] be removed from the home because he was 'psychotic'. This document also indicates that two days later [24 September 2018], [BB] assaulted his grandfather who feared his leg may have been broken" CDIII, p.9). All for no apparent reason.

Yes, a sad pathetic story, one unfortunately (I'm told by Medics, Nurses, Physicians, Psychologists, Police Officers, Law Enforcement Officers, Peace Officers, Parole Officers, The Crown Prosecutor, Lawyers, Judicial Assistants, etc.) is but the tip of the proverbial (child Crime) 'iceberg', not an anomaly, not an exception; but all too common, the run of the mill (as it were).

I'm reminded of Elvis Presley's tragic ballad: "In the Ghetto!".

But I'm ahead of the story....

Let's start from the beginning:

The Background (To the Events of 26 September 2018, the Day of the Assault)

Prior to going to work (to drive the Public Transit bus for ETS, Edmonton Transit Service) on that fateful day 26th September 2018, to arrive at Mitchell Garage for 20:00 hours to begin my shift (ending at 04:00 hours), I had determined to empty out my storage space at Sentinel Storage, as the rental promo was about to expire that weekend. I had to transport several full carloads of goods (temporarily) from storage into my two-bedroom apartment (over the past few days).

There was very little time to rest (or to sleep), but somehow, skipping all my meals, and not taking any long breaks, I was able to do it: just in time to begin my night shift for 20:00 hours. I reasoned that I could 'rest' while driving the bus as it was a late-night shift, and the ETS patron ridership was typically rather light.

After all, it was a Tuesday night (not a weekend, or a 'Freaky Friday', nor a 'Manic Monday").

What could possibly go wrong, or happen, to spoil my plans to 'take it easy tonight'?!

But from the get-go, I seemed to have unexpected issues with bus unit number 4764, the bus in which I was to later almost lose my life. The seat belt buckle took forever to release, due to a defective release button, as I concluded. But to ask ETS Control for a change-over bus for a defective release button was (then) out of the question. I had attempted to do so before, and the usual routine is, as follows:

(Control would ask the Operator): "When you snap the seat belt buckle into the sheath, does it stay in place?" I would answer: "Yes!" (but then would quickly add: "But it's a real pain to quickly release the seat belt!")! Then Control would repeat the exact same question: "When you snap the seat belt buckle into the sheath, does it stay in place?" According to Control, that was all that was necessary: That the seat belt does not come apart, or dislodge, while one is driving. But what remained unanswered was my follow-up query: "What would happen were I to be attacked and the seat belt release button would refuse to release my seat belt?" The answer (unanswered by Control) became obvious to me: I would be a 'dead duck'!

Yet again, I am ahead of myself. Allow me to state the facts of this case as best as I can remember them! And how could I forget them (ever?) come to think of it! As my future forensic psychologist (also a Métis) would tell me: "It's necessary to let go of tragic events, so that your life can move forward!" Easy to say, no doubt.

But I find that the only way I can effectively accomplish that end is to practice my Christian beliefs: to learn to forgive even my enemies, and (to push the point even further!): to learn to love even my enemies! That would be to practice what we Christians love to preach: The Gospel of John, "The Gospel of Love" (as John the Beloved Apostle describes it).

Well, that eventful day, 26th September 2018, one day before my 65th birthday, proved most eventful, to put it mildly. I had spent the previous two days moving a lot of storage items (many carloads, in fact) from a nearby Sentinel Storage site, and did not allow myself sufficient R&R (Rest & Relaxation). Indeed, the very day of the aggravated assault, I was deeply sleep-deprived, and had moved about five carloads of possessions (to and fro) from the storage site to my apartment, prior to starting my eight-hour shift.

As it turned out, my apartment shortly became full of boxes from the storage site, so that there was hardly any room to walk about. But I was not overly concerned, as I had intended to move everything out of the suite the very next 'off-day' (from work). Little did I know that Fate would determine otherwise.

For it would be many months, into the next year, before I would recover from the events of this most fateful night:
The night of nightmares.

The Assault Proper

I began to prepare for my night shift after 7 p.m. as it was an 8-hour shift (as I kept reminding myself). I looked forward to being able to simply sit down in a comfortable seat after all that heavy lifting, and virtually non-stop 'moving activity' earlier in the day. This night shift would be a breeze. After which, I would take a nice hot bath (to relax my overly exerted muscles) and take a much-deserved sleep, a deep sleep, no doubt.

But from square one, there would be problems. To begin with, (as referred to earlier), the seat belt on bus unit #4764 was defective. No doubt about it. [The Day-Operator working the earlier shift for that day on the same bus shared the same issue with me, when I met with him several months later: he recalled that bus specifically because of the unusual nature of the seat belt release button: it was very difficult to remove quickly and/or easily]. Even earlier in that fateful shift on that fateful night, I recalled how difficult it was to release that release button to rush to the washroom for a short layover break.

But with an earlier discussion with an ETS Inspector only a few weeks prior to my assault, I was told point-blank that there would be a one-to-three-day suspension (loss of pay) if an Operator were found (or, 'discovered') without his seat belt securely fastened around his waist at all times he is in the Driver's seat, even if the bus is fully secured (parked) and not in operation. Hence, to be obedient to the wishes of upper ETS management (although not required by Alberta Highway Traffic Laws), I dutifully complied and kept the seat belt locked into place, even though I fully realized it would be rather difficult to release in an emergency, or in a life-threatening situation.

This new seat belt policy came into effect (February 2018) under a newly recruited Deputy Manager to ETS who insisted that all bus drivers follow this policy on threat of suspension. Yet this new seat belt policy in hindsight almost became my death sentence. For little did I know but that I would be fighting for my very life over a defective seat belt release button in only a few short hours.

The night shift went through without a hitch, although I noted that it was rather unusually busy (almost like a weekend) until almost midnight. Then things slowed down, which allowed me to finally rest (somewhat) before this shift would finally play out (be over), like the last sands in an hourglass, a moment I looked forward to with more than the usual delight. There was a humorous saying among Operators: (That) you would work your entire shift simply for the good feeling you would (expect to) experience once your shift ended. For 'How sweet it is!' (or can be) at times. No truer words were ever spoken for this night in question. I wanted to sleep, oh so badly.

On my last trip (as a route #8 heading to Mill Woods Transit Centre, my final destination) departing from Downtown, I picked up one female East Indian patron, and en route to Bonnie Doon for 03:09 hours I picked up a male East Indian patron: these two passengers became my only two patrons at that time. Then turning from Argyll Road WB to go SB onto 86 street, I crossed the Railroad Tracks (at 61 Avenue/Wagner Road). While I began to pick up speed (to the 50 Kph speed limit), a young boy running East to West (like a frightened deer from the neighbouring park) cut directly in front of my bus.

He was not at a designated bus stop, so his abrupt jumping in front of the bus (forcing me to stop!) was highly suspicious. I almost drove over him, but he walked back a few steps to avoid the bus driving on top of him. Once he saw that he had my attention, he began lifting both windshield wipers with both his hands and letting them drop to the windshield noisily.

I had no intention to open my front doors to such a basket case. I already judged him to be either high on drugs, or an inmate from a mental asylum?! My gut instinct was not to allow him on the bus but to press the red button to alert Control that Police assistance was required. But I had two bus patrons who wondered why I was not opening my doors to let on yet another bus patron. Also, I knew that I was the last bus of the night going in this direction. And then again, the intruder was a small, short Métis youth who appeared harmless, who had no discernible weapon, and whose only 'crime' seemed to be erratic behaviour. As I was the last bus of the night, perhaps that would explain the fact that this youth was running like a scared rabbit trying to flag down my bus? Hmm? But something deep inside my gut told me otherwise: I would have to watch this one closely.

I kept the front doors to the bus closed as the youth 'bounced' towards them and tried to pry them open with his hands. As the bus patrons reminded me that this kid wanted to get on the bus, I relented and let him on, and prepared for the worse. But he bounced onto the bus (as he was bouncing in front of the bus) as if he were a big rubber ball. I wondered at his bizarre behaviour, keeping an eye open to see if he had some hidden weapon. But he had no coat or jacket on and did not appear to have anything in his hands.

The fare was never discussed, nor was it an issue at all. [I state this fact because later it came to my attention that some people at my workplace (even in the Training Division of ETS) apparently concluded that this ensuing issue concerned fare evasion. Little did they know how utterly ridiculous that claim actually was. I had never bothered with fare evasion since I was 'talked to' by an ETS Inspector in 1977 (when I first joined ETS) and told not to bother patrons about fares: so, I dutifully never did. Ever since that formal reprimand.]

As soon as the youth boarded the bus, he began to demand (while he began to hyperventilate) that the bus leave immediately. Oddly enough, he kept looking backwards towards the direction from whence he came, as if he suspected he was being followed. [Later, much later, I learned that this feeling of being followed was a typical standard symptom of persons suffering from Borderline Personality Disorder, a branch of *psychopathic* behaviour.] I asked him whether he required Police assistance (due to his strange behaviour of always looking over his shoulder and down the dark pathway from whence he came) but he loudly stated (in a sharp confrontational tone): "NO! just drive this bus! Isn't that what you're supposed to do, as a bus driver? You are supposed to drive this bus!"

At this point, I once again was about to press the red button to call for Security but somehow I needed more evidence?! Evidence of what? I didn't know? But I began to ask routine questions of B.B.: "Where was he going? Was he sure that he was on the right bus? Did he know that this is the last bus of the night and that I am not driving back this way? Why was he in such a hurry to go somewhere tonight?" and: "Did he require help in any way?"

But he did not reply to these additional queries. Indeed, all these questions seemed to infuriate BB even more. So much so, that he began to hyperventilate (again), a fact that caused the female patron on the bus to offer BB some water to drink, but he refused to accept any water (at that time).

I slowly proceeded with the bus (deliberately driving slower than usual) towards Mill Gate Transit Centre (passing Ferrier Garage, which I knew would be open for help in an emergency). As I was a couple of minutes early at my timing point in Mill Gate TC, I parked the bus and took yet another closer look at this strange kid: Why was he so hyper? And what was he so afraid of? At this point in time, the female bus patron again offered BB a drink of water. To everyone's amazement, he said: "Yes!" and grabbed the bottle of water from her hand without even saying: "Thank-you!".

I noted his self-serving behaviour, and again was tempted to call Control. I felt a distinct urge to do so, but thought that as this was my last trip and as this kid insisted that he knew where he was going, what complaint could I state to Control: That I had a kid that bounced up and down like a rubber ball? Perhaps? But nothing seemed dangerous or life-threatening at this point. A bit unusual behaviour admittedly, but I've had so many instances of unusual behaviour (in my many years, even decades as a bus driver) that ended up as totally harmless. Yet something told me that this kid was neither: neither harmless, nor simply unusual: he had to be watched very carefully.

Once BB accepted the bottle of water, he tore off the cap, and standing up, put his head backwards so as to swallow the entire bottle in one long gulp?! Again, unusual behaviour?! But at least there was some sort of cooperation between BB and the only two remaining bus patrons of the night.

The next stop was at Lakewood Transit Centre for 03:23 hours: I was a minute or so early, and so I asked BB once again if he required any assistance, if he knew where he was going, if he understood that the next stop would be Mill Woods Transit Centre; and I would then be *Not In Service*; to return to the Bus Barns; that there would be no more bus service for the night.

But BB insisted that everything was okay, that he simply wanted the bus to keep on rolling, that I should do the job I was paid to do, to drive the bus to where he wanted to go. I began to sense that BB was ignoring the bottom line, the gist of what I had just stated, that he was lost inside his own private world, that he was going to pull a fast-one on me, and likely state that he wanted to go somewhere else once we arrived at Mill Woods Transit Centre.

But what could I do differently? I had not enough evidence (I thought) to push the red button to call Control, as BB kept insisting that he was on the right bus, that he knew where he was going, and that all he wanted me to do was to stop asking him silly questions, and to simply drive the bus to Mill Woods Transit Centre. So, I reluctantly complied. After all, he appeared to know where he was going, despite the fact that he appeared stone-faced, his eyes looked glazed over, and I distinctly sensed that he was in some sort of a trance.

So, finally, a few minutes later, the bus arrived at Mill Woods Transit Centre for 03:30 hours. Both East Indian bus patrons stepped off the bus through the rear door, wishing me a 'Good Night', as they glanced at BB who appeared even more agitated than before. Once the bus was empty with only BB and myself on board, I reminded BB that this bus was *Not In Service*; and that it was time for me to head back to the Garage.

I asked him if someone was supposed to meet him here, because now we are at the destination, I told him we would arrive at, the destination that he insinuated he wanted to go to, the end of the line. BB looked furtively around him as if to see if someone was here to meet him. [But later in hindsight I realized that BB was simply scouting the area to ensure that he was actually alone with me.] I repeated myself: that I had to leave the Terminal at this point to go to the Garage as this bus was now *Not In Service*.

Then BB surprised me as he asked me (in a small childlike voice): "Does this bus go Downtown?". I told him, that I did not, but that there would be additional bus service here in an hour or two, for the early morning service of the new day. He could wait in the bus shelter for the next Downtown bus if he liked.

BB then approached me and told me that he had to go to his Grandfather's place, that his Grandfather lived downtown. I asked for the address, but he did not know it. He said that his cell phone didn't work but that he knew his Grandfather's phone number. He began to recite it to me: "--780...". I interrupted him and said not to worry. I would contact ETS Control and they would send someone to give him a courtesy ride home to his Grandfather's house.

I then began to call ETS Control and was surprised to find someone live on the phone almost instantly, without delay. I relayed my situation, that I was now *Not In Service* and that I had a youth, a minor, on my bus who appeared to be lost and disoriented, but who wanted to go to his Grandfather's home 'Downtown.' Control said that the nearest Party (Peace Officer's car) was in the University Area but that they would head down that way to pick him up in about fifteen to twenty minutes.

Control asked me for his age. I asked BB his age: He said that he was twelve years old. I then knew that something was highly unusual: he appeared to be about fourteen or fifteen at the youngest. [But why would BB lie about his age?!] I told ETS Control that he claimed to be twelve years old, but that in my estimate, he appeared to be fifteen. We ended the conversation; and upon hanging up the phone, I turned to face BB.

BB appeared even more agitated, as if he were beginning to hyperventilate again. I asked him what did he wish to do. He said that he wished to remain on the bus; and that I should drive him home to his Grandfather's. I reminded BB that the public Transit buses were not private taxi cabs, that we did not drive people to their private homes. If he would wait here for only fifteen or twenty minutes, he would meet with the ETS Security Officers ("Peace Officers") who would gladly drive him to his home, where his Grandfather lived.

BB then became angry, and loudly demanded that I should drive him home, and that I should drive him home right now. I then saw the true face of this troubled youth: not someone simply looking for a free ride, but instead someone who demanded to have his own way no matter how unreasonable it might be. I assumed that he must be tired and frustrated, as a lost and confused 'child.' So (feeling partly empathetic to his predicament), I politely said to him that even though it is somewhat unusual, I will see whether Control would give me permission to drive him to his home, his grandfather's place.

Of course, I knew that Control would likely not even consider the request (as it was against policy), but I was also 'buying time' to let Control know that I had a situation here on my hands, with an erratic youth who demanded to be driven home by an ETS bus. I expected that perhaps Control would expedite an ETS Inspector, or a Police car to my location, as a precaution as (I was told) the nearest Peace Officer was likely twenty minutes away).

No sooner had I begun to call Control (the second time) to relay the situation of this youth on my bus, when I felt the strongest premonition to turn around, to see what BB was up to, what was he doing? For he was awfully silent all of a sudden.

The "Aggravated Assault" On My Life!

No sooner had I turned my head to the right, to look into the face of BB, then I saw the flash of his knife blade as he rapidly stabbed it towards my eyeball.

Instinctively, I dropped the hand phone (and shouted that I was being attacked), as I ducked my head down (with my left elbow over my eyes) so that the flurry of his knife blade stabbed repeatedly into my left elbow and into my scalp (as if he wished to penetrate it). [Later, doctors would tell me that I was very fortunate that although the knife blade scrapped several parts of my scalp, it never penetrated the skull or cranium, which could have proved fatal.]

As BB paused for a few seconds, I lifted up my head (now dripping in blood) and saw that BB began to redirect his blade towards various parts of my face. I shouted to BB: "Why are you stabbing me? What's wrong with you?"!

[But BB would not answer throughout the remainder of this aggravated assault. He simply wanted to kill me as quickly as possible, to get it over with (as it were), perhaps so that I would stop asking him questions (or so it seemed to me)?! I had decided as well: *Not* to talk to him, not to break his trance, as I needed every available second to try to second-guess where the next knife stab would be directed. Later, I discovered that my 'suffering in silence' did actually unnerve BB: he could not figure out why I never cried out for my life? As his other victims perhaps did?! He no doubt felt as if he were stabbing into a dead corpse: no verbal response! no 'fun' in that at all!]

I pulled my head back banging it against the driver's side window, as I tried to avoid the full thrust and impact of each rapid knife stab.

I could clearly see BB's small perfectly black and seemingly lifeless pupils of his eyes, that appeared glazed over as if by some other being from the unseen world: he appeared to be in some sort of a trance. His facial muscles were extremely tight, taut, and tense. His eyebrows were raised very high as he peered with a hysterical look down upon me.

I thought I was looking into the eyes of perfect hate, the eyes of a living devil, but I had no time for further reflection:

The point of his knife blade tipped my forehead, my left eyebrow, my left ear, my left nostril, my left upper lip, my left part of the chin, my left part of the Adam's apple, as he began to work down from there. Each time the knife blade came to my face, I had quickly jerked back to strike my head against the driver's windowpane splashing it with my blood.

At the same time, the realization came over me in a flash: I had to get out of my driver's seat to face my attacker. To do so, I had to unfasten the seat belt that trapped me as a helpless victim! But the seat belt would not unfasten. [To aggravate matters even worse: the sheath holding the seat belt buckle was wholly defective: loose, wobbly, and flabby. It flapped about every which way, which made it nigh impossible to focus on unsnapping the seat belt, especially when one is being stabbed to death.]

[Later, I discovered a large black and blue bruise about an eight-inch square over my right hip where the seat belt buckle was. So desperate to be released, I had frantically tried to break free from it, but to no avail; hence, the dark superficial bruise.]

BB was now serious. No more messing around with my face and throat without success; now, he aimed directly for my heart. I turned my left shoulder to deflect a few of the initial stabs that were pointedly directed into the heart. But soon I found I could only wiggle a few times one way or the other, as I was trapped by a defective seat belt. So, of his many thrusts into various parts of my chest, as I pulled quickly away towards the driver's window (my only outlet), two of the several chest stabs did come within less than half a centimetre from my heart. [Later, I was told, that had the tip of BB's blade actually penetrated into the heart, I would likely not have survived the ambulance ride to the U of A Hospital Trauma unit.]

Then, BB decided to stab me in the stomach. I could tell from the fixed gaze of his beady eyes: he looked directly at my midsection and pulled his hand back for a quick deep stab. A silly smirk, a sickening grin came over his overwrought face, as he launched forward with all his might into my stomach. But I pulled my right hand (which was all this while trying to unfasten the seat belt buckle) to cover my stomach, just as BB plunged his knife smack into the middle of the back of that hand. (I had thereby protected the soft muscles of the stomach and the delicate internal organs from this unhinged youth.)

It was at this precise moment that I realized I was in a death-and-life struggle with an apparent maniac, a wild kid who appeared to be (I assumed) some sort of psychopath or severely mentally ill patient. I knew that I had to do something quickly or perish. [It was also at this precise moment that the Police Constables later told me (as they watched the assault video) that they were at the edge of their seats in anxious anticipation: waiting for that seat belt to be released! But it was not yet to be!].

I swung my right foot around as the kid was about to plunge into me yet another time; and kicked him squarely in the stomach so that he landed right outside the front door of the bus. He went sprawling onto the concrete sidewalk, dazed and stunned. I then quickly moved the bus handle (on the dash) to close the bus doors, but the rear door closed first, then the front door, which gave BB just enough time to squeeze through the front doors as they were closing in on him. Seeing that he appeared to be coming into the bus, I swung both doors open again.

This time, BB was rip-roaring mad. He took his blade and with his eyes on my groin, plunged it as hard and as far as he could into the genital area. But I shifted my waist just in the nick of time so that his blade missed (most of) the crotch area and stabbed high into the upper right thigh. I could see from BB's silly smirk on his face that he likely believed: To now finish me off would be as easy as to kill fish in a barrel. After all, he could see that I was not able to release the seat belt from around my waist. I was more than a captive audience: I was a sitting dead duck. He knew it! And I knew it! There was a sense for a split-second in which I realized that one of us would soon meet his Maker. And I didn't want it to be me!

As soon as BB pulled his knife blade out of my upper right thigh, hot blood spurted out like a water fountain down the inside of my pant leg as if someone had spilled a hot cup of coffee on it. [Later,

I was to learn, many weeks later, from an ultrasound scan, that the tip of his knife blade was less than one centimetre from the main artery in that leg. If it had penetrated into the main artery, I would not have lived to arrive at the U of A Trauma centre. Because of my many knife stabs (twenty-two all told, creating thirteen major wounds) there would not be any possible way that the surgeons could operate on me to patch up that open artery without jeopardizing the rest of my immune system].

The will to live, the sheer force of my desire to be free from this fate, this certain death, caused me to drop all focus on BB for the next few seconds; and to manipulate the seat belt release button, much like one would a combination lock: to move it this way to the left, then that way to the right, then back to the left: then that way to the right, then back to the left, to wiggle it inwards, then outwards; up, then down, pushing the centre release button (while wiggling it every which way) until finally, *Yes!* It finally gave way and released! [At this point, the Police watching this video all stood up to cheer, they later told me!]

As soon as BB realized that the seat belt button was now released, he instantly stepped backwards, almost falling down but quickly caught his balance. He began to shout, then to plead, then to beg for me to step off the bus. (I could clearly see that BB had become unhinged by my total silence. He was definitely unnerved.) I stood much taller than him and didn't blink an eye. BB didn't like what he saw in my eye, my one right eye, my only 'good eye' (as the left eye was covered in a stream of blood dripping steadily down from my bleeding scalp). I must have been a sight to behold!

BB was visibly shaken! He was clearly frightened! What I then saw was not a dangerous threat to me anymore, but an out-of-control youth pleading for me to get off 'his' bus.

Now, I will admit that for a second or two when I initially stood up to face my killer, the thought crossed my mind to take him out, to end his life as he had tried to end my life.

But I saw two obstacles simultaneously:

I had lost a fair amount of blood (more than half a quart in just the driver's seat, the Police later told me!) and was feeling quite faint and rather fatigued at this point.

And, secondly, the sleep deprivation of the past few nights, along with the strenuous adrenaline-filled struggle to survive the past few moments (which seemed like an eternity!) took up all my available nerve energy.

Even were I to attempt to retaliate, and to redeem myself from this on-going threat to my life (while I still had some reserve energy to do so) what if I should faint from sheer lack of blood? Then, no doubt, BB would stab me endlessly as if I were a human pin cushion.

I then decided to step off the bus, as BB directed, so that (as I assumed) BB and I could end this fiasco one way or the other. But no sooner did I step off the bus, then BB hopped into the driver's seat to attempt to drive the bus (perhaps to his Grandfather's place downtown?)! But BB had no idea where he was, nor did he know his Grandfather's address, let alone how to drive an ETS bus, nor how to steer and operate the ETS bus to his Grandfather's place. So insane!

Now I realized that my killer was likely mentally challenged. What was he doing on the streets anyway, so late at night, and without any supervision?!

The Aftermath

Listening to BB trying to move the bus into gear, into motion (as I had simply left the interlock brake on because I expected to quickly drop off BB at the final Terminal, and then to return to the Garage), I dragged my left foot towards the interior of the Mill Woods Transit Centre. As I was parked on the West side of the Terminal, I tried to scan the locked doors but to no avail. I then realized that only one set of doors was left unlocked for Operators so late at night. So I assumed it must be on the other (East) side of the Terminal. I continued to drag my left foot along looking behind me to see if BB had decided to follow me.

[This left kneecap injury was seriously damaged as I sat in the driver's seat and attempted to deflect the dozens of knife stabs in my direction: only twenty-two knife stabs (according to the Police, analyzing the assault video) had penetrated into my body, creating thirteen serious wounds, (as many knife stabs were into the same wound site). The left kneecap and left heel kept smashing hard against the steering wheel column positioned between the driver's legs, as I would turn rapidly and sharply to the right to face BB who was plunging his knife into my body.]

For what seemed to take forever, I finally arrived at the East side of the Terminal, where (as an answer to prayer) the scan card was finally accepted. I made a beeline to the Men's washroom which was located ironically next to where BB was attempting to drive the bus away. (We were separated only by this one wall.)

I scanned myself into the washroom and looked at the large wall mirror. I could not believe my eyes! I looked like a victim from a *Halloween 9* slasher movie! As I looked down to the floor, the entire bathroom floor became red with my blood. [Later, the washroom cleaner (sent to this site that morning) told me that he took a photo (with his cell phone camera) of the bathroom floor completely covered in my blood.]

I picked up my cell phone to find it literally drenched in my blood, and wiped it off against my sweater, saying a silent prayer that it would still work. It did! I called Control to tell them that I was in the Men's washroom. They said that they knew it already, that I was being watched *live* on camera throughout the entire assault. They emphasized that the Police and Ambulance were on their way, that I should not hang up, and that I should try not to faint because I need to be able to open the washroom door when the Police arrive (as the Police did not have a scan card for this door).

At this very instant, I heard the loud screech of tires from (what turned out to be eight) Police cars as they arrived at the scene! I could hear their shouts for BB to drop to the ground; and soon the Police were at my door. When I opened the bathroom door, the Police Constable who first saw me was visibly aghast! He stepped back (almost as if in horror or amazement) and said: "OMG!"! He blinked his eyes as if to hold back tears and then directed me through the west exit door, telling me to stand at the curb, as he waved the Ambulance to come toward me.

The Constable then used a pair of shears to slice off all my clothes from top to bottom, told me to remove my socks and shoes, as I awaited a young blonde female Medic who assisted me onto a stretcher. I could hear several people (Ambulance attendants) who first viewed me quietly muttering, "OMG! OMG! Will he make it?"

I simply laid me down to rest upon the stretcher (looking up into the stars at the night sky) as the stretcher was moved into the Ambulance. And the race to the University of Alberta Trauma Unit began.

For some heretofore unknown reason, my life was to be spared. For some purpose, by the Grace of God, and known to God alone, I was to be given a second lease, another chance to live out my life!

My time on this earth was not yet over!

Youth Feedback:
____

____

____

DISCLAIMER: N.B. (*Nota Bene*)
All tunes/songs/video clips/links/quotes/etc. are herein provided to assist in Group Therapy Sessions, or privately, for individual study (to assist in learning) and for educational purposes *only*.

[#2: U-Tube Reference]
Elvis Presley - Amazing Grace
https://www.youtube.com/watch?v=B3XdXEJEI4E&list=RD8H9T7 427Ebl&index=11

Amazing Grace (Alternate Take 2)

Amazing Grace! How sweet the sound
That saved a wretch like me
I once was lost but now am found

Was blind but now I see

Through many dangers, toils and snares
I have already come
'Tis Grace has brought me safe thus far
And Grace will lead me home

Scene i:

What to make of the "Aggravated Attempt" on My Life?: The Story of the Two Wolves

The Story of the Two Wolves inside each one of us:

Long, long, long ago, there was a meeting, a causal night-time counsel, around a fireside in the middle of a dark forest. The sound of wolves baying and howling could be heard all around in the pitch-black darkness of this otherwise quiet night. An old Cherokee Chief was teaching his many grandchildren about the facts of life. He was telling a story about the 'two wolves' inside each one of us:

"One wolf (the black wolf) was a very bad rotten wolf. You could tell he was very bad because of his characteristics: He was always angry, arrogant, biased, constantly critical, fearful, greedy, hell-bent, jealous, judgmental, lying, lustful, sacrilegious, self-destructive, thieving, treacherous, vulgar, and just plain wicked! The other (white) wolf was easy to spot as well: He was always confident, exhibiting an excellent spirit, fair-minded, friendly (as an 'ideal friend'), harmless, helpful, honest, kind, loving, obedient, peaceful, self-reliant, temperate, tender-hearted, thankful, upstanding, and of course: always vigilant! These two wolves are fighting to the death inside our soul, our spirit."

Then the wise old Chief paused a long time to let his words sink into the minds and hearts of his young offspring. But his littlest grandchild was impetuous and impatient. He could no longer contain himself. He impolitely blurted out: "But Grandpa! Which wolf wins?!" The kindly Grandpa smiled and looked deep into the eyes of his youngest grandchild: *"The One You Feed!",* he said!

And so it is: The good or bad 'wolf' inside each one of us will live or die if we feed it. And how do we know which wolf to feed? Well, that is the thrust and main theme of this book, a type of workbook, that allows interaction among ourselves. We can use this book as a group-therapy book (not necessarily around a campfire at night, but then: why not? If that works best for all concerned?).

The key point to bear in mind is that through our own internal scrubbing, our own introspection, we are able (firstly) to recognize the negative character traits we may be harboring (heretofore unbeknown to us), and so work to root them out, as well as (secondly) to replace the empty vacuum with 'goodly works', the good habits and traits we need to adopt, in order to reform.

And perhaps even to convert our nature into a more pleasing, and goodly nature, as we allow the Spirit Above to work through our spirit so that we can become the (adopted) sons and daughters of God, our Heavenly Father. Admittedly, to do so, to convert our human weaknesses into a divine-like character is a tall order. But with God's help, all things are possible. The march of a thousand miles begins with the first step.

Scene ii:
Seventeen Different *Points of View* (POV)

1. The Ambulance Ride (to The U of A Trauma Centre) POV:

What was seemingly *'impossible'* in the Ambulance Rescue was the ride to the U of A (University of Alberta) Trauma Centre. Because of the loss of blood, potentially high risk of blood infection throughout the body, time became the deciding factor. How much blood I had lost was not known, nor the extent or number of wounds. The wound of most concern was in the genital area: Because the stabbing wound next to the genitals, in the high upper right thigh was still pumping out blood, one could not be certain whether the genitals (the penis or scrotum) were also injured. Everything was soaked in blood in all directions.

The young blonde female Medic tried unsuccessfully three times over to meticulously check out the genitalia to see if anything there was bleeding, but the blood from the adjacent thigh wound kept squirting out covering the entire pelvic area. I did complain of a stinging sensation below the head of the penis, but nothing could be discerned with the non-stop bleeding of the thigh wound.

Hence, it became critical to bandage and apply pressure on the upper thigh wound to stop the wound from oozing out blood spontaneously. As I had thirteen major wounds oozing out blood simultaneously, the usual Ambulance driver had to assist the other Medics. A Police Constable took over and became the new Ambulance Driver, and what a ride it was!

The Police Constable now driving the Ambulance went far above and beyond the call of duty. Hardly did it seem that the tires of the Ambulance touched the ground! Trying to place two IVs (intravenous needles) into my veins while hitting a bump and flying into the air was a bit of a challenge. I think I had several bruises as the young Medic tried and even her assistants but finally, they gave up [to place the needles into my veins]. They managed to apply bandages and do a quick count of all the wounds and before you knew it, we had arrived at the Trauma Centre (some ten miles away or so).

According to the Ambulance staff, the crucial point was to assess the damage and to radio ahead to the Trauma unit to describe the nature and extent of my wounds, so that they could have staff and medication ready for me when I arrived. Thirteen major wounds were counted in the Ambulance by multiple persons (counting from the scalp down to the thigh), as well as a significant loss of blood was noted.

As the Ambulance arrived at the U of A Hospital, I was switched over from the Ambulance stretcher to the hospital bed on wheels. Rushing at high speed and running at a full gallop, I went from corridor to corridor, until I was brought to a veritable full team of surgeons, physicians, and nursing staff awaiting my arrival. They literally pounced upon me (in a very orderly manner) each group taking different parts of my body and vocalizing out loud to their assistants what meds and equipment they needed. Then I was prepped to enter the CAT scan for a quick review to determine the extent of internal injuries and/or bleeding.

This 'Impossible Dream' was soon to become a reality!

Youth Feedback:

____

____

DISCLAIMER: N.B. (*Nota Bene*)
All tunes/songs/video clips/links/quotes/etc. are herein provided to assist in Group Therapy Sessions, or privately, for individual study (to assist in learning) and for educational purposes *only*.

[#3: U-Tube Reference]
Elvis Presley The Impossible Dream Live 1972
https://www.youtube.com/watch?v=wRAluyj2ztA

Impossible Dream
Elvis Presley

This is my quest, to follow that star
Without question or pause
To be willing to march into hell

For a heavenly cause

And the world would be better for this
That one man scorned and covered with scars
Still strove with his last ounce of courage
To reach the unreachable star.

Songwriters: Joe Darion / Mitchell Leigh

2. BB's (The Assailant's) POV:

The point of view of Billy Bundy (B.B., for short!) my assailant (whose real name I can never use in public or in my books or to the Media, although the Media well knows his real name already from their attendance in Court) for the rest of his natural life! Why? Why not? Who is being best served here to keep his identity totally secret?

BB's "Licence to Kill"

From the Assailant's Point of View, BB may have felt he was justified to try to kill this bus driver who refused to drive him to his Grandfather's home at 03:33 hours (in the wee hours of the morning?!)! Reflecting upon this possibility, I thought of the words of Johnny Cash (in "Folsom Prison Blues"): " I killed a man just to watch him die!". [See, as well, the movie *Compulsion* (1959, with Orson Welles) in which two teenage youth, after killing a young boy, state: "You know why we did it? Because we damn well felt like doing it!"].

This 'License to Kill' is not limited to a James Bond persona only: BB appeared to have little hesitation, no deterrent, to kill me (when he saw that he was alone with me). His sole mode of communication is 'violence' and his 'risk' to resort to violence is 'high,' according to his 35-page Psychiatric Report, which states: "In the opinion of the assessment team, [BB's] risk for future violence is HIGH. [BB] appears most likely to engage in reactive violence or violence that is impulsive and done in an angry or retaliatory emotional state. He also appears to possess a hostile attribution bias, of a tendency to perceive malevolence or ill-intent where there is none" (CD III, pp.28-30). A case in point was BB's Facebook entry in September 2017 (a year prior to trying to kill Mike Kostelny, the bus driver). BB posted that he was "seeking a weapon with which to kill his Grandfather" (CD III, p.10).

BB's Mental Health Status

BB was also prone to psychopathic and psychotic tendencies as Court Documents disclose: "[BB's case worker from Child and Family Services (CFS)] indicated the subject [BB] was assessed for his mental health in January 2018. She advised the subject

[BB] was diagnosed with Conduct Disorder [CD] and substance-induced psychosis" (CD I, p.15].

Conduct Disorder (CD), we learn is defined as: "a repetitive and persistent pattern of behaviour in which the basic rights of others or major age-appropriate societal norms or rules are violated" (CD III, p.31). BB was also diagnosed with ODD (or, "Oppositional Defiant Disorder") which is defined as: "a pattern of angry or irritable mood and argumentative or defiant behaviour" (CD III, p.31). As a result of BB's tendency to react violently as a standard mode of communication, and "because of his symptoms of a psychotic disorder as well as his demonstrated inability to maintain his mental health in the community, [BB] was certified under the Mental Health Act on November 30, 2017" (CD III, p.7).

BB's Criminal Record

Since early childhood, BB's criminal record indicated crimes of violence to include threats to injure or to kill several different persons, but no behavioural improvement or implementation thereto proved successful. Prior to the 6th of March 2019, BB's list of offenses includes the following:

    (1) 18 counts of 'threats to cause death and/or bodily harm'.

    (2) 14 counts of possession of a dangerous weapon.

    (3) 14 counts of stolen goods.

    (4) 7 counts to cause mischief or property damage.

    (5) 6 counts of aggravated assault.

    (6) 6 counts to carry a concealed weapon.

    (7) 6 counts of a breach to a condition of an undertaking requiring him to "keep the peace and be of good behaviour".

    (8) 5 counts with an assault with a deadly weapon (CD II, Misc.: "Alberta Justice Court Appearance List").

BB's Recidivism

As to BB's behavioural improvement vs. his risk of 'recidivism' (his tendency to revert back to his negative behaviour), his psychiatric report reveals that "[BB] is at HIGH risk for both violent and general recidivism" (CD III, p.32). The explanation given is that "[BB's] glorification of gangs and criminal activity, appeared, at times, to border on infatuation. Without a significant reduction in his veneration of antisocial behaviour, [BB] is at risk of seeking out opportunities to engage in violence and criminal activity, which further increases his risk of future recidivism" (CDIII, p.30).

Indeed, while BB was awaiting the final trial (for 26 April 2019) for 9 criminal counts involving his 'aggravated assault' against 'yours truly' on 26th September 2018, he assaulted (on 13th of January 2019) "a co-patient [in the dining room of the Alberta Hospital] in a pre-meditated and malicious manner" as well as two nurses of the Hospital staff sometime earlier (on 12th October 2018). "[BB] did not express remorse for his conduct or empathy towards the staff members he assaulted" (CD III, p.10; CD I, p.10). As to the 9 criminal counts against BB for his 'aggravated assault' against Mike Kostelny, the first two counts read as follows:

"COUNT 1: On or about the 26th Day of September 2018, at or near Edmonton, Alberta [BB] did attempt to murder Mike Kostelny, contrary to Section 239(1)(B) of the Criminal Code of Canada"; and

"COUNT 2: On or about the 26th Day of September 2018, at or near Edmonton, Alberta [BB] did unlawfully wound, maim, disfigure or endanger the life of Mike Kostelny, thereby committing an aggravated assault, contrary to Section 268 of the Criminal Code of Canada" (CD II, Misc., Peace Officer Report).

BB's Intelligence Quotient (IQ)

BB had attended only a few days of school in the past several years. His Intelligence Quotient was estimated in the low 60s, far below the average for boys his age. As BB's Psychiatric Report reveals: "[BB's] intellectual ability was measured in the 'Extremely Low' range. His score might be artificially low due to his failure to regularly attend school since Grade 2" (CD III, p.34). BB was "assessed to have an Intelligence Quotient (IQ) in the low sixties" (CD I, p.15). As his Psychiatric Report points out: "According to the school records, [BB] has not completed any Junior or Senior High School classes due to lack of attendance. In 2018, [BB] was placed into extremely modified scholastic programming; he only attended a total of twenty-six days" (CD III, p.18).

It is claimed that BB's mom had to abandon BB when he was an infant so that BB was passed on from one foster home to another. Indeed, from 2009 to 2018, BB was "evicted from six different places [or foster homes] due to his behaviour" (CD I, p.12). The object of abuse became the subject of abuse [CD I: p.16]. The abused became the abuser, a story very much like that related by Elvis Presley in his ballad: "In The Ghetto!". So predictable! So pathetic! Yet so poignant!

BB's Libertarianism

Apparently, BB followed his version of Libertarianism (which espoused 'extreme liberty' as the preferred mode of 'therapy'). If BB does not wish to attend school, he simply refuses to attend. If BB does not like one foster home, he simply leaves it for another. If BB wishes to end an interview prematurely (as he did with the Psychiatric report) he simply walks away [CD III, p.3]. It appears that BB feels that he has a right to live his own life exactly the way he wants to, whether or not anyone else objects to it. "It's my life!", BB clearly believes (in keeping with the Billy Joel tune).

BB's mom states that her son does "not follow rules and that he 'comes and goes as he pleases' from the family home" [CD III, p. 5]. If he wants to do drugs, then he does drugs, regardless of what anyone else would say or do to regulate that behaviour. In July 2017, BB admitted in an assessment interview, that he was "using cannabis and crystal methamphetamine 'a couple of times a week'" (CD III, p.11; also, pp.6,7,9).

Since 03 January 2018, BB "continued his pattern of substance abuse, [and] out of control psychotic behaviour" (CD II, LCYPR, p.4). In his aggressive behaviour to assault his own mother, his own grandfather, a social worker, and a bus driver during the week of 22-26 September 2018, BB admitted to having used heroin (CD II, LCYPR, p. 6; CD III, pp. 9-10).

And in keeping with his desire for 'extreme liberty', BB followed his defence lawyer's advice to avoid all further psychiatric advice as well as to waive the necessity to receive any potential benefits from mental health therapy. As the Magistrate pointed out in his concluding remarks: Because these procedures are not required, nor mandated by law, BB has the right to reject all such mental health programs which right he exercised. As BB's Psychiatric Report sums up the issue: "[BB] sees no need for addiction treatment. Any attempt to require [BB] to attend addiction treatment when he does not see the need for it will likely be futile" [CD III, p.32).

BB's Lack of Remorse

But as BB's psychiatric report warns: "[BB] appears to identify with and idolize gangs and antisocial behaviour. Since early adolescence, he has engaged in criminal conduct with little apparent remorse or acknowledgment of the harm of his actions" (CD III, p.31).

And what is the conclusion of BB's psychiatric report, you may ask? Well, it's no surprise: "[BB] possesses minimal frustration tolerance, and when his requests are not met, his frustration erupts in violence. Because caregivers are the most likely individuals to deny his request, they are the most likely victims of [BB's] aggression... [BB] is at significant risk of committing acts of violence whenever he uses substances, and thus his risk of aggression and violence extends to the general public" (CD III, p.30).

Furthermore, the EPS Police Constable in charge of the aggravated assault case on the bus driver pointed out that in the 24 months prior to 26 September 2018, BB was involved in 38 criminal occurrences that involved "arrests, mental health, and social disorder". The Police Officers who actually arrested BB "found that he had no remorse for his actions towards the bus driver." The Constable in charge advised: "I strongly believe that [BB] is a threat to the community" (CD I, p.9).

Crime *without* Punishment

Since this aggravated assault on my life, I've had more than two years (now) to reflect that if this 'young offender' [BB] were properly retained, reprimanded, and restricted in custody (based upon his prior offenses), he would not have been able to attempt to kill me. If he were obliged to undergo mental health therapy (as a required or mandatory treatment for prior offenses) perhaps a future aggravated assault could be thwarted or avoided altogether?

I'm reminded of the true-crime case of Jack Unterweger who was found guilty of murdering several young women but who was released from prison after serving only 15 years of a life sentence, due to 'good behaviour'. Then once released (on 23 May 1990), he murdered nine more young women before he was caught and sentenced to life in prison. (He committed suicide by hanging in prison on 29th June 1994 at age 43). My argument is that had Jack Unterweger remained in prison (for his 'life sentence'), these 9 women would not have been murdered by him.

On the other hand, there is the true story of Rocky Graziano (as played by Paul Newman in the movie, *Somebody Up There Likes Me,* 1956). This seemingly unredeemable hoodlum (whose own mother appears to give up on him and threatens to abandon him in prison) is given a second chance in life through his skill as a boxer. Thanks to the undying moral support of his devoted wife, he comes around and truly reforms. So, in a few exceptions, it seems that the proverbial 'leopard' can 'change its spots' (cf. Jeremiah 13:23).

Having reflected over these child crime issues since my aggravated assault on 26 September 2018, it is clear to me that our current (Canadian) Young Offenders Act can be so misconstrued, so misinterpreted, that the Law itself can allow (false) 'interpretations' to excuse virtually any criminal act that anyone who is a minor may commit with unabashed impunity. No longer do we have 'Crime *and* Punishment' so that the punishment fits the crime, but now we have 'Crime *without* Punishment' so that the punishment *of* crime is in itself a 'crime' (as whacky as that may sound!).

Only time will tell (for certain) whether BB is a 'bad seed' worthy of punishment for his crimes, or whether he is simply a mixed-up kid who needs a second chance to get it right as it were. More will be commented on this conundrum throughout this book and at the conclusion.

Youth Feedback: ___________________________________

____

____

DISCLAIMER: N.B. (*Nota Bene*)
All tunes/songs/video clips/links/quotes/etc. are herein provided to assist in Group Therapy Sessions, or privately, for individual study (to assist in learning) and for educational purposes *only*.

[#4: U-Tube Reference]
Folsom Prison Blues [Johnny Cash]
https://www.youtube.com/watch?v=wG0fS4DoGUc

Folsom Prison Blues

When I was just a baby
My Mama told me, "son
Always be a good boy
Don't ever play with guns"
But I shot a man in Reno
Just to watch him die
When I hear that whistle blowin'
I hang my head and cry

Songwriters: John R. Cash

[#5: U-Tube Reference]
Licence To Kill (1984 movie)
https://www.youtube.com/watch?v=nMSwiMCWa4A

[#6: U-Tube Reference]
Billy Joel - My Life (Official Video)
https://www.youtube.com/watch?v=h3JFEfdK_Ls

My Life

I don't need you to worry for me 'cause I'm alright
I don't want you to tell me it's time to come home
I don't care what you say anymore, this is my life
Go ahead with your own life, leave me alone

I never said you had to offer me a second chance
I never said I was a victim of circumstance
I still belong, don't get me wrong
And you can speak your mind, but not on my time

Writer: Billy Joel

[#7: U-Tube Reference]
The Junkie's Prayer (by Johnny Cash)
https://www.youtube.com/watch?v=OkDJt5GutqA

The Junkie's Prayer

That bed that I lay on is narrow and cold
This sickness inside me tears at my soul
And the devil awaits me, he calls me his son
For he knows I'm cornered and too weak to run

My mind's filled with torture my body's in pain
But the needle is warm as it sinks in my vein
Just a matter of seconds then my mind will be free
From the coldness and darkness that dominate me

3. BB's Family, Friends, Grandfather, and Mother's POV:

To meet BB's mother Roda [FAKE Name] for the first time was quite a jolt. My second visit to the Courtroom (Part two of the three-part Trial process as a result of this aggravated assault on my life) was full of surprises: When Roda (a short slender petite Métis woman) confirmed that I was the victim of her son's unrestrained and ferocious rage resulting in twenty-two knife stabs into my body, she looked me directly in my eyes and said that she was so very sorry, so very ashamed for what her son had done to me, and that she begged for my forgiveness.

She then fell on her knees on the floor outside the entrance to the Law Courts Courtroom (in front of all the spectators awaiting entrance to the Chamber) outside the very room where her son was awaiting further sentencing for his crimes. I could actually sense (or feel) Roda's pain, never having met her before, not knowing anything about her at that time.

Subsequently, I was to learn how BB's mom at age twelve "found her roommate dead hanging in the closet" at the Yellowhead Youth Centre. Later, at age seventeen, BB's mom witnessed her first husband, stab "himself in the heart and [die] while standing in front of [BB's mom]" (CD II, LCYPR, p. 2). Quite possibly, these are some of the reasons or causes that may have led BB's mom to a long road of depression and drugs, whereby she may have felt inadequate to take care of her son, BB?! For alcohol and illicit drugs have become BB's mom's "biggest enemy"! [CD I: p.11]

As BB's Psychiatric Report states: "[BB's] mother has a history of significant substance abuse and involvement with the criminal justice system. She has previously been admitted to [the] hospital for unidentified psychiatric concerns. Her past charges include assault; aggravated assault; weapons charges; arson; possession of stolen property; theft; driving while intoxicated; possession of marijuana and fail-to-follow conditions and fail-to-attend Court. Her most recent Court was on February 13, 2019, where she was dealing with charges of aggravated assault, possession of a weapon, and possession of stolen property" (CD III, pp.12-13). BB's mom also admitted that "she had a history of crack cocaine use" [CD III, p.5]. Little wonder, perhaps, when news of what her son, BB, did to a bus driver, she was brought to her knees in despair?! (See, CD II: LCYPR, p. 4)

What happened to the honour of motherhood? How can BB simply assault his own mother, and then only a few days later try to kill me?! No conscience? No remorse?!

And then to assault his own Grandfather days earlier (confined to a walker due to health reasons)?! As the Court Documents reveal: "[BB] has been demanding, threatening, and has physically assaulted both his mother and grandfather" (CD III, p.13). Since January 2016, BB's "behaviour had progressively deteriorated" (whereby he would attack his own mother even in front of the Police and Medical Staff [CD III, p.7]) to specifically include: "yelling, swearing and physical abuse (scratching, punching, hitting, kicking, pulling her hair" [CD III, p.5].

As to BB's friends, they tell me they could no longer connect with him after he turned twelve years old when BB "was supposed to go to Vancouver for a big [skateboard] competition... but did not end up going" (CD I, p. 12). Apparently, they skateboarded with him until then (CD I, p. 12), but because of BB's use of street drugs, they found his behaviour towards them, too violent, too threatening, and too frightening, and unpredictable. One day he would be your best friend, and then without warning, he would fly off the handle, like a bat out of hell and threaten the jeepers out of you (they would tell me). Even to the point of attempting violence against your person!

BB was out of control. But even more terrifying to his closest friends, it became apparent that he could not seem to control his own behaviour, even if he wanted to do so! That was beyond scary, even to BB himself, one would think?! As one EPS Police Constable put it: "I do feel [BB] is a threat to the Community as his violent acts appear to become more severe through time as he ages" [CD I, p.9].

Youth Feedback:

____

____

____

[#8: U-Tube Reference]
Suspicious Mind - Elvis Presley
https://www.youtube.com/watch?v=SBmAPYkPeYU

Suspicious Minds

So, if an old friend I know
Stops by to say hello
Would I still see suspicion in your eyes?

Oh let our love survive
Or dry the tears from your eyes
Let's not let a good thing die
When honey, you know
I've never lied to you

Songwriter: Francis Zambon

[#9: U-Tube Reference]
Cher - Gypsys Tramps And Thieves
https://www.youtube.com/watch?v=TOSZwEwl_1Q

Gypsies, Tramps & Thieves

Picked up a boy just south of Mobile
Gave him a ride, filled him with a hot meal
I was sixteen, he was twenty-one
And papa woulda shot him if he knew what he'd done

I never had schoolin' but he taught me well
With his smooth southern style
Three months later I'm a gal in trouble
And I haven't seen him for a while, uh-huh.

Songwriter: Bob Stone

[#10: U-Tube Reference]
Abba - Knowing Me, Knowing You (Official Video)
https://www.youtube.com/watch?v=iUrzicaiRLU

Knowing Me, Knowing You

We just have to face it
This time we're through
Breaking up is never easy, I know
But I have to go
Knowing me, knowing you
It's the best I can do

Memories, good days, bad days
They'll be with me always

Songwriters: Benny Goran Bror Andersson / Bjoern K. Ulvaeus / Stig Erik Leopold Anderson

[#11: U-Tube Reference]
Brenda Lee - The end of the world (1963)
https://www.youtube.com/watch?v=KLkLs6SvyDM

End Of The World
(originally by Skeeter Davis)

Don't they know it's the end of the world
'cause you don't love me anymore, Yes
It ended when I lost your love
Why does my heart go on beating
Why do these eyes of mine cry
Don't they know it's the end of the world
It ended when you said "Goodbye!"

Writer(s): Sylvia Dee, Arthur Kent

[#12: U-Tube Reference]
Brenda Lee - I'm Sorry
https://www.youtube.com/watch?v=r-TkjEdB1kE

I'm Sorry

I'm sorry, so sorry
That I was such a fool
I didn't know
Love could be so cruel
You tell me mistakes
Are part of being young
But that don't right
The wrong that's been done

Writer(s): Ronnie Self, Dub Allbritten

4. COE (City of Edmonton) My Employer's POV:

COE (City of Edmonton) POV

I was dubbed, the '$20 Million Man' because (an estimated) $20 million was to be spent to provide plastic-guard shields on the Operator's door of every ETS bus; and to place 24/7 Security Guards at every major ETS Transit Centre (as well as to increase Police, Peace Officers, and ETS Inspectors' presence by 20% for late night service).

Upon receiving a distress call for help (on 26 September 2018), ETS Control Centre immediately related the Emergency Distress Call (at 03:33 hours) to EPS (Edmonton Police Service). Help was on its way almost instantly. All sound and video recordings were working; so, Control was able to view and hear (and record) the entire aggravated assault *live* as it happened (I later learned).

For some undisclosed reason, however, even though I was clearly told subsequent to the crime that a Master digital tape recording (including sound) was made (even to the exultation of surprise that Control was able to match or overlay the soundtrack perfectly in synch with the video track) all such recordings were not released outside of the Control Centre: neither to the Edmonton Police investigating the crime, nor to the Crown Prosecutor's Office who handled the attempted "aggravated assault" case. Several persons employed by ETS told me personally and directly that they had viewed (and heard) this recording.

For some unknown reason, both my forensic psychologist and the COE staff refused to allow me to view that 'Master tape recording', although a muted version was permitted that was taken from a distant camera angle and which did not clearly indicate the knife stabbings into my person. The Police apparently had a different viewing of the "attempted assault" scene as they could count the twenty-two individual knife stabs into my person (which resulted in thirteen major wounds, as many of the knife stabs were in the identical spot or location).

The secondary question I was asked the most (after the primary query: "Why did you come back to work?") was always: "So, how much did the City of Edmonton, your employer, compensate you for this traumatic "aggravated assault" that occurred while you were under their employment and protection?" The answer usually stuns or at least surprises most people (including the Mass Media): that not only did I not receive any monetary compensation but that during my six months of unemployment on WCB (Workman's Compensation Board) benefits, I lost an estimated: $10,380 that I would normally have received. The $10,380 is based upon the Gross pay indicated on my ETS pay stubs less the total deductions, leaving a shortfall of approximately $800 per two-week pay period on average for the entire (six-month) WCB period, as indicated by the Net Pay reduced by that amount).

There was no initial explanation for this shortfall in pay, except (after two Union Grievance meetings spread ten months apart), my Employer (COE) admitted to me that they invoked an old clause in the Union Contract (after WWII) that stated anyone sixty-five years of age or older (I had turned sixty-five years old just hours after my assault) was only entitled to receive the average *net* pay paid prior to the WCB claim, during his entire WCB period [regardless of any additional funds due to him, or regardless of any additional deductions no longer valid (after the assault), such as CPP (Canada Pension Plan) premium payments, or LTD (Long-Term Disability) payments. Also, Vacation time was not "earned" during this WCB period, nor coffee-break allowances.]

Hence, instead of receiving any anticipated financial assistance or compensation for this aggravated assault (due to lack of security at the workplace, and due to a defective seat belt release button), I was hard hit financially with a significant loss of money.

So, I hope that the bubbly over-the-top cheery inquiries asking me exactly how much compensation my Employer gave me (while I was recovering from twenty-two knife stabs) would cease and desist immediately. It's like adding salt to an open wound. Yet to add insult to injury, WCB reminded me in one of my many emails and conversations with them that the key reason I am receiving WCB benefits (and that my employer insists that I receive these WCB benefits) is that unless I receive these (reduced) WCB benefits from my Employer, I would have a legal right and option to sue my Employer for compensation (likely far exceeding anything that I would receive under WCB benefits).

In fact, on 24th June 2020, the "Legal Services Department" of WCB sent me a personal registered two-page letter to emphasize the following point (and I quote from their own correspondence): "Pursuant to Section 23 of the *Workers' Compensation Act*, legal action between workers and employers by WCB is barred."

Why twenty-one months after the aggravated assault against my person (while fully employed by COE) did WCB feel compelled to remind me that I cannot sue my employer (COE)? Did it have anything to do with the fact that my two-year moratorium (to begin to launch a lawsuit, or to litigate, against COE) was scheduled to expire on 26th September 2020, in three short months after this letter was penned. Were COE and WCB that afraid (or 'concerned') that I just might decide to sue them after all? Could that be the reason?

I am grateful that COE (finally) did pay my $385.00 Ambulance ride bill which was due in September 2018, but which the Ambulance Department (which was hounding me for delinquent payment in February 2019) told me that this bill was (finally) paid in April 2019.

Even when Figaro (FAKE Name) a representative from ETS Management came to see me later that morning (around Noon on 27th September 2018) for my birthday, and brought me a large birthday cake, I commented how nice it was to receive at least something from my Employer, COE. But he quickly negated that assumption and told me point-blank that ETS refused to allow any funds for this birthday cake, that this cake was from his own pocket (I think his wife made it for me, as I recall?).

Then the Union representatives, Macaroni and Marshmallow, alias M&M (FAKE Names) came to greet me as well with a $20 Costco birthday cake. They commented that although they were truly sorry for what happened to me personally, they had to tell me that as a result of my assault, they received phone calls from four City Counsellors asking the Union: "What could they do to rectify this situation?" Hence, the labelling of myself as the *$20 Million Dollar Man* arose. (I gave both cakes, by the way, to the Trauma Hospital staff who were elated to receive anything from anyone. Many people do not know how over-worked and under-appreciated this staff really is, in my opinion.)

Later, the next month in October 2018, Macaroni advised me to write a direct (open) letter to City Hall, regarding the need to replace defective seat belts, as Macaroni stated that City Hall promised to do so but have been since negligent to follow up on their "promise". Accordingly, I sent a letter addressed to a certain man, Humpty-Dumpty (FAKE Name) or HD for short, The City of Edmonton, City Hall, Edmonton, Alberta, but received no reply. I waited patiently until 19 November 2018, and again sent the same letter addressing the key issue or concern, as follows:

"RE: The Need to replace inadequate seat belts to improve ETS Operator Safety

Dear HD:

It has come to my attention that little, or nothing is being done (or is intended to be done) to replace inadequate ETS Operator seat belts. Is this rumor true? I hope not.

Let me explain why this issue is of chief concern to me.

I am the ETS Operator (Badge 1252), Mike Kostelny, who was grievously assaulted (stabbed at least thirteen times [actually stabbed twenty-two times but as many knife stabs were in the same spot, the medics counted only thirteen *major* wounds]) by a fifteen-year-old native youth on 26 September 2018 at 03:30 a.m. while on duty.

As the bus video (for Bus Unit 4764) will clearly show, there was a problem with the seat belt (that recent ETS Policy required to be worn by Operators at all times when seated).

As the youth attacked me mercilessly multiple times with his knife, I had to deflect and protect vital parts of my body with my left arm (and once with my right hand).

It was critical to my life and safety that the seat belt would release immediately, but it refused to do so. It was wobbly and unsteady and would not release without a two-hand operation.

(I will assume that the belt bolt was repaired and/or the seat belt problem was 'fixed' since the date of the assault).

The reason for this letter is to clearly state to you, HD, (before any comment is made to the Media, or any newspaper interview) that the only reason I am alive today is that finally after an excess of thirteen knife stabs in my direction, the inadequate seat belt did release (but only because I was finally able to use both hands to release it).

I solemnly testify to you, HD, that had the seat belt not released, I would have been stabbed not thirteen times but thirty or more times; indeed: stabbed to death without question.

The key problem in my ability to defend myself and to save my own life was this inadequate seat belt. (Yes, I've been told by ETS Officials that if a seat belt locks into place and does not unlock while driving, that it is deemed: 'Safe and Adequate'. But although I distinctly complained several times about this mandatory ETS Policy [not required under the Alberta Highway Traffic Act within the City limits] for all Operators to fasten and secure their seat belts at all times while in the driver's seat, the only reply to me was a threat that should I not wear that seat belt, I would lose one to three days of pay as a 'progressive disciplinary' penalty.)

Please feel free to address this issue with ETS Local Union ATU 569 at your earliest convenience.

Of course, I would also appreciate a timely and personal reply to this pressing concern as you may understand.

I would like to be able to tell (in future meetings with) all press releases and in Union meetings with my ETS (Union) Brothers and Sisters of Local 569 that I have your serious commitment to see to it that this life and death struggle would never happen again.

Question: What can be done to prevent this near-death experience from happening again, one may ask?

Answer: In my case, a simple correction or replacement of an inadequate seat belt, a seat belt that simply required too much time to properly release while this deranged youth attempted to kill me.

Very Sincerely yours,

Mike Kostelny

PS Should you wish to meet with me in person, I would be pleased and delighted to share the details of my story with you (before I meet with the Media, whom the Police Department tells me are still trying to locate me for an exclusive interview). --M.K."

Still no reply, not to this very day! I returned to Macaroni, to ask his opinion in this 'refusal to respond' to my personal request by HD to ensure the health and safety of all Transit Operators in the use of their seat belts, to ensure that these seat belts are not defective, but that they function normally. Macaroni's response was intriguing to say the least. He believed that HD no doubt received legal counsel not to respond to my letter, nor to my safety concerns.

Then in February 2019 (five months after my assault) in conversation with Macaroni again regarding this identical issue, Macaroni informed me that the ETS City Manager had called him to come to his office to view a video they created. It was a video (created end of January 2019) taken on the bus unit I was attacked in (Unit 4764). It showed that there was absolutely no issue at all with that seat belt: It was not wobbly at all and had no defective seat belt release button. Why, even a small child could easily and lightly depress that (new) release button, and (presto!) it would instantly release and quickly retract to its proper resting place. Macaroni said that they showed this operation several times over in the video, that one can easily see that this seat belt release button would release, and quickly retract, over and over again without a glitch or a problem.

I then asked Macaroni: "Why did the COE feel compelled to make a separate high-definition digital recording specifically for this bus unit, #4764, and specifically on the seat belt issue when I am not in litigation, nor have I filed a lawsuit against the COE regarding a defective seat belt issue? Why this trouble to create this video some four months after the assault?"

Furthermore, I asked Macaroni point-blank: "If bus unit #4764 actually had no original defective seat belt issue, why the necessity to create a video to show that bus unit #4764 has no seat belt issue?!". Macaroni then seemed surprised and seemed amazed, as if he had just discovered something highly unusual: "Yes", he said to me, "you're right, Mike! Neither this Union, nor yourself, officially declared to the City of Edmonton that you or the Union intended to sue them over a defective seat belt issue".

But more recently (as of 9th September 2020), I was called into the ETS Office of my GS (Garage Supervisor) for "progressive disciplinary" action. Although I did not have any incident whatsoever since January 2018 (aside from the aggravated assault against my person on 26th September 2018) until July/August 2020 (more than two years ago), I was told that should I have a single additional incident within the next twenty-four months (two years), my employment would likely be 'terminated'.

As I reflected upon these rather severe and draconian measures (in my view), I then more fully understood the oft-spoken phrase 'woke movement', in particular, what this 'cancel culture' (specifically, against 'aging white males') is all about. As our current City Hall agreed to defund our (magnificent) EPS Police by $11 million this next budget year (in 2021) in direct response to the BLM (Black Lives Matter) request, my eyes were opened to see (and understand) that our Civic Government is 100% behind this 'woke' revolution and seeks to appease (akin to the 'Stockholm syndrome') whatever these new revolutionaries may order them to do.

My employer's attitude towards me makes perfect sense: That is (likely the reason) why there was 'no cake' from City Hall (on my birthday, the morning after the aggravated assault against me), no urgency to pay even my Ambulance tab of $385.00 (for over six months, until April 2019), the reason why HD refused to answer my two letters to him calling attention to defective seat belts on

ETS buses, as well as why all this $10,380 went missing from my Net Pay while I was recovering for six months from twenty-two knife stabbings (which occurred while on duty and while working for my employer COE). No mystery here anymore.

[See, the U-Tube Reference below, "Canceling Cancel Culture," for further insights]

Youth Feedback:

____

____

____

DISCLAIMER: N.B. (*Nota Bene*)
All tunes/songs/video clips/links/quotes/etc. are herein provided to assist in Group Therapy Sessions, or privately, for individual study (to assist in learning) and for educational purposes *only*.

[#13: U-Tube Reference]
Ain't That A Kick In The Head - Dean Martin
https://www.youtube.com/watch?v=huKSm0tAvhs

Ain't That A Kick In The Head?

How lucky can one guy be?
I kissed her and she kissed me

The room was completely black
I hugged her and she hugged back

Tell me quick ain't love a kick in the head?

She's telling me we'll be wed
She's picked out a king-size bed
I couldn't feel any better or I'd be sick

Songwriters: S. Cahn / J. Van Heusen

[#14: U-Tube Reference]
Johnny Cash - Man in black with lyrics
https://www.youtube.com/watch?v=dY8_vZXo8oY

[#15: U-Tube Reference]
Johnny Cash - Man in Black (Man in Black: Live in Denmark)
https://www.youtube.com/watch?v=1Okt0-Y38Pc

Man In Black

I wear the black for those who never read,
Or listened to the words that Jesus said,
About the road to happiness through love and charity,
Why, you'd think He's talking straight to you and me.

Well, there's things that never will be right I know,
And things need changin' everywhere you go,
But 'til we start to make a move to make a few things right,
You'll never see me wear a suit of white.

Songwriter: Johnny Cash

[#16: U-Tube Reference]
Cancelling 'Cancel Culture': The Rise and Fall of the 'wokerati'
[July 2020]
https://www.youtube.com/watch?v=_3MccCsSuU0

5. Care Providers, Doctors, Nurses POV:

Tell the truth and shame the devil:
Nurses who daily treated my wounds

The key issue with my care providers (to include the many Doctors, and Nurses) was that they insisted this story be told. And it is because of their almost daily insistence, that I actually put this work together (not for any vanity of my own, not to toot my own horn, as it were, but) because they were so frustrated that my story was not an isolated case: But something they experienced on a much-too regular basis. To keep my promise to them, I have dedicated this work trying to finish it to the best of my ability, to do it 'justice' according to their expectations.

As these Care Providers are at the frontlines (in the trenches, as it were) to try to deal with the fall-out and aftermath of so much Native violence (especially among the Métis youth) I am in large part dedicating the creation and existence of this Book to their story, on their behalf. Virtually every day (seven days a week) for five weeks, I listened to my care providers (as they changed my bandages) recount 'stories' (true accounts) of the violence they witnessed caused by an indigenous youth gone amuck. Several of the nurses related to me how they had their face or body disfigured (in one case, her jawbone shattered) by Native youth while these 'care providers' were trying to assist, to patch up, 'to provide care' for these troubled teenagers.

No proper adequate education, no life-skills training, no social preparation, or personalized instruction is provided for these youth to receive the help they need (the basic fundamental knowledge or understanding necessary in order to integrate and to become part of mainstream or civilized society). These forgotten youth assume that they can do whatever they wish; and that in doing so they will be treated with 'white kid gloves'.

True, many of them are (were) the innocent victims of 'Adult' Society, social workers, and 'other' care providers (in the Child Welfare System) in which some workers abused them (in many instances since they were little children). I've heard of so many cases (names provided) of little Native children who were sexually molested, raped, and even killed (arguably, 'murdered') by rather sick individuals within our very own Social Welfare System, without redress, and with total impunity (almost surreal as in a Charles Dickens novel). So, yes, these 'survivors' are well aware of the harm done to them, and to many of their peers, or 'Elders' (when they were children themselves).

The abuse cycle is still not broken but actually appears to continue unhindered by time. Current Liberal Government policies (although fiscally generous to a fault) along with numerous social programs do not adequately address or redress these past harms done to these innocent children but seem to (or appear to) acquiesce or appease the perpetrators of these 'crimes against this race' as if there is nothing that anyone can (or will?) do about this on-going abuse cycle either now or in the near future?!

The feeling of despair and utter hopelessness is truly pervasive; and hence, the only way these 'cornered' (or 'boxed in') youth believe they can cope with their deeply depressing status is to either: commit suicide (which an alarming number of them do); or to develop explosive and extremely violent forms of behaviour. Hence, the BBs of this world! Little wonder, one might conclude.

The intent and the main thrust of this book, therefore, is to, first of all, define the problem, state the story, the structure, we (as a society) are faced with; and, secondly, to provide a (proposed) solution to this sorry state of affairs. To some extent, my story is a springboard to a discussion, to open up a can (or a barrel?) of worms, to unlock Pandora's Box, and to let 'the cat' out of the proverbial 'bag': that ferocious wild exotic monster as a saber-tooth tiger from prehistoric days, to prey upon the minds, and conscience of society at large; to, in essence, make us, as a people, as a possible force for healing, to become keenly aware of the abject, deplorable state that these Native youth have found themselves in.

I do contend that we do have a moral obligation, a social duty to address this growing out-of-control problem: Not by throwing money at it, but by kneeling in prayer, and in searching our souls for a truly permanent and effective solution to this heretofore truly negative cesspool of abuse.

Youth Feedback:

DISCLAIMER: N.B. (*Nota Bene*)
All tunes/songs/video clips/links/quotes/etc. are herein provided to assist in Group Therapy Sessions, or privately, for individual study (to assist in learning) and for educational purposes *only*.

[#17: U-Tube Reference]
Abba - One Of Us (Official Video)
https://www.youtube.com/watch?v=IIKAe8Wi0S0

One of Us

They passed me by, all of those great romances
You were, I felt, robbing me of my rightful chances

I saw myself as a concealed attraction
I felt you kept me away from the heat and the action
Just like a child, stubborn and misconceiving
That's how I started the show
One of us had to go
Now I've changed and I want you to know

Songwriters: Benny Goran Andersson / Bjoern K. Ulvaeus

[#18: U-Tube Reference]
Susan Jacks - You Don't Know What Love Is - Poppy Family
https://www.youtube.com/watch?v=th46UYi_cfE

You Don't Know What Love Is

But you don't know what love is
And I can't understand
'Cause I've got so much love to give
And you're my only man

You've got to know what makes it tough
Is that I just can't seem to give you enough
You've got to know, I need love too
And yet I haven't ever got it from you.

6. Educational, Mass Media, Social Media POV:

Jean Jacques Rousseau wrote a classic novel entitled: *Émile* (in 1762), the story of a boy raised outside the norms of civilized culture. The premise (or theme) of this story is that this innocent (naive) boy (untainted by societal norms) is actually the product of a futuristic more promising social order that focuses on the natural unfettered 'goodness of humanity'. The difficulty that Rousseau did not at first realize is that human nature (being what it is) tends to go downhill instead of uphill unless higher powers are at play (or 'at work').

Karl Marx fell into that similar naiveté when he proposed a Socialist Utopia, called: "Communism": "From each according to his ability, to each according to his needs" was the all too simplistic slogan (in 1875); but as History portrays all too vividly: It is the nature of virtually all men (and women) to exercise *'unrighteous dominion'* once pure unadulterated power is put into their hands. Hence, the collapse of the Soviet Union, and currently, the total collapse of Venezuela. The all-too-human greed and the failure to consider one's fellow citizen as one's own brother and sister (under the Marxist vision) proves that there needs to be something more, something 'higher', than the mere mortal wish to return to the Garden of Eden lifestyle.

And so it is today with the free-love movement of 'libertarianism', ("the freedom to enjoy extreme freedoms"): based no doubt on the premise that if a troubled Métis youth is simply set free into society, he would have a much better chance to 'get it right' (similar to 'herd immunity', I suppose?) than if he were retained in custody for the greater good and protection of society at large. If you truly love the children of the world, set them free, let them do whatever they bloody well like, and then things will be better off in the long run?!

Whoever thought of this approach to child discipline, obviously never had children, and quite frankly, in my view: doesn't even like children, for children appreciate knowing their limitations. To simply say: Go and integrate into Society, when these children (Métis youth, in particular) have no real social or life skills to succeed, is setting them up to fail. What these young people need and would appreciate is to grow up with people who truly love them. And as Scripture, so emphatically declares: The Lord chastens those whom he loves! (Revelation 3:19) Indeed, the Bible warns parents to: "Chasten thy son while there is hope" (Proverbs 19:18), Why is there this need to give direction to children 'while there is hope'? The implication is that there may be a point of no return? Something even Ted Bundy points out rather vividly in his own confession before his execution:

"It's a very difficult thing to describe: the sensation of reaching that point where you know, or I knew, that it was something that, say, 'snapped,' that I knew that I couldn't control it anymore, that **these barriers that I had learned as a child**, that had been instilled in me, were not enough to hold me back, with respect to seeking out and harming somebody."

As Ted Bundy makes it clear from his own point of view: "I don't want to die, I kid you not, but I deserve the most extreme punishment Society as to offer. I believe **Society deserves to be protected from me, and from others like me.** That's for sure!"

Mass Media and our current educational system, the incessant intent of our liberal propaganda, pretends to be a benefit (an improvement) to these social anomalies, to society as a whole but once again we are re-learning the painful lessons of History. To quote Ted Bundy's last words hours before his death:

"Basically, I was a normal person: I wasn't some guy hanging out at bars, or a bum. I wasn't a pervert in the sense that people look at somebody and say: 'I know there's something wrong with him,' and [they can] just tell. **I was essentially a normal person.** I had good friends. I lived a normal life, except for this one small but very potent, and very destructive segment of it, that I kept very secret, and very close to myself, and that I didn't let anybody know about it."

Human nature, unlike the unfounded optimism of a Rousseau or Marx, unconverted to the purity of Spirit envisioned by the Christian Brethren, appears to revert (if unrestricted) to the lowest common denominator: the 'Me First', 'Me above all else' generation, whereby the old minority, now the New Majority, unabashedly proclaims that (their) 'might makes right'! To conclude with Ted Bundy's chilling condemnation of this approach (as a product of this libertarian philosophy):

"It was like coming out of some kind of horrible trance or dream... Then, the next morning, to wake up from it, to remember what happened and to realize that basically in the eyes of the Law, and certainly in the eyes of God, you're responsible! To wake up in the morning and to realize what I had done. **With a clean mind and with all my essential moral and ethical feelings intact,** that at that moment absolutely horrified that I was capable of doing something like that!".

 Youth Feedback:
____

____

____

DISCLAIMER: N.B. (*Nota Bene*)
All tunes/songs/video clips/links/quotes/etc. are herein provided to assist in Group Therapy Sessions, or privately, for individual study (to assist in learning) and for educational purposes *only*.

[#19: U-Tube Reference]
Bad Moon Rising - Creedence Clearwater Revival (HQ - 5.1 Studio)
https://www.youtube.com/watch?v=w6iRNVwslM4&list=RD9QFSp RlElmY&index=2

Bad Moon Rising

I see a bad moon a-rising

I hear hurricanes a-blowing
I know the end is coming soon
I fear rivers over flowing
I hear the voice of rage and ruin

I hope you got your things together
I hope you are quite prepared to die
Look's like we're in for nasty weather
Songwriter: John C. Fogerty

[#20: U-Tube Reference]
Cher - Half Breed
https://www.youtube.com/watch?v=Z6E98ZRaU1s
RE: The Métis question: half-French and half-Native

Half Breed

My father married a pure Cherokee
My mother's people were ashamed of me
The Indians said I was white by law
The White Man always called me "Indian Squaw"

We weren't accepted and I felt ashamed
Nineteen I left them, tell me who's to blame
My life since then has been from man to man
But I can't run away from what I am

Songwriters: Al Capps / Mary Dean

[#21: U-Tube Reference]
SONG: Indian Reservation
Indian Reservation [Disco Version]
https://www.youtube.com/watch?v=9QFSpRtEImY&list=RD9QFSp
RtEImY&start_radio=1

[#22: U-Tube Reference]
Paul Revere & The Raiders - Indian Reservation HQ Sound
https://www.youtube.com/watch?v=21ixwlaN7qw

Indian Reservation
(The Lament Of The Cherokee Reservation Indian)

They took the whole Cherokee nation
Put us on this reservation
Took away our ways of life
The tomahawk and the bow and knife
Took away our native tongue
And taught their English to our young
But maybe someday when we've learned
Cherokee Indian will return

Writer: John D. Loudermilk

[#23: U-Tube Reference]
To Sir With Love - Lulu (Lyrics)
https://www.youtube.com/watch?v=PT5OmavfOWg

To Sir With Love

Those schoolgirl days
Of telling tales and biting nails are gone

But how do you thank someone
Who has taken you from crayons to perfume?

I know that I am leaving my best friend

A friend who taught me right from wrong
And weak from strong, that's a lot to learn

But I would rather you let me give my heart.

Writer(s): Black Don, London Mark, Black Don, London Mark

[#24: U-Tube Reference]
Help Me Make It Through the Night! [Rita Coolidge & Kris Kristofferson]
https://www.youtube.com/watch?v=HKh6ZqVKmN4

Help Me Make It Through The Night

I don't care what's right or wrong
I don't try to understand
Let the devil take tomorrow
Lord, tonight I need a friend
Yesterday is dead and gone
And tomorrow's out of sight
And it's sad to be alone
Help me make it through the night

Writer: Kris Kristofferson

[#25: U-Tube Reference]
Joni Mitchell Both Sides Now on Mama Cass Show 1969
https://www.youtube.com/watch?v=4NdsnFZm0X4

[#26: U-Tube Reference]
Joni Mitchell - Both Sides Now (Lyric Video)
https://www.youtube.com/watch?v=BOPwviOUenA

Both Sides Now

But now it's just another show
You leave 'em laughing when you go
And if you care, don't let them know
Don't give yourself away

I've looked at love from both sides now
From give and take, and still somehow
It's love's illusions I recall
I really don't know love at all

7. EPS (Edmonton Police Service) POV:

The 'boys in blue' proved true to the old adage: "The Calvary to the rescue!" with an eight-car Police escort and an ambulance ride to the U of A Trauma Centre, I arrived in record time: and none too soon. The impact of the Trauma Team taking care of all my entry wounds, and the moral support of the EPS Forensic and Criminal Investigative Team cannot be overrated. Without the speed of the EPS arriving at the scene of the crime, and their Police escort for me to the U of A Trauma Unit, I doubt I would have survived. I cannot praise the EPS too highly: as they deserve the best accolades as 'Edmonton's finest'.

The most memorable scene I recall after the escort to the Trauma Centre was the following morning when the lead Police Constable visited me in person to see how I was doing. He commented that his dad was a 'bus driver'; that when he heard that a bus driver was being knifed to death, he thought of his dad, and reacted accordingly. With an eight-car Police escort racing to the rescue, all bets were off. The rules looked the other way, as a life-or-death decision had to be made: to arrive ASAP. And thanks to that one critical decision, my life was spared.

He told me that when he heard of the seriousness of my many wounds (that blood infection could lead to blood poisoning which would then be fatal), and especially when he viewed that attack video, it was only by the Grace of God that I lived for more than one angel was present to protect me! The entire ordeal was a miracle: that I should have survived.

Although he viewed and saw the attack on my person, he could not believe his own eyes. He stated that he had watched dozens upon dozens of these attack videos and that invariably with only a few knife stabbings, the victim rarely lives. But the fact that I survived twenty-two of these stabbings speaks volumes for the goodness of God in my life.

These religious descriptions (coming from a veteran Police Detective) made me realize how true they really are. That indeed I was given a second lease on life, thanks to the tender mercies of our God and Creator of all life.

[PS: The EPS Police Sergeant in charge of this attempt on my life told me that his team had worked twenty-three hours overtime without pay to prepare this case against BB. They were quite familiar with BB's track record. They wanted to ensure that justice would prevail to keep BB from further harming members of the public.]

Youth Feedback:

____

____

____

DISCLAIMER: N.B. (*Nota Bene*)
All tunes/songs/video clips/links/quotes/etc. are herein provided to assist in Group Therapy Sessions, or privately, for individual study (to assist in learning) and for educational purposes *only*.

[#27: U-Tube Reference]
Elvis Presley - If I Can Dream ('68 Comeback Special 50th Anniversary HD Remaster) (Official Video)
https://www.youtube.com/watch?v=u-pP_dCenJA

If I Can Dream

If I can dream of a better land
Where all my brothers walk hand in hand
Tell me why, oh why, oh why can't my dream come true

There must be peace and understanding sometime
Strong winds of promise that will blow away the doubt and fear
If I can dream of a warmer sun
Where hope keeps shining on everyone
Tell me why, oh why, oh why won't that sun appear

Writer: Earl Walter Brown

[#28: U-Tube Reference]
GALE GARNETT --" We'll Sing In The Sunshine" 1966
https://www.youtube.com/watch?v=1w9gb9ZEvMs

We'll Sing In The Sunshine

I will never love you,
The cost of love's too dear.
But though I'll never love you,
I'll stay with you one year.

I'll sing to you each morning,
I'll kiss you every night.
But darlin' don't cling to me,
I'll soon be out of sight.

8. Family, Fiancée, and Friends POV:

'He Ain't Heavy: He's my brother!' basically sums up in a sentence, my family support. My sisters, Wendy and Holly, were the first to arrive in person to see me the very next morning (for my birthday). They were pleased that my face was not all cut up, although it had six or seven nick marks from the tip of BB's blade: my left ear, my left nostril, my left cheek, my left part of my chin, the left part of my neck (just past the Adam's apple), the left eyebrow, the left part of my lip, etc.

They seemed in positive spirits to see that I was still alive and not badly sliced up (that they could see). Notwithstanding, we all felt as if we were at the "Rivers of Babylon", for it was an appropriate time to weep: to weep for this evil in our midst, in our society, but also to weep for joy, that my life was spared, thanks to the Angels sent from above, to protect me from that ultimate enemy, Death, the Grim Reaper.

My fiancée, Victoria (in Ukraine) told me that when she first heard of this aggravated assault on my life, the little hairs at the back of her neck all stood up! She was in shock. Never could she believe that such a thing was possible (as she lived in East Ukraine, where the children are all so well-behaved)?!

Ukrainian youth think of signing up to serve as Ukrainian volunteers, to fight the barbarian invasion from the East, to go freely and willingly to the Eastern Front, to give their lives if need be to protect their own families, and loved ones, and society. They believe in doing what is right, what is morally right for the greater good of their own people, not thinking of their own safety or loss of limb or life. Never would it even enter their minds to harm or to disrespect a hard-working bus driver who is only doing his job, his duty to help others who need his help (and especially so late in the night).

Even among my own siblings, my younger brothers and sisters, it is utterly incomprehensible how such a murderous fiend could design to harm someone whom they all knew all their lives to be a decent sort of guy, one who was continually trying to the best of his ability, to live the Christian life.

Youth Feedback: ______________________________

____

____

[#29: U-Tube Reference]
Boney M Rivers of Babylon Lyrics HQ
https://www.youtube.com/watch?v=vz6LRBLPKSM

Rivers of Babylon (Psalms 137:1)

By the rivers of Babylon, there we sat down
Yeah, we wept, when we remembered Zion

There the wicked
Carried us away in captivity
Required from us a song
Now how shall we sing the Lord's song in a strange land?
Let the words of our mouth and the meditation of our heart
Be acceptable in thy sight here tonight

Songwriters: Brent Dowe / Frank Farian / George Reyam / Trevor McNaughton

[#30: U-Tube Reference]
Johnny Cash - Me and Bobby McGee (Man in Black: Live in Denmark)
https://www.youtube.com/watch?v=Mc7qmE5CiuY

Me and Bobby McGee

Freedom's just another word for nothing left to lose
And nothing isn't worth nothing but its free
Bobby shared the secrets of my soul
Standing right beside me through everything I done

Then somewhere near Salinas, Lord, I let her slip away
She was looking for the love I hope she'd find
Well I'd trade all my tomorrows for a single yesterday
Holding Bobby's body close to mine.

[#31: U-Tube Reference]
TOPPOP: Terry Jacks - If You Go Away
https://www.youtube.com/watch?v=ByaexIa0EXU

If You Go Away
(originally by Rod McKuen)

But if you go away
When I love you so
There'll be nothing left
In the world, you know

Just an empty room
Full of empty space
Like the empty look
I see on your face

Writers: Rod McKuen, Jacques Romain Georges Brel

[#32: U-Tube Reference]
The Hollies - He Ain't Heavy, He's My Brother
https://www.youtube.com/watch?v=Jl5vi9ir49g

He Ain't Heavy, He's My Brother

He ain't heavy, he's my brother
If I'm laden at all
I'm laden with sadness
That everyone's heart
Isn't filled with the gladness
Of love for one another
It's a long, long road
From which there is no return

Writer(s): Bob Russell, Robert William Scott

9. Forensic Psychologist POV:

Ironically, the forensic psychologist (arranged for me via WCB) was a Métis, a lovely well-educated quite fascinating young woman, who openly confessed her Métis background to me. She is working on her Doctorate Degree in Psychology (which allowed us a common platform for discussion on a personal level, that of the Doctoral or Ph.D. education program). We shared a total of fifteen one-hour sessions together (the maximum allotted under the WCB program). I was required to attend these sessions, in order to ensure that I was mentally fit and capable to return to work (one day) to work with the vulnerable public in particular.

I accepted this 'ruling' as City Policy and as a precondition to returning to work to full-time employment as a Public Transit bus driver (or Transit Operator). I could have left the City employ, and worked full-time in my own Real Estate Company (*Sir Realty Ltd.*) but I chose for the time being to get back on the horse I was thrown off: To get back in the saddle, back in the same job I was doing when I almost lost my life so doing. I have no regrets for having made that decision: I had to prove to myself, first of all, that I could still '*cut* the mustard' (excuse the pun!) despite all the 'cuts' ('slings and arrows') I had gone through when I turned sixty-five years old.

Of course, the matters (or issues) we talked about, my psychologist and I, are confidential (and will remain so!). Client privilege and all that. I'm sure the reader will understand. But one thing I can share relates to the steady stream of nightmares that I endured (not to be killed or not to lose my life but): How my brain was reinventing the scenes of that night: to imagine that the seat belt release button (or latch) came off much sooner than it did in reality.

What I then did (in this dream-state) to this poor unfortunate kid would make even Ted Bundy look like a Saint. Hence, the nightmares. Somewhere in this life-and-death struggle, a dark part of my own brain (or mental processes) came unglued, became unlocked: I felt no hesitation (but intense mental relief) in the macabre solemn-like insane release of intense mental anger which needed to be 'experienced' even if only as a fantasy, a freak show of sorts.

But after 6.5 months of WCB and mental health therapy, after the fact, so to speak (the fact that I was almost killed) things began to normalize once again: I could see light at the end of the tunnel, the light of life and hope, and a renewed vision to once again take the bull by the horns. Life is good. To be alive, to really live life to the fullest, felt (oh!) so good! Yes, no matter what happens to you in life, always remember (that): "Life goes on!".

 Youth Feedback:
____

____

____

DISCLAIMER: N.B. (*Nota Bene*)
All tunes/songs/video clips/links/quotes/etc. are herein provided to assist in Group Therapy Sessions, or privately, for individual study (to assist in learning) and for educational purposes *only*.

[#33: U-Tube Reference]
The Beatles - We Can Work it Out
https://www.youtube.com/watch?v=Qyclqo_AV2M

We Can Work It Out

Life is very short, and there's no time
For fussing and fighting, my friend.
I have always thought that it's a crime,
So I will ask you once again.

Try to see it my way,
Only time will tell if I am right or I am wrong.
While you see it your way
There's a chance that we may fall apart before too long.

Songwriters: John Lennon / Paul McCartney

[#34: U-Tube Reference]
Susan Jacks - We Had It All
https://www.youtube.com/watch?v=R4hAT_0j9zA

We Had It All

Remember how I used to touch your hair
While reaching for the feeling that was always there
You were the best thing in my life I can recall
You and me we had it all.

I know that we can never live those times again
So I let my dreams take me back to where we have been
Then I'll stay with you as long as I can
Oh, it was so good, oh, it was so good

Writer(s): Troy Harold Seals, Donnie Fritts

[#35: U-Tube Reference]
Live Josh Groban_smile_brilliant
https://www.youtube.com/watch?v=KM0wNNpUW3c

Smile [Charlie Chaplin's favourite song]

Smile, though your heart is aching
Light up your face with gladness
Hide every trace of sadness
Although a tear may be ever so near

That's the time you must keep on trying
Smile, what's the use of crying
You'll find that life is still worthwhile
If you just smile

Writer(s): Parsons Geoffrey Claremont, Chaplin Charles, Phillips
James John Turner

[#36: U-Tube Reference]
Terry Jacks - Seasons In The Sun
https://www.youtube.com/watch?v=YG9otasNmxI&list=RDwB9Yls
KIEbA&index=14

Seasons In The Sun
(originally by Jacques Brel)

Goodbye papa, please pray for me
I was the black sheep of the family
You tried to teach me right from wrong

Goodbye papa, it's hard to die
When all the birds are singing in the sky
Now that the spring is in the air

Goodbye Michelle, my little one
You gave me love and helped me find the sun

Writer: Rod McKuen

[#37: U-Tube Reference]
Don McLean performs American Pie live at BBC in 1972 - Newsnight archives
https://www.youtube.com/watch?v=RciM7P9K3FA

American Pie

No angel born in Hell
Could break that Satan's spell
I saw Satan laughing with delight
The day the music died

And the three men I admire most
The Father, Son and the Holy Ghost
They caught the last train for the coast
The day the music died.

Writer: Don Mclean

10. (The Forgotten) General Public POV:

Cornelius Wilder once said: 'The Public be Damned!'. In a sense, there is a large grain of truth to that statement. Throughout history, especially during the French Revolution (of 1789), we see that: *"Damned be the public!"* (And so, in that past) bloody Revolution seemed to be the only answer: to break the cycle of social abuse and exploitation, the enslavement of one people by another. We saw that in the liberating of the Hebrews from Ancient Egypt, God by His prophet, Moses, chosen of God, declared to Pharoah to: "Let My People Go!" (Exodus 5:1; 7:16; 8:1,20; 9:1,13; 10:3).

Today, the same refrain repeats itself: whether in the mistaken Russian Revolution (of 1917), or that of Chairman Mao's "Cultural Revolution" (of 1966), a lot of 'false prophets' pretend to give the working class their freedoms, in the Universal slogan: 'Workers of the World Unite!'. So did the dictatorships of Africa and Europe throughout the Ages: all as a power grab, nothing to benefit the downtrodden, only to become a new ruling class, as leaches to the working poor.

Currently, in 2021 (despite the pandemic that still is spreading like an Ancient Egyptian plague), there is hope that this 'new normal' may not last forever, that while we (as the General Public) may learn to live with surging crime (and this spreading pandemic), we will overcome. We will survive. We will see light at the end of this International tunnel, for the General Public will not be forgotten any longer.

As to public safety here in Edmonton (particularly with ETS) there has been a real eye-opening alarmist reaction since my assault, which is in some ways reassuring (that with the $20 million dollars Edmonton City Council has allotted to ETS for General Public Safety): Things may be on the mend, although quite frankly there is still a lot left to be desired.

Youth Feedback:

____

____

____

[#38: U-Tube Reference]
Neil Diamond--I Am I Said--B B C Live Concert 1971
https://www.youtube.com/watch?v=3OgQjEXVyOl

I Am...I Said

"I am"... I cried
"I am"... said I
And I am lost and I can't
Even say why

But I got an emptiness deep inside
And I've tried But it won't let me go
And I'm not a man who likes to swear
But I never cared For the sound of being alone.

Songwriter: Neil Diamond

[#39: U-Tube Reference]
Elvis Presley - I'm So Lonesome I Could Cry
(Aloha From Hawaii, Live in Honolulu, 1973)
https://www.youtube.com/watch?v=itdSGRnjdFl

I'm So Lonesome I Could Cry

Hear that lonesome winter bird
He sounds too blue to fly
The midnight train is whining low

Did you ever see a robin weep
When leaves began to die
That means he's lost the will to live

And as I wonder where you are
I'm so lonesome I could cry

Writers: Williams Hank

[#40: U-Tube Reference]
Beatles - Yellow Submarine
https://www.youtube.com/watch?v=krIus0i9xn8

Yellow Submarine

In the town where I was born
Lived a man who sailed to sea
And he told us of his life
In the land of submarines

As we live a life of ease
Everyone of us has all we need
Sky of blue and sea of green
In our yellow submarine.

11. Medical Staff at the U of A Trauma Unit POV:

When the Ambulance arrived with much fanfare at the U of A Hospital, I was quickly whisked from the Ambulance stretcher to the Hospital one, and then raced over to the U of A Trauma Unit, where I met a warm reception: about thirteen doctors, surgeons, nurses, assistants all awaiting my arrival (all eyes were on me).

The General Surgeon (in charge) gave me a handful of multi-coloured, multi-shaped pills and capsules: it appeared to be two dozen or more. He simply said: "Don't Ask! just swallow. They've been carefully selected just for you for your situation to give you the best possible outcome [modern medicine can provide]!". I promptly complied: Down the hatch they went, with a sip of water.

Then all the assembled medical staff selected various parts of my body to inspect, disinfect, and to cauterize, and bandage up, to stop the incessant bleeding, the spillage of blood everywhere. One took one foot; the other, the other foot; one took the chest, another the stomach; then the arms, and the scalp, and so on.

But the most troubling and worrisome wound was, of course, the deep penetrating knife stab into the right upper thigh. The blood would simply not coagulate, nor stop bleeding. So, they stuffed it with gauze, taped it up, and then rushed me into a quick CAT scan. Their thinking was that possibly the tip of the knife blade cut into the main artery; and if so, then they would have to do life-threatening surgery. There would be no other option. The chance of survival, in that case, would be rather slim.

So, off I went into the CAT scan, but when the results came back, the angle of the X-ray experience was not very informative. There was no internal bleeding that could be detected, which was a good thing; but the view of the deep thigh wound was obscured and not easily discerned (from what I gathered second-hand from the lively chit-chat out loud among the surgeons).

There was the option to do yet another CAT scan, but more slowly, with more detail. However, the prevailing objection was that it would involve too much additional radiation and with so many open wounds, the option was vetoed. After all, they concluded: We had at least determined that there is no internal bleeding, which the Medical staff found to be almost incredulous. With these thirteen major open wounds, they could not believe what they were witnessing: Divine intervention, they commented softly: Someone smiling down from above, for whatever reason?!

Youth Feedback:

____

____

____

[#41: U-Tube Reference]
Abba - SOS • TopPop
https://www.youtube.com/watch?v=brxvxksq9CY

S.O.S.

Where are those happy days, they seem so hard to find
I tried to reach for you, but you have closed your mind
Whatever happened to our love?

You seem so far away though you are standing near
You made me feel alive, but something died I fear
I really tried to make it out
I wish I understood
What happened to our love, it used to be so good

Songwriters: Stig Erik Leopold Anderson / Benny Goran Bror Andersson / Bjoern K. Ulvaeus

[#42: U-Tube Reference]
Michael W. Smith - Angels Unaware
https://www.youtube.com/watch?v=FsiSPiGrgAY

Angels Unaware [See, Hebrews 13:2]

Maybe we are entertaining *angels unaware*
Maybe there's a place where we will fly
But some say "God is dead" (like Nietzsche said)
and faith has made me a fool

Let me take you by the hand
Lead you to the promised land
And trust Him with your heart
He'll lead you home.

Songwriters: Michael W. Smith / Wayne Kirkpatrick

12. My Own POV (as the Victim):

Of course, the thought crossed my mind multiple times: "Why me, Lord?". Yes, there's that inner query: the wonderment, the curiosity, the grateful praise: Why was I spared? I read a passage of Scripture just a day or two earlier, which read: "Blessed is he that considers the poor: the Lord will deliver him in time of trouble. **The Lord will preserve him, and keep him alive**, and he shall be blessed upon the earth: and Thou wilt not deliver him unto the will of his enemies... By this, I know that Thou favours me because mine enemy does not triumph over me" (Psalms 41:1-2,11).

In hindsight, such a sacred passage was surely prophetic: the confidence it instilled in me inspired me to face all my (wanna-be) enemies, without fear or timidity, as the Lord promised to me (as I read that passage) that He would so protect me. Yes, one can say that it is easy to so conclude after the fact, after the "aggravated assault" on my life; but if the truth be known: that particular reading greatly strengthened my resolve to do what is right, to be obedient to the paths of righteousness, and to go forward in my day-to-day activities knowing (in a personal intrapsychic sense) that God, our Heavenly Father promised to look out for me.

Such was the rather personal experience I had as I read those particular words! I need not (and would not) make such a confession except for the fact that I do know it to be true. Ironically, as life turned out, I did meet an 'enemy' (intent to kill me as if by the dark powers of the unseen world). But after the aggravated assault (while I recovered at the U of A Trauma Unit) I reflected upon these words that I had read only a short time earlier.

As to the formal legal description of BB's aggravated assault on my person, allow me to cite in full (by permission of myself as the 'subject' or in this case 'the victim') the words from BB's own Probation Officer, as follows:

"Mike Kostelny (victim) was contacted for the purposes of this report on February 2019. [Dr.] Kostelny indicated the subject [BB] was not known to him before the incident... He stated he was stabbed 14 times by the subject [BB] and indicated, 'I was fighting for my life that night'. He expressed he was in the [U of A] Hospital for three days before he was released. Even though he was released from the hospital after three days, [Dr.] Kostelny was required to meet with a nurse daily for approximately 8 weeks to get his wounds cleaned and bandaged. He stated one of the responding officers estimated he lost approximately half of a litre of blood while he was still on the bus. [Dr.] Kostelny advised a physician informed him that an ultra-sound imagery revealed his thigh wound was less than one centimeter away from the main artery in his leg. He communicated his stab wounds have now healed; however, he is now dealing with the secondary injuries that occurred during the incident. [Dr.] Kostelny expressed his kneecap and some of the tendons in his arm were injured during the assault. He indicated his injuries affected him greatly, not only physically, but also financially. He stated he has been off work on the Worker's Compensation Board (WCB) Program since being assaulted and estimates he has lost approximately $8,000.00 as of January 21, 2019. [Dr.] Kostelny advised he has been meeting with a Psychologist since the incident to help him through this traumatic event. He stated his quality of life has decreased, as he is no longer able to go for long walks, something he enjoyed doing before his knee was injured. [Dr.] Kostelny expressed he does not want to see the subject released back into the community, without some type of therapeutic counseling" [CD I: p.7].

With regard to my relationship with the Métis people, I have had a great many positive experiences prior to this very dastardly dark and demonic one, the night in question. I still recall with youthful fondness, the name: Roy McBeth, a Métis fellow-soldier who (in my teenage years) befriended me as I went through military training at Boot Camp in Camp Wainwright, Alberta. The stories he would share with me about his former (civilian) life in the Indian Reservation, really surprised, and shocked, and even stunned me, as I still distinctly recall. So much (unnecessary) abuse. So much living-hell on earth he went through.

Partly for this reason, Roy was well-prepared for the tests and trials of military Boot Camp. No matter what the Drill Sergeant said to him, no matter how much he swore at him two inches from his eardrum, no matter how much he was punished for grinning, no matter what he was put through (as part of the military training to 'break your spirit'), Roy never budged, never moved, never gave in! Roy appeared as solid as the Rock of Gibraltar! How I envied him and looked up to him. I truly admired him, his spirit was so strong. So, in short, we became the best of friends. I learned a lot from Roy: It was a learning curve I shall never forget.

Since those early formative years (or in the first of four years of military summer camp training), I have forgotten all the names of my Commanding Officers (except for Lieutenant Taylor, a man's man), and the name of all my fellow soldiers (except for Orville, whom later I met as a bus driver); but I shall never forget Roy McBeth.

As a streetfighter, Roy had a remarkable knack of spunk and self-confidence: you could never hold him down for long, and even if you did, he sprung right back stronger than ever. Yet Roy learned the one secret all youth need to learn (in my view): He was not openly disobedient to authority, he was no 'rebel without a cause'. He played by the rules of 'the Game' both written and unwritten. And it was the 'unwritten rules' that he mastered so well. That's what I now realize made him a genuine 'Billy Jack', a true legend to his people (and to me).

Now, what can be said of my thoughts regarding my 'wanna-be killer'?! How can there be any animosity or animus against a mental basket case who is a raging bull gone out of control? He was clearly not in control of his own faculties, nor of his actions, nor of his own emotions, nor of his own thoughts. The Police openly stated to me that BB had not a drop of drugs in his blood at the time of his arrest that fateful night.

So, what are we to take away from that disclosure (of fact), that discovery, except that all those bleeding-heart libertines who tried to excuse BB's actions as those of a drug addict have not a leg to stand on. Even I, admittedly, assumed BB to be acting out as a result of street drugs but now in the face of this irrefutable evidence, we see that BB's problem is a lot deeper: We can't simply dismiss it as the actions of a drug-crazed junkie?!But do BB's actions mirror those more akin to a Ted Bundy or Billy the Kid? It would appear so. According to BB's Psychiatric Report, BB expresses no remorse whatsoever for his violent outbursts he causes others: "[BB] had no remorse for his actions towards the bus driver" (CD I, p.90). As his psychiatric report states specifically: "[BB] did not express remorse for his conduct or empathy towards the staff members he assaulted" (CD III, p.10).

It is my view in preparing the material (and thought and reflection) that went into the composition of this book, that we as a country (as Canadians) need to change the scope and application and restrictions of our Mental Health laws, especially as they apply to convicted convicts with a criminal history. These are young people crying out for help as their criminal records clearly indicate.

People like BB who commit an act of aggravated assault (and but for the Grace of God, I would certainly have been killed, a thought that crosses my mind every day) even if they do not succeed at first to complete their intended aggravated assault, need to be compelled by law to seek mental health therapy. Just as I had to see a forensic psychologist (for fifteen one-hour sessions) in order to return to work (there was no choice in the matter unless I did not wish to return to my workplace); so, BB should be obliged to do likewise (for at least fifteen one-hour sessions), if he wished to return to society, to be among 'vulnerable persons' again.

To do so is simply common sense; for no one in their 'right mind' should or would release a mad 'rabid dog' into the defenceless body of society (to remove the leash off his collar) until this mad dog (full of rage and anger) is fit to mingle with society again; until it is determined that this (previously *mad*) dog is no longer a danger (or threat to the safety of society).

One is reminded of the Disney movie, *Old Yeller!* (1957), in which an old yeller dog saves his master from the attack of a wild boar, only to discover that the boar had rabies, which Old Yeller later soon contracts. As there was no cure for rabies, the boy has to shoot his best friend, his beloved pal (whom he slept with before the attack) who had saved his life from certain death.

I'm not suggesting that anyone shoot BB, of course not. But to release someone with obvious 'mental rabies' back into society without any medical therapy and without any psychiatric help (which the Psychiatrist states in his report BB had refused and is free to do so [see, CD III, p.33]) is a classic case of having the Asylum run by the inmates (as we oft say in jest!).

But my twenty-two wounds cry out to me and to all the world reading this story, that this is no laughing matter! We have an insane response to an insane situation (no pun intended): We need a sane remedy, a surer solution than simply echoing the libertarian viewpoint of extreme liberty. We need not shoot Old Yeller if there is an alternate answer to this problem of 'rabies' (or, in BB's case, 'mental rabies').

Until we find that answer, however, the Old Yellers and BBs of the world who suffer incurable illnesses, need to be kept the hell away from the Public. Do we need to wait until Old Yeller (now released from his leash) attacks and kills someone before we keep him 'penned up'? Or, more direct to home: Do we need to wait until BB (now released from protective custody) attacks and kills someone before (like 'Old Yeller') we learn that he needs to be penned up, not only for his own safety but for the safety of others?

Really now, let us think this issue through clearly: We know that Ted Bundy was an awfully nice and polite gentleman (in the daytime or when in the presence of others) but at night, or when others were not present, we became a veritable serial murderer.

In fact, after he was captured and held in custody, he befriended all the staff around him with his intellectual quips and good humour; but once he figured out how to escape from prison, he managed to murder another four beautiful women, one of the last being a twenty-year-old girl (leaving his dental impression on her left buttocks, whether she was alive at that time or not, was never ascertained). Grotesque, you say! How dare you relate such a disgusting tale for us to read, you say? Well, sadly, this account is true: but guess what?

If Ted Bundy had been kept in prison (until his trial and later execution), these four beautiful women would not have been murdered, right? I think you see what I am trying to say: Today, we voluntarily released BB without any medical or mental health assurance that he was psychologically fit to be free as a bird in the world at large?!

Why this basic assumption that because one is under-age, one is under-rated as a possible re-offender? True, Ted Bundy broke out of prison so that he could re-offend, which he quickly did, but after

May 2020 when BB was no longer under 'probation' (as he was released from "Protective Custody" shortly after Halloween 2019) who can say that he will not try to re-offend?

As BB's psychiatrist points out: BB's "recidivism" (his 'probability to re-offend') is quite HIGH, or to quote precisely the verdict: "[BB's] risk for future violence is HIGH" [CD III, p.30]. Remember BB was under (protective) probation when he attacked me for no apparent reason, which is still baffling to this very day! Not a mentally healthy sign at all! Indeed, in BB's own words to his Probation Officer he admits that he "lashed out at the bus driver because he would not drive him home" (CD I, p.9). Not a rational reason to attempt to kill someone now, is it?!

Youth Feedback:

____

____

____

DISCLAIMER: N.B. (*Nota Bene*)
All tunes/songs/video clips/links/quotes/etc. are herein provided to assist in Group Therapy Sessions, or privately, for individual study (to assist in learning) and for educational purposes *only*.

[#43: U-Tube Reference]
One Tin Soldier - The Original Caste [Original]
https://www.youtube.com/watch?v=cTBx-hHf4BE

One Tin Soldier

Go ahead and hate your neighbor,
Go ahead and cheat a friend.
Do it in the name of heaven,
You can justify it in the end.
There won't be any trumpets blowing,
Come the judgment day,
On the bloody morning after
One tin soldier rides away.

Songwriters: Brian Potter / Dennis Earle Lambert

[#44: U-Tube Reference]
Neil Young - Heart Of Gold
https://www.youtube.com/watch?v=Eh44QPT1mPE
Heart of Gold

"I wanna live, I wanna give
I've been a miner for a heart of gold"
It's these expressions I never give
That keeps me searching for a heart of gold

I've been to Hollywood, I've been to Redwood
I crossed the ocean for a heart of gold
I've been admired by, it's such a fine light
That keeps me searching for a heart of gold

Songwriter: Neil Young

[#45: U-Tube Reference]
Why Me Lord Story - Told and Sung By Kris Kristofferson
https://www.youtube.com/watch?v=1tA7E7pbUws

[#46: U-Tube Reference]
Why Me Lord? [Johnny Cash]
https://www.youtube.com/watch?v=CYBlyMX1e8M

Why me Lord?

What have I ever done
To deserve even one
Of the pleasures I've known

Lord help me Jesus
I've wasted it so help me Jesus

Maybe Lord I can show someone else
What I've been through myself
On my way back to you.

13. My Mother's POV:

When I think of my mother and what she has gone through in life (even before my assault), the heartaches she had to endure (losing two husbands so early in life and then choosing to never remarry), to struggle through life alone (having raised eight children), I'm reminded of Mary, the Mother of our Lord. Mary (as the Scriptures indicate) had given birth to Jesus (our Lord) and to at least six other siblings (see, Matthew 13:53-56).

But when Simeon blessed Jesus shortly after His birth, he said to Mary these prophetic words: "Yea, a sword shall pierce through thy soul also, that the thoughts of many may be revealed" (Luke 2:35). The Scriptures then add that: "But Mary kept all these things and pondered them in her heart" (Luke 2:19,51).

So, likewise, I've noticed through the years, that my mother (like so many other mothers I'm sure) tended to keep certain sayings in her heart and would ponder over them through the years. We may also ponder how it is that Joseph (Mary's husband) was not present at the Wedding in Cana, nor at the Crucifixion. Legend has it that he had died earlier, having been considerably older than Mary when they married. Again (as with my mother) Mary was left at a young age to fend for herself, without a husband (we may assume).

As my mother had just had a stroke only twenty-two months prior to my assault (the murder attempt against my life), I determined not to tell her at first about the murder because I feared for her safety, her own reaction, and concerns on my behalf. I asked all my siblings to keep this assault secret from her. But then when I met her several weeks later (after my release from the U of A Trauma unit), she seemed startled by my appearance and my subsequent story, but not overwhelmed by it.

Perhaps all our prayers helped significantly, to cushion the blow to her. She could see that I was "All Right" [or as Bob Dylan would say it (in his parody): **"I'm All Right, Ma, I'm only Bleeding"**, perhaps reminiscent of our Savior **bleeding on the cross** as He turned to His own mother and said: "Woman, behold thy son!" (John 19:26)]

In thinking in particular of the relationship between our Lord and his earthly mother, Mary (as well as my own rapport with my own mother, my sisters, my fiancée!), I'm reminded of that most fitting poem by Margaret Scoutton, entitled: "For Honor of Her!", which reads:

"She loves you, trusts you, breathes in prayer your name.
Soil not her faith in you, by sin or shame.

Somewhere, a woman--mother, sweetheart, wife,
Waits betwixt hopes and fears, for your return.
Her kiss, her words, will cheer you in the strife,
When death itself confronts you, grim and stern.

But let her image, all your reverence claim
When base temptations scorch you with their flame."

Youth Feedback:
____

____

____

DISCLAIMER: N.B. (*Nota Bene*)
All tunes/songs/video clips/links/quotes/etc. are herein provided to assist in Group Therapy Sessions, or privately, for individual study (to assist in learning) and for educational purposes *only*.

[#47: U-Tube Reference]
I believe" - Elvis Presley
https://www.youtube.com/watch?v=ODtExxkW0ws&list=RD8H9T7427Ebl&index=23

I Believe

I believe for everyone who goes astray,
someone will come To show the way

I believe above a storm the smallest prayer
Can still be heard
I believe that someone in the great somewhere
Hears every word.
Every time I hear a newborn baby cry,
Then I know why, I believe

Songwriters: Drake Ervin M / Stillman Al / Shirl Jimmy / Graham Irvin

[#48: U-Tube Reference]
Mama - Connie Francis
https://www.youtube.com/watch?v=rKXRYqmL06w

Mama

When the evening shadows fall
And the lovely day is through
Then with longing I recall
The years I spent with you

Safe in the glow of your love
Sent from the heavens above
Nothing can ever replace
The warmth of your tender embrace

Songwriters: Geoffrey Parsons / James John Phillips

[#49: U-Tube Reference]
Bob Dylan 1986--It's Alright Ma, (I'm only Bleeding)
https://www.youtube.com/watch?v=oYFGxUqfo5U

[#50: U-Tube Reference]
Bob Dylan - It's Alright, Ma (I'm Only Bleeding) (Audio)
https://www.youtube.com/watch?v=_CJHbfkROow

It's Alright, Ma (I'm Only Bleeding)

While them that defend what they cannot see
With a killer's pride, security
It blows the minds most bitterly
For them that think death's honesty
Won't fall upon them naturally
Life sometimes Must get lonely.
And if my thought-dreams could be seen
They'd probably put my head in a guillotine

Writer: Bob Dylan

14. OHS (Occupational Health & Safety) POV:

As is apparent from the attack video, bus unit #4764 was equipped with a defective seat belt release button. Since my assault, that bus unit seat belt (soaked in my blood) has been changed.

On my first day officially back to work, the first bus I was assigned to drive was (yes, you guessed it): Bus Unit #4764. I worked an 8.0-hour shift on that bus that first day. The seat belt sheath that was loose, and flabby, and wobbly every which way, was repaired or replaced with a sheath that could not move in the slightest budge even with a sledgehammer. A major improvement, to say the least. The seat belt release button worked wonderfully well. One only had to touch it with only one hand, and (presto!) it released and retracted as if brand new?!

It was interesting to me that two OHS reps came to the foot of my bed in the U of A Trauma Unit to ask me if there are any suggestions, or improvements that could be made as a result of my assault. They gave me their personal business cards with their personal cell phone numbers. They seemed to be in earnest as one of them frantically jotted on a (paper) notebook things I would say. I clearly outlined to both of them that seat belt safety is paramount (for obvious reasons). Thanks to a defective seat belt release button, I nearly lost my life!

In addition to replacing all defective seat belts and flabby, wobbly sheaths (that receive the seat belt male end), I commented on the fact that ice scrapers, and brooms (especially those with broken handles, made sharp as a wooden spear) were routinely seen on the buses. Hardly, a day goes by, but that I'm assigned a bus with the broom (and/or ice scraper) left unsecured and in plain view, over the front right wheel mound, easily available for any psycho-kid (or mentally deranged patron) to grab it and to (potentially) use it against the bus Operator, as a lethal weapon.

If the Operator were to drive a bus without at least a plastic door shield, imagine the mayhem (and bloodletting) that could conceivably occur under an unprovoked or unsuspecting attack? Mind-boggling, actually! Yet, everyone I talk to at OHS acknowledges my comments, writes them down (or writes something down in their notepads) but to date, absolutely nothing is being done to correct that (potentially) dangerous scenario.

Despite my numerous attempts to correct this potentially lethal situation, to make the workplace healthier and safer, still to the date of this writing (two years after the murder attempt against my person), all the bus unit 7000 series, and all the High-way buses within the ETS bus fleet still have loose, flabby, and wobbly seat belt sheaths.

True, I have not been killed, but that is because I take the precaution every single time, I enter an ETS bus to place those brooms (broken or otherwise) and ice scrapers immediately behind the driver's seat, and out of harm's way, thereby being proactive and avoiding a possible life-or-death outcome.

Youth Feedback:

DISCLAIMER: N.B. (*Nota Bene*)
All tunes/songs/video clips/links/quotes/etc. are herein provided to assist in Group Therapy Sessions, or privately, for individual study (to assist in learning) and for educational purposes *only*.

[#51: U-Tube Reference]
Barry McGuire - Eve Of Destruction
https://www.youtube.com/watch?v=qfZVu0alU0I

Eve of Destruction

Yeah, my blood's so mad, feels like coagulatin',
I can't twist the truth, it knows no regulation,
Handful of Senators don't pass legislation,
And marches alone can't bring integration,
When human respect is disintegratin',
This whole crazy world is just too frustratin',
And you tell me over and over and over again my friend,
Ah, you don't believe we're on the eve of destruction.

Songwriter: P. F. Sloan

15. (The) Theological POV:
    "They know not what they do!" (Luke 23:34)

It's often quoted that 'love makes the world go 'round!' and that: 'All you need is love!" to solve all problems. Some philosophers claim that there is no such 'thing', or 'reality' as *love*, that *love* (like the existence of God Himself) is a mere mental (or at best, moral) construct. But the concept of love (as an intellectual point of discussion) betrays the cold hard-hitting truth that every human heart yearns to be loved, to be accepted, to be considered as uniquely special to someone else. As the song sung by Susan Jacks so bluntly states: "I want you to love me!" is a desire (or request from one lover to another) that says it 'as it is'!

From the Theological Point of View, BB not only lacks a loving disposition, but he is a 'snake', as Al Wilson points out in his poem: 'The Snake'. In this account, a beautiful young woman takes into her own home a cold half-frozen snake. When the snake revives, it bites her fatally. As she is dying, she demands to know what did she ever do to the snake to deserve such lethal ingratitude?! But the snake smilingly replies: "Well, you knew that I was a snake!" to imply, 'What can you expect more (or better) from a deadly reptile?'.

The moral of this story is: The Good Samaritan needs to be more selective of his choices. It's a matter of 'casting pearls before swine'. Our Lord advised against such actions. (Matthew 7:6) But, speaking of snakes, advised us that we should be 'wise as serpents' to know good from evil, and thereby to choose the good, to 'avoid' the evil, as He says: "Behold, I send you forth as sheep *in the midst of wolves:* be ye therefore *wise as serpents,* and harmless as doves" (Matthew 10:16).

Yes, there is 'karma': for as one sows, so shall he reap (Galatians 6:7). On the one hand, as Johnny Cash says it in *"God's Gonna Cut You Down":* There is the Judgment of God; but on the other hand, our Heavenly Father tempers Judgment with mercy, as Elvis says in his moving rendition of *'Life'*.

Youth Feedback: _______________________________

____

____

DISCLAIMER: N.B. (*Nota Bene*)
All tunes/songs/video clips/links/quotes/etc. are herein provided to assist in Group Therapy Sessions, or privately, for individual study (to assist in learning) and for educational purposes *only*.

[#52: U-Tube Reference]
Johnny Cash - God's Gonna Cut You Down (Official Video)
https://www.youtube.com/watch?v=eJIN9jdQFSc

God's Gonna Cut You Down

Well my goodness gracious let me tell you the news
My head's been wet with the midnight dew
I've been down on bended knee talkin' to the man from Galilee
He spoke to me in the voice so sweet
I thought I heard the shuffle of the angel's feet
He called my name and my heart stood still
When he said, "John, go do my will!"

What's done in the dark will be brought to the light.

Songwriter: John R. Cash / Traditional

[#53: U-Tube Reference]
Donald Trump--Al Wilson The SNAKE with Lyrics VERY ACCURATE HQ
https://www.youtube.com/watch?v=8axWyK8nGuQ

[#54: U-Tube Reference]
AL WILSON--THE SNAKE (RARE VIDEO FOOTAGE)
https://www.youtube.com/watch?v=fHIcVuqQgVo

The Snake

A tender hearted woman saw a poor half frozen snake

"Oh well," she cried, "I'll take you in and I'll take care of you"

Now she clutched him to her bosom, "You're so beautiful," she
cried
"But if I hadn't brought you in by now you might have died"
But instead of saying Thanks, that snake gave her a vicious bite

"And you know your bite is poisonous and now I'm gonna die"
"Oh shut up, silly woman," said the reptile with a grin
"You knew damn well I was a snake before you brought me in.

[#55: U-Tube Reference]
Elvis Presley "You'll Never Walk Alone" best version, with
beautiful slideshow .mp4
https://www.youtube.com/watch?v=8H9T7427Ebl&list=RD8H9T74
27Ebl&index=1

You'll Never Walk Alone
[Elvis narrates this Intro]

You've never stood in that man's shoes
Or saw things through his eyes
Or stood and watched with helpless hands
While the heart within you dies
So, help your brother along the way
No matter where he starts
For the same God that made you
Made him too....

[Then Elvis begins to sing: "You'll Never Walk Alone!"]

When you walk through a storm hold your head up high
And don't be afraid of the dark.
At the end of a storm is a golden sky
And the sweet silver song of a lark.

Walk on through the wind,
Walk on through the rain,
Tho' your dreams be tossed and blown.
Walk on, walk on with hope in your heart

Songwriters: Oscar Hammerstein II / Richard Rodgers

[#56: U-Tube Reference]
ELVIS PRESLEY--Life
https://www.youtube.com/watch?v=ZAgKCPskmrA

Life

And so he sent His chosen Son,
To let us know,
That love had surely made us all,
and hate would surely make us fall,

So from the cross,
Well He showed the world that dreadful day,
That love could be the only way,
or all is lost of life,

Words & Music by Shirl Melete

[#57: U-Tube Reference]
Susan Jacks - I Want You To Love Me (Stereo)
https://www.youtube.com/watch?v=fs79G1Mqemk

I want you to Love me!

And I'm gonna miss you
When you are gone!
'Cuz you left me something
That will live on

But baby, baby, it's gonna explode in me
It's hard to control, you see
I want you so badly!

16. Workers' Rights (ETS ATU Union 569) POV:

When the Union Representatives Macaroni and Marshmallow [M&M: FAKE Names] arrived to see me on my birthday at the U of A Trauma Unit, they commented that although it was a horrible thing that I was almost killed, this assault was actually a classic case of serendipity. For four years they were trying desperately to gain the attention of City Hall as to the plight and public dangers Bus (Transit) Operators routinely face late at night without (adequate) Security and protection from late-night bus patrons (some of whom proved violent time and time again).

Now Macaroni said to me with a broad smile (that) he had no less than four City Councillors phone him directly hours after my aggravated assault, asking him what he could suggest they do to improve Operator safety. They immediately acquiesced to spend upwards of twenty million dollars ($20,000,000.00) to implement all the measures that Macaroni outlined to them. These improvements included: a 20% increase of all Peace Officers and EPS Police drive-throughs late at night (at the major ETS Transit Centres), as well as full-time security guards (at all the ETS Transit Centres 24/7), and of course the much-sought-after and long-over-due plastiglass security door shields for all the buses, along with improved seat belt maintenance.

I was dubbed: "The $20 Million Dollar Man" by Macaroni (from the TV series, *The $20,000,000 Man!*). We all smiled and remarked how hard it was to obtain this critical financial assistance for the Workers' rights, for our Local Union until now.

What I endured that 'Night of Horrors!" was clearly not in vain. A fair amount of my blood was spilt (at least half a quart just in the Driver's Seat, EPS later confirmed to me), as well as a bleeding trail from the bus to the Male Operator's washroom at the Millwoods Transit Centre. The entire floor of that washroom went red with my blood in minutes, as I witnessed with my own eyes (and as the cleaning staff later photographed on their cell phones later that morning).

I paid a high price for this victory, this $20,000,000 Award (as it were), but at least something good came out of all this nightmare.

The Workers' rights to have improved safety and security at the ETS Transit Centres late at night became a living reality.

Youth Feedback:

____

____

____

DISCLAIMER: N.B. (*Nota Bene*)
All tunes/songs/video clips/links/quotes/etc. are herein provided to assist in Group Therapy Sessions, or privately, for individual study (to assist in learning) and for educational purposes *only*.

[#58: U-Tube Reference]
ABBA - The Winner Takes It All (1980) HD 0815007
https://www.youtube.com/watch?v=iylOl-s7JTU

The Winner Takes it All

I was in your arms
Thinking I belonged there
I figured it made sense
Building me a fence
Building me a home
Thinking I'd be strong there
But I was a fool
Playing by the rules

Songwriters: Benny Goran Bror Andersson / Bjoern K Ulvaeus

[#59: U-Tube Reference]
LESLEY GORE "YOU DON'T OWN ME" 1963 HD
https://www.youtube.com/watch?v=4QEqLTbEXy0

You Don't Own Me

And please when I go out with you
Don't put me on display, 'cause
You don't own me, don't try to change me in any way

You don't own me, don't tie me down 'cause I'd never stay

I'm young and I love to be young
I'm free and I love to be free
To live my life the way I want
To say and do whatever I please

Writer: Medora John L

17. (The) Youth Courts POV:

Child crime, in particular Child Murder, is still a difficult conundrum for the Youth Courts today as it was yesterday, in yesteryear. I'm reminded of the sensational Court Trial of Cheryl Crane, the fourteen-year-old daughter to the world-famous movie star, Lana Turner (age 37), which involved the murder of Johnny Stompanato (at age 32) Lana Turner's fifth husband.

On Good Friday, 4th April 1958, Lana Turner had a loud altercation in her bedroom with her husband. In the adjoining bedroom, Cheryl (Lana Turner's daughter) over-heard death threats to her mother and went to the kitchen to obtain a 9-inch knife. She entered the bedroom and (unseen by both parents) she sunk the knife into the mid-section of her stepfather. He reeled over and died in minutes. In the Court Trial, the mother (Lana Turner) convinced the Court that her daughter ('Cherie') was only trying to protect her. The Court was emotionally moved and judged the case as 'justifiable homicide'. The fourteen-year-old killer, but 'a child', was set free without sentencing.

I mention this case of a fourteen-year-old girl who killed her stepfather (as 'justifiable homicide') to contrast it with my case in point: There was no justification of any kind for BB to attempt to kill me! BB served his mandated twelve-month sentence of 'restrictive custody' (no prison time, as he has a mental illness, I was told), and was then promptly set free to mingle in our society.

I asked the Crown Prosecutor (out of sheer curiosity) what sentence would BB likely receive had he succeeded in his attempt to kill me?! I was stunned to learn that the maximum sentence attributed to Canadian youth for murder would be: two years (twenty-four months).

He would be 'entitled' ('entitlement', you know, is a big deal today among the youth, in particular) to three square meals a day, as well as Cable-TV (to help pass the boredom of confinement) and of course access to the Internet (but as I recall he would not be able to transmit or send, only to receive digital information). No harsh punishment here because (after all) under the libertarian (or extreme liberty) point of view, 'punishment' is an out-dated notion. It actually is a crime. Yes, you read it right: the phrase used today is: "The Crime *of* Punishment"!

The pendulum has swung to the other end. Recall when the Kingston Penitentiary was first built in Kingston, Ontario Canada (even before Canadian Confederation of 1867), one of the earliest inmates was an eight-year-old boy, Antoine Bucher, from Montreal who was incarcerated for three years (for pickpocketing). He was routinely whipped (to correct his childish behaviour) and suffered meal deprivation on numerous occasions [see, "Tales From KP" in the *Doc Zone* on youtube.com].

Of course, these extreme measures to force 'penitence' on prison inmates no longer exist in any Canadian prison today (Thank God!). But the reverse is now the standard: We now have 'Crime *without* Punishment', as my case (the aggravated assault on my life) is a prime example on full display.

But what to make of this continual saga of troubled unwanted youth? Elvis Presley put it best perhaps in his ballad: "In The Ghetto!", a story in song that portrays all too vividly what happens when a child is born in the Ghetto: As a social misfit, who cannot find his niche, his identity, and so joins a gang, and becomes [as in the classic movie, *Rebel Without a Cause* (1955, with James Dean)], a rebel, an enemy, alienated disenfranchised by mainstream society.

Such appeared to be the life of BB: like a fish out of water, not wanted in the various foster homes he had been assigned to. In the latest home (that he was to stay in), the foster family changed their mind, especially given his violent track record. Then sometime after 23:00 Hours (11 p.m.) on the night of my assault, BB ran away from Child Placement Services in the Mill Woods area who were going over the paperwork with an 'emergency family' (a Middle Eastern family) who presumed they would know how to keep BB in check.

According to the Court Documents, BB who "was seriously psychotic, out of control and [had] just assaulted [his mother, his Grandfather, and a social worker] ... on or about September 25, 2018... refused to stay with a middle eastern family so he left" [CD II, LCYPR, p.6].

BB was on the lam for over four hours until he spied my bus (the last bus for the night) heading towards Millwoods Transit Centre (with only two adult bus patrons on board, one male and one female). No one from Child Welfare Services contacted either EPS (the Police) or ETS (Public Transit) to warn the public at large that there was a potentially dangerous youth out on the loose with potentially a dangerous weapon!

It has been stated repeatedly throughout the Court Documents that BB assaulted his mother before he tried to kill me "with a knife" [CD II, LCYPR, p. 6; CD III, p.7]. Indeed, it appears that BB "was frequently verbally and physically aggressive, especially towards his mother" (CD III, p.11) These allegations of 'mother abuse' remind me of a quote I read (when but a lad myself) written by Adolf Hitler (in 1923) in his book *Mein Kampf* ('My Struggle'). I believe the quote is chilling in its prophetic insight into the nature of 'delinquent youth', as Hitler says it:

"The three-year child has become a fifteen-year-old **despiser of all authority**... Now he begins the same life which all along his childhood years he has seen his father living. He hangs around the street corners and bars, coming home God knows when; and for a change now and then **he beats the broken-down being which was once his mother**, curses God and the world, and at length is convicted of some particular offense and sent to a house of correction. There he receives his last polish."

Here we can see that according to a man like Hitler such waifs have a rather bleak predictable future. Let's hope (and pray) that BB reforms, that his fate is not the fate of those guttersnipes who amount to nothing but a crying shame, and a deplorable disgrace to "the broken-down being which was once his mother".

As to being a 'despiser of all authority,' it is noteworthy that when BB was but ten years old (on 9th December 2013), he posted a selfie photo "putting up a middle finger and pointing what appears to be a handgun at his head [with] the caption on the bottom [that] says, 'F--- THE POLICE!" (CD III, p.13); [swear word is uncompleted by Author].

Of course, I get it: the 'child' who attempted to kill me has 'his rights'. Anyone in the Courtroom (including myself) who knows this 'child's' identity cannot reveal his name, or give a detailed description, or release a photo of this child's true identity (because he cannot be 'branded' as a criminal). All his previous 'crimes and misdemeanours' are to be forgiven, to be wiped clean, to be whitewashed entirely, when he becomes an adult (age 18) in August 2021. That is the Law in Canada!.

Until that age (it can be argued that) youth in Canada (just like James Bond) actually do have (in effect!) a "License To Kill" (as in the 1989 movie of the same title). There appear to be no serious impediments to those 'psycho kids' so inclined mentally, emotionally, or otherwise. In theory at least, a very rich man wishing to do away with his soon-to-be-ex-wife can approach one of these Canadian youth and ask him for a favour. A large sum of money can be promised (say in a Swiss bank account), the details passed onto the youth; and (Bingo!) another ex-wife bites the dust.

Sounds macabre? Sounds chilling? Yes, I wholly agree! It's like releasing a (young) Frankenstein monster (one that our society appears to be able to manufacture willy-nilly, thanks to our Youth Courts?!). But to say that such a scenario is utterly impossible? No! That much we now know (based on legal precedent) cannot be dismissed with the wave of our hand. It is entirely within the realm of the possible, thanks to the monstrous loopholes in our Youth Justice system. The days of the 'Wild West' (although far behind us) haunt us still, don't they? And the disturbing outcome, the basis for this verdict? Why, it's all *legal*, ain't it?!

In a few US States, however, it is possible for a juvenile (i.e., a person under 18 years of age) to be tried as an 'adult' in an Adult Court. Although no death sentence is possible for juveniles both in Canada and in the USA, in some cases a juvenile can be tried and convicted as an 'adult' regardless of his age, or his/her status as a 'child'.

As Steven Briggs (a "nationally recognized criminal justice expert" and a former US criminal prosecutor) puts it (in his book, *Criminology for Dummies*, 2009): "I once tried a seventeen-year-old boy *as an adult* because he stabbed the boy he was babysitting 86 times and then set off down the street to find a girl to rape and murder. He was sentenced to life in prison after serving a period in a youth correctional facility" (p.335; italics added).

See as well, U-Tube Reference #67A (Trystin Bailey stabbed 114 times . . .).

 Youth Feedback:
____

____

____

DISCLAIMER: N.B. (*Nota Bene*)
All tunes/songs/video clips/links/quotes/etc. are herein provided to assist in Group Therapy Sessions, or privately, for individual study (to assist in learning) and for educational purposes *only*.

[#60: U-Tube Reference]
Elvis Presley-- in the Ghetto (with Lyrics)
https://www.youtube.com/watch?v=ZXBMQKnpj6s

[#61: U-Tube Reference]
Elvis Presley - In The Ghetto (Music Video) (1969)
https://www.youtube.com/watch?v=6am8V5KNJ4A

In the Ghetto

People, don't you understand
The child needs a helping hand
Or he'll grow to be an angry young man some day?
Take a look at you and me
Are we too blind to see
Do we simply turn our heads, and look the other way?

So he starts to roam the streets at night
And he learns how to steal, and he learns how to fight

Songwriter: Mac Davis

[#62: U-Tube Reference]
Elvis Presley - Tomorrow Never Comes
https://www.youtube.com/watch?v=QhYtB7pjkS0&list=RDm_nD4o
myX4l&index=49
Tomorrow Never Comes

Oh you tell me that you love me
Yes you tell me that you care
That tomorrow we'll be married, oh
But tomorrow's never there

Many weeks now have I waited
Oh many long nights have I cried
But just to see that happy morning
When I have you right by my side

Songwriters: Johnny Bond / Ernest, Est. Of Tubb

[#63: U-Tube Reference]
Linda Ronstadt - It Doesn't Matter Anymore
https://www.youtube.com/watch?v=wGQXTJQTLM0

It Doesn't Matter Anymore

There's no use in me a-crying
I've done everything now I'm sick of trying
I've thrown away my nights
Wasted all my days over you

Now you go your way baby and I'll go mine
Now and forever till the end of time
I'll find somebody new and baby
We'll say we're through

Writer: Hal David

[#64: U-Tube Reference]
Delta Dawn - Helen Reddy
https://www.youtube.com/watch?v=afsp7MU-nTI

Delta Dawn

She's forty-one and her daddy still calls her "Baby"
All the folks around Brownsville say she's crazy
'Cause she walks downtown with a suitcase in her hand
Looking for a mysterious dark-haired man

In her younger days they called her Delta Dawn
Prettiest woman you ever laid eyes on
Then a man of low degree stood by her side
Promised her he'd take her for his bride.

Writer(s): Alex Harvey, Larry Collins

[#65: U-Tube Reference]
The Beatles- Eleanor Rigby- Digitally Remastered
https://www.youtube.com/watch?v=twFbweJfUUo

Eleanor Rigby

Eleanor Rigby picks up the rice in the church where a wedding
has been
Lives in a dream
Waits at the window, wearing the face that she keeps in a jar by
the door
Who is it for?

Eleanor Rigby died in the church and was buried along with her
name
Nobody came
Father McKenzie wiping the dirt from his hands as he walks from
the grave
No one was saved.

Writer: Lennon John Winston

[#66: U-Tube Reference]
Send in the Clowns [sung by LizTaylor]
https://www.youtube.com/watch?v=UxTbTfsn1iU

Send in the Clowns

Isn't it rich? Are we a pair?
Me here at last on the ground, You in mid-air,
Don't you love farce? My fault, I fear
I thought that you'd want what I want

Isn't it rich? Isn't it queer?
Losing my timing this late in my career
But where are the clowns? There ought to be clowns
Well, maybe next year.

Songwriter: Stephen Sondheim

[#67: U-Tube Reference]
HELEN REDDY - I DON'T KNOW HOW TO LOVE HIM - THE
QUEEN OF 70s POP - ANDREW LLOYD WEBBER
https://www.youtube.com/watch?v=WOCwE5D9Ghk&pbjreload=1
0

I Don't Know How To Love Him

Don't you think it's rather funny
I should be in this position
I'm the one who's always been
So calm, so cool, no lover's fool
Running every show
He scares me so

Yes, if he said he loved me
I'd be lost, I'd be frightened

Writer(s): Lloyd-Webber Andrew, Rice Timothy Miles Bindon

[#67A: U-Tube Reference]
Trystin Bailey stabbed 114 times by a 14-year old boy
(who will be tried as an adult) [27 May 2021]
https://www.youtube.com/watch?v=TyzjwSg71hc

Scene iii:
What to make of all of these many differing opinions (Points of View)

The bottom line is that the Métis problem is a problem spiraling out of control. That is not to say that the Canadian Government is not doing anything to correct the situation. On the contrary, the perks and benefits, the incentives, and outright grants and financial assistance is currently very enticing. One almost half-wishes he was a half-breed (or, "Métis" which is what 'half-breed' means in French), as the economic benefits have rarely been better anywhere else.

But then we arrive at the crux of the problem: Throwing money to the Métis to try to assimilate (or integrate) them into mainstream society, may not work, may not be adequate in and of itself. The psychosis of the Métis 'madness' defies most psychological descriptions.

We need answers to the questions such as:

(1) Why the high suicide rate among the Métis, especially among the youth, and the young generation?

(2) Why the continual reliance on drug addiction (especially, alcoholism)?

(3) How do these messed up and forgotten kids fend for themselves when they have little or no life skills?

(4) How can these Métis youth survive on their own when they can't even cook their own meals, or balance their own budget?

In so many ways, these unfortunates (*Les Misérables*) are like fish outside their waters. But the question or issue is not to return these Métis youth to their former habitat or reservation because they have none: They have burned their own bridges, so to speak. They are figuratively (and even literally, in many respects) a people disenfranchised, disengaged from the rest of mainstream society. 'Normal' to them is the setting on a washing machine. They are outsiders looking inward into society, like passerby's window-shopping: They can't afford to buy anything, but they sure like to stare.

What is the answer to these questions? Is there an answer? Is there a happy solution, or do we still need to ask the right questions? Do the Métis people by and large wish to integrate into mainstream society, to become part of a greater mosaic? Or, do they prefer to be a distinct people, to withdraw into their own inner circles, separate and different from the rest of us? Who can say for sure what they want?

The question remains unanswered: How can a Government give any people, including the Métis people, what they want, when the people themselves don't know what it is that they want?

At the end of the day, life goes on. And the issues of today are either plowed over or treated with white kid gloves. As a famous line in a movie (*Cool Hand Luke,* 1967) goes: "What we have here is a failure to communicate!" Perhaps it's as simple as that.

Youth Feedback:

____

____

____

DISCLAIMER: N.B. (*Nota Bene*)
All tunes/songs/video clips/links/quotes/etc. are herein provided to assist in Group Therapy Sessions, or privately, for individual study (to assist in learning) and for educational purposes *only*.

[#68: U-Tube Reference]
John Denver / Some Days Are Diamonds [1986]
https://www.youtube.com/watch?v=gnf_cWYj1Uw

Some Days Are Diamonds

When you ask how I've been here without you,
I like to say I've been fine, and I do.
But we both know the truth is hard to come by.
And if I told the truth, that's not quite true.

Now the face that I see in my mirror,
More and more is a stranger to me.
More and more I can see there's a danger
In becoming what I never thought I'd be.

Writer(s): Marshall Morgan, Troy Johnson

[#69: U-Tube Reference]
The Tremeloes - Silence is Golden
https://www.youtube.com/watch?v=n03g8nsaBro

Silence Is Golden

Talking is cheap; people follow like sheep
Even though there is no where to go
How could she tell? He deceived her so well!
Pity she'll be the last one to know

How many times will she fall for his lines
Should I tell her or should I be cool
And if I tried I know she'd say I lied
Mind your business don't hurt her you fool.

Writers: Bob Crewe, Bob Gaudio

ACT II:
Seventeen Negative character traits (to avoid)

Scene i:
The Colour of the "Big Bad Wolf"

Much can be said (and much has been said) about the colour of 'darkness'. Jude (a blood brother to our Lord, born of the same mother), refers to 'the blackness of darkness' as a negative factor of those who forfeit their divine destiny, and choose to become *wandering stars*', souls lost to Satan. (See, Jude 13) In Children's folklore, and fairy tales, the symbol of evil is usually: the 'big bad wolf' (as in *Little Red Riding Hood*). Typically, this wolf is a black wolf, not a white wolf. And so in keeping with that tradition, I have referred to the *black* wolf, as a 'big bad wolf'. No racist slurs or remarks are intended.

Youth Feedback:

____

____

____

DISCLAIMER: N.B. (*Nota Bene*)
All tunes/songs/video clips/links/quotes/etc. are herein provided to assist in Group Therapy Sessions, or privately, for individual study (to assist in learning) and for educational purposes *only*.

[#70: U-Tube Reference]
The Beatles - Help!
https://www.youtube.com/watch?v=2Q_ZzBGPdqE

Help!

When I was younger so much younger than today
I never needed anybody's help in any way
But now these days are gone and I'm not so self assured
Now I find I've changed my mind, I've opened up the doors

And now my life has changed in oh so many ways
My independence seems to vanish in the haze
But ev'ry now and then I feel so insecure
I know that I just need you like I've never done before.

Writers: John Winston Lennon , Paul James Mccartney

Scene ii:
Seventeen Negative Character Traits

Upon consultation of linguistic Philosophy (to examine word analysis and the ways that synonyms relate to each other), I have compiled a list of seventeen of the major categories of negative character traits. Each main character trait consists of sub-categories that connect or support that particular quality.

Because this First (Youth) Edition is an interactive volume (as an eBook), I have allowed for feedback (or comments) to be made by the participants as they join in a group therapy session (or, for individuals simply wishing to improve their inner moral nature). As one writes down his admission of this or that negative trait, the hope and aspiration is that he will upon the recognition of this particular fault, seek redress, to (eventually) correct this error at some point in his progression; thereby, improving his character.

In the next section ("The Seventeen Positive Character Traits"), a replacement of these negative traits (so admitted) can be achieved.

Youth Feedback:
____

____

____

DISCLAIMER: N.B. (*Nota Bene*)
All tunes/songs/video clips/links/quotes/etc. are herein provided to assist in Group Therapy Sessions, or privately, for individual study (to assist in learning) and for educational purposes *only*.

[#71: U-Tube Reference]
Poppy Family - Where Evil Grows (1971 - HD - 720p)
https://www.youtube.com/watch?v=QfeEcCLMtxk

Where Evil Grows

I should have steered away from you
My friend told me to keep clear of you

But something drew me near to you
I never knew where evil grew

Evil grows in the dark
Where the sun it never shines
Evil grows in cracks and holes
And lives in people's minds

Angry:

Abusive

Aggressive

Argumentative

Brawling

Clamouring

Contentious

Discordant

Disputing

Easily-provoked

Exasperated

Fighting

Furious

Hot-tempered

Indignant

Insulting

Irritating

Maddening

Offending

Profane

Provocative

Quarrelsome

Raging

Resentful

Reviling

Ridiculing

Shouting

Strife-like

Striking

Swearing

Vexing

Wrathful

FOOD FOR THOUGHT:

For the Natural Man Striving to Become Spiritual

Meditation: (To Chew over one's Thoughts!)
Listen to what your child is trying to tell you *not* to do!:

Don't spoil me. I know quite well that I ought not to have all that I ask for. I'm only teasing you. Don't take too much notice of my small ailments. If you do, you will find that I stop asking and seek my information elsewhere.

Rule #1: For Raising Delinquent Children:

"Begin with infancy to give the child everything he wants. In this way he will grow up to believe that the world owes him a living."

Youth Feedback:
____

____

____

Rule #1: For Repentance (to turn your life around):

Recognize that an attitude or action is out of harmony with God's will.

Youth Feedback:
____

____

____

Angry

When I think of an angry animal, I think of a baboon beating his chest. When I think of an example of an angry person, I think of Adolf Hitler ranting and raving over one of his many political tirades, screaming at the top of his lungs with eyes bursting with rage! It's been said: "There's a raging tiger inside every man whom God put on this earth. Every man spends his life building inside himself a cage to pen this tiger in!" (Murray Kempton)

The proactive approach to a build-up of anger should be one as the world-renown psychiatrist, Karl Menninger, puts it: "We need to neutralize the aggressions that well up within us: Often, strangely enough, against those who have the most in common with us. To understand all is to forgive all, and to know one another well enough should not be to hate one another the more but to love one another the more."

Although it is true (as Ralph Waldo Emerson says) "we boil at different degrees," we should try to emulate Aristotle's advice: "Anybody can become angry--that is easy: but to be angry with the right person, and to the right degree, and at the right time, and for the right purpose, and in the right way--that is not within everybody's power, and is not easy."

Even Buddha advises against anger in this vivid analogy: "Holding on to anger is like grasping a hot coal with the intent of throwing it at someone else: you are the one that gets burned".

1A.   Angry:

Youth Feedback:
____

____

____

1. Abusive

Youth Feedback:
____

____

____

2. Aggressive

Youth Feedback:
____

____

____

3. Argumentative

Youth Feedback:
____

____

____

4. Brawling

Youth Feedback:
____

____

____

5. Clamouring

Youth Feedback:
____

____

____

6. Contentious

Youth Feedback:

____

____

____

7. Discordant

Youth Feedback:

____

____

____

8. Disputing

Youth Feedback:

____

____

____

9. Easily-provoked

Youth Feedback:

____

____

____

10. Exasperated

Youth Feedback:

____

____

____

11. Fighting

Youth Feedback:

____

____

____

12. Furious

Youth Feedback:

____

____

____

13.   Hot-tempered

Youth Feedback:

____

____

____

14. Indignant

Youth Feedback:

____

____

____

15. Insulting

Youth Feedback:

____

____

____

16. Irritating

Youth Feedback:

____

____

____

17. Maddening

Youth Feedback:

____

____

____

18. Offending

Youth Feedback:

____

____

____

19. Profane

Youth Feedback:

____

____

____

20. Provocative

Youth Feedback:

____

____

____

21. Quarrelsome

Youth Feedback:

____

____

____

22. Raging

Youth Feedback:

____

____

____

23. Resentful

Youth Feedback:

____

____

____

24. Reviling

Youth Feedback:

____

____

____

25. Ridiculing

Youth Feedback:

____

____

____

26. Shouting

Youth Feedback:

____

____

____

27. Strife-like

Youth Feedback:

____

____

____

28. Striking

Youth Feedback:

____

____

____

29. Swearing

Youth Feedback:

____

____

____

30. Vexing

Youth Feedback:

____

____

____

31. Wrathful

Youth Feedback:

____

____

____

Arrogant:

Assuming

Behaving-(as-an-upstart)

Boastful

Cocksure

Conceited

Disdainful

Dogmatic

Egotistic

Empty-(inside)

Frustrated

Haughty

Having-hubris

High-minded

Imperious

Insolent

Lofty

Lordly

Pompous

Presumptuous

Proud

Seeming-superior

Self-exalting

Self-important

Self-willful

Stubborn

Vain

Vainglorious

Worldly

FOOD FOR THOUGHT:

For the Natural Man Striving to Become Spiritual

Meditation: (To Chew over one's Thoughts):
Listen to what your child is trying to tell you *not* to do!:

Don't be afraid to be firm with me. I prefer it. It lets me know where I stand. Don't let my fears arouse your anxiety. Then I will become more afraid. Show me courage.

Rule #2: For Raising Delinquent Children:

"When he picks up bad words, laugh at him. This will make him think he's cute!"

  Youth Feedback:
____

____

____

Rule #2: For Repentance (Turning your life around):

Remorse: Feel genuinely sorry with a broken heart and contrite spirit.

  Youth Feedback:
____

____

____

Arrogant

What better example of a puffed-up arrogant animal than a proud peacock strutting its fan of colourful feathers (especially during the mating season). When I think of an arrogant man, proud as a peacock, the image of Benito Mussolini vividly comes to mind with his jaw outwardly strutting out, and his hands astride his waist as he bellows out his political tirades from the balcony overlooking Piazza Centrale across the Duomo in Milan, Italy.

His many standoffish mannerisms remind me as well of Shakespeare's famous lines in *Measure for Measure*:

"Man, proud man,
Dressed in a little brief authority,
Most ignorant of what he's most assured;
His glassy essence, like an angry ape,
Plays such fantastic tricks before High Heaven
To make the angels weep"!

2B. Arrogant:

Youth Feedback:

____

____

____

  1. Assuming

Youth Feedback:

____

____

____

  2. Behaving-(as an-upstart)

Youth Feedback:

____

____

____

  3. Boastful

Youth Feedback:

____

____

____

  4. Cocksure

Youth Feedback:

____

____

____

  5. Conceited

Youth Feedback:

____

____

____

6. Disdainful

Youth Feedback:

____

____

____

7. Dogmatic

Youth Feedback:

____

____

____

8. Egotistic

Youth Feedback:

____

____

____

9. Empty-(inside)

Youth Feedback:

____

____

____

10. Frustrated

Youth Feedback:

____

____

____

11. Haughty

Youth Feedback:

____

____

____

12. Having-hubris

Youth Feedback:

____

____

____

13. High-minded

Youth Feedback:

____

____

____

14. Imperious

Youth Feedback:

____

____

____

15. Insolent

Youth Feedback:

____

____

____

16. Lofty

Youth Feedback:

____

____

____

17. Lordly

Youth Feedback:

____

____

____

18. Pompous

Youth Feedback:

____

____

19. Presumptuous

Youth Feedback:

____

____

20. Proud

Youth Feedback:

____

____

21. Seeming-superior

Youth Feedback:

____

____

22. Self-exalting

Youth Feedback:

____

____

23. Self-important

Youth Feedback:

____

____

24. Self-willful

Youth Feedback:

____

____

____

25. Stubborn

Youth Feedback:

____

____

____

26. Vain

Youth Feedback:

____

____

____

27. Vainglorious

Youth Feedback:

____

____

____

28. Worldly

Youth Feedback:

____

____

____

Biased:

Adhering-to-kangaroo-justice

Having-lynch-mob-mentality

Imbalanced

Partial

Playing-favourites

Prejudiced

Prepossessing

Rendering-evil-for-evil

Respecter-of-persons

Skewed

Unfair

Unjust

Warped-thinking

FOOD FOR THOUGHT:

For the Natural Man Striving to Become Spiritual

Meditation: (To Chew over one's Thoughts):
Listen to what your child is trying to tell you *not* to do!:

Don't use force with me. It teaches me that power is all that counts. I will respond more readily to being led.

Rule #3: For Raising Delinquent Children:

"Never give him any spiritual training. Wait until he is 21 and then let him 'decide for himself.'"

Youth Feedback:

____

____

____

Rule #3: For Repentance (to turn your life around):

Resolve and truly desire to make a permanent change.

Youth Feedback:

____

____

____

Biased

Today (in the 2020s) it is commonplace to use the term, 'Fake News!", to describe what once upon a time used to be professional journalism, unbiased news reporting. But (alas) the bias of Mass Media (even mainstream TV, and newspaper articles) is so rampant and rancid that it reeks to High Heaven.

The self-serving 'me first' attitude is so prevalent in social circles nowadays (especially in political cliqués) that it makes one wonder whether it will ever be possible to one day return to any modicum of fairness, of a sense of fair play in normal social intercourse? We live in Machiavellian times (it appears) without much hope or prospect of things ever returning to normalcy (in our lifetime).

In the animal world, I think of the cuckoo bird which is so biased against its own brood that it parks its eggs in the nest of other birds (to do the job of hatching them). Then there's the ostrich which is noted for hiding its head in the sand when pursued. Hence, people who are biased against the truth are commonly described as: 'ostrich-like'.

Robert H. Jackson claims that: "The most odious of all oppressions are those which mask as Justice". As Thomas Fuller also points out: "A fox should not be on the jury at a goose's trial".

Or, as Bill Maher says: "In this country, you're guilty until proven wealthy". Even the famous poet Robert Frost acknowledged that: "A Jury consists of twelve persons chosen to decide who has the better lawyer". To which Peter F. Drucker agrees: "Everyone is prone to look for the facts that fit the conclusion they have already reached".

Historically, we see through the most famous Trials of history, that prejudice, and bias (arguably) stacked the *kangaroo court* (to list but a few):

#1: The Trial of O.J. Simpson, a famous football player found "Not Guilty" (in 1995) under the criminal code but 'Guilty" under the Civil Code (in 1997) for the double homicide (on 12th June 1994) of his ex-wife (Nicole Brown Simpson) and her lover (Ron Goldman), a clear travesty of Justice on all counts.

#2: (Commencing 09 January 1431 AD), the Trial of Joan of Arc (a simple French maid, Jeanne d'Arc, who claimed God spoke to her, who led Charles VII of France to military victories as a result, and who was burned as a heretic on 30th May 1431 by the biased English Military Courts).

#3: The (secret military) Trial of Alfred Dreyfuss on 19th December 1894 (a French Artillery Officer) falsely accused of being a 'Judas' (to France) in that he (as falsely alleged) betrayed military secrets to the enemy (Germany). He was sentenced on 05 January 1895 to Devil's Island for life imprisonment.

#4: The Trial(s) of Joseph Smith, Jr. (all fake charges by biased antagonists) resulting in his murder (while awaiting trial) on 27th June 1844.

#5: The Trial of Socrates (by his highly biased civic leaders) for "corrupting the youth" (moral corruption) and "impiety" (to the gods) resulted in his sentence: To commit suicide by drinking hemlock.

#6: And the most famous Trial of all time (before Pontius Pilate): The Sanhedrin (and Roman) Trial of Jesus Christ (an innocent man crucified to satiate the biases of certain Jewish religious leaders of his day in 33 AD).

3C. Biased:

Youth Feedback:

____

____

____

   1. Adhering-to-kangaroo-justice

Youth Feedback:

____

____

____

   2. Having-lynch-mob-mentality

Youth Feedback:

____

____

____

   3. Imbalanced

Youth Feedback:

____

____

____

   4. Partial

Youth Feedback:

____

____

____

   5. Playing–favorites

Youth Feedback:

____

____

____

6. Prejudiced

Youth Feedback:

____

____

____

7. Prepossessing

Youth Feedback:

____

____

____

8. Rendering-evil-for-evil

Youth Feedback:

____

____

____

9. Respecter-of-persons

Youth Feedback:

____

____

____

10. Skewed

Youth Feedback:

____

____

____

11. Unfair

Youth Feedback:

____

____

____

12. Unjust

Youth Feedback:

____

____

____

13. Warped-thinking

Youth Feedback:

____

____

____

Constantly-critical:

Asking [silly questions]

Begrudging

Blaming [non-stop]

Caustic

Condemning-unjustly

Crabby

Denouncing

Exacting

Gossiping

Grumbling

Ignorant

Immature

Impractical

Impulsive

Judging-prematurely

Mis-communicating

Nagging

Naive

Provocative

Rebuking

Roasting

Scathing

Scornful

Selfish

Self-pitying

Self-seeking

Slamming

Sneering

Sniping

Unrelenting [complaints]

FOOD FOR THOUGHT:

For the Natural Man Striving to Become Spiritual

Meditation: (To Chew over one's Thoughts!):
Listen to what your child is trying to tell you *not* to do!:

Don't be inconsistent. That confuses me and makes me try harder to get away with everything that I can. Treat me the way you treat your friends; then, I will be your friend too!

Rule #4: For Raising Delinquent Children:

"Avoid the use of the word 'wrong'! It may develop a guilt complex: This will condition him to believe later, when he is arrested for stealing a car, that society is against him, and he is being persecuted."

Youth Feedback:

____

____

____

Rule #4: For Repentance (to turn your life around):

Report, confess sins to the Lord, and talk with people whom you trust.

Youth Feedback:

____

____

____

Constantly-critical

Elvis Presley in his song: *You're Nothing but a Hound Dog!* points out the unhappy love affair in which the woman is "Crying all the time". The gist of the song (as I understand it) is not about abuse, that is: it is not the case that the girl in the relationship is being abused, as it is that she is crying (or, whining) all the time constantly critical of her lover.

In my cinematic repertoire, I think of Dr. Zachary Smith in the original (classic) TV Series, *Lost In Space*, played by Jonathan Harris: He was always saying how terrible everything is, nothing went right for him, it seemed. He never stopped complaining.

The Apostle James in his Epistle states: "If any man offend not in word, the same is a perfect man, and able also to bridle the whole body" (James 3:2). To be constantly critical is 'to offend another person,' not to be confused with legitimate and well-deserved criticism: the catchword is to be *constantly* critical, to not let up, to keep hounding away at the person that (if habitual) can become a negative character trait.

As James explains: "The tongue is a little member [of the body] and boasts great things. Behold, how great a matter a little fire kindles! And the tongue is a fire, a world of iniquity... it defiles the whole body, ... and is set on fire of hell. For every kind of beasts, and of birds, and of serpents, and of things in the sea, is tamed, and has been tamed of mankind. But the tongue can no man tame; it is an unruly evil, full of deadly poison... For where envying and strife is, there is confusion and every evil work." (James 3:5-8,16)

Perhaps no greater example of the negative result of this 'fire of hell' resulting in an 'evil work' is that of the last weekend in the life of Marilyn Monroe. Having had literally perhaps the worst month of her life (July 1962), Ms. Monroe began to fight back, to try to regain some sort of sanity, some sort of dignity through all the ugly filthy morass she was put through in July.

She decided to advertise to everyone (the Kennedy brothers, in particular) that come Monday morning 6th August 1962 she was going to the Media, she had an appointment with *Look* magazine, and with other notables, for there would be hell to pay: she wasn't going to take it anymore, as a 'woman scorned' by those who seemed to willingly and continually take the most intimate advantages of her!

But as Dr. Bill Truels points out (in his YouTube video, *"The Mafia Murder of Marilyn Monroe"*) perhaps Marilyn crossed a 'red line' in continually criticizing her failed relationship with the Kennedy's. Marilyn would not hold back her tongue as the Kennedy brothers had cut off all phone conversation and she had to go through Peter Lawford (married to Patricia Kennedy) and her good friend, Jeanne Carmen, to convince Bobby Kennedy to come to see her at 4 pm (4th August 1962) at her Brentwood home in L.A. Several witnesses attested to his visit (twice) to her place (later at 10:00 pm that night as well).

This book is not the place to settle the issues of Marilyn Monroe's 'mysterious death'. In 2039 (we're promised), there will be total declassification of all documents held by the CIA and FBI on Marilyn. But before that date, let me simply say (as pertains to this part of my book) that it is quite reasonable to suppose that had Ms. Monroe simply held back from 'shaking the apple tree' or from 'rocking the boat' (choose your own analogy), she quite likely would not have died.

A controversial point, some may say, but the evidence carefully analyzed can easily prove the point (to those who care about 'the truth of what really happened that fateful night'). Numerous witnesses (who lived in that era and who gave their inside knowledge albeit much later in life, to avoid hostile repercussions from 'the powers that be', shall we say) have carefully crafted the events of that weekend.

As I say, my point in alluding to this tragic story is not to prove anything definitively but to simply say, if you have eyes to see, then see for yourself all the staggering evidence that is currently available which proves beyond any doubt that Marilyn Monroe was murdered. See, for instance, Jeanne Carmen's book (published by her children after her death) entitled: *My Wild, Wild Life* (2006); as well as Anthony Summers classic research work, entitled: *Goddess: The Secret Lives of Marilyn Monroe* (1983), just to name one or two.

Perhaps it's a moot point today, but I conclude that if MM had not threatened to 'spill the beans' on what she knew, her life may have been spared?! MM granted was no whiner (as a rule), but even though her complaints were likely legitimate, silence would have been not only *golden,* but more prudent given the unpredictable political power-play in 1962.

My favorite Scripture with regard to the tongue as 'an unruly evil' is from Proverbs: "A soft answer turns away wrath: but grievous words stir up anger"! (Proverbs 15:1) James says that to do so, to be wise and "endued with knowledge" would constitute 'a perfect man', but then as Marilyn Monroe famously said: "But I'm not perfect"! And there's the rub: Which one of us is perfect? (Although as the thrust or theme of this book attempts to demonstrate, we can certainly try to become so with Divine Guidance.)

4D. Constantly-critical:

Youth Feedback:

____

____

____

1. Asking [silly questions]

Youth Feedback:

____

____

____

2. Begrudging

Youth Feedback:

____

____

____

3. Blaming [non-stop]

Youth Feedback:

____

____

____

4. Caustic

Youth Feedback:

____

____

____

5. Condemning-unjustly

Youth Feedback:

____

____

____

6. Crabby

Youth Feedback:

____

____

____

7. Denouncing

Youth Feedback:

____

____

____

8. Exacting

Youth Feedback:

____

____

____

9. Gossiping

Youth Feedback:

____

____

____

10. Grumbling

Youth Feedback:

____

____

____

11. Ignorant

Youth Feedback:

____

____

____

12\. Immature

Youth Feedback:

____

____

13\. Impractical

Youth Feedback:

____

____

14\. Impulsive

Youth Feedback:

____

____

15\. Judging-prematurely

Youth Feedback:

____

____

16\. Mis-communicating

Youth Feedback:

____

____

17\. Nagging

Youth Feedback:

____

____

18. Naive

Youth Feedback:

____

____

19. Provocative

Youth Feedback:

____

____

20. Rebuking

Youth Feedback:

____

____

21. Roasting

Youth Feedback:

____

____

22. Scathing

Youth Feedback:

____

____

23. Scornful

Youth Feedback:

____

____

24. Selfish

Youth Feedback:

____

____

____

25. Self-pitying

Youth Feedback:

____

____

____

26. Self-seeking

Youth Feedback:

____

____

____

27. Slamming

Youth Feedback:

____

____

____

28. Sneering

Youth Feedback:

____

____

____

29. Sniping

Youth Feedback:

____

____

____

30. Unrelenting [complaints]

Youth Feedback:

____

____

____

Fearful:

Alarmed	Indecisive
Anxious	Nervous
Apprehensive	Palpitating
Being-ashamed	Phobic
Conforming-easily	Quaking
Cowardly	Quivering
Dismayed	Scared
Double-minded	Shaken-(in mind)
Dreadful	(Terribly)-shocked
Faint-hearted	Timid
Fear-mongering	Trembling
Feeling-shameful	Uncertain
Fickle	Unstable
Fluctuating	Unsteady
Frightened	Vacillating
Guilt-ridden	Volatile
Having-consternation	Wavering
Having-misgivings	Worrisome
Horrified	
Inconsistent	

FOOD FOR THOUGHT:

For the Natural Man Striving to Become Spiritual

Meditation: (To Chew over one's Thoughts!):
Listen to what your child is trying to tell you *not* to do!:

Don't make too many promises: you may not be able to keep them all. That will discourage my trust in you.

Rule #5: For Raising Delinquent Children:

"Pick up everything he leaves lying around: books, shoes, and clothes! Do everything for him so that he will be experienced in throwing all responsibility on others."

Youth Feedback:

____

____

____

Rule #5: For Repentance (to turn your life around):

Rely on the merits and mercy of God and put yourself in His hands.

Youth Feedback:

____

____

____

Fearful

For a squirrel racing up the tree, or the trembling of a shell-shocked sailor, every slight movement (or change in the scenery) would cause either a flight, or fear response, or both. Sophocles once said: "To him who is afraid everything rustles"! Macbeth (in Shakespeare's play by that name) seemed always fearful that his crime of murder would be discovered. So did the murderer in Fyodor Dostoevsky's classic novel: *Crime and Punishment!*

Guilt riddled with fear (and constant dismay) is perhaps one of the worst psychological states of the human mind. In many cases, it is the natural consequence of having committed a horrendous act or an unconscionable crime.

As Ted Bundy relates: [just before being executed] "I don't want to die, I kid you not, but I deserve the most extreme punishment Society has to offer. I believe Society deserves to be protected from me, and from others like me. That's for sure!" As Voltaire put it: "Fear follows crime and is its punishment."

'FEAR' has been described as: "False Evidence Appearing Real"; as 'the parent of cruelty' (James A. Froude); as "the tax conscience pays to guilt"; 'as a fine spur'; as 'the absence of faith' (Paul Tillich); as 'the prison of the heart'; as 'the father of hate'; as 'the main source of superstition' (Bertrand Russell). For (as John Witherspoon puts it): "It is only the fear of God that can deliver us from the fear of men"! Franklin D. Roosevelt claimed that: "The only thing we have to fear is fear itself!" To which Marie Curie noted: "Nothing in life is to be feared: It is only to be understood".

To realize the guilt we may feel is to realize that we sometimes shut the door to the feelings of guilt about the things that perhaps we should feel guilty about; perhaps it is because "we are continually stifling our deepest impulses" (Henry Miller)? A lot is made of the benefit of 'fear' over that of 'love': (as Machiavelli explains) "Love is held by a chain of obligation which men, being selfish, break whenever it serves their purpose; but fear is maintained by a dread of punishment which never fails."

R.D. Laing puts it bluntly: "If we can stop destroying ourselves, we may stop destroying others. We have to begin by admitting and even accepting our violence, rather than blindly destroying ourselves with it, and therewith we have to realize that we are as deeply afraid to live and to love, as we are to die."

Machiavelli concludes: "Since love and fear can hardly exist together, if we must choose between them, it is far safer to be feared than loved". But as Jean Pierre Camus contends: "Those who love to be feared, fear to be loved"! For "nothing is more despicable than respect based on fear" (Albert Camus). "Fear is something learned: we are born with love" (Marianne Williamson). Indeed, to "live with fear and not be afraid is the final test of maturity" (Edward Weeks).

My favorite quote is by Richard Halverson: "Men who fear God face life fearlessly. Men who do not fear God end up fearing everything"! Martin Luther King, Jr. had this amazing insight with regard to the origin of our fears: "Men hate each other because they fear each other; they fear each other because they don't know each other; they don't know each other because they are separated from each other".

5E. Fearful:

Youth Feedback:

____

____

____

1. Alarmed

Youth Feedback:

____

____

____

2. Anxious

Youth Feedback:

____

____

____

3. Apprehensive

Youth Feedback:

____

____

____

4. Being-ashamed

Youth Feedback:

____

____

____

5. Conforming-easily

Youth Feedback:

____

____

____

6. Cowardly

Youth Feedback:

____

____

____

7. Dismayed

Youth Feedback:

____

____

____

8. Double-minded

Youth Feedback:

____

____

____

9. Dreadful

Youth Feedback:

____

____

____

10. Faint-hearted

Youth Feedback:

____

____

____

11. Fear-mongering

Youth Feedback:

____

____

____

12. Feeling-shameful

Youth Feedback:

____

____

____

13. Fickle

Youth Feedback:

____

____

____

14. Fluctuating

Youth Feedback:

____

____

____

15. Frightened

Youth Feedback:

____

____

____

16. Guilt-ridden

Youth Feedback:

____

____

____

17. Having-consternation

Youth Feedback:

____

____

____

18. Having-misgivings

Youth Feedback:

____

____

____

19. Horrified

Youth Feedback:

____

____

____

20. Inconsistent

Youth Feedback:

____

____

____

21. Indecisive

Youth Feedback:

____

____

____

22. Nervous

Youth Feedback:

____

____

____

23. Palpitating

Youth Feedback:

____

____

____

24. Phobic

Youth Feedback:

____

____

____

25. Quaking

Youth Feedback:

____

____

____

26. Quivering

Youth Feedback:

____

____

____

27. Scared

Youth Feedback:

____

____

____

28. Shaken-(in mind)

Youth Feedback:

____

____

____

29. (Terribly)-shocked

Youth Feedback:

____

____

____

30. Timid

Youth Feedback:

____

____

____

31. Trembling

Youth Feedback:

____

____

____

32. Uncertain

Youth Feedback:

____

____

____

33. Unstable

Youth Feedback:

____

____

____

34. Unsteady

Youth Feedback:

____

____

____

35. Vacillating

Youth Feedback:

____

____

____

36. Volatile

Youth Feedback:

____

____

____

37. Wavering

Youth Feedback:

____

____

____

38. Worrisome

Youth Feedback:

____

____

____

Greedy:

Avaricious

Covetous

Extravagant

Loving-luxury

Loving-money

Materialistic

Mercenary

Miserly

Usurious

FOOD FOR THOUGHT:

For the Natural Man Striving to Become Spiritual

Meditation: (To Chew over one's Thoughts!):
Listen to what your child is trying to tell you *not* to do!:

Don't fall for my provocations when I may do things just to upset you. Then I'll try for more such victories. Don't forget that I love to use experimenting. I learn from it; so please put up with it.

Rule #6: For Raising Delinquent Children:

"Let him read any printed matter he can get his hands on. Be careful that the silverware and drinking glasses are sterilized but let his mind feast on garbage."

Youth Feedback:

____

____

____

Rule #6: For Repentance (to turn your life around):

Respond to guidance from Church and Community leaders (who are imbued with the Spirit of God).

Youth Feedback:

____

____

____

Greedy

When I think of *greed*, I think of the movie by the same name [1924 silent film by Director Erich von Stroheim]: it's worth watching to obtain a visual reminder just how distasteful *greed* really is, and yet how prevalent it is in our Society. The hog, or swine, or fat pig is the standard universal symbol for greed.

One thinks of George Orwell's *Animal Farm*, in which all the animals are declared 'equal' but some (i.e., the ruling 'Pigs') are 'more equal' than all the others. That is the essence of *greed*: To have and want more all the time, to never have enough, to feel as if one can never satiate his (greedy) desires.

Seneca perhaps put it best (and in the simplest way): "Believe me, of all people in the world those who want the most are those who have the most". To better understand this miserly nature with respect to *money*, one need but watch (or read) Charles Dickens' masterpiece: *A Christmas Carol*, on the self-centred life of Ebenezer Scrooge, a miser who thinks only of himself. Zeno describes this sentiment near-perfectly: "The avaricious man is like the barren ground of the desert, which sucks in all the rain and dew with greediness but yields no fruitful herbs or plants for the benefit of others."

Socrates, the Ancient Greek philosopher, asks the question: "Are you not ashamed of heaping up the greatest amount of money and honour and reputation; and caring so little about wisdom and truth and the greatest improvement of the soul?" to which Henry George answers: "Nature laughs at the miser. He is like the squirrel who buries his nuts and refrains from digging them up again."

Immanuel Kant (1724-1804) explains this conundrum in more detail:

"Avarice arises from a process of misguided logic. We see about us the good and pleasant things of life, and we wish to possess and enjoy them, but because we have not the wherewithal, we make up our minds to obtain the necessary funds by saving. We accustom ourselves to do without one thing after another, and in the process of time we gradually wean ourselves from all pleasures; we cease to care for them, and we become indifferent to their very existence. By the time that we have acquired the means, so that the good and pleasant things are within our reach, we have lost the taste for them, and it has given way to the taste for saving and hoarding; we go on saving and laying by when it is no longer necessary for us to do so."

It was Gandhi who rightly said: "There is sufficiency in the world for man's need but not for man's greed!": No gain, apparently, satisfies a greedy mind! This dark side to 'greed' is clearly seen in the words of Thomas Fuller: "The pleasures of the rich are bought with the tears of the poor".

My most thought-provoking quote on *'greed'* is the question asked by our Savior: "For what is a man profited, if he shall gain the whole world, and lose his own soul?" (Matthew 16:26)

6F. Greedy:

Youth Feedback:

____

____

____

  1. Avaricious

Youth Feedback:

____

____

____

  2. Covetous

Youth Feedback:

____

____

____

  3. Extravagant

Youth Feedback:

____

____

____

  4. Loving-luxury

Youth Feedback:

____

____

____

  5. Loving-money

Youth Feedback:

____

____

____

6. Materialistic

Youth Feedback:

____

____

____

7. Mercenary

Youth Feedback:

____

____

____

8. Miserly

Youth Feedback:

____

____

____

9. Usurious

Youth Feedback:

____

____

____

Hell-bent:

Acting-with-dark-humour

Agitated

Bragging

Dare-devilish

Easily-excitable

Emoting-fiery-feelings

Hot-headed

Impetuous

Issuing-oaths

Jesting-(in a coarse way)

Light-minded

Ludicrous

Swearing

Threatening

Vaunting

FOOD FOR THOUGHT:

For the Natural Man Striving to Become Spiritual

Meditation: (To Chew over one's Thoughts!):
Listen to what your child is trying to tell you *not* to do!:

Don't be too upset when I say, 'I *hate* you!' I don't mean it, but I want you to feel sorry for what you have done to me.

Rule #7: For Raising Delinquent Children:

"Quarrel frequently in the presence of your children. In this way, they will not be too shocked when the home is broken up later."

Youth Feedback:

____

____

____

Rule #7: For Repentance (to turn your life around):

Request forgiveness from the Lord.

Youth Feedback:

____

____

____

Hell-bent

Whenever I think of a 'hell-bent' animal, I can't help but think of a frightening vicious-looking bat, or as the phrase goes: "like a bat from Hell!".

In the Cinema world, I think of that character, Tony Montana played by Al Pacino in *Scarface* (1983), who is truly hellbent from the get-go. He works his way up the criminal underworld bent upon creating 'hell' everywhere he goes. But the story is a sad one as is all too typical with this negative character trait: Tony Montana ends up killing his sister's husband, estranging himself from all his family, and then is killed himself. There is a saying that Satan the Devil will never support his own children on the last day, and this cinema tale sends that grueling message in spades.

There is a common saying that unless we rule our passions, they shall rule us. As our Lord put it much more clearly: "Whatsoever thing from without enters into the man, it cannot defile him; Because it enters not into his heart, but into the belly... That which comes out of the man, that defiles the man. For from within, out of the heart of men, proceed evil thoughts, adulteries, fornications, murders, thefts, covetousness, wickedness, deceit, lasciviousness, an evil eye, blasphemy, pride, foolishness: All these evil things come from within, and defile the man". (Mark 7:18-22)

Yet perhaps the best example in all literature (that I'm aware of) of the 'Hell-bent' persona is that of Richard III as Shakespeare describes him:

"If any spark of life be yet remaining,
Down, down to hell, and say I sent thee thither,
I, that have neither pity, love, nor fear.
Indeed, 'tis true that Henry told me of;
For I have often heard my mother say
I came into the world with my legs forward.
Had I not reason, think ye, to make haste
And seek their ruin that usurped our right?

The midwife wondered, and the women cried,
'O, Jesus bless us! He is born with teeth!

and so I was; which plainly signified
That I should snarl and bite and play the dog.
Then, since the heavens have shaped my body so,
Let hell make crook'd my mind to answer it.
I have no brother, I am like no brother;
And this word 'love,' which greybeards call divine,
Be resident in men like one another,
And not in me. I am myself alone."

Henry VI, Third Part

7G. Hell-bent:

Youth Feedback:
____
____
____

1. Acting-with-dark-humour

Youth Feedback:
____
____
____

2. Agitated

Youth Feedback:
____
____
____

3. Bragging

Youth Feedback:
____
____
____

4. Dare-devilish

Youth Feedback:
____
____
____

5. Easily-excitable

Youth Feedback:
____
____
____

6.   Emoting-fiery-feelings

Youth Feedback:

____

____

____

7.   Hot-headed

Youth Feedback:

____

____

____

8.   Impetuous

Youth Feedback:

____

____

____

9.   Issuing-oaths

Youth Feedback:

____

____

____

10. Jesting-(in a coarse way)

Youth Feedback:

____

____

____

11. Light-minded

Youth Feedback:

____

____

____

12. Ludicrous

Youth Feedback:

____

____

____

13. Swearing

Youth Feedback:

____

____

____

14. Threatening

Youth Feedback:

____

____

____

15. Vaunting

Youth Feedback:

____

____

____

Jealous:

Antipathetic	Malevolent
Being-disturbed	Malignant
Bigoted	Odious
Bitter	Psychopathic
Blind [refusing to see]	Racist
Damnable	Rancorous
Detestable	Repugnant
Degrading	Resentful
Discriminatory	Revengeful
Disgusting	Revolting
Envious	Sociopathic
Green-eyed	Sorrowful
Having-animus [ill will]	Spiteful
Indifferent	Vile
Loathing	

FOOD FOR THOUGHT:

For the Natural Man Striving to Become Spiritual

Meditation: (To Chew over one's Thoughts!):
Listen to what your child is trying to tell you *not* to do:

Don't make me feel smaller than I am. I will make up for it by behaving like a 'big shot'! Don't let my 'bad habits' get me a lot of attention. It only encourages me to continue them.

Rule #8: For Raising Delinquent Children:

"Give a child all the spending money he wants. Never let him earn his own. Why should he have things as tough as you had then?"

Youth Feedback:
____

____

____

Rule #8: For Repentance (to turn your life around):

Receive God's gift of forgiveness.

Youth Feedback:
____

____

____

Jealous

When I think of that 'green-eyed monster', jealousy, I think of the cuckoo bird who raids the nests of other birds, full of jealousy of their 'home', and when that other mother bird is not 'home' (looking for food for it's young) pushes out one of the eggs and supplants it with its own egg. Amazingly, the cuckoo egg almost perfectly matches the colour, size, and appearance of the egg it just destroyed.

Then when the cuckoo bird egg hatches (which nature allows it to hatch a lot earlier than the other eggs), it breaks through its shell and immediately pushes the eggs of the other birds out from the nest to fall broken to the ground. What a jealous little creature! This action far exceeds sibling rivalry! But then this 'cuckoo' is not their sibling, now is it?! What strange logic of a most jealous creature. (Perhaps this bird is the origin of that other behaviour, to be a "cuckold"? Or a husband whose wife is unfaithful?)

Among humans, the classic tale of extreme jealously is most assuredly that described in Shakespeare's *Othello, The Moor of Venice!* As Gerald Bentley once said: Othello "intensifies the emotional impact of blind self-destruction". And that is typical of the nature of jealousy, so clearly captured by Iago's encouragement to Roderigo: "I hate the Moor. My cause is hearted; thine hath no less reason. Let us be conjunctive in our revenge against him. If thou canst cuckold him, thou dost thyself a pleasure, me a sport".

The gist of jealousy is captured by Iago's own words to his Master, Othello: "O, beware, my lord of jealousy! It is the green-eyed monster, which doth mock the meat if feeds on. That cuckold lives in bliss Who, certain of his fate, loves not his wronger; But O, what damned minutes tells he o'er who dotes, yet doubts--suspects, yet strongly loves!"

As John Milton puts it: "Jealousy is the injured lover's hell"! Or to quote Iago (from Othello) once again: "Trifles light as air Are to the jealous confirmations strong As proofs of holy writ"! for "to be direct and honest is not safe"! I like Henri Amiel's insight into this rage from love to hatred turned: "Jealousy is a terrible thing. It resembles love, only it is precisely love's contrary. Instead of wishing for the welfare of the object loved, it desires the dependence of that object upon itself, and its own triumph".

A sad tale to a jealous lover is that role played by James Mason, in *Islands in the Sun* (1957), a story taken in part from Dostoevsky's *Crime and Punishment*. In both tales, the protagonist who has committed a secret murder through an act of jealousy (compounded with guilt in having committed this heretofore 'unsolved murder') plays into the hands of the Police Detective investigating the crime, and later surrenders to his conscience, eventually confessing his guilt.

In the Bible, jealousy is purported to be as "cruel as the grave" (Song of Solomon 8:6). And as in the case of Desdemona (Othello's wife), it proves to be literally true.

Perhaps the best example of jealousy (in Scripture) is the story of Joseph and his brethren, in which Joseph's brothers sell Joseph for twenty pieces of silver as a slave in bondage "into Egypt" (Genesis 37). Donny Osmond captures this raw sentiment very well (in my view) in his (musical) stage production: *Joseph and His Amazing Technicolor Dream Coat* (1999).

8H. Jealous:

Youth Feedback:

____

____

____

1. Antipathetic

Youth Feedback:

____

____

____

2. Being-disturbed

Youth Feedback:

____

____

____

3. Bigoted

Youth Feedback:

____

____

____

4. Bitter

Youth Feedback:

____

____

____

5. Blind [refusing to see]

Youth Feedback:

____

____

____

6. Damnable

Youth Feedback:

____

____

____

7. Detestable

Youth Feedback:

____

____

____

8. Degrading

Youth Feedback:

____

____

____

9. Discriminatory

Youth Feedback:

____

____

____

10. Disgusting

Youth Feedback:

____

____

____

11. Envious

Youth Feedback:

____

____

____

12. Green-eyed

Youth Feedback:

____

____

____

13. Having-animus [ill will]

Youth Feedback:

____

____

____

14. Indifferent

Youth Feedback:

____

____

____

15. Loathing

Youth Feedback:

____

____

____

16. Malevolent

Youth Feedback:

____

____

____

17. Malignant

Youth Feedback:

____

____

____

18. Odious

Youth Feedback:

____

____

____

19. Psychopathic

Youth Feedback:

____

____

____

20. Racist

Youth Feedback:

____

____

____

21. Rancorous

Youth Feedback:

____

____

____

22. Repugnant

Youth Feedback:

____

____

____

23. Resentful

Youth Feedback:

____

____

____

24. Revengeful

Youth Feedback:

____

____

____

25. Revolting

Youth Feedback:

____

____

____

26. Sociopathic

Youth Feedback:

____

____

____

27. Sorrowful

Youth Feedback:

____

____

____

28. Spiteful

Youth Feedback:

____

____

____

29. Vile

Youth Feedback:

____

____

____

Judgmental:

Agnostic

Atheistic

Cynical

Disbelieving

Distrusting

Doubtful

Excessively-inquisitive

Heretical

Incredulous

Non-believing

Skeptical

Superstitious

Suspicious

Unbelieving

Unduly-interrogatory

Unrighteous

FOOD FOR THOUGHT:

For the Natural Man Striving to Become Spiritual

Meditation: (To Chew over one's Thoughts!):
Listen to what your child is trying to tell you *not* to do!:

Don't do things for me that I can do for myself. It makes me feel like a baby, and I may continue to put you in my service.

Rule #9: For Raising Delinquent Children:

"Satisfy his every craving for food, drink, and comfort. See that every sensual desire is gratified. Denial may lead to harmful frustration!"

Youth Feedback:

____

____

____

Rule #9: For Repentance (to turn your life around):

Restitution: Repair all possible damage to relationships with God or man!

Youth Feedback:

____

____

____

Judgmental

Whenever I think of the ideal animal symbol representing *'Judgment',* I invariably think of the hawk or eagle, in particular of The American Eagle, a majestic stunningly beautiful bird that has piercing eyes (that seem to look right through you), and a-quick-to-react demeanor! In literature, I'm reminded of Hamlet (in the Shakespeare play by that same name) who judged his stepfather to be an evil man; and judged his mother to be a moral weakling.

But from such judgment Hamlet admits to his girlfriend, Ophelia, that he did love her once but that now she should go to a nunnery! In prejudging his stepfather, the King, to be hiding behind near-by curtains while he talked with his mother, the Queen, Hamlet rashly decides to plunge his sword into that curtain only to discover that it was the father to Ophelia who falls dead, not the King, whom he hated.

Ophelia, who, in being grossly neglected by her lover (Hamlet) and discovering that her lover killed her father divides herself "from her fair judgment" and shortly commits suicide. Hamlet's mother, the Queen, concludes that her son is mad, but Hamlet argues that he must be 'cruel in order to be kind' citing paradoxes to prove his point: "A man may fish with the worm that hath eat of a king, and eat of the fish that hath fed of that worm".

The willy-nilly nature of Hamlet's 'judgment' is noted in his reply to Horatio, his best friend (who rightly predicts that Hamlet will lose 'the gentle entertainment to Laertes, the brother to Ophelia'): "There is a special providence in the fall of a sparrow. If it be now, 'tis not to come; if it be not to come, it will be now; if it be not now, yet it will come. The readiness is all." This 'wager' or 'gentle entertainment' is a sword duel by which Hamlet does die, as foretold. Shakespeare's Hamlet is a play full of misjudgments, pre-judgments, and prejudices. As John Locke famously put it: "Men see a little, presume a great deal, and so jump to conclusion"!

Jesus makes this point quite emphatically: "Judge not, that ye be not judged. For with what judgment ye judge, ye shall be judged: and with what measure ye mete, it shall be measured to you again. And why behold you the mote [that tiny speck of dust] that is in your brother's eye, but consider not the [large wooden] beam that is in your own eye? Or how will you say to your brother, Let me pull out the mote out of your eye; and behold a beam [of wood] is in your own eye? You hypocrite, first cast out the beam out of your own eye; and then shall you see clearly to cast out the mote out of your brother's eye." (Matthew 7:1-5)

The Russians have a saying: "When you meet a man, you judge him by his clothes; when you leave, you judge him by his heart." Seneca put it this way: "He who decides a case without hearing the other side, though he decides justly, cannot be considered just." And that is the rub, the gist of pre-judging a situation. In speaking of our conscience as our moral guide, Immanuel Kant argues: "The judge within us is just. He takes the action for what it is and makes no allowance for human defectiveness if only we have the will to listen for his voice and do not stifle it."

Kant further explains: "The moral disposition of others is for God to judge, but we are competent judges of our own. We cannot judge the inner core of morality: no man can do that, but we are competent to judge its outer manifestations. In matters of morality, we are not judges of our fellows, but nature has given us the right to form judgments about others and she also has ordained that we should judge ourselves with judgments that others form about us." Woodrow Wilson put it bluntly: "One cool judgment is worth a thousand hasty councils. The thing to do is to supply light and not heat." For anyone convinced against his will, will remain of the same opinion still.

Thomas à Kempis leaves us with this sobering thought regarding Judgment: "Of a surety, at the Day of Judgment it will be demanded of us, not what we have read, but what we have done; not how well we have spoken, but how holy we have lived. In all that thou doest, remember the end, and how thou will stand before a strict Judge, from Whom nothing is hid, and Who is not bribed with gifts, and accepts excuses, but will judge righteous judgment".

9I. Judgmental:

Youth Feedback:

____

____

____

  1. Agnostic

Youth Feedback:

____

____

____

  2. Atheistic

Youth Feedback:

____

____

____

  3. Cynical

Youth Feedback:

____

____

____

  4. Disbelieving

Youth Feedback:

____

____

____

  5. Distrusting

Youth Feedback:

____

____

____

6. Doubtful

Youth Feedback:

____

____

____

7. Excessively-inquisitive

Youth Feedback:

____

____

____

8. Heretical

Youth Feedback:

____

____

____

9. Incredulous

Youth Feedback:

____

____

____

10. Non-believing

Youth Feedback:

____

____

____

11. Skeptical

Youth Feedback:

____

____

____

12. Superstitious

Youth Feedback:

____

____

____

13. Suspicious

Youth Feedback:

____

____

____

14. Unbelieving

Youth Feedback:

____

____

____

15. Unduly-interrogatory

Youth Feedback:

____

____

____

16. Unrighteous

Youth Feedback:

____

____

____

Lustful:

Adulterous

Carnal

Engaging-in-prostitution

Erotic

Flirtatious

Fornicating

Having-love-affairs

Having-sexual-hangups

Perverse

Promoting-pornography

Sensual

Sexist

Seeking-sexual-deviations

Sexually-stimulating

Whore-mongering

Wishing-to-appear-nude

FOOD FOR THOUGHT:

For the Natural Man Striving to Become Spiritual

Meditation: (To Chew over one's Thoughts!):
Listen to what your child is trying to tell you *not* to do!:

Don't correct me in front of people. I'll take much more notice if you talk quietly with me in private. Don't try to discuss my behaviour in the heat of a conflict. For some reason my hearing is not very good at this time, and my cooperation is even worse. It is all right to take the action required, but let's not talk about it until later.

Rule #10: For Raising Delinquent Children:

"Take his part against neighbours, teachers, and policemen. They are all prejudiced against your child!"

Youth Feedback:

____

____

____

Rule #10: For Repentance (to turn your life around):

Renew your life through a realization of Redemption!

Youth Feedback:

____

____

____

Lustful

The concept of being 'lustful' involves virtually every facet of life, as well as life itself! The 1956 movie, entitled: *"Lust for Life"*, the life story of Dutch artist Vincent Van Gogh (played by Kirk Douglas) tells it all. Webster Dictionary defines 'lust' as: "a strong uncontrollable desire, especially for sexual pleasure" and gives the example: "old men lust after young girls".

Given the sexual (reproductive) overtones of this concept, I think it fitting to refer to rabbits as the animal best representative of this 'desire', as in the oft-quoted phrase: 'to multiply like rabbits'. Playboy magazine uses the symbol of a 'bunny' as its logo.

Everywhere in Scripture, we read that men are to cease to lust after a woman but to love her instead. The powerful warning comes from our Lord Himself, when He says: "Ye have heard that it was said by them of old time, Thou shalt not commit adultery: But I say unto you, That whosoever looks on a woman to lust after her has committed adultery with her already in his heart"! (Matthew 5:27-28) Jesus makes it clear that it is what comes "out of the man" defiles the man, not merely the physical act itself (see, Mark 7:20-23).

Pope John Paul II while visiting the City of Edmonton (on 16 September 1984) quoted this self-same passage of Scripture; and then added that this 'lusting' (looking upon a woman "to lust after her") includes the relationship within marriage, between a husband and his wife (which created no small stir as I still vividly recall from that comment). Lusts are considered 'ungodly' (Jude 18); to be desires of the flesh (I Peter 2:11); to be worldly (Titus 2:12); to be 'foolish and hurtful' (I Timothy 6:9); to be 'deceitful' (Ephesians 4:22); and, to be 'unclean' (Romans 1:24). The Apostle Paul clearly indicates that we are not to 'lust after evil things' (I Corinthians 10:6), for the 'flesh lusts against the Spirit' (Galatians 5:17).

Apostle James

James in his Epistle gives us a deeper analysis of what 'lust' actually means: "Let no man say when he is tempted, I am tempted of God: for God cannot be tempted with evil, neither tempts He any man: But every man is tempted, when he is drawn away of his own lust, and enticed. Then when lust has conceived, it brings forth sin: and sin, when it is finished, brings forth death"! (James 1:13-15)

James further explains: "From whence come wars and fightings among you? Come they not hence, even of your lusts that war in your members? [Think of the two wolves fighting each other inside each one of us.] Ye lust, and have not: ye kill, and desire to have, and cannot obtain: ye fight and war, yet ye have not, because ye ask not. Ye ask, and receive not, because ye ask amiss, that you may conceive it upon your lusts." (James 4:1-3)

James then hits dead-centre to the core of the problem: "Ye adulterers and adulteresses, know ye not that the friendship of the world is enmity with God? whosoever therefore will be a friend of the world is the enemy of God. Do ye think that the scripture says in vain, The spirit that dwells in us lusts to envy?" (v.4). Then James offers the one and only solution to this 'lust-problem': "Submit yourselves therefore to God. Resist the devil, and he will flee from you. Draw nigh unto God, and He will draw nigh to you. Cleanse your hands, ye sinners; and purify your hearts, ye double-minded. Be afflicted, and mourn, and weep: let your laughter be turned to mourning, and your joy to heaviness. Humble yourselves in the sight of the Lord, and He shall lift you up." (Vv. 7-10)

Tamar, as an Object of Lust

Perhaps the best well-known example of "lust" is that found in the Old Testament in II Samuel, chapter 13, in which Amnon lusts after his half-sister Tamar, and forces her to have sex with him. The Scriptures say that Tamar was "fair" and that Amnon "loved her" (again, we shall see that 'love' is used as the excuse for what is actually 'lust') (v.1): "And Amnon was so vexed, that he fell sick for his sister Tamar; for she was a virgin; and Amnon thought it hard for him to do anything to her". (v.2)

So as we shall we see: in order to entrap a woman that a man 'lusts' after, he needs a partner. In this case, "Amnon had a friend, whose name was Jonadab... Jonadab was a very subtil [subtle] man" (v.3). Then as the story goes, both Amnon and 'his friend'

Jonadab concoct a plan to entice Tamar to come to see Amnon alone (vv.4-10). Then Amnon grabbed Tamar and "would not hearken unto her voice: but, being stronger than she, forced her and lay with her." (vv. 11-14).

What happened next is so telling: it reveals that this entire sex act was not an act of love but one of lust: "Then Amnon hated her exceedingly; so that the hatred wherewith he hated her was greater than the love wherewith he had loved her. And Amnon said unto her, Arise, be gone." (v. 15)

And what was the result of this 'desire to love Tamar'? The Scriptures relate the classic case of a woman scorned, one used and abused: "Then [Amnon] called his servant that ministered unto him, and said, Put now this woman out from me, and bolt the door after her...Then his servant brought her out, and bolted the door after her. And Tamar put ashes on her head, and rent her garments of divers colours that was on her, and laid her hand on her head, and went on crying." (vv. 17-18)

Sexual Morality

As Immanuel Kant (the Rationalist philosopher) so adeptly put it: "Sexual love [lust] makes of the loved person an object of appetite. As soon as that appetite has been stilled, the person is cast aside as one casts a lemon which has been sucked dry." In contrast, Bertrand Russell (another philosopher) states that love (or 'sexual morality'): "consists essentially of respect for the other person, an unwillingness to use that person solely as a means of personal gratification, without regard to his or her desires."

Although 'lust is like rot in the bones', Barbara de Angelis' insightful comment distinguishes it from sex: "I like to call sex a training camp for how to behave with people. Just 'making love' with someone is, in itself, an act of trust: I offer you my naked body; I trust you will not hurt me; that you will be loving to me. When you make love with someone, you make yourself completely vulnerable to them."

Matthew Henry contends as well that: "Nature is content with little; grace with less; but lust with nothing". And that is the nub of the problem here: As Seneca, the ancient Roman thinker explains: "If sensuality were happiness, beasts would be happier than men; but human felicity is lodged in the soul, not in the flesh"!

Even Adolf Hitler appears to agree: "Parallel to the training of the body, a struggle against the poisoning of the soul must begin. Our whole public life today is like a hothouse for sexual ideas and stimulations. Just look at the bill of fare served up in our movies, vaudeville, and theaters, and you will hardly be able to deny that this is not the right kind of food, particularly for the youth."

Marilyn Monroe: The Classic Case for Lust

In this regard, we can see that the classic case of the object of 'lust' has been undoubtedly Marilyn Monroe, a woman who from her rape at eight years of age (and on), has been objectified into a sex (or specifically a lust) symbol, someone arguably more desirable than any other woman in the world! It has often been said by narrators and commentators on her life that she perhaps was not even aware of the extent and pervasiveness of this symbolism, appearing almost surprised at the amount of adulation that was heaped upon her throughout her brief and tragic life.

When she was but twenty-six years old, a music crew including Mickey Rooney (1920-2014) put together a song in her honor entitled: "Marilyn" in which one line of the lyrics tells all: "But if luck is with me, she'll be my bride forevermore"! Labeled the "It' girl in 1952, Marilyn was the wholesome 'girl next door' that every man (or so it seemed at the time) wanted to have as his 'bride forevermore'! But this tale of such a charming loveable lass does not have a happy ending.

After Marilyn Monroe had accepted the Whitehouse invitation (on 17th April 1962) and had received approval from Fox studio to attend this Democratic Party Fundraiser on Saturday the 19th May 1962, to sing: "Happy Birthday, Mr. President" (ten days before his actual birthday), she received nothing but criticism from virtually all quarters thereafter. Fox studio (her employer) fired her a few days after her 36th birthday (1st June) on 8th June 1962, citing 'failure to appear for work' (during these two weekends, totaling 12 days of sick time over 32 days of shooting).

Dean Martin who worked with Marilyn refused to have her

substituted and so he was fired along with the entire film repertoire. Not to be undone, and somehow feeling responsible for this extreme action by Fox Studios, Marilyn worked very hard to contact all 104 members of the crew and asked if she could renegotiate a deal with Fox to be rehired, would they agree to return to work. They all said: "Yes!" And so, Marilyn contacted *Life* Magazine, *Look* Magazine, and several personal photographers she knew to update her public image and to have a lot of positive publicity going in all directions. The last photoshoot was on 13th July 1962 with George Barris.

And then came the bad news: on 17th July the White House cut off all future contact with Marilyn telling her not to attempt to call either JFK or RFK anymore. Marilyn was devasted. She wanted one last conversation with at least RFK to find out what happened, and why the sudden silent treatment? She contacted several of her 'phone buddies' and sought their sympathy and empathy on the way she was being treated, as a woman scorned. Then in the middle of all of this kerfuffle, things only became worse, much worse for Marilyn.

Marilyn Monroe's Penultimate Weekend (at Lake Tahoe)

The Chicago crime boss, Sam Giancana (also known as "Momo", a psychotic killer) had lusted after Marilyn for some time and wanted (like Amnon of old) to 'lie with her' but didn't know how to coax her to come to his lair (at Cal Neva next to Lake Tahoe, which he co-owned with Frank Sinatra). And, as in the biblical example of 'lust' and sexual depravity, MM's friend, Patricia Kennedy Lawford (perhaps a 'subtle' woman?) 'tricked' MM to accompany her husband Peter Lawford and herself to Frank Sinatra's Lodge as one pair of researchers describe it:

"Since [Marilyn] Monroe had become intimate with Patricia Kennedy Lawford, Bobby [Kennedy] apparently prevailed on Pat Lawford to get Monroe out of town during his visit to Los Angeles the weekend of July 27 to 29. The Attorney General was flying in for a public appearance and several conferences on the progress of *The Enemy Within* [a movie production of RFK's book by the same title written in 1960]. Monroe later told [Robert] Slatzer that the Kennedys had tricked her into leaving Los Angeles. But this deception or decoy (to bring MM to Cal-Neva) so that RFK can do his thing in LA without MM present, did not sit well with MM.

"She [MM] also expressed considerable anger at Pat Lawford... The Lawfords persuaded Monroe to accompany them on a weekend jaunt to Lake Tahoe, ostensibly to attend Jack Jones's opening at Frank Sinatra's lavish Cal-Neva Lodge. Weak from the effects of the abortion [of RFK's 'potential child'] and furious over Bobby's hypocrisy, the actress delivered herself into the Lawfords' hands and, again, virtually disappeared until late Sunday night, when the Attorney General was safely back in Washington." (*Marilyn: The Last Take*, pp.282-284; henceforth referred to simply as: MLT)

The previous year, in 1961, Sinatra had a summer affair with Marilyn but broke it off when marriage was discussed. Frankie appeared to relent, however, when he gave MM a pair of emerald earrings (perhaps as a consolation gift?). Quite naturally then, Marilyn was led to believe that 'old blue eyes' could possibly have a change of heart?! So, Marilyn (who had just been passed around 'like a piece of meat' [her own words] from both Kennedy brothers, JFK and RFK) was faintly hopeful at the prospect that Frankie might soothe her 'ruffled feathers,' so to speak. She accepted his invitation (on behalf of the Lawfords) for a private meeting on the weekend of 27-29 July 1962 (the last weekend before her untimely death).

When Marilyn arrived, she was surprised to see Sam Giancana (whom she met many years earlier before she became famous) anxiously awaiting her arrival. Frankie introduced Marilyn to Sam, and then whispered to her: "Be nice to Sam!", and instantly disappeared (to attend to his many other guests for this special weekend, no doubt) leaving Marilyn to fend for herself.

What followed is detailed in various commentaries and biographies on Marilyn, but noteworthy in Daniel Bates' exposé: "Marilyn spent her last night with Mafia boss at Frank Sinatra's Lodge" (in *Lexis Nexis Academic*, 29 April 2011). Marilyn was fully aware of the lust many men had for her, as she adeptly reveals (as a 'changeable nature') in the lyrics of a song ("After you Get What you Want") she once sang: "There's a longing in your eye, hard to satisfy And here's the reason why: 'Cause after you get what you want, you don't want it. You're like a baby: you want what you want when you want it; but after you are presented with what you want, you're discontented!"

Leonard Cohen in one of his esoterical ballads ("Take This Longing") describes the romantic side of yearning for a beautiful woman as: "Everyone who wanted you. They found what they will always want again. Your beauty lost to you yourself. Just as it was lost to them. Oh, take this longing from my tongue. Whatever useless things these hands have done. Let me see your beauty broken down. Like you would do for one you love!"

The key problem with this encounter with (the much older) Sam "Momo" Giancana was that there was no soft romance here, no intention to 'be nice' to Marilyn, but only the one component: to break Marilyn's spirit, to have her agree to meet with RFK, to threaten to expose the Kennedy affair, so that Sam could exact his revenge on these two men whom he despised and hated above all others. We see here the correlation with Amnon and Tamar, as now (after he had his 'jollies'), Sam "Mooney' Giancana hates Marilyn enough to watch her end her own life. (cf. II Samuel 13:15)

To ensure Marilyn's cooperation, Sam degrades Marilyn in front of photographers (who took a total of 14 Instant Polaroid photos with Frank Sinatra's own new camera which just came out the previous year). As in the recent movie, *La Dolce Vita* (Feb/1960), Marilyn was driven like a donkey and had so many degrading sex acts performed on her that she couldn't pop enough pills, drink enough Champagne, and force herself into a semi-comatose state fast enough!

When Frankie finally returns to see what became of his 'guest', he is disgusted and appalled. He asks to see the (Polaroid) photos: he sees that Marilyn has been compromised and is certainly not having a good time, to put it mildly! He asks the photographer to burn all those photos. And then when he finally musters the courage to go to see Marilyn (who retired to building #3), he finds her in a near drug overdose. Rushing her to Emergency to save her life, he must have been reminded of the several times he himself attempted suicide (the first two over Ava Gardner) and how he likewise cheated death by the skin of his teeth.

Who will 'Throw the First Stone'?

But to return to this concept of 'lust', we can see from the words of Laurence ("Larry") Olivier (in his affair with Vivien Leigh) that Marilyn's fellow actors struggled to understand what 'lust' really meant: "I couldn't help myself with Vivien. No man could. I hated myself for cheating on Jill [Olivier's current wife] but then I had cheated before, but this was something different. This wasn't just out of lust! This was love that I really didn't ask for but was drawn into" (*Wikipedia*, "Laurence Olivier").

Another more flamboyant example perhaps was that of Elizabeth Taylor with Richard Burton on and off the set of *Cleopatra* (in which they both co-starred) which affair was openly plastered on all the tabloids. Liz Taylor was then married to Eddie Fisher (whom she had taken away from Debbie Reynolds, while Eddie was still married to Debbie). Sounds a lot like *Peyton Place*, true to the motto: "All's fair in love and in war!".

So, who can throw the first stone at Marilyn Monroe? Who of all her peers was without sin? (See, John 8:1-12) They say the 'nickname' some people tag on others is the hardest stone that the devil can throw at a woman! In this regard, Marilyn had her share of 'nicknames': Darryl Zanuck (head of Fox Studios, her employer) used to refer to her regularly as: 'that straw head!". Movie critics would call her anything from 'The Cheesecake Queen' to that 'blonde bimbo with the horizontal walk"!

Yet through it all, Marilyn was a fighter: she was a survivor! She well knew (as she said in *"Gentlemen Prefer Blondes!"*): "I can be smart when it's important, but most men don't like it!". Yes, Marilyn accepted herself as a 'national institution' (as well-known as 'hot dogs, apple pie, or baseball'); but she knew her place was with her public, as she put it so well: "I knew I belonged to the public and to the world, not because I was talented or even beautiful, but because I had never belonged to anything or anyone else." The public became Marilyn's surrogate mother (in a sense) as she lacked the sympathy and warmth than normally would be granted most children in life.

A Love Bond is not Lust

As Katherine Butler Hathaway puts it so well: "Everybody knows that a good mother gives her children a feeling of trust and stability. She is their earth. She is the one they can count on for the things that matter most of all... She is the one they want to be near when they cry... There is no substitute for her. Somehow even her clothes feel different to her children's hands from anybody else's clothes. Only to touch her skirt or her sleeve makes a troubled child feel better."

In some magical way of transference, Marilyn was able to receive this sort of moral support from her fans. She often spoke of the upbeat way in which the men (the US Marines) fighting in Korea praised her and accepted her with unabashed adulation when she performed ten shows there in four days (during her honeymoon to Joe DiMaggio). She even kept a photo of that event in her purse to the time of her death. She bonded so well with her audience. And likewise, her audience bonds with her even to this day.

It has been noted that the famed singer Mariah Carey bought Marilyn Monroe's baby Grand piano for $600,000 at an auction a few years ago. In addition, her famous birthday dress in which she sang "Happy Birthday, Mr. President!" to JFK in May 1962 (and for which she paid $12,000 back then) sold in 1999 at Christie's Auction for $1.4 million. And then a few years later the same dress at Julien's Auction sold for a whopping $4.81 million, to become the most expensive dress in all history. Even her Raven Black 1956 Ford Thunderbird sold in November 2018 at Julien's Auction for $490,000). Why all this adulation? Why is it so special to actually want to possess something that Marilyn Monroe once wore or once played or once owned? It makes you wonder: Marilyn was not simply a physical symbol, someone who appealed to men only; she equally (or perhaps even more so) appealed to women too.

Accolades for Marilyn Monroe

As Marvin Runyon, the US Postmaster General described Marilyn (on the announcement of US postage stamps made in her honour): "Being the most famous face in the world would be plenty for a lot of us. The camera loved her and so did we. But she fought to master her craft and earned the respect of the critics in the same way that she won the hearts of millions of fans. Today, more than thirty years after her death, her comedic style still makes us laugh. Her big-girl looks and little-girl voice still makes us smile. And her incredible beauty still stirs our hearts. There is only one: Marilyn!"

But my favourite tribute to Marilyn will always be her eulogy by her mentor, Lee Strasberg (President and founder of the New York Actors' Studio) on Wednesday after 1 p.m. on 8th August 1962 at Westwood Village Park Memorial Cemetery: [Here it is greatly truncated due to copyright restrictions: Please check it out on U-Tube in its entirety].

"Marilyn Monroe was a legend!... Despite the heights and brilliance, she had attained on the Screen, she was planning for the future. In her eyes and in mine, her career was just beginning... She had a luminous quality: a combination of wistfulness, radiance, and yearning that set her apart, and yet made everyone wish to be part of it, to share in the childish naiveté which was at once so shy and yet so vibrant. This quality was even more evident when she was on the stage."

Following this eulogy, Joe DiMaggio (her second husband who had just formally proposed re-marriage with Marilyn on 1st August 1962, days before her death) kissed Marilyn on the lips saying: "I love you! I love you!" as they permanently closed the lid of her casket. Years later when Joe was dying (in 1999), his lawyer stated that 'Jolting Joe's' last words were: "I'll finally get to see [my] Marilyn!".

10J. Lustful:

Youth Feedback:
____
____
____

1. Adulterous

Youth Feedback:
____
____
____

2. Carnal

Youth Feedback:
____
____
____

3. Engaging-in-prostitution

Youth Feedback:
____
____
____

4. Erotic

Youth Feedback:
____
____
____

5. Flirtatious

Youth Feedback:
____
____
____

6.   Fornicating

Youth Feedback:

____

____

____

7.   Having-love-affairs

Youth Feedback:

____

____

____

8.   Having-sexual-hangups

Youth Feedback:

____

____

____

9.   Perverse

Youth Feedback:

____

____

____

10. Promoting-pornography

Youth Feedback:

____

____

____

11. Sensual

Youth Feedback:

____

____

____

12. Sexist

Youth Feedback:

____

____

____

13. Seeking-sexual-deviations

Youth Feedback:

____

____

____

14. Sexually-stimulating

Youth Feedback:

____

____

____

15. Whore-mongering

Youth Feedback:

____

____

____

16. Wishing-to-appear-nude

Youth Feedback:

____

____

____

(Some of the) Sources Consulted:

Wikipedia [under the names referred to in this Section]
See as well, "Sources Consulted" under the "Lying" Section

DISCLAIMER: N.B. (*Nota Bene*)
All tunes/songs/video clips/links/quotes/etc. are herein provided to assist
in Group Therapy Sessions, or privately, for individual study (to assist in
learning) and for educational purposes *only*.

[#72: U-Tube Reference]
MM's last weekend at Cal-Neva Lodge
https://www.youtube.com/watch?v=gbyZIU09vZw

[#73: U-Tube Reference]
MM Did not commit suicide (Hard Copy)
https://www.youtube.com/watch?v=U3qgGji7UoQ

[#74: U-Tube Reference]
Double Cross - Giancana and Marilyn Monroe
https://www.youtube.com/watch?v=3JgKlMR0PvE&t=3s

[#75: U-Tube Reference]
Double Cross - Giancana and The Kennedys
https://www.youtube.com/watch?v=EGFilkbzfZ4&t=1s

[#76: U-Tube Reference]
Sam "The Cigar" Giancana's Demise
https://www.youtube.com/watch?v=c_qhgXKQKI4

[#77: U-Tube Reference]
Momo: The Sam Giancana Story
https://www.youtube.com/watch?v=obn1Y-bMk34&t=5s

[#78: U-Tube Reference]
The Mafia Murder of Marilyn Monroe [Dr. Bill Truels]
https://www.youtube.com/watch?v=0vHOcTO3rmc&t=6s

[#79: U-Tube Reference]
Jeanne Carmen - Marilyn Monroe
https://www.youtube.com/watch?v=2QDfofFXPJg&t=1491s

[#80: U-Tube Reference]
Shelley Winters on MM
https://www.youtube.com/watch?v=cRvwjm3eq3g&list=RD2QDfof
FXPJg&index=9

[#81: U-Tube Reference]
Jeanne Carmen - 2nd Interview on MM
https://www.youtube.com/watch?v=tmTDs_0EjmQ&t=2s

[#82: U-Tube Reference]
Jeanne Carmen - on MM (National Inquirer)
https://www.youtube.com/watch?v=pt3ug9Pbg2E

[#83: U-Tube Reference]
Jeanne Carmen on MM [Entertainment Tonight]
https://www.youtube.com/watch?v=t1PM-SNPkQE

[#84: U-Tube Reference]
Jeanne Carmen on MM [History Buff]
https://www.youtube.com/watch?v=KfcBarDpOel

[#85: U-Tube Reference]
Jeanne Carmen on MM [Channel 9 News]
https://www.youtube.com/watch?v=Rdep_Xunl_k

[#86: U-Tube Reference]
The Marilyn Monroe Files
https://www.youtube.com/watch?v=biYs3hR4w_8&t=2541s

[#87: U-Tube Reference]
MM interviewed by George Belmont for Marie Claire Magazine
[April 1966]
https://www.youtube.com/watch?v=3wfMzdlMA00

[#88: U-Tube Reference]
MM sings: "Specialization!"
https://www.youtube.com/watch?v=FLhTrjQU8Pk

[#89: U-Tube Reference]
After you get what you want, you don't want it! [Marilyn Monroe sings]
https://www.youtube.com/watch?v=jlooRreqEt4&list=RDMM&index=25

[#90: U-Tube Reference]
Leonard Cohen: Take This Longing [with Lyrics]
https://www.youtube.com/watch?v=Y2cafzCEokk

Lying:

Beguiling

Crafty

Cunning

Deceiving

Defrauding

Dishonest

Equivocating

Exaggerating

Excusing

Falsifying

Forked-tongue

Full-of-trickery

Hypocritical

Inaccurate

Insincere

Loquacious

Mendacious

Plagiarizing

Propagandizing

Saying-white-lies

Serving-'father-of-lies'

Stating-whoppers

Taking-unfair-advantage

Untruthful

FOOD FOR THOUGHT:

For the Natural Man Striving to Become Spiritual

Meditation: (To Chew over one's Thoughts!):
Listen to what your child is trying to tell you *not* to do!:

Don't try to preach to me. You'd be surprised how well I know what's right and wrong. Don't nag. If you do, I shall have to protect myself by appearing deaf.

Rule #11: For Raising Delinquent Children:

"When he gets into real trouble, apologize for yourself by saying: 'I never could do anything with him'. And Prepare for a life of grief: You will be likely to have it!"

  Youth Feedback:
____

____

____

Rule #11: For Repentance (to turn your life around):

Reform your conduct by adopting new patterns of behaviour.

  Youth Feedback:
____

____

____

Lying

The story is told of the old Greek philosopher Diogenes who went around Athens in broad daylight with a lit lantern shining it in all the faces of the prominent leaders of Ancient Greece! When asked what did he think he was doing flashing that bright lantern during High Noon into everyone's face, he replied simply: "I'm looking for an honest man!".

Today, we think: Things may not be any different?! Perhaps we still are looking to find that honest individual, that person who can speak the truth without a forked tongue, as the 'redskins' used to say back in the day when the West was wild and free?!

Karl Menninger, the President and Founder of the American Psychiatric Association, used to say: "One of the most untruthful things possible, you know, is a collection of facts; because they can be made to appear in so many different ways". He also added: "Truth to the lawyer is something one tells or does not tell; to the psychiatrist, it is something that we (or at least 'some' of us) strive wistfully and perpetually to discover; and to others: something in which they have no interest". (*Crime of Punishment*, p.97)

When it comes to an animal that best represents the 'lie', I think of the crocodile, who when it opens it's mouth wide enough to swallow large prey, releases tears from its eyes, as if it were crying, or feeling sorry for its victim; hence, the phrase: 'crocodile tears'! When I think of a person in history best represented as 'the mother of all liars' there are so many.

But to choose just one: I would say, without a doubt, the Minister of Nazi Propaganda, Josef Goebbels. He said that: "Truth is the mortal enemy of the lie, and thus by extension, the Truth is the greatest enemy of the State". What Goebbels was referring to indirectly was his boss, Der Fuehrer, Adolf Hitler's own explanation of the benefits of the "Big Lie" theory: "In the big lie there is always a certain force of credulity; because the broad masses of a nation... more readily fall victims to **the big lie** than the small lie, since they themselves often tell small lies in little matters, but would be ashamed to resort to large-scale falsehoods" (in *Mein Kampf*, 1925) .

The principle needed to succeed in telling a 'Big Lie' is to "make the lie big, make it simple, keep saying it, and eventually, they [the public] will believe it"! This process is quite an art and has been exemplified in 1948 by George Orwell's book, *Nineteen Eighty-Four*, as follows: "The keyword here is black-white. Like so many Newspeak words, this word has two mutually contradictory meanings: Claiming that black is white, in contradiction of the plain facts!" This is 'doublethink', as Orwell defined in his futuristic book.

In this 'art of lying' one must tell 'deliberate lies', to genuinely believe in them, so as to be able to forget any fact that has become 'inconvenient'! The key is to preserve 'loving feelings', and not to be 'brutally frank', not to tell the 'whole truth', for to do so would be perceived to be more 'brutal' than 'frank'.

Hence the creation of the 'white lie', the lie which (as we lie to ourselves) states only a 'little inaccuracy' so as to save a world of explanation. In so doing, we can see that a 'big lie' (as simply an 'alternate point of view') is actually more (publicly) plausible than the Truth!

The art of lying is the art of knowing how to believe lies. As Lord George Byron once said: "And after all, what is a lie? 'Tis but the Truth in masquerade!". To state just a little itty-bitty small lie could be passed off as a 'terminological inexactitude', or attributed to inaccurate memory, or temporary memory loss, which cannot be held to be a really bad thing after all, as no one can be expected to always have a perfect memory at all times, now can they?!

One can easily see the slippery slope involved in justifying these small 'white lies' as no one actually 'lies': People simply do what they have to do, and say what they have to say, to make their story sound just right. That's all! Hence, we see that: "A liar begins with making falsehood appear like truth" (as William Shenstone puts it) "and ends with making truth itself appear like falsehood". But lying is not always done with words alone; it can be done with silence: "For the cruelest lies are often told in silence" (Robert Louis Stevenson).

As John Locke, the British philosopher, so aptly surmised: "Men see a little, presume a great deal, and so jump to conclusions". If the Truth (as it is told) has a very big hole in it, well, we can put into that 'hole' (that 'absence of truth') whatever filler (or lie) we wish, now can't we? Or, as Bill Vaughn mocks the Truth: "We all want to get 'The News' objectively, impartially, and from our own point of view". We see that when it comes to *fake* news, we must learn to read between the lies.

But for me, Truth is the 'safest lie', for if a lie is a handle that fits every sin, the misunderstanding behind every truth, then Truth is the only means to set the record straight, let the chips fall where they may! As Shakespeare says (in *Hamlet*): "This above all: to thine own self be true, and it must follow as the night the day, Thou canst not then be false to any man"! For what is 'sin' except as the Bible puts it: "He who knows to do good, and does it not, to him it is sin"! (James 4:17) So there it is: we cannot sin in ignorance, as James says: Sin is knowing what is true and the refusal to do it, to admit it, to confess it, to let Truth prevail!

Now wouldn't it be nice, wouldn't it be easy to spot the liar: If like Pinocchio every time one tells a fib (a real whopper) that his nose would grow longer and longer? Of course, I'm being just a tad facetious! Everyone knows that 'flatterers look like friends, just like wolves look like dogs!" (George Chapman); but then do they? What would happen if people actually confuse what they read in the Newspapers as actual "News"? What would happen if people confuse Television News with Journalism? For as we now know to be true: Never have so many been manipulated by the Media so much (or so often) by so few.

The danger with lying 'so often' (to appear perhaps more clever, or to achieve more attention or fame, or power) is that if one does so habitually, he will not only not be able to believe anything told to him, but neither will anyone believe what he says. It's the *'boy who cried: Wolf! too often'* syndrome: "When men no longer have the least fear of saying something untrue, they very soon have no fear whatsoever of doing something unjust" (Theodor Haecker"). The danger is that some people (accustomed to lying) may "tell enough white lies to ice a wedding cake" (Margot Asquith).

On the one hand, there is the argument (as Lin Yutang says): "Society can exist only on the basis that there is some amount of polished lying and that no one says exactly what he thinks"; but on the other hand, "Men are able to trust one another, knowing the exact degree of dishonesty they are entitled to expect" (Stephen Leacock). If (as Nietzsche argues) "the lie is a condition of life", we need to begin to analyse why is it that so many people today (more so than in the past?!) don't want honest answers? Why is honesty not considered by so many (especially political) parties to not be the 'best policy'?

Is it because the public does not wish to hear disturbing or unpleasant news? Is it because people believe there is some falsehood mingled with all truth? Is it because (as Hitler argued) that there is 'a certain factor of credulity' in a big black lie as opposed to a little or small white lie? Is it because people by and large no longer believe that there is simply one truth, that a liar can represent two truths, be a person that lives a double life, simply because he 'feels' something to be true irrespective of the facts?

In the Scriptures, it states that a double-minded man is unstable in all his ways (James 1:8; 4:8). The Lord our God does not lie (Numbers 23:19); nor does the Lord make His people to trust in a lie (Jeremiah 28:15). Indeed, those who 'delight in lies' are cursed of God (Proverbs 19:5; Psalms 62:4) for "no lie is of the truth" (I John 2:21). Those who plow wickedness and reap iniquity will eat 'the fruit of lies' (Hosea 10:13). The Lord God condemns all liars, for no one who 'makes and loves to make a lie' can enter into His kingdom (Revelation 21:1-2,27).

John, the Beloved Apostle, makes it crystal clear that "if a man says, I love God, and hates his brother, he is a liar: For he that loves not his brother whom he has seen, how can he love God whom he has not seen?" (I John 4:20). Isaiah, God's prophet of Old, states a truth eternal that never can change: "Woe unto them that call evil good, and good evil; that put darkness for light, and light for darkness; that put bitter for sweet, and sweet for bitter! Woe unto them that are wise in their own eyes, and prudent in their own sight!" (Isaiah 5:20-21).

But our Lord Jesus (who is the Christ) perhaps said it best of those (fake) religious leaders of His day (who sought to kill Him): "Ye are of your father the devil, and the lusts of your father ye will do. He was a murderer from the beginning, and abode not in the truth, because there is no truth in him. When he speaks a lie, he speaks of his own: for he is a liar, and the father of it". (John 8:37-44).

Jonathan Swift adds an interesting insight to this prevalence of lies within our society today: "But although the devil be the 'father of lies', he seems, like other great inventors, to have lost much of his reputation by the continual improvements that have been made upon him."

In considering the concept of lying, we do well to note this analysis: "There are three essential elements to a lie: the material must be untrue; it must be known to be untrue; and it must be told with the intention to deceive" (Terence H. Qualter). Now that is all well and good in a Court of Law, but in the real world, we see that we appear to live in a state not unlike a 'moral earthquake' in which everywhere we may turn, there can be deception abounding. Where can we stand on solid ground, when everywhere we turn to for support is based on the quicksand of lies?!

The only 'Gatekeeper' of what is true, of what is right, of what we can wholeheartedly place our trust and faith in is our Lord, our God! The devil appears to have made a heyday from so many willing subjects who love the spoils of political office, of power, of control over others, of fame, or simply put, who love to lie.

Can we feel comfortable in a world that thrives on the material necessity to lie, to spread propaganda, misinformation, disinformation, and a steady barrage of 'Big Lies'?! I hardly think so! As Boris Pasternak, the famous Russian novelist (no doubt speaking of life in the former Soviet Union), puts it so well: "The great majority of us are required to live a life of constant duplicity. Your health is bound to be affected if, day after day, you say the opposite of what you feel, if you grovel before what you dislike, and rejoice at what brings you nothing but misfortune."

Goebbels once boasted that if he could control the Mass Media (the Newspapers and outlets of communication) of any nation that he would assuredly convert them into "a herd of pigs". Quite the boast, yet we see that not everyone can be so easily deceived today, or at least we would like to think so. As the saying goes:

you may deceive some of the people all of the time, and all of the people some of the time, but you cannot deceive all of the people all of the time.

I would like to include a bit of a 'thinking or thought experiment' to demonstrate how a long-held Big Lie today may be finally laid to rest. And that big lie (in my view) is the (Fake) News claim that: Marilyn Monroe killed Marilyn Monroe!

To present this case of The Biggest Lie, to demonstrate that it is Fake News, I have compiled a summary taken from over fifty different sources, each one of which has provided a piece or two of this puzzle, this mystery, to put them all together, as one big picture, to see what has often been cited: (that over time) "Truth will finally prevail!"

The Argument That Marilyn Monroe Did Not Kill Marilyn Monroe!

The approach I will use in this 'thought experiment' consists of two key elements: (1) The Sherlock Holmes approach of deductive logic: For example, granted that A and B are true, then C follows. To quote a simple instance: If all birds can fly, and if a crow is a bird, then it follows logically that a crow can fly; and (2) the Socratic approach (as commonly used in our Court system), which is to ask a series of questions that strongly suggest a certain outcome.

For example: Consider the series of questions that follow the case in point, which is:

"Did Mr. Brown kill Mrs. Brown with her own revolver?"

(a) **Question #1:** Has a bullet been fired from Mrs. Brown's revolver?

Answer #1: It is an indisputable fact that no bullet has been fired from the revolver.

(b) **Q#2:** Has Mrs. Brown received any bullet in her person from her own revolver?

A#2: Mrs. Brown has not received any bullet in her person from this revolver.

THEREFORE,

(c) **Q#3:**   Can the claim still be made that Mr. Brown killed Mrs. Brown with her own revolver?

     A#3:   Of course not!

[This claim is made invalid through the Socratic approach.]

As so many books and articles and dozens of documentaries have been made to suggest this or that cause to be the sole reason for Ms. Monroe's untimely death, I will not dwell upon all the various points of view. Instead, after having done extensive research on my own, and weighing the evidence so presented along with the timetable of events in the last weekend of Ms. Monroe's life, I have plotted my own conclusion, as presented by the following statements of evidence.

[The Author will reference (only some of) the remarks in the remainder of this Section from the book, *Marilyn: The Last Take*, which references will be abbreviated from henceforth as: "MLT" followed by the page number, of course.]

It is my understanding that commencing on 1st January 2039, UCLA (The University of California in Los Angeles) will provide an official release of all documents and private recordings held previously by Marilyn Monroe's psychiatrist, Dr. Ralph Greenson, to the public at large. There will also be (it is expected at that time if not sooner) a full release of all (redacted and unredacted) files currently held by the CIA and FBI on Marilyn Monroe's life and death, in particular her complete unredacted phone log on that fateful last weekend of her life.

[I understand that Anthony Summers, author of *Goddess: The Secret Lives of Marilyn Monroe*, was able to obtain a partially declassified or unredacted phone log of Marilyn Monroe's last weekend calls after nine years of solicitation. (MLT, 354)]

Therefore, this current exercise in this book will be at best a precursor to the eventual full release of all of these documents and accumulated evidence heretofore held by the departments and agencies so expressed. "Why do you not simply wait to see what the full story of Ms. Monroe's death will entail in eighteen years or so?" one may ask.

Well, simply put, because there has been a truly significant outpouring of details pertaining to her demise (to date) so much so that I do believe my current point of view will be largely (if not fully) substantiated by these future revelations (in 2039). In other words, I doubt that there is a need to wait another eighteen years or so to see what actually transpired during those last three days of her life (3rd to 5th August 1962).

What is disconcerting to me is that the detailed phone log of Ms. Monroe is still being detained and withheld (redacted) by the CIA and FBI who (as we shall see) were apparently involved in her untimely death.

Opponents to the status quo will hastily label this 'theory' (or any other theory) as a 'conspiracy theory' which to do so is to throw mud onto the evidence thus far accumulated. We need to have an open mind and no pre-conceived notions as to Marilyn Monroe's cause of death in order to discover the true course of events, as well as the true nature of her death. Anyone can concoct any kind of tale (or absurdity) as they wish, but the genuine lovers of truth will stick to the facts of the case as we now know them to be.

Many thanks of course to the peers and relations of those persons involved in Marilyn Monroe's life, as well as those who knew her personally, for their testimonials and assistance in creating this timeline leading up to her death.

A Few Notes Leading Up to Marilyn Monroe's Last Weekend Alive:

December 1961

Marilyn Monroe [henceforth, known as 'MM'] was told on 16th December by Fox Studio that she had to complete one more film entitled: *"Something's Got To Give"* in order to be released from her movie contract. She tried to refuse to make any more movies with Fox (especially after her disastrous relationship with Director George Cukor in *"Let's Make Love"*, shot in 1960) but her lawyer Milton Rudin advised MM that she had no choice, legally speaking. Even her Swiss-trained psychoanalyst, Ralph

Greenson, persuaded MM that she should 'work' for her 'emotional health' (MLT, p.44).

To make matters even worse, the openly Gay Director (dubbed "the Little Dictator"; MLT, pp. 32,53,111,119), George Cukor, was ordered by Fox to work as Director for MM in *"Something's Got To Give"*, also his final legally-binding commitment to Fox (MLT, p.51). As the following months (in 1962) would reveal, Cukor loathed and even downright hated MM with an unrelenting passion (because as rumors still have it, he was snubbed by bi-sexual Yves Montand in *"Let's Make Love"*, who clung onto MM instead; MLT, pp. 28-33,60,114-116).

Cukor who had MM perform dozens of (now believed to have been) utterly senseless yet painstaking re-takes (in an attempt to demoralize her apparently) made a written request to Fox (on 6th June 1962) to have MM fired which Fox did on 8th June 1962 (MLT, pp. 52,199). As Cukor put it: 'She [MM] is a spoiled, pampered Superstar and represents all that is bad about Hollywood today". (MLT, p.52) Cukor's (not so secret) wish to 'derail' *Something's Got To Give* finally brought down the curtain with MM's (arguably) unjustified dismissal (MLT, p.175-177).

Thereafter, MM's personal life for several reasons also begins to spiral downwards. But I'm ahead of this (tragic) tale.

MM attends a Christmas party hosted by Patricia Kennedy Lawford at the Lawford Beach Mansion where she meets Jack Kennedy (JFK). Private detective Fred Otash later testifies that his 'bugs' in the Lawford Mansion "picked up the steamy love scene between politician [JFK] and movie star [MM] during the posh Christmas party" (MLT, p. 71). So began the fatal attraction between the world's 'sexiest' movie star and the world's 'sexiest' politician (as RFJ would later describe it) (MLT, p.133).

January 1962

This New Year was the turning point for MM. She wanted finally to own her own house. With ex-hubby Joe DiMaggio's timely aid, she purchased a lovely hacienda-style home (listed for $77,500) for only $52,500. [This hacienda remained unsold after MM's untimely death until 2017 when it sold in ten days for $7.25 million.]

MM was so elated about her new home (at 12-305 and Fifth Helena Drive, in Brentwood, Los Angeles 49, California) that she exclaimed to her masseur, Ralph Roberts: "I have finally arrived in a point of my life in which I am truly happy. It's so good to finally own my own home! I feel like laughing again! It feels so good!". Ironically, MM's new home had the motto *Cursum Perificio* written into The Coat of Arms (in the pavement entrance) which translated means: "My Journey ends here!".

February 1962

MM flies to Mexico City on the 10th of February (for ten days) to meet with several people including ex-hubby Joe DiMaggio (who hints at remarriage but does not formally propose). MM's main goal in Mexico City is to look to buy Mexican-style furniture for her newly acquired hacienda, which is being custom-built to MM's specifications (MLT, p.61). She apparently prepays for a distinctive sofa which does not arrive at her home until 04th August, the last day of her life. [The sofa remains in its original shipping crate until it is 'sold as is' in Christie's Auction in 1999.]

On 27th February 1962, J. Edgar Hoover (head of the FBI) notifies Bobby Kennedy (RFK) that the FBI discovered JFK had an intimate affair with Judith Campbell Exner, "a sometimes mistress of Sam Giancana, the Chicago crime boss. The implication is that Frank Sinatra had 'fixed Kennedy up' with Campbell (MLT, p.167). Although Sinatra spent $1.2 million to enhance his Lake Tahoe hideaway (the Cal-Nev Lodge) anticipating a JFK visit thereafter, JFK's political advisors declares Sinatra as "an undesirable person". He is therewith dropped by JFK and completely ostracized from the White House on 28th February 1962. As Giancana would occasionally stay at the Cal-Nev Lodge (being part-owner), it became too dangerous politically for JFK to be seen there. In only three months, Sinatra would be giving the same (hard) advice to MM, that the Kennedy's would be dropping her (as they did him), and that she would likewise become ostracized.

March 1962

MM begins to undertake a few renovations. She has plans to redo the landscaping of her hacienda. Inside the walls surrounding her home (which were two feet thick and seven feet high) was a secret garden. "Hillocks of baby's breath and veins of German moss stretched along a flagstone walkway. Brilliant bougainvillea vines made crimson splashes against white-washed walls" (MLT, p.273). Already early in the year, MM adds "flowering bushes, Oriental bulbs, and sweet olive trees" (MLT, p.273). She wants to add her 'personal stamp' to her 'secret garden'. Eunice Murray, MM's housekeeper, gives Marilyn a gift, a book on horticulture, which can be seen on MM's night-table (next to her bed) the day of her death.

As MM needs to re-wire the house, she is approached by several different persons: Bernard Spindall (formerly from the Military Signal Corps), and Fred Kotash, among others, who apparently offer MM a deal too good to refuse. But as it turns out, these men are professional conmen who wiretap and bug MM's home to include orders from: (1) J. Edgar Hoover (of the FBI); (2) The CIA; (3) Jimmy Hoffa (of the Teamsters' Union); and (4) Sam Giancana, a Chicago Mafia boss. (MLT, pp. 254,308-309). Their motives are simply to tape-record all the phone calls and activities that MM undergoes, especially with her liaisons with the Kennedy brothers, JFK (John Fitzgerald Kennedy, the 35th US President); and RFK (Robert Francis Kennedy, the 64th US Attorney General).

In later months, MM becomes suspicious that people are listening on her line (due to 'clicks' she hears), and so she begins to call (whenever convenient) from a nearby payphone. Peter Lawford's beach home (located at 625 Pacific Coast Highway in Santa Monica) not far from MM's home is also bugged and wiretapped by the CIA and FBI (MLT, p.71). This beach home becomes the rendezvous for RFK later in June and July of this year. It consists of 27 rooms (14 of which are bedrooms and hidden suites), along with a heated marble pool (MLT, pp. 252-253).

[The excuses later made by these Security Agencies is that it was necessary to bug and wiretap all the various homes of JFK's lovers as he would repeatedly 'duck' from these Secret Service Agents to rendezvous with his 'sweethearts'. Because of political tensions with Cuba at the time, it was imperative that the 'nuclear football' suitcase be close at hand to JFK at all times. In plain language, the Security protecting the President had to know where he was at all times. In addition, J. Edgar Hoover (head of the FBI) had created a file for MM as a potential Communist agent, as she had defended her ex-husband Arthur Miller (whom Joe McCarthy had accused of attending Communist rallies in the 1940s). The Monday after MM's death (the 6th August 1962) it is reported that J. Edgar Hoover declared that a victory against Communism had been achieved.]

MM receives a Golden Globe Award this month (for several film roles including) for her role in *The Misfits* (Arthur Miller's 'Valentine' to MM). MM had completed the film in Nevada in October 1960 but had to re-do the ending with Clark Gable in the Studio in November of that year. Two days after completing the final take, Clark Gable has a heart attack and dies 16th of November 1960, leaving MM so devastated that she couldn't seem to function normally, nor work throughout 1961. To console MM, Frank Sinatra gives her a white terrier which she names "Mafia Honey" (or Maf, for short) because of Frankie's purported connections to the Mafia. (Marilyn's sense of humour). [The two original Polaroid photos MM had of Maf sold in Christie's Auction in 1999 for $100,000 each.]

April 1962

On 8th April, MM is to begin to work for Fox Studios (under the basement bottom price of only $100,000) along with Dean Martin, her co-star (who is paid $500,000). But the Director, George Cukor, didn't like the script. And so, it all had to be rewritten. Production would have to be delayed until the 23rd of April. (MLT, p.66)

On the 17th of April, MM receives an official invitation from the White House to attend JFK's 45th Birthday Gala held jointly at the Democratic National Convention Saturday 19th of May. Fox Studio initially replies (though not officially) that MM could go to Madison Square Garden for the Gala celebration. (Later, they would renege on their 'permission' and demand MM work even on Saturdays (to include 19th May) but MM listens to RFK who reassures her that he will take care of Fox Studio for her (but to no avail). (MLT, pp.129,132-135) MM goes ahead and orders a special dress for the occasion, which would increase in price from $5,000 to

$12,000 (MLT, p.133). [This Jean Louis dress would later sell in November 2016 at Julien's Auction for $4.81 million, the most expensive dress in recorded history! (MLT, pp.136-141)]

MM could now phone directly to the Oval Office and speak directly to JFK's secretary, Evelyn Lincoln, to arrange a rendezvous with "Jack" wherever he wished: the Carlyle Hotel, the Lawford Mansion, the Beverly Hilton Hotel, or even aboard Air Force One. "When the President beckoned, Marilyn responded" (MLT, pp.68-74). MM's trip therefore on the 18th of April to pick up her drama coach, Paula Strasberg, was actually (in part) a cover to meet with 'Jack' (JFK) (MLT, pp. 74-75) But MM's trip to NYC to visit her mentor, Lee Strasberg, ensured she caught his viral cold just as MM had to return to L.A. to continue her work (MLT, pp.74-75).

May 1962

Having returned from NYC to LA on 19th April 1962, MM became quite ill by 20th April. Filming for *Something's Got To Give* was to commence on Monday, 23rd April 1962; but by Sunday, 22nd April, MM was dangerously ill and had to be rushed to Cedars of Lebanon Hospital for 2 p.m. Tests there confirmed that MM's acute viral cold from a few days ago "had developed into a massive sinus infection. She suffered high fevers [of 101 degrees] and dizziness, unbearable headaches, and lethargy. The tests also showed that she had contracted the most severe form of the disease, 'chronic sinusitis,' which usually required a month of massive antibiotic treatment to cure" (MLT, pp.76-79). Lee Siegel, Fox Studio's physician (who had treated MM since 1951) recommended that MM be given a month's rest.

But Fox Executives (especially Phil Feldman) refused to accept that request, stating (privately) that as this was MM's last film with the Studio that she should be given 'hot shots' to artificially shock her back into health. The Fox Studio Executives attitude (as related by her physician Lee Siegel) was (to quote them verbatim): "Let Marilyn collapse after we finish"! (MLT, p.81) (This treatment was not uncommon in Hollywood Studios having been used with marked success particularly with racehorses when the stakes are high and the horse's life after the race is of no consequence to its owners.)

For MM, therefore, she would be given these 'hot shots' twice daily to perk her up and have her back to work in no time. MM had been given these injections previously during the filming of *The Misfits* when Arthur Miller insisted MM finish that filming in the hot Arizona desert ASAP! As Dr. Siegel described their composition: "They contained methamphetamines, a few vitamins glucose to give an immediate lift, and a small amount of Librium to smooth out the effect of the uppers" (MLT, pp.81-82). These man-made chemical pills were merely another tool to keep MM working far beyond her normal body tolerance (MLT, pp.83-84).

Given these semi-daily 'hot shot' injections, MM was able to come onto the Studio set briefly on 30th April, fainted on 1st May, then worked 9 hours straight on 7th May, suffering a relapse on 8th May, and therefore being forced to confinement until the 14th May (MLT, p.112). The irony was that although MM was ready to go at it, back to work in full swing on the 14th May, no one else in the Studio, especially the Director George Cukor was up to it. The previous three months of a virtual total standstill (as MM was in almost every scene) resulted in a demoralizing resentment to MM (MLT, p.104).

To make matters even worse, MM was scheduled to leave Friday the 18th to rehearse in NYC for the Presidential Gala on Saturday the 19th. Fox Studio intervened and demanded MM not leave for the Gala, having rescinded their previous permission allowing her to leave, on pain of being fired. Bobby Kennedy, however, reassured MM that he would take care of everything (MLT, pp. 132-135).

Fox Studio was upset that MM's three weeks off work cost them almost $100,000 in production costs (as they had 104 employees on the set). What Fox did not disclose however was that MM's chief Fox rival, Elizabeth Taylor (the 'world's most famous femme fatale', MLT, p.90) had cost Fox Executives $8,000,000 (that's eight million dollars!) due to her "bouts of pneumonia and bronchitis" which delayed the production of *Cleopatra* for seven months! (MLT, p.78)

The intimate relationship between MM and JFK (having met six times before May) came to a climax on 19th May for MM's 'swan song' as she sings "Happy Birthday, Mr. President" to JFK. A jubilant Bobby Kennedy had arranged this entire spoof for his elder brother JFK. But many people simply felt that MM's appearance at Madison Square Garden "would be like Marilyn making love to the President publicly after doing it privately all these months" (MLT, p.70). Joseph Kennedy, JFK and RFK's father (who had suffered a stroke in December 1961 and), who wanted his son, JFK, to run for re-election in 1963, put his foot down demanding JFK end his liaisons with MM (which RFK as the dutiful brother was ordered to perform).

To appease Fox Studio Productions, MM did a nude swimming scene on 23rd May after 5 p.m. which still photographs "eventually appeared on the covers of seventy-two magazines in thirty-two countries--some of them behind the Iron Curtain" (MLT, pp.156-161). But her plan did not work! Fox Studios was not pleased with MM's 'swan song' to JFK. RFK and Peter Lawford had lied to her. They did not guarantee her job with Fox as they promised they would (MLT, pp.132-135,169,189,191).

To make matters even worse, it appeared that JFK had just used her, and now intended to throw her away. MM could see herself now as a world-wide joke, nothing more than a high-class call-girl at best. As of 25th May, all her calls to the White House were disconnected. JFK had cut her off completely. But according to one of MM's closest actress friends, Terry Moore, Bobby Kennedy "had been delegated to put an end to the affair" (MLT, pp.168-169).

Just as Cleopatra of old awaited the arrival of Mark Antony who was delegated by Rome to discipline her, to put her in her place, so MM looked forward to the arrival of RFK. (RFK had, after all, insisted to dance five times with MM the evening of the Gala "while an angry Ethel Kennedy looked on" MLT, p.150-151)

Between 21 May and 1st June, MM worked nine days and completed ten key scenes, while she was 'emotionally shattered. "Her appearance at the Gala now promised to destroy her career. And, in repayment, the First Family had cut her adrift" (MLT, p.169). As Frank Sinatra confirmed with MM (via phone) on 26-27th May, JFK was through with her. MM disappeared for those two days but returned to work on 28th May, Monday. It was rumoured she might have had a "clandestine abortion" (MLT, p.166).

June 1962

On 1st June, MM turned 36 years old, a pivotal age for an actress. Clara Bow, Joan Crawford, Greta Garbo, and Gloria Swanson all were considered 'box-office poison' when they turned thirty-six (although actresses, such as Joan Crawford, did make a comeback in later years) (MLT, p.173-174). Yet when Jane Fonda shared with MM her wish once all the youthful 'vapid sex symbol' is gone, an actress could then finally "begin to play character roles and rely on acting alone," MM expressed a "despair akin to that of a painter who discovers that he is going blind, or of a pianist whose hands are becoming arthritic" (MLT, p.174,178-179).

For Elizabeth Taylor's 30th birthday in February 1962, Fox Studios spent almost $5,000 but for MM's 36th birthday MM's stand-in, Evelyn Moriarty, bought her a "five-dollar sheet cake", and Fox Studios only bought her a large urn of coffee (from the Fox snack bar), but they later billed it back to MM's estate (after she died). Marilyn could feel all of their bad vibes. She was denied all the prerogatives of a Star (MLT, p.116). She was not allowed time off for her birthday until after 6 p.m. as if she were 'a bad child' (MLT, pp.176-177). So, MM has a very low-key birthday party at her home late in the evening, with Dean Martin present, Director George Cukor, and a few photographers. Her home is still under renovation and appears quite empty of furniture (as she is still awaiting the custom-built furniture from Mexico). But everyone makes the best of it.

Unbeknown to MM, Fox Studio had planned to fire her on the 8th of June, the same day they intended to fire Elizabeth Taylor but for a lot more reasons (MLT, p.182,202). Liz Taylor's living expenses alone reached $228,000 (more than double MM's entire salary for *Something's Got to Give*). Her overtime rates (at $10,000 per day) along with 10% of the gross (whether or not the film turned a profit), and her insistence that *Cleopatra* be filmed in Todd-A-O, "the wide-screen process created by her late husband, Michael Todd" ensured that her initial $1,000,000 salary more than double to a final profit (to include royalties, etc.) estimated to be: $7,000,000! (MLT, pp.91-95)

Yet more important than these financial losses incurred by incessant delays due to Liz Taylor's delicate health (for which no Insurance Company would ensure her as an employee of Fox since her near-death in March 1961 which required a tracheotomy; MLT, p. 92), was the very public very open love affair between Liz Taylor and Richard Burton while Burton was still married to Sybil, and Taylor to Eddie Fisher (MLT, pp. 366-367). They were referred to as "The Hollywood Jezebel and her Welsh gigolo' (MLT, p.367). The USA refused them entry; and Italy (prompted by the Vatican) condemned Liz Taylor as "an undesirable person" (MLT, pp.124-128). To add insult to injury, Richard Burton on full salary had "worked only five times in the first seventeen weeks, and only thirty days in the entire first year" (MLT, p.97).

But Liz Taylor threatened to sue Fox and to "tie up the film [*Cleopatra*] for years" if she were fired [MLT, p.187]. Her ruse (or bluff?) worked. The Fox Executives "couldn't get rid of Taylor, so they decided to show they were strong men and fired Monroe--in Taylor's place" (MLT, p.205). But MM was "cushioned by a false sense of security". "Abandoned by her erstwhile friends in the media, and isolated by the rigours of her illness, Monroe was in the eye of a corporate hurricane" (MLT, p.205).

MM had no idea that Fox was really going to fire her until "the studio shut down production without even informing her" on the 6th of June (MLT, p.206). MM (who had previously believed filming would resume on the 11th of June) was devastated when she was told by her own psychoanalyst, Ralph Greenson, on the 8th of June that she was fired. MM had never been fired before.

She felt betrayed by her own support group, which 'substitute family' (she concluded) had "done more harm than good" on her behalf (MLT, p. 206, 277). She felt that she should dismiss all the following 'family members' from her payroll (as they did not properly protect her from being fired by Fox): Pat Newcomb (her so-called publicist); Paula Strasberg (her drama coach, whom MM was paying $3,000/week); Ralph Greenson (and others to whom she paid more than $150,000 for psychiatric services since 1957; MLT, p. 220); Eunice Murray (her so-called housemaid hired by Dr. Greenson, but who was secretly a psychiatric nurse collecting data on MM), and the list goes on (MLT, pp. 205-207, 241-242).

But the worse was yet to come: Fox Studios set out to destroy MM's reputation as a superstar. "The publicists dredged up two of Marilyn's most private heartbreaks: her fear of insanity, and her long-hidden history of learning disabilities. Cleverly and insidiously, they turned these faults into a firestorm." (MLT, p. 219). Even George Cukor, MM's director, wrote to Fox Studios that MM "the poor dear has finally gone around the bend" (p.217). Monroe was depicted as 'half-mad' (MLT, p. 211). Then the knock-out punch came from Fox's own Chief of Production, Peter G. Levathes, to *The Times* that: "Miss Monroe is not just being temperamental; she is mentally ill, perhaps seriously" (MLT, p. 215).

On the 8th of June, Fox Studios officially fires MM ("one of the most financially successful stars in Fox's history"; MLT, p. 190), and charge her with a $500,000 lawsuit on the grounds that she violated her Fox Contract and did not show up for work when required to do so. They try to replace her with Kim Novak or Lee Remick, but Dean Martin (MM's co-star) insists on the exact wording of the Fox Contract. He thereby refuses to work with anyone but MM, stating: "No MM, No Martin!" (MLT, pp. 224-225). So, Fox dutifully fires Dean Martin and all the rest of the staff, including Cyd Charisse. Dean Martin later retaliates on the 24th of June with a $6.8 million lawsuit against Fox (MLT, p. 246).

Marilyn truly appreciates the loyalty of Dean Martin; and sends a telegram to each of the 104 cast and crew members who were all laid off (on the 11th June) to say to each one of them regarding their lay-offs: "It was none of my doing: I hope you know that"! (MLT, pp. 227-231) MM feels the heat on her, and being a good sport, renegotiates the Fox Contract by promoting her image, posing for various photographers from *Look* magazine, *Life* magazine, and other professional photographers all throughout June, and up until the 13th July.

Summer of Love

Since the first week of June, Marilyn (MM) & Bobby (RFK) became an item. Their initial contact (following the magic chemistry in the post-Gala evening celebration of JFK's birthday on 19th May 1962) was in MM's garden. MM's maid (Hazel Washington who viewed the 'courtship') compared it to "making love over the phone. And I do mean 'making love'"! (MLT, p. 253) MM and RFK became "soulmates, from the beginning" (MLT, p. 251) as their places of rendezvous varied from the Presidential Suite at the Beverly Hilton in LA, MM's apartment in Hollywood, MM's own Brentwood hacienda, and the Lawford's Mansion in Santa Monica.

The Lawford neighbours, Lynn Sherman and Peter Dye, not only saw Bobby and Marilyn spending the weekend of 23-24 June 1962 walking together along the Santa Monica beach but were both "convinced that overnight trysts were involved" (MLT, p. 254). Detectives working for the Mafia and who had bugged the Lawford Beach Home could attest to the many 'on-again, off-again' affairs in their love nests (MLT, p. 254) [See also, FBI File 66-1700-39; MLT, p. 410]. MM was "absolutely starstruck" with RFK, sharing her "far from sexless" intimate evenings with Bobby "repeatedly during June and July 1962]" (MLT, pp. 252-258).

These sexual encounters were well known by many persons in MM's inner circle, News reporters, researchers, and local politicians including the following: (1) Ralph Roberts; (2) LA Mayor Sam Yorty; (3) James Spada (Peter Lawford's biographer); (4) Anthony Summers; (5) Mike Carroll (LA Deputy District Attorney); (6) Hazel Washington (MM's personal assistant); (7) Gene Allen; (8) Natalie Jacobs; (9) Rupert Allan; (10) Pat Newcomb; (11) Dorris Johnson; (12) Dorothy Manners; (13) Ed Guthman; (14) Robert Slatzer (MM's masseur); (15) Terry Moore (actress); (16) James Bacon (Journalist); (17) Eunice Murray (MM's housekeeper); (18) Jeanne Carmen (MM's confidante), and others (MLT, p.386). MM was of the belief that "Sex isn't wrong if there's love in it"! (MLT, p. 260).

MM's seemingly endless 'summer of love' was shortly to come to a brutal finale. As with the true story of Mark Antony who was sent (by the Roman Emperor Octavian) to rule over Egypt, but who became seduced instead by the Egyptian Queen Cleopatra, so Bobby Kennedy was sent by his brother Jack to discipline (or control) Marilyn, to break off all relations between MM and JFK.

But instead, RFK became embroiled in an intimate ongoing love tryst with MM. And as Mark Antony was already married to Octavian's sister, Octavia, but continued the affair with Cleopatra, so Bobby (Kennedy) who was married to Ethel (Kennedy) apparently followed suit. The key difference was that only MM died not long after her love affair with Bobby, whereas both Cleopatra and Mark Antony committed suicide.

Meanwhile, on the other side of the world, in Rome, Elizabeth Taylor and Richard Burton who were supposed to only 'pretend' as actors (and as a publicity stunt to advertise the movie *Cleopatra*) to be passionately in love (playing the roles of Cleopatra and Mark Antony, respectively) actually became sexual lovers on and off the screen (although both persons were married to other spouses).

Indeed, Liz Taylor, in particular, seemed to have rehearsed this role (as a home breaker; MLT, p. 90) with her then-current husband, Eddie Fisher. After the tragic death of Liz Taylor's third husband (Michael Todd), Liz's 'best friend', Debbie Reynolds, sent her husband, Eddie Fisher, to 'console Liz'. Elizabeth instead (as the story goes) seduced Eddie Fisher, had him divorce his wife, Debbie Reynolds, and marry her (MLT, p. 389). Then, not long thereafter (during the filming of *Cleopatra*) Taylor repeatedly seduced Richard Burton off-screen (as was her part, or role, in the movie on-screen) much to the chagrin of the movie moguls!

July 1962

MM had lost 27 pounds for her last contractual obligation with Fox Studios, *Something's Got to Give*, and as the many photo-shoots (of June and July 1962) and the many out-takes from that final film still clearly indicate: She never looked better, perhaps even ten years younger! (MLT, pp. 36-37,114-115, 274) In compliance with the demands of Fox Studios to become reinstated with a new contract, MM had to dismiss her entourage of 'consultants', to include: Pat Newcomb, Paula Strasberg, Dr. Ralph Greenson, Eunice Murray, and so forth (MLT, pp. 203, 206-207, 241-242, 277-278, 293-294).

Perhaps it is for this reason that MM (after her last photo-shoot of 13th July) decided to record a 42-minute reel-to-reel tape recording for her psychoanalyst, Ralph Greenson? It has been noted that MM had begun to resent these endless hours of counselling with Dr. Greenson, as she began to see them as totally fruitless. She even taped 'fake monologues' and "offered them to Greenson in lieu of an agonizing session of analysis" (MLT, p. 220).

On this final recording she ever made (for Dr. Greenson) she declared that she was finally free of all her past hangups, that she felt she no longer needed his services, that she was free of all her past love trysts, that she found happiness to simply go on with her life, to live her own career, and to be free and single as she is now (according to John Miner's notes from this tape Dr. Greenson had allowed him to listen to).

[This final recording is to be released, declassified, to the public on 1st January 2039 (together with all other collected materials in Box 39, to contain correspondence, letters, and notes in the Special Collections located at UCLA, as set up by the late Dr. Greenson. Greenson had played this final recording for John Miner before he, Dr. Greenson, died (on 24 November 1979). Apparently, this final recording contained rather intimate and personal comments MM made to Greenson, which comments Greenson asked John Miner not to disclose to the public. Miner felt after Greenson's death that he could relay at least the less intimate details on that recording.

The one detail of note that Miner released was the final verbatim quote MM had read into her last taped recording that pertained to Bobby Kennedy. MM purportedly disclosed the following personal confession: "As you see, there is no room in my life for him (RFK). I guess I don't have the courage to face up to it and hurt him. I want someone else to tell him it's over! I tried to get the President to do it, but I couldn't reach him." (*Wikipedia*, "John Miner") Miner did say that having listened to this tape made only two weeks prior to MM's death, that there is no possible way she would have wanted to commit suicide.]

MM believed simply that "A girl doesn't need anyone who doesn't need her!". And so, with the gnawing and growing realization that both the Kennedy brothers were simply using her, and that they would drop her "once that got what they wanted" (MLT, p. 265), she decided to be the one to leave first. As MM was noted to have said before: "A wise girl kisses but doesn't love, listens but doesn't believe, and leaves before she is left"!

But sometime in mid-July, MM discovers that she is pregnant for approximately one month (during her period). Doing the math in reverse, she realizes that it could only be RFK's baby (MLT, pp. 282-284). As MM wanted to do the right thing: To quietly have another 'clandestine abortion' (she had six previously along with four miscarriages; MLT, p. 103), she thought she should at the very least let Bobby know that she was 'in the way'.

As MM wanted one last encounter with Bobby Kennedy (possibly to simply state that she was pregnant with his child and wanted to see if he objected to an abortion as he was Catholic), to her amazement when she called the White House, she was told emphatically not to call anymore, neither for JFK, nor for RFK! MM believed that "we all have insecurities of one kind and another, but it's hardly an excuse for bad manners or bad behaviour". She knew that JFK was sexually prolific, that he had many sex partners, and that she was only one pebble among many on the beach (MLT, pp. 73-74).

But to sing: 'Happy Birthday, Mr. President' was an honor so high, so desirable that it is said Marilyn would have "come back from the dead" to sing it! (MLT, p.144) Picture this scenario, as Henry Weinstein points out: "Here's a girl who really did come from the streets, who had a mother who wasn't all there; and a father who had disappeared; a girl who had known all the poverty in the world. And now she was going to sing 'Happy Birthday' to the President of the United States in Madison Square Garden. There was no way for her to resist that!" (MLT, p. 135).

MM eventually realized that neither of the Kennedy brothers would leave his spouse to marry her. As in the movie created in that same year, *Love With The Proper Stranger*, there is a fair amount of stress for a woman to go through an abortion because of unrequited love, a lop-sided love, a love that is not returned. MM simply wanted a 'Goodbye kiss', to be let down gently, with respect, with a sense of admiration she (falsely) assumed the Kennedy brothers had for her. She could "never understand why the President, and later the Attorney General, hadn't the courage or the gallantry to tell her 'Goodbye' themselves" (MLT, p. 278).

Bobby Kennedy ended Monroe's 'bittersweet romance' in a "particularly brutal manner": "He did it cruelly, like a rich college boy dumping a girlfriend from the wrong side of the tracks. She had been fun; she had been exciting. But she was used up." Bobby's heartless dismissal of MM was "a macho act of a sort highly regarded within the Kennedy clan".

As Patricia Seaton Lawford describes it: "It seems as though Joe Kennedy's children, and the men and women they married, have a history of emotional and physical abuse. The men have a tendency to use women sexually and then discard them. This masks their own ability to feel." (MLT, pp. 264-265) According to Pat Seaton Lawford (in her conversation with MM about 'Bobby' false promises'): "Bobby's still a little boy wanting to play like a little boy!" (MLT, p. 281)

But MM couldn't simply let the lost love affair come to an end as a 'silent treatment' from both the Kennedy brothers, without the courtesy of an explanation. She felt used, abused, and discarded as a lemon sucked dry, as an object of lust, not as a friend or former confidante. She had wanted to end the affair herself in a gentlemanly and polite way. Not like this, not to be dropped like a hot potato, to be treated like a tramp, as a saloon girl (MLT, p.18, 255).

So, after contacting her former gynecologist, Leon Khron, on 19th July 1962, MM went incognito (under an assumed name) into Cedars of Lebanon Hospital for a 'quickie abortion'. She returned home on the evening of 21st July 1962. (MLT, pp. 282-283).

MM then called Bobby Kennedy (between 22-26 July 1962) at his home in Hickory Hill in Arlington, Virginia having obtained his personal phone number from movie producer Jerry Wald (who was working on Bobby's film, *The Enemy Within*). Bobby who was trying to distance himself completely from MM was "furious with Marilyn for taking this liberty" (MLT, p. 280).

RFK then requests Peter Lawford to ensure that MM was out of LA for the weekend of 27-29th July 1962 as he plans to be there for several public appearances. Peter of course complies and arranges matters for MM letting her believe that Frank Sinatra wants to be with her in Lake Tahoe at his "Cal-Neva" Lodge (named after the fact that it is located on the California-Nevada border). Reports state that Peter Lawford gives MM an abundance of drugs to prepare her for her arrival at the Lodge.

As MM still carries a torch for Sinatra (who had given her a pair of emerald earrings last Summer), she thinks perhaps Frankie is thinking to propose. But MM is to suddenly learn upon arrival that Frankie ('Blue Eyes') is actually now engaged to dancer Juliet Prowse! (MLT, pp. 285-286, 289) Instead of finding comfort and understanding in Frankie's 'hideaway' Lodge, MM meets Chicago Crime Boss, Sam Giancana, who wants more than ordinary sex with her. As one account states, Frankie simply says: "Be nice to Sam, Marilyn!" and leaves her to her own devices.

In Bungalow 52, MM becomes the sex-toy and plaything of this known psychopath, Sam Giancana (a man who hates the Kennedy brothers and wishes MM to feel likewise as he sets her up for the last weekend of her life). The fourteen Polaroid photos, taken at this scene (and photos from regular film later developed) are so offensive that when Frankie sees them he has them all burned (MLT, pp. 286-287). One could only imagine what may have occurred, although leaked reports indicate that *La Dolce Vita* (an Italian 1960 movie that mimicked the sex-suicide culture of the idle rich) captured the mood in that Lodge that Saturday night.

On this day, Saturday the 28th July 1962 (the last day of filming for *Cleopatra*), MM is overwhelmed by the many betrayals and honey-traps of those she considers 'friends' that she collapses into a complete emotional meltdown. The non-stop flow of drugs that Peter Lawford keeps supplying to MM together "with the aftereffects of the abortion" become too much for her. She was a 'good sport', for the Kennedy brothers got rid of her pregnancies, which they arguably caused, once they 'got what they wanted' (as she puts it; MLT, p. 264), but cannot shake the shameful realization that she was but 'a 'sex object' to them, nothing more than "the butt of filthy corporate jokes" (MLT, p. 18). Her future appears bleak; there appears to be no light at the end of this long dark tunnel.

MM likely wishes only to be rubbed out, to escape from all these sudden pressures she faces on virtually all fronts. She keeps taking the pills Peter keeps giving her, realizing the degradation her 'friends' are putting her through; and then (as could well be expected) she overdoses, and has to be rushed to emergency to have her stomach pumped.

Joe DiMaggio appears on Sunday 29th July 1962 and has a private quiet chat along the water's edge with MM away from everyone else. (MLT, p. 285) (No one knows what is being said but, in a day, or two it becomes apparent: Joe, MM's ex-hubby, formally proposes marriage.) MM flies back to LA with Pat and Peter Lawford in a private jet. But en route (in a limousine) from the LA International Airport, Peter Lawford leaves the limo to chat with Bobby Kennedy (for more than half-an-hour to warn him "Marilyn had begun making threats"). (MLT, pages 286-287)

03 AUGUST 1962, Friday

On this last weekend of MM's life, she appeared to be in a super good mood (according to witnesses, in particular, her 'housemaid' Eunice Murray).

She expects an expensive sofa to be delivered to her place this weekend as she had "ordered truckloads of furniture from Mexico" (where it was being 'manufactured') (MLT, p. 61).

"Whatever her source, Monroe knew by midmorning that Bobby [Kennedy], Ethel, and their children were on a jet headed for San Francisco. It was a combined business and vacation trip" (MLT, 298). ["Kennedy and his family spent most of the three-day weekend at the Bates Ranch in Gilroy, California. The Bar Association provided a suite at the St. Francis Hotel for use as an office and retreat during its convention" (MLT, p. 298n.).]

As *Life* magazine was promoting MM's nude swimming scene at airport gift shops and newsstands everywhere, this exposé likely reinforced in RFK's mind that any hint of a liaison with MM (especially at that time) could prove damaging to his career, not to mention JFK's! (MLT, p. 299) To make matters even worse, by early afternoon, as MM keeps her pre-scheduled appointments both with her internist, Hyman Engleberg, and her psychoanalyst Ralph Greenson, she stops at least three times to call RFK at his St. Francis suite. But RFK refuses to return her calls.

Perhaps by appointment, MM stops in at Frank's Home Nurseries (a tree farm) to select "several citrus trees, flowering plants and succulents" for her new landscaping plans with delivery arranged for the following day. "Very likely she planned her wedding [to Joe Dimaggio (on Wednesday, August 8th] to be set outdoors, and the garden and pool area needed plantings and colour." (Donald Spoto, *Marilyn Monroe: The Biography*, 1993: pp. 549, 565)

She continues to call Bobby repeatedly but without success.

MM calls Robert Slatzer (who had requested her return call a day earlier before she would take 'action' against the Kennedy brothers) to state emphatically that she wants "Bobby to end 'it' [the dangling unfinished 'Goodbye'!] himself". RFK (it appears) had made many promises to marry MM, to lead her on, to continue their most intimate affair, an affair that involved not mere sex, but apparently MM's feelings, mind, heart, and soul!

MM initially believed Bobby's words, and was sold hook, line, and sinker that he would marry her. Now MM knows that to be a lie, something she wants Bobby to say to her face: That he was a liar and that he lied to her, something she already knows but wants to hear him say 'it'! She does not at all appreciate Bobby's crass 'tragic brushoff' and will not settle for less than a full in person apology (especially as he left her alone to deal with aborting 'his' baby, as researchers currently maintain. (MLT, pp. 282-284, 288, 290, 299-300)

To Slatzer, MM renews her threats (to go public) against the Kennedy brothers. "If I don't hear from Bobby Kennedy before the end of the weekend, I'm going to call a press conference, and blow the lid off this whole damn thing!... I'm going to tell about my relationship with both Kennedy brothers... that the Kennedys got what they wanted out of me, and then moved on!" MM exclaims (MLT, p. 299).

MM begins to leak out her disgust and dismay with the way the Kennedys treated her to her confidante, Jeanne Carmen, as well as to Jean Louis's head fitter, Elizabeth Courtney, and others (MLT, p. 299). She demands to meet with her (paid) publicists Rupert Allan and Pat Newcomb, but only Newcomb initially responds. "She felt like a spurned woman and that she had been deliberately used." (MLT, p. 300)

MM speaks with a photographer, John Barris (who was in NYC) to come to see her (at her home in LA) on the weekend (because she has something very important to discuss with him); but he postpones the visit until Monday (6th August, two days after MM's unexpected death). Rupert Allan finally agrees to meet with MM after the weekend, as well, on 6th August 1962, Monday (MLT, p. 328).

Bobby no doubt (worried about MM's flurry of phone calls) decides to arrange a "wine-and-candlelight approach to ease Monroe out of the picture" (MLT, p. 301). He requests Peter Lawford and Pat Newcomb (who actually works closely with RFK, although on MM's payroll) to arrange a meeting with MM at their favorite cozy Italian restaurant in LA, La Scala. MM agrees. According to employees at La Scala (MLT, pp. 253-254), as Pat and Marilyn meet Bobby and Peter things shortly escalate to a heated exchange at a back table (MLT, pp. 300-301).

MM and Pat Newcomb retreat to MM's Brentwood home where Pat spends the night in the Guest Room. MM is beside herself and simply cannot sleep. She is interrupted by mysterious phone calls beginning at 11:00 P.M.: "A female voice screamed at her, 'Leave Bobby alone, you tramp!' Then the woman hung up. A second call came at 12:45 A.M. It was the same woman. 'You'll be sorry if you ever see Bobby Kennedy again!' The calls continued intermittently until 5:30 A.M." (MLT, p. 307).

[Author's Note: As certain parties may speculate, "How is it possible for RFK to meet with MM that Friday night given that he was already at the St. Francis Hotel in San Francisco earlier that day?", I would relay the explanation given by some as follows:

"The Attorney General, having received Monroe's increasingly strident messages at the St. Francis Hotel..., may have flown down to Hollywood to make a quick nonaggression pact with her. Since he was in San Francisco very early the next morning, he must have flown back to Northern California immediately after dinner. By jet, San Francisco was only a forty-five-minute flight from Los Angeles." (MLT, p. 301)]

04TH AUGUST 1962, Saturday
Marilyn's last night alive!

08:30 A.M.

Bright and early on this rather hot August morning, at 8:30 a.m., Norman Jefferies (Eunice Murray's nephew) begins to bring in all his work materials to lay tile in Marilyn's kitchen.

09:00 A.M.

Marilyn awakes to see what he was doing and has a light breakfast.

Patricia (Newcomb) lies peacefully asleep in her bed until she is fully rested (until about Noon), whereas MM has had a fitful night with little to no sleep at all.

Marilyn awaits delivery of a new sofa (from Mexico) [which, as a side note, remains in the shipping crate in MM's home until it is resold (along with Marilyn's other 'effects' from the house) at Christie's Auction in 1999].

11:00 A.M.

Peter Lawford calls MM from the Fox lot to tell MM that RFK's chopper is scheduled to land just after 11:00 a.m. and that they would like to visit MM in her home in Brentwood later this afternoon.
(MLT, pp. 303-306)

MM takes this moment (before RFK's arrival) to once again check out her earlier selection of trees and shrubs at Frank's Home Nurseries (possibly to arrange payment and delivery date?).

12:00 Noon

MM returns around Noon to her home just as Pat (Patricia Newcomb) is awakening. There is a hot discussion between the two of them (according to Norman Jefferies) pertaining to Bobby Kennedy's supposed arrival (which possibly is no surprise to Pat?!). Marilyn seems to suspect that Pat is currently having an affair with Bobby. Marilyn then tells Pat that her services are no longer required.

01:00 P.M.

Marilyn says that her (psychiatric) 'Nurse' Eunice Murray could also leave (as she typically did leave weekends to go to her own apartment). MM writes a check for severance pay to Mrs. Murray (for $206, which was a lot of money back then); and said that her services were no longer required either.

[Greg Schreiner bought MM's last canceled check (written on 4th August 1962 for $206 USD to Mrs. Eunice Murray) for $100 USD at Christie's Auction in 1999; as well as her still-unpacked sofa which remained in the original shipping crate with the delivery tag date of 4th August 1962.]

Mrs. Murray, however, takes matters into her own hands and immediately calls Dr. Ralph Greenson (who hired Mrs. Murray and who lived less than 2 miles away) to say that Marilyn requires his services.

01:30 P.M.

Dr. Greenson shows up shortly thereafter and states bluntly that Marilyn requires an immediate therapy session with him. Marilyn then accuses Mrs. Murray of being a spy for Dr. Greenson; and sees (for the first time what she often suspected) that they both work together spying on her privacy.

Then MM adds that Dr. Hymen Engelbeg (her regular physician, who also lives close by) was likely in cahoots with Greenson and Murray against her. She also expresses the desire to dismiss him,as well, saying that she was well, and so no longer requires their services.

MM plays a tape recording she made two weeks earlier (as part of her therapy routine) to share with Dr. Greenson that she now feels free of the necessity of all of these $1400/month sessions, that she is free of her romantic ties with the Kennedy brothers (except that she did not like the way they 'dropped her' like a hot potato).

She states that she really did not know how to break it to Bobby that she is no longer interested in him as she has decided to accept Joe DiMaggio's proposal of re-marriage! In fact, she is scheduled to 'fit the dress' she ordered on 6th August, Monday! (MLT, p. 300) (Marilyn had written earlier that she believed "a wise girl leaves [a relationship] before she is left"! Marilyn had wanted to be the one to break up her relationship with Bobby, not the other way around).

She appreciates what Drs. Greenson and Engelberg had done for her but states emphatically that she no longer requires their services. She also states a few very intimate details (we are left to presume) that regard her relationship with Dr. Greenson (which relationship Dr. Engelberg declares later was not professional, nor normal given MM's dependency on him). This tape as well as all the other taped sessions, MM had with Dr. Greenson were confiscated by the Probate Officer (as Dr. Greenson's "property") and were donated to UCLA to be released to the public at large on 1st January 2039.

What possible good reason could necessitate this very long delay (for 8 decades!) has led many to speculate that Dr. Greenson likely has something to hide, to say the least, in his relationship with MM. He did play the last tape with Mr. John Miner (under a pledge not to reveal the 'intimate contents' portion (in 1962). However, in 2005, John Miner publishes his extensive notes from these tape recordings in the *L.A. Times* (although not disclosing all the intimate details we may infer).

Miner (as a former L.A. District Attorney) was convinced beyond any reasonable doubt that MM was murdered. As could be expected, with his death on 25 February 2010, everything he said is currently being discounted by the 'Peter Lawford/Arthur Jacobs Big Lie' theorists who refuse to give up the Big Lie that MM killed MM. (MLT, pp. 286, 312-315, 325-327)

[Author's Sidenote: With both Greenson and Miner deceased at this time, the question remains: Why should we the public have to wait until 2039 to listen to something that should affect neither man? Both men (later) insisted that MM did not commit suicide either accidental or otherwise.

The conclusion, therefore, is that she was murdered! So why is this vital information still retained from public knowledge? There is no moratorium on murder: MM's case for murder should be opened up so that the Grand Jury could indict these tapes along with all other evidence (from CIA and the FBI files) to investigate the painfully obvious fact: (that) MM was murdered; and, to come to the legal conclusion as to whom the killers were, and the motives of all parties involved.

But Dr. Greenson (who apparently had sex with Marilyn, his patient, as disclosed by Marilyn's close friend, Jeanne Carmen, with whom Marilyn confided in all her secrets) felt that MM could be a threat to not only himself but to the Kennedy's should she be allowed to speak to the media Monday morning (06th August 1962) as she had threatened to do so (as disclosed by Mrs. Murray to Greenson).]

MM receives calls at this time from Ralph Roberts (her masseur), Jeanne Carmen, Joe DiMaggio Jr., and even Arthur Miller's dad but they are all answered by Eunice Murray (MM's 'maid') and/or Dr. Greenson himself: MM answers these calls later this evening. ["If someone wants to seriously commit suicide, as Peter Lawford maintains MM did, why should she bother to answer any of these calls?", one may reasonably infer.]

03:00 P.M.

Greenson meets with MM until 3 p.m. at which time he prepares to leave but then instructs Pat (Patricia Newcomb) to leave the premises (as Marilyn had told Dr. Greenson that Pat refused to leave when asked to do so). Pat (who was sunning herself at the back of Marilyn's pool) leaves as requested.

Dr. Greenson instructs Mrs. Murray to stay with Marilyn 'to protect her' this night! [Strange words one would think considering what would happen next?!] Mrs. Murray happily agrees to do so (but does not return her severance-pay cheque for $206 that MM wrote for her earlier!). Norman Jefferies remains as well until 7:30 Sunday morning, 5th August 1962.

As Greenson had given Marilyn a sedative (which made her temporarily drowsy and somewhat unsteady), Mrs. Murray had to drive Marilyn to Santa Monica beach to meet with movie director, Elia Kazan (according to one commentator). Kazan and MM meet for an informal discussion. Kazan had directed Marlon Brando in *On the Waterfront* (1954) and earlier in *Streetcar Named Desire* (1951).

As Brando had romantic interests in MM for many years, even sending her flowers and birthday greetings for her 36th birthday (MLT, pp. 39, 87-88, 163, 175, 179), and as MM's contract with Fox would expire soon, it should be no surprise that MM was looking ahead for different and better movie contracts. Kazan had confessed to a previous love affair with MM in a private letter to his wife, Molly Day Thacher, dated 29th November 1955 (released to The Hollywood Reporter in April 2014). It is possible that Kazan felt sympathy to MM's mistreatment by Fox and offered her alternate options.

MM returns home to be meet with RFK and Peter Lawford.

04:15 P.M.

Bobby Kennedy and Peter Lawford are both awaiting MM when she arrives home with Mrs. Murray (according to Norm Jefferies' 1993 testimony). Bernard Spindell (a former Military Signals Corps technician) had a pirated copy of MM's last day on earth, attests likewise. [He had planted wiretapping devices in MM's home under orders from Jimmy Hoffa (who apparently had a bone to pick with RFK) back in March that year.]

Spindell was later arrested on 15 December 1966. His pirated tape recordings were confiscated from his home by the FBI under Hoover's orders. Although Spindell repeatedly requested the return of those tapes, the FBI has kept them until this day (we are to presume, as they were never returned to Spindell).

According to Spindell's account (from the actual tape recordings of the day's events), Bobby Kennedy was initially soft and polite with MM when they first met in the guest area. But when he asks for 'it' [the listeners presumed he was referring to the 'Red Address/Diary' book in which MM kept a few notes to herself of discussions she had with the Kennedy brothers], MM replies emphatically she does not have 'it'.

Bobby blows a gasket and raises his voice demanding to have that Address book ASAP. He then marches into MM's private bedroom and begins to ransack (the little that was there) in search of this book, which he claims could mean MM's life if he cannot locate it! MM becomes hysterical (it is claimed) and demands that both men leave her house.

Bobby ignores her demands and keeps opening up drawers and wall panels: He comes across the mesh of wiring hidden by the secret service (and others) behind one of the panels in the closet area. He then realizes that everything he said was likely already recorded and that his visit with MM was a setup.

His first reaction is to blame MM for setting him up for a political fall (along with JFK). MM denies she knows anything about this wiretapping to which Bobby gives her a direct life-and-death threat! He knocks MM against an object which leaves a large bruise on her left hip [which bruise is noted in the later autopsy report]. MM becomes totally unhinged at Bobby's crude manhandling and has an emotional meltdown [MLT, pp. 373-374).

At which point, Peter Lawford intervenes and says to Bobby: "That's enough, Bobby! She really doesn't know anything!" As Bobby leaves, he asks Mrs. Murray to send for Dr. Greenson because MM obviously needs something to calm her down. Mrs. Murray dutifully complies.

04:35 P.M.

Bobby and Peter then left MM to her musings over this whole affair. MM discloses to both Mrs. Murray and Norm Jefferies that Bobby Kennedy had given her a direct 'threat' and that she now feared for her life. Dr. Greenson arrives and gives MM a sedative. He remains with her until 7:00 P.M. shut inside her bedroom. What they may have discussed or done together in the privacy of MM's bedroom has not been disclosed. But quite likely if the tapes recorded by the various parties that day have still survived, they would likely release what Spindell (and others who listened to MM's murder that day) have earlier hinted at: That Dr. Greenson became privy to the danger to MM's life that afternoon.

Note of Explanation:

Now it became apparent to all parties listening in at the events that occurred earlier this day at MM's house, that Bobby Kennedy visited MM in her Brentwood home in Hollywood. The trap was set and now it was sprung: Sam Giancana's pressure on the impressionable MM the earlier weekend had borne fruit. Unwittingly MM had demanded Bobby to see her, and unwittingly Bobby complied.

As Sam Giancana already had a CIA contract (through CIA rogue President Sheffield Edwards as admitted and relayed to J. Edgar Hoover) to take out MM only when RFK should arrive at her home, the murder plot swung into full action. Sam (Momo) Giancana was staying at Palm Springs (nearby) awaiting confirmation of MM's death.

[His sickening mindset was typical of psychopaths (as he was thus diagnosed by the military psychiatrists when he went to sign up under the WWII draft: A classic casebook study of a psychopath, they concluded). As the famed psychiatrist, Karl Menninger put it: "In kind, if not in degree, [the psychopaths] then line up with the Marquis de Sade, who believed in pleasure, especially pleasure derived from making someone else feel displeasure." (*Crime of Punishment*, p. 201)]

In a sense, Momo believed that his killing of MM (to blame it on RFK) would be the 'doublecross of the doublecross'. It would be sweet revenge for what RFK and his brother JFK had done to him (and others) in the Bay of Pigs fiasco (17 April 1961) also known as Operation Mongoose. Since WWII, the secret service (through the US military) had worked with criminals in Italy (as Operation Gladio). The motto of the CIA back then was: 'The enemy of my enemy is my friend' meaning that they would or could work together with the Mafia (in particular with Sam Giancana) to take down Fidel Castro, their mutual 'enemy'. "Momo" was banking on 'making a killing' in Cuba through Casinos run by the Mafia and controlled by himself. The Bay of Pigs disaster (whereby JFK reneged on USA Air Support) ended those 'get rich quick' schemes permanently.

Former US President Dwight D. Eisenhower had passed on this

legacy (to take out Castro) to JFK in March 1960, a legacy JFK (and especially RFK) detested. But when the Mafia (and especially Johnny Rosselli, former military sharpshooter, and sniper marksman, had convinced about twelve hundred mercenaries to attempt to take out Castro (believing that the US Airforce would back them up), virtually the entire group was captured except for about one hundred who were killed.

Rosselli somehow escapes and lives to get his revenge on JFK on 22nd November 1963. But unbeknown to "Handsome Johnny" Rosselli, his crime boss, Momo, had accepted the CIA contract to take out MM as soon as RFK would visit her in her Brentwood home.

People have criticized MM for her involvement with the Kennedy brothers saying: "If you are afraid of wolves, stay out of the forest". But then as MM believed she was 'in love,' she truly believed that she was being loved in return (for so is the nature of love: "Love is kind... seeks not her own, is not easily provoked, thinks no evil... bears all things, believes all things, hopes all things, endures all things!" (I Corinthians 13:4-7)

At some point, MM realizes that she has to break it to Bobby (Kennedy), that it is over between them. Most likely, this painful realization sinks in (as the therapy tapes to Greenson of 15th July reveal) even before the Kennedys had told her (on 17th July) not to call them anymore.

06:00 P.M.

The third call from Ralph Roberts to MM that day is intercepted by Greenson who bluntly barks out to Roberts that MM is not home. This unpleasant tone of voice to Roberts bothers him, as well as the obvious lie that MM is 'not home': He muses that at least Greenson could have been more polite and said simply: "MM is not available" or that "MM is busy at this time."

07:00 P.M.

Greenson leaves MM but does not give her any pills or additional medication at this time as MM calls her friend Jeanne Carmen (for the second time) to see if she has any sleeping pills but is not able to get through to her. MM begins to return her several calls of the day.

Joe DiMaggio, Jr. calls MM (for the third time) which phone call she answers. They have a pleasant chat about his break-up with his girlfriend, which (for whatever reason?) MM greets with enthusiasm believing it to be a good thing! Later, Joe DiMaggio Jr. testifies that MM was in a superb mood, and rather upbeat.

07:15 P.M.

When the conversation with Joe DiMaggio, Jr. ends, Marilyn in her excitement calls Greenson (who lives only two miles away and), who is preparing for a dinner with (movie star) Eddie Albert and his wife Margo for 8:00 P.M. Greenson notes that Marilyn is in excellent spirits and shares her enthusiasm for Joe DiMaggio, Jr.'s breakup. He reminds Marilyn that should she need him, she should ask Mrs. Murray for Eddie Albert's number.

07:30 P.M.

Peter Lawford calls Marillyn (to apologize for the earlier treatment she went through with Bobby Kennedy and) to invite her for dinner with Pat (Newcomb) and himself. She declines and tells Lawford (according to Lawford's later testimony) to say: "Goodbye!" to Jack, Bobby, and himself as she is 'through with love' and all that nonsense she endured. It is clear for a long time now that MM distrusted Peter Lawford. To put it bluntly, she "hated him" as he was "awfully mean" to her. "Her only relationship was with Pat Kennedy Lawford, Peter's wife" (MLT, pp. 317-318).

Later, Peter thinks that it is an odd message and comments that her speech sounded tired and slurred (which both Greenson and Joe DiMaggio Jr. dispute later saying that MM spoke clearly and distinctly). What is interesting to note, however, is that several people said that it was Peter who was thoroughly inebriated that night, and not Marilyn at all.

08:15 P.M.

MM is going to retire early for the night and bids Mrs. Murray a "Goodnight!" but still keeps her phone by her bedside (according to Mrs. Murray). Normally, when MM is ready to sleep, she leaves the phone in another room and covers it with pillows to muffle its loud ringing sound. She apparently can't sleep despite the earlier sedative Dr. Greenson gave her but continues to phone her phone buddies and to return calls.

08:30 P.M.

Peter Lawford, still puzzled by MM's "Goodbye!" comment to Bobby and himself, calls his brother-in-law, Mickey Rudin (MM's attorney), to ask if he could call Mrs. Murray to see if MM is all right (as he had just called her an hour ago and felt something was amiss). Rudin calls Mrs. Murray to ask if MM is okay, and to check on her, but Mrs. Murray insists that all is well, and that MM had just gone to bed early tonight.

09:30 P.M.

Still excited by the events of the day no doubt, MM finds that she simply cannot drift off to sleep, and as she has no additional medication or pills available, phones her dear friend Jeanne Carmen and does manage to catch her on the phone (on this, the third attempt). She asks Jeanne if she has any extra sleeping pills as MM is completely out of them, but Jeanne tells MM she too has no pills (as the two friends typically shared Nembutal tablets). Marilyn likely tells Jeanne of Bobby's visit and what transpired earlier today. (MLT, 342-343)

10:10 P.M.

As Marilyn tries to sleep, she receives a call from Bill Bonocanno which she quickly interrupts to tell him that she heard some sort of commotion in the house. Marilyn leaves the phone off the hook and goes to investigate the noise. She never returns to the phone.

When MM comes to the Guest room (where she thought the noise came from) she is met with two strangers, Leonard 'Needles' Gianola and James 'Mugsy' Tortorella, two Chicago hitmen sent by Sam Giancana to murder her. The hired thugs act quickly. They disrobe MM, pin her face down [bruise marks are noted on both her shoulders and lower back during the autopsy], tape her mouth shut, and place the CIA specially designed poison capsule (intended originally for Fidel Castro) as a suppository into MM's rectum. They tape it shut and allow its fast-acting lethal poison to enter into her bloodstream. Within minutes, MM is comatose and non-responsive. They remove the tape and leave.

Meanwhile, both Mrs. Murray and her nephew Norman Jefferies have been detained by two other plain-clothes men: They do not identify themselves but threaten both Eunice and Norman with their very lives should they attempt to call the Police or to intervene in any way. Norman later testifies (in 1993) that he believed they were either CIA or FBI agents because of their dress and demeanor.

10:25 P.M.

Once the men leave, Eunice and Norman enter into the Guest room where MM's body lay motionless; and sense that she is dying. Mrs. Murray immediately calls Peter Lawford and tells him what just transpired. He arrives in minutes with Bobby Kennedy and Patricia Newcomb. Pat Newcomb has a hysterical meltdown upon seeing MM apparently dead, saying out loud: "Marilyn is dead! Marilyn is dead!". Both Bobby and Peter try to calm her down and ask Mrs. Murray to call an Ambulance.

10:35 P.M.

While Natalie Trundy (Jacobs) is attending a Henry Mancini concert at the Hollywood Superbowl for her 21st birthday with her (future) husband, Arthur P. Jacobs (MM's publicist for Fox Studios), they receive a phone call message (from Arthur's employee, Margot Patricia Newcomb) to say that MM is dead. [Arthur Jacobs later disappears for two days without contacting Natalie as to his whereabouts]. He arrives at MM's place before 11:00 P.M.

The Schaeffer Ambulance arrives promptly with James Hall (as the Ambulance driver) and Murray Leibowitz, the attendant. Dr. Greenson is also summoned (probably by Mrs. Murray). After several attempts at CPR with MM, and applying mouth-to-mouth respiration, MM appears to subconsciously react, and color returns to her cheeks.

The Ambulance Driver relates what happens next: A doctor with a black bag arrives (Greenson, it is later confirmed). He states that he is MM's doctor. He takes out a long (heart) syringe from his bag, fills it with a brown fluid, and immediately injects it into MM's heart, moving her naked breast aside with one hand. The syringe is misdirected, hits a rib, but Greenson does not pull it out for a re-try: instead, he forces it down into MM's heart cracking a rib in the process (the distinct rib-cracking sound is heard by the Ambulance driver). He then releases the contents of the large syringe into MM's heart and tells the party present that they must now rush her to the Hospital.

11:10 P.M.

The party present hastily carry MM's nude body into the Ambulance and rush off to the Santa Monica Hospital nearby, leaving Pat Newcomb behind possibly to make a few phone calls, and to chat with her boss, Arthur Jacobs (whom she had likely called earlier at 10:30 P.M.; MLT, p. 310). During the trip, someone notes that Bobby Kennedy says a prayer for MM's recovery.

Before they arrive at the Santa Monica Hospital, Dr. Greenson realizes that MM is gone. The 'candle blowing in the wind' [Elton John] has been snuffed out. Marilyn is no more. RFK, Peter (Lawford), and Dr. Greenson now realize that the jig is up (that MM's death has been orchestrated by devious powers to obviously blacken Bobby's reputation and as a ploy against his brother JFK's bid for re-election). The decision is made not to continue en route to the hospital but to do damage control ASAP. They return to the scene of the crime (MM's Brentwood home) shortly before midnight (to have MM's body placed back into the Guest suite, as before).

11:45 P.M.

The next-door neighbor, Arthur (Abe) Landau (a LA financier), returns from a party and notes that there is an Ambulance present.

After the Ambulance leaves, Bobby contacts LAPD Police Chief, William Parker, a personal friend of his (and one to whom he had hinted he might make Director of the FBI, as RFK did not like J. Edgar Hoover). Chief Parker agrees to send over his best hand-picked officers for the cover-up.

Bobby Kennedy asks Peter Lawford and Dr. Greenson to accompany him in Peter's dark grey Lincoln Continental sedan as he needs to check out of his L.A. Beverly Hilton Hotel before he takes the helicopter (parked at Fox Studios, MLT, pp. 303-305) to the L.A. Airport, to catch the 2 A.M. flight from L.A. to San Francisco (where RFK will later claim he was present during this entire weekend).

05 August 1962, Sunday

12:10 Midnight

En route to the Beverly Hilton Hotel, Peter Lawford drives (without headlights on) between 70 to 80 miles per hour going East on Olympic Boulevard In L.A. and is stopped and told to pull over at the Robertson intersection by a Hollywood LAPD traffic cop, Officer Lynn Franklin. Officer Franklin immediately recognizes Peter Lawford and shining his bright flashlight into the back seat, he acknowledges Bobby Kennedy as 'Sir'! But he does not know the passenger in the front seat who is addressed simply as a 'doctor' (until he later sees his photo in the newspaper depicting MM's death).

Although he notes that Peter is inebriated and has the shakes (he keeps trembling as if cold despite the hot summer night), he does not issue them a speeding ticket but instead gives them the correct direction to turn around to arrive at the Beverly Hilton Hotel. He reminds them not to speed and acknowledges (in response to Bobby's question) that they are free to go.

Bobby checks out of the Beverly Hilton Hotel. They then drive Bobby to his 'dark' (tinted) helicopter parked at the Fox Studio lot. Bobby takes off (where a Secret Service agent is waiting for him) to the L.A. Airport.

Lawford and Greenson return to MM's place.

[Sometime later, the Police Officer Franklin puts two and two together, realizing that the location where he pulled Lawford's car over was only a short distance from MM's place; and discovers that Greenson was MM's psychoanalyst. Franklin notes as well the time of MM's death: The same night that he caught Lawford speeding away from the direction of MM's home.

[As a result of these 'coincidences,' Franklin seriously contemplates (in a later media interview) whether Greenson and RFK had something to do with MM's sudden death. He concludes that it likely was murder.]

12:15 A.M.
[Meanwhile at MM's home]

Within minutes, several Police cars arrive, and the LAPD Intelligence Department (part of a 57-member team that specializes in 'Intelligence work' or coverups for the Police Chief) goes to work. According to an eyewitness, Norman Jefferies, the LAPD Intelligence Agents carry MM's (nude) body from the Guest room to her bedroom, where a suicide attempt is staged.

Mrs. Murray is told to wash all the linen sheets and to help clean up MM's soiled body (possibly together with Pat Newcomb?) so that no foul play can be suspected. As a result of the suppository being forced into the rectum of the still struggling MM, there were likely remnants of feces, urine, and blood samples present or excreted.

The Intelligence Officers wipe down all fingerprints of the crime scene (even MM's own prints) in both rooms. Neatly placed empty pill bottles (none of which were prescribed by either Drs. Greenson, or Engelberg) are placed with their caps tightly sealed all in a row next to MM's bed.

She is placed face down (initially) with a phone receiver in her right hand (as seen in one photo). MM is staged as if in a provocative photoshoot position (with a white bedsheet partly covering her nude backside). In their haste, the Agents forget to place an empty glass next to the pill bottles. They make MM's bedroom look completely clean of any evidence of wrong doing.

[But (as later investigators were wont to say) it looks 'too clean, too perfect, too staged'!]

12:30 A.M.

The Intelligence Officers are left to do their duty, to make the murder of MM appear as a suicide.

Meanwhile, Johnny Rosselli having gained word that MM was indeed murdered (although he initially believed it was done by the Kennedys), goes to Jeanne Carmen's home to tell her that MM has been murdered; and to warn her that her life is therefore in danger (as MM had shared many secrets with her). As Rosselli had first introduced Jeanne (as he did Marilyn) to his boss Momo, he feels partly responsible for her safety. He tells Jeanne that she needs to flee right now and that he will help her to relocate in Nevada (with her two children). She instantly packs and rushes off for the next fourteen years to live under a new name far away from Los Angeles, never to contact anyone, nor to return until 1976 (after the death of Sam Giancana on 19 June 1975).

[Although never confirmed by Police records who really killed Momo, Jeanne Carmen discloses in an interview that the 'Silver Fox' "Handsome Johnny" Rosselli told her he did it. The actual killing was somewhat graphic. According to this record, Roselli, who was completely trusted by Momo, had come to Momo's place for breakfast. And in the course of their discussion, Rosselli shot Momo, his boss, one bullet in the back of the head. Then as Momo lay dying on his back in a puddle of blood, Rosselli told him (that): "This is for what you did to Marilyn!"; and shot six bullets directly into his face!]

[Apparently, it's explained in various sources that mobsters are okay when they kill their own, but when someone totally innocent, as for example a child, is deliberately 'taken out' on a contract, then other mobsters have a problem with that. Momo's role in the death of both the Kennedy brothers was acceptable for Rosselli (as Rosselli himself by his own admission was involved in JFK's murder).

[But for Momo to have MM killed bothered Rosselli to the point that he simply had to end this monster's life, knowing full well that his own life would be over not long thereafter. (Indeed, Rosselli disappeared on 28 July 1976). For you cannot kill your own Mafia boss and live long to tell about it.]

01:00 A.M.

MM's next-door neighbor, Arthur (Abe) Landau, again testifies that he saw several police cars and a lot of other persons running around MM's property shortly after 1:00 A.M. They did not begin to leave until sometime around 2:00 A.M. Greenson remains on the scene but ducks all photos that were taken.

Peter Lawford and a private detective (Fred Otash) go over MM's home with a fine-tooth comb to ensure that there is no evidence of a crime anywhere. MM's closet and bedroom which were messed up by Bobby Kennedy (earlier that day) are put in order. A search is out for MM's 'Red Diary' book but it is not located at this time.

[Later, on Monday morning 6th August 1962, Mrs. Murray passes on the Red Diary/Address book (which she was hiding for MM) to the Coroner who arrives to pick up information on Ms. Monroe's last known relatives (so that someone may bear the burden of the funeral expenses, as so far no one stepped up to the plate). MM's much-sought-after Red Diary is glanced through by Dr. Lionel Grandison (one of several coroners for MM's death) who places it for safe-keeping in the mortuary safe intending to go through it more carefully the following morning (in order to locate the next of kin).

[But by the next morning, Tuesday, 7th August 1962, it disappears from the locked safe never to be returned! Grandison and Deputy Chief Coroner Noguchi by now both conclude that MM's autopsy is being tampered with by higher powers, that the entire procedure has become a farce, that MM's death has been treated as a joke, that a well-orchestrated coverup is the only logical explanation (MLT, pp. 325-329].
02:00 A.M.

The Police are packing up, cleaning up the property, and preparing to leave.

Bobby Kennedy catches his 02:00 A.M. flight to San Francisco, about 320 miles away, and arrives there without a hitch.

Mrs. Murray is still doing laundry all through the night, as she has several loads to wash and to dry.

Pat Newcomb, Peter Lawford, Fred Otash, and possibly 'other guests' (Arthur Jacobs, etc.) leave to their respective homes.

Dr. Greenson and Mrs. Murray (with Norman Jefferies present) plan the details of the staged suicide: MM's bedroom window is apparently broken with a fireplace poker from the inside, as most of the shards of glass are found outside the window and some distance from the window frame. The place where the window is broken however is miscalculated as one arguably cannot easily reach one's arm through the broken window to reach the window latch without cutting oneself!

No one believes that Mrs. Eunice Murray ran to MM's window and "looked through the window and saw Monroe on her bed 'looking strange'" (MLT, p. 326) or that Dr. Greenson actually entered MM's bedroom through her bedroom window, as he attests in this coverup story. It's just not feasible. Eunice Murray and Ralph Greenson were lying to the Police (and they knew it!) when they said that 'nothing was out of the ordinary'.

"Everything was out of the ordinary. Monroe never went to sleep in the nude, with the lights on and the curtains open... The thick blackout curtains [in her bedroom] were tacked shut each evening." [These were a special drapery that "fitted over the windows and were attached to the walls with tacks in order to plunge the bedroom into blackness even at noon."] "Then Monroe would slip on a fresh brassiere... to keep her breasts from sagging." "Monroe did none of these things on her last night. Her having fallen asleep nude in a room ablaze with light should have alerted Murray to foul play unless, of course, Murray was fully aware of what happened." (MLT, pp. 276, 348)

Notwithstanding these glaring inconsistencies, Dr. Greenson's statement on the record is considered gospel truth: It becomes the accepted course of events. (MLT, pp. 326-327)

As to MM's door being locked, the only key to the house was a skeleton key that Mrs. Murray used to lock the front and rear doors late at night. (Mrs. Murray's copy which she always kept with herself is the only key ever found.) As was later noted, none of the doors within the house had keys as the previous owner never gave them to Marilyn, because they were too old and did not work properly anyway.

[According to later testimony (in 1985), Mrs. Murray stated that MM never locked her bedroom door (which did have a deadbolt lock) because of the fear she had ever since her highly traumatic experience on 1st February 1961 when she unwisely admitted herself into the Payne Whitney Psychiatric Clinic (after the death of her idol, Clark Gable) having blamed herself for his unexpected heart attack on 16th November 1960).

[She had been locked into a small confinement for long periods of time as part of her therapy. The Psychiatric Nurses forcibly gave her several baths a day occasionally assisted by several staff members who indiscriminately grabbed various parts of her body to submit her to their version of what 'cleanliness' meant. Her treatment was so invasive and intrusive, that she later had to have her gall bladder removed (in July 1961) as well as experienced intermittent bleeding in her vagina for some time thereafter.

[Marilyn eventually (after a week of this 'therapy') broke down completely. She called Joe DiMaggio to help her and told him that she was trapped inside a Clinic which refused to release her. She felt so stressed out as if she were to die there. As one account describes it, Joe instantly sensed her pain and became her 'white knight'. He arrived at the Clinic almost immediately to demand that they release 'his wife' this very minute.

[Although the Psychiatric Nurses there realized that Marilyn and Joe were legally divorced, Joe created such a loud and angry scene (threatening to tear apart the Clinic with his bare hands) that they quickly released Marilyn to Joe's custody. In one of her darkest moments, Marilyn had no one else to turn to (to escape that 'house of horrors') but Joe DiMaggio.

[MM later comments that when she initially entered the Clinic, she thought that she was experiencing a mental breakdown (as did her mother), but once inside the Clinic she soon realized that the staff members themselves were the 'insane people,' that they were crazier than the inmates, and that the inmates were genuinely 'crazy' people, much more than she thought she could ever be. As a result of this nightmarish treatment, Marilyn (Mrs. Murray admitted) could never again lock her bedroom door.]

03:00 A.M.

Although Mrs. Murray is still doing laundry so late at night, she is called to review the storyline for MM's staged suicide (as follows): Mrs. Murray apparently found MM locked inside her bedroom and notices through the bedroom window (which by the way has a rather heavy blackout curtain) that her light was still on, and sees that she is holding her phone in her right hand. She calls Dr. Greenson, who comes over, uses a fireside poker to smash the window, enters the bedroom through the broken window, and opens the bedroom door. This was the Big Lie that was to be perpetuated through all mainstream media right to this very day. (MLT, pp.326-327)

No one (initially) appears to notice that there is no empty glass next to MM's several empty bottles of pills. As MM apparently could not swallow even one Aspirin without a large sip of water, how she could swallow the 70 to 90 capsules they (later) claimed she swallowed (based upon the extremely high overdosage found in her liver, at least 3-5 times the lethal dosage) remains a mystery: a gross miscalculation by the 'suicide' theorists! One would think that if all these capsules were orally ingested, that MM would have long died before she reached the minimum 3-5 times the lethal dosage limit?!

"The most likely argument against suicide or accidental death came from the Suicide Prevention Team. 'Marilyn would have had to gulp down those pills, all of them [70 to 90], within a matter of minutes, a very few minutes,' said Robert Litman, the UCLA psychiatrist who headed the Team. 'If she had taken those pills a few at a time, she would have been unconscious before she could ingest the amount needed to achieve that degree of barbiturates in her bloodstream.'" (MLT, p. 345)
If for instance it were presumed MM had by some magic feat been able to swallow 70-90 capsules without water, how could her suicide be 'accidental'? It had to then be a deliberate suicide!

But to be deliberate was utterly ridiculous: MM had too many exciting things to live for! She was planning a remarriage to Joe DiMaggio. She was in excellent (albeit a bit fatigued) spirits that night. But most important of all: There was absolutely not the slightest trace of any drugs or remnants of capsules throughout her entire digestive tract: not a speck!

Her liver was overloaded with deadly chemicals that could only have entered through the anus: the lower part of her large intestine next to the rectum being darkly discolored. An enema or suppository was the only means possible, as no needle marks were to be discovered anywhere. But a forced enema was not likely because an involuntary enema would have caused serious internal damage, and no such injury was noted in the autopsy (MLT, pp. 342-247).

[The large syringe that Greenson placed into MM's chest did not leave a trace apparently as MM had been turned face down in her 'death position' for several hours allowing the blood to surface to that area and effectively erase that needle mark, we are told. This phenomenon of erasing possible needle marks is known as lividity; that is, "when the blood in the body drops to the lowest point of gravity the part (of the body) the victim is lying on (as, for example 'face down')"; Webster's Dictionary.]

03:15 A.M.

Dr. Greenson decides to call Dr. Hymen Engelberg, MM's personal physician, to confirm MM's death.

03:45 A.M.

Dr. Engelberg (who is not privy to this Big Lie theory and staged suicide) arrives and confirms MM is dead. Dr. Greenson already knows that MM was dead (for several hours), but it is necessary to have Dr. Engelberg come over to make the 'story of MM's suicide' appear more credible.

The word eventually leaks out to several key media centers over the next hour that MM is dead! Then the news begins to spread like wildfire to well over 400 outlets.

04:25 A.M.

Dr. Greenson then calls the LAPD to report a death, that MM is dead.

04:35 A.M.

Sergeant Jack Clemmons, a 15-year-old veteran of the LAPD (who happened to be only minutes away), arrives to investigate Ms. Monroe's death. He is stunned to see that this suicide has clearly been staged. He states in his report that MM did not commit suicide and that her death, if not accidental, was therefore 'murder' by deductive logic. He notices that her body position is not in a convulsive state (typical of drug overdose victims) and that there was no white mustache around the lips, or vomit on the sheets or any excretions whatsoever, which would typically be present for overdose suicide victims.

He also noted that the housemaid was still doing laundry all through the night and that there was no drinking glass for the empty tablet bottles, every bottle cap of which was screwed on tightly and the bottles neatly placed in a row. The window was broken in from the inside (despite the loud rebuttals by Dr. Greenson) as most of the broken glass could be seen outside the window. He could not find any key to lock or unlock Ms. Monroe's door. It apparently could not be locked by a key from the inside.

Sgt. Clemmons also notes that when he called the phone service to see to whom MM had last spoken, he was told that all MM's phone records have already been seized by the FBI, and that they are not available to be seen by anyone. The puzzling query that could not escape Sgt. Clemmons's mind was: How did the FBI know that MM was already dead? Jack Clemmons thought that he was the first Official Police Officer to know of MM's death?! Clemmons concludes that whoever seized the phone records likely knew who killed MM. So noting all of these discrepancies, Sgt. Clemmons files his report.

Sgt. Clemmons wants to declare MM's death as a 'crime scene' but senior (actually, 'hand-picked') officers (Sergeant Robert Bryon and Lieutenant Grover Armstrong, Chief of Detectives in West L.A.) arrive from the LAPD and take over the investigation. They refuse to declare this 'obvious suicide' (as Dr. Greenson claims it to be), as a 'crime scene'. Sgt. Clemmons overhears one of the investigative team members present saying: "Just another case of a Hollywood junkie overdosing." As they could not see any evidence of a struggle or of violence, all fingerprints having been wiped clean, all evidence (what little was left on the scene) is therefore not saved, nor tagged, nor documented. The Jury, they assume, is in: MM murdered MM.

05:00 A.M.

Patricia Newcomb, MM's (former) publicist, arrives wearing dark sunglasses (which she never removes) to introduce several News Reporters and Fox Studio personnel to the death scene. MM's private home becomes a veritable Grand Central Station, as no attempt is made by the Police or anyone else to control the flood of media photographers from traveling throughout MM's home. "After the Secret Service, the Los Angeles Police Department, and the publicity department at Twentieth Century-Fox were through at Monroe's house, not a scrap of paper remained. Even the five drawers of Twentieth Century-Fox contracts had disappeared... Evidence shows that much of the document-burning and political tidying up was a collaboration between [Peter] Lawford and Twentieth Century-Fox." (MLT, pp. 350-351)

Many personal items disappear (MM's panties placed on her bedside lampshade, for example, as originally noted in one of MM's early bedroom photos). As well as any possible evidence of a murder or crime scene, while MM's nude body lies partly draped in her private bedroom. Mrs. Murray attempts to restrict passersby from going throughout the house as if it were a museum but to little avail.

05:30 A.M.

Possibly because it is rather early on a Sunday morning, the Los Angeles County Coroner's Office is still not available to do an autopsy until after 08:30 A.M. As MM's body has been decomposing in the rather hot LA August heat since her death approximately 10:30 P.M. earlier that night, a phone call is made from an 'unknown party' [or a party that wished to remain anonymous, whom I suspect by deductive logic was Patricia

Newcomb] to Allan Abbott and Ron Hast of the Abbott & Hast Mortuary Accommodation Company to come to the Westwood Village Mortuary (at Westwood Village Park Memorial Cemetery) to meet with the (ambulance-style) station wagon that will transport MM's body to them for an initial inspection.

There is no funeral hearse (or limousine) for MM at this time. She is wheeled out in an ambulance stretcher wrapped in a blue blanket. And then driven to be viewed by the Mortuary staff. However, the paparazzi follow the car to the Westwood Village Mortuary attempting to take more photos of MM. To reduce the near violence of dozens of reporters clamoring to catch a photo of MM through the windows of the Mortuary, her nude body is wheeled into a large maintenance closet.

[It is solely my personal judgment in piecing together this narrative from over fifty disparate sources, that one possible explanation for this temporary relocation of MM's corpse is simply to allow her a little respect (if even in death) from the flood of photographers and news reporters who were literally inundating this small somewhat modest abode in Brentwood, especially entering at random into the privacy of her bedroom where her nude body lay displayed partly clad on her bed face down.

[As Pat Newcomb was truly emotionally overwhelmed at MM's sudden death (and suspecting 'foul play' at work), the least she could do, one would think, is to hide MM's body (as an act of human dignity) from the leering gaze of so many strangers and photographers (whom she swore at, calling them, "Vultures!"].

[Hopefully, when the books are open and the records disclosed in 2039, all controversies will be made abundantly clear. For now, there are (admittedly) a lot of missing pieces of MM's last day on earth. Thankfully, sufficient testimonials have been disclosed until now to yield a somewhat focused (if not perfectly clear) kaleidoscope of the events of that fateful day as they unfolded virtually hour by hour.]

05:45 A.M.

Sergeant Clemmons files his official Police Report on the mysterious death of MM claiming that in his opinion MM did not murder herself but that foul play was at work here. Although submitted, his report is never filed (unbeknown to him). Years later, when he asks to see his previously filed report for a television interview, it cannot be found. It disappeared without a trace, not even a record posted that it was indeed ever filed.

06:04 A.M.

Peter Lawford calls JFK to inform him that MM is dead. They chat for about twenty minutes (according to the White House phone log). No need to call RFK, as he already knows.

07:30 A.M.

Norm Jefferies leaves MM's home at this time (according to his 1993 testimony) as the aftermath of MM's death and subsequent intrusion into her home winds down. Coroner Bob Dambacher and Deputy Coroner Cleet Pace receive a phone call to arrange for the pickup of MM's body which is waiting at The Westwood Mortuary.

08:00 A.M.

MM's nude body is covered with a blue blanket as she is transported from the Westwood Village Park Cemetery Chapel by the Morticians Abbott & Hast to the L.A. Coroner's Office (amid a swarm of photographers who want to take photos of MM's nude corpse. But they are denied access to her autopsy (which autopsy lasts five hours).

08:45 A.M.

Chief Deputy Coroner Thomas Tsunetomi Noguchi begins to examine MM's body together with John Miner, the Legal Medical Official who is also the Assistant Deputy Attorney for L.A. They both use magnifying glasses, and both go over every square inch of MM's nude body examining all her orifices, etc. looking for possible needle marks. They conclude that they could not locate anything suspicious.

Upon slicing up MM and taking out her internal organs (her heart, lungs, liver, kidneys, stomach, intestines, colon, etc.), Dr. Noguchi makes the startling discovery that there are absolutely zero remnants of pills or capsules within MM's entire digestive tract. The only organ to show any sign of a death caused by drug overdose is the liver.

Dr. Noguchi takes samples of all of the organs and of MM's blood, and places MM's organs in a safe place for future evidence to show that MM did not die a suicide, but that clearly foul play was at work. As there were no needle marks, and no indication of ingestion of pills, the only way she could have received such a very high lethal dosage (estimated at least 3 to 5 times the lethal limit) was through a very deadly enema or suppository. MM's lower colon (next to the rectum) indicated a dark purplish discoloration obviously from an extremely lethal suppository. (MLT, pp. 342-346)

Later, Dr. Noguchi will return to his lab to discover all MM's internal organs and samples to be missing (which could substantially prove she did not die from ingesting pills, as was hastily assumed) except for her liver and blood sample (which indicated a high degree of Nembutal and Chloral Hydrate, the latter drug never having been prescribed by any physician to MM). (MLT, p. 334)

[The six CIA specially designed poison pills that were given to Sam Giancana to use for Fidel Castro (of which at least one was used on MM the night of her murder) contained lethal overdosages of both Nembutal and Chloral Hydrate, estimated at fifteen times the lethal dosage per pill.]

09:30 A.M.

Robert Kennedy attends mass at St. Mary's Roman Catholic Parish with his wife Ethel and their 4 children in Gilroy CA 79 miles south of San Francisco. He claims he was in San Francisco for the entire weekend, that he never visited MM's place since 27th June 1962 (when he was noted to speak to her about ending her relationship with JFK). He is not at all surprised to hear of MM's death, we are told.

02:00 P.M.

After MM's autopsy, her body is then driven back to Westwood Village Mortuary where Abbott & Hast prepare her body for viewing, for the Funeral Services to be held 1 P.M. Wednesday on 8th August 1962 at Westwood Village Park Memorial Chapel.

06th August 1962, Monday

MM's red address/diary book (which was finally located and) given by Mrs. Eunice Murray to the Coroner's office Monday morning, 6th August 1962, (to facilitate the knowledge as to her next of kin) goes missing the same night it was discovered and placed in the safe in the mortuary. Again, criminal activity is suspect here: No notes of supervision, no record-keeping, no documentation of MM's death, and the proceedings of her autopsy can be located to this day.

When police detectives finally begin to ask questions to suggest that Monroe might have been murdered, Dr. Noguchi calls for his test results from the Lab. But he is curtly informed by his superiors that the test results have been discarded. "An official memo said that 'further tests are unnecessary as the death has been declared to be a suicide.' Noguchi's carefully preserved tissue samples had been inexplicably discarded on orders of Chief Toxicologist Raymond Abernathy." (MLT, p. 334).

All Deputy Chief Coroner Thomas Noguchi could do to inform the public of these charades is to publish his book *Coroner to the Stars*, (in 1983). He states that he did not believe MM committed suicide based on the evidence he had originally examined, which evidence conveniently disappeared from a safe and secured location, so as to take away the possibility to prove medically that MM was murdered. As a result of these disclosures in his book, Dr. Noguchi is demoted as "Deputy Chief" Coroner in 1983.

In the fall-out from MM's untimely death, a deal is struck between RFK and J. Edgar Hoover. In exchange for the coverup assistance from the FBI, with J. Edgar's promise not to release MM's highly sensitive phone log (records), J. Edgar demands that RFK make his position as Director of the FBI permanent effective immediately.

And given that J. Edgar did not intervene to protect MM from these murderous thugs (although his agents were dutifully recording all the events in a van nearby), J. Edgar wanted RFK to state that due to J. Edgar's great work in stemming the flow of Communism (MM being the most recent victim as an undoubtedly 'communist agent', via her marriage with her former husband Arthur Miller) he, J. Edgar, would be awarded a lifetime position as Director of 'his FBI'.

Early Monday morning, 6th August 1962, RFK did just that. A trade-off was struck: MM's life for J. Edgar's tenured position. With MM's death, business as usual resumed.

What we can take away from this gross injustice to MM is that "power [especially political power] always has to be kept in check; power exercised in secret, especially under the cloak of national security, is doubly dangerous" (William Proxmire). Or as C.S. Lewis so aptly described it: "The greatest evil... is conceived and ordered (moved, seconded, carried and minuted) in clean, carpeted, warmed, well-lighted offices, by quiet men with white collars and cut fingernails and smooth-shaven cheeks who do not need to raise their voices"!

Wednesday, 08th August 1962

MM's funeral is held at Westwood Village Memorial Park Cemetery and is completely paid for by Joe DiMaggio who restricts attendees to only close friends of MM, totaling 31 persons. Frank Sinatra, Dean Martin, Peter Lawford, Pat Kennedy Lawford, and other Hollywood celebrities (as well as all the Kennedys) were excluded.

Both Joe DiMaggio and his son, Jr., felt that MM's death was not a suicide. They suspected foul play but could prove nothing conclusive at the time. No one (who was present at and privy to MM's death) would volunteer to speak the truth of what actually occurred.

17th August 1962: Inquest Day

Ironically, on the very day of MM's Inquest (to determine whether she committed suicide or was murdered) the two key witnesses, Mrs. Eunice Murray, and Patricia Newcomb, each received generous amounts of (hush) money, and given plane tickets to leave the USA for Europe (France, Germany, Italy, Switzerland!) for the next six months!

Mrs. Murray after six weeks of traveling across Europe became bored (as she admitted) and returned home to L.A.; whereas, Patricia Newcomb after two months of globe-trotting returned to a rather prominent executive position next to RFK's office. She never again spoke of MM, nor of that last day of MM's life, even though she was officially MM's publicist (a somewhat contradictory role one might think?)!

[Mrs. Murray, however, did break down in 1985 when interviewed by Anthony Summers for his new book, *Goddess: The Many Lives of Marilyn Monroe* (1985), in which she stated (when she thought the recorders were turned off), that MM did not die a suicide, and that RFK did visit her in her home on that last day of her life.]

Both Assistant Coroners, Thomas Noguchi, and Lionel Grandison refused to sign the cause of death in MM's autopsy report "as a suicide". They said that there was insufficient evidence to demonstrate suicide, as well that the disappearance of all key evidence to prove otherwise is highly suspicious of a cover-up.

But the Chief Coroner, Theodore Curphy, promised them that the evidence and proof of suicide were forthcoming, that they should trust his judgment and decision, and that they should sign the cause of death as: "suicide." But they adamantly refused: They said they would sign it as a 'possible suicide' at best; but Curphy argued for a 'probable suicide' judgment, which (with the promise of further proof and documentation forthcoming [which never came]) they reluctantly, and under protest, did finally agree to label MM's death as a 'probable suicide' just before the 23rd August 1963.

20th August 1962

Under pressure from the Inquest Committee and numerous News reporters hounding Dr. Greenson for a more detailed summary, for more information regarding that last day on Marilyn Monroe's life, Dr. Greenson slips this wild remark into one of his interviews: "If you really want to know what happened to MM, why don't you ask Robert Kennedy?". He then refuses to comment further.

Two years after MM's mysterious death (in August 1964), Greenson is asked once again what did he mean by his caustic remark (in 1962) to "ask Robert Kennedy" if we want more answers to MM's death?

Greenson gives the following noteworthy response (which I quote in his own words): "I can't talk about it, because I can't tell the whole story. I can't explain myself or defend myself without revealing things that I don't want to reveal. You can't draw a line and say: 'Well, I'll tell you this, but I won't tell you that.' It's a terrible position to be in: to have to say, I can't talk about it, because I can't tell the whole story... Listen, you know, talk to Bobby Kennedy!". Greenson never again spoke publicly about MM's death but became a sort of recluse, saying he tried to save MM but in the end he 'hurt her'?! We are left to draw our own conclusions.

23rd August 1962: The Chief Coroner's Summary Report and Conclusion

Chief coroner, Theodore Curphy, provided the following 'proof' and summary of the 'probable suicide' of MM, as his 'opinion':

[As will be noted in this 'conclusion or summary report', there is absolutely zero scientific or medical evidence of anything remotely resembling 'proof of suicide'; in fact, the exact opposite is true: This report is based on hearsay and subjective assumptions made of the psychological and mental state of Ms. Monroe, something coroners have no training, nor expertise to even comment on. But such it is, and so it passed as a 'coroner's opinion', as the cause of MM's death:]

"Ms. Monroe had suffered from psychiatric disturbance for a long time. She had often expressed wishes to give up, to withdraw, and even to die. On more than one occasion in the past when disappointed and depressed, she has made a suicide attempt using sedative drugs. On these occasions, she had called for help and had been rescued. From the information collected about the events of the evening of August the 4th, it is our opinion that the same pattern was repeated except for the rescue. On the basis of all information obtained, it is our opinion that the case is a probable suicide."

My own conclusion on the matter:

Susan Strasberg, one of MM's closest friends, described the legacy of MM as that of the lotus that grows in the mud! Ms. Strasberg added: "MM continues to rise [in posthumous fame] no matter how people try to pull her down"! There is a large grain of truth to Susan Strasberg's words: The implication is that there are still people who would like to "pull her down"! I see this verdict, this slur of "probable suicide" as one such instance.

The week following MM's 'suicide' (falsely so claimed), the suicide rate in the USA initially doubled and then tripled for the rest of August! Incredible how negative the effect was on those 'close to the edge', who looked up to MM and therefore who concluded (wrongly) that if MM can simply give up, a woman 'so sunny and so funny', then why should I resist the temptation to also commit suicide?

Such a travesty of Justice. Marilyn Monroe did not murder Marilyn Monroe! To conclude otherwise is The Biggest Lie yet perpetrated on Western Civilization! Consider MM's own words: "There are only three choices in life: Give up, Give in, or Give it all you've got!". These do not sound at all like the words of a basket case, a drug floozy, someone who gives up ending it all!

Consider who would benefit if MM should be labeled as a victim at her own hand:

The #1 Party: JFK and RFK: If MM's death is determined to be a suicide, RFK then could not have murdered her. So, his political power is secured as well as that of his elder brother JFK. But their desire for political fame was to be short-lived, as history points out. It was all for nothing: To dismiss MM as a junkie, as a joke, as someone who did not deserve to have the truth told about the reality of her death, the true nature and hidden motives behind her untimely death was a grave moral mistake. But one which given time will eventually be set straight.

The #2 Party: Fox Studios: To benefit from a 'probable suicide' judgment Fox Studios had a $13 million Agent Insurance clause on MM. If she was murdered by an outside party, then Fox could not collect that large bounty on her head (because 'that party' would have to pay for those legal costs and 'damages').

Recall that no one (at first) stood up for this orphan girl? No one came to the mortuary to claim her body, no family member, no member of the Strasberg family, or Dr. Greenson, or any of her relatives, all to whom she gave large sums of money and who would inherit her possessions! Not even Fox Studio offered to cover MM's funeral costs. Imagine that! It has been estimated that in the ten years MM made movies for Fox, they earned over $200,000,000 from her top-notch performances! Yet they never gave her any credit, not as an actor, only as a Box Office Star!

Today, those two hundred million dollars MM earned for Fox are estimated to be worth (in 2019) not less than $2,000,000,000.00 (that's $2 Billion)! For all this money, yet Fox would not cover MM's basic funeral expenses. Only Joe DiMaggio stepped up to the plate and hit another home run. He proved his love for MM and made it public for eternity. He agreed, in the absence of anyone else, to cover all MM's funeral costs.

But if MM's death could be deemed a 'suicide' or at least a 'probable suicide', then Fox Studio could collect from that 'straw head' (as Darryl Zanuck, the head of Fox Studios, liked to call her) the $13 million they needed to help finance their dud of a movie, *Cleopatra*, which originally cost $44 million (but eventually reached $62 million by the end of production)! It appears even to this day that the only value Fox Studio (and other movie moguls) could see in MM was as a 'cash cow'.

But thanks to a flood of testimonials in the past six decades, we have a much different story than that of The Big Lie (that "MM murdered MM"): In order for the evil of big lies to succeed, all that is necessary is for good people to do nothing. Perhaps the world needs more anger for the disrespect and disgrace heaped upon MM in this major cover-up of her murder? Perhaps the world allows evil to succeed, simply because it isn't angry enough? As John Steinbeck asks: "Must the hunger [for justice] become anger and the anger fury before anything will be done?". Or as MM puts it in her own words: "Always be yourself. Retain individuality. Listen to the truest part of yourself."

In Conclusion

Some may consider this 'thought-experiment' to be a work of fiction, a product of an overactive imagination; whereas others, may see this work for what it is: An exposé into probably the biggest whopper ever put across the thinking minds of the world today. Either way, in 2039, when (the masks come off and) all known documents (currently hidden in secret CIA and FBI files) come to light, what an explosive event that should prove.

But until then, allow me to leave this thought that should be chewed over carefully: "If they can kill MM, the most popular (and, arguably, the most well-beloved) female movie star in history, and completely 'get away with it', then they can kill anyone in the world, even the President of the United States, with total impunity."

What a chilling thought! How pervasive this Big Lie has become! How glorious the day when it shall be exposed, and the myth exploded that MM murdered MM!

In honor of MM's memory, allow me to share this concluding thought (as she always did say: "Hold a good thought for me!"):
(from *Romeo & Juliet*)

"Death lies on her like an untimely frost,
Upon the sweetest flower of all the field"!

[Or as MM said of herself: "I never wanted to be Marilyn: It just happened. Marilyn is like a veil I wear over Norma Jean."]

If I were present the day MM died, I would have liked to have paraphrased the following:

(as originally exclaimed by Gaius Octavius upon hearing of the death of Mark Antony, in *Cleopatra*)

"Is that announced as simply as that?

Marilyn is dead?
Marilyn Monroe is dead!

The soup is hot!
The soup is cold!
Marilyn is living!
Marilyn is dead!

Shake with terror when such words pass your lips...
The dying of such a woman
Must be shouted, SCREAMED!

It must be echoed back from
The corners of the Universe!

Marilyn is Dead!
Norma Jeane is dead!
Marilyn Monroe lives no more!"

11K. Lying:

Youth Feedback:
____

____

____

1. Beguiling

Youth Feedback:
____

____

____

2. Crafty

Youth Feedback:
____

____

____

3. Cunning

Youth Feedback:
____

____

____

4. Deceiving

Youth Feedback:
____

____

____

5. Defrauding

Youth Feedback:
____

____

____

6. Dishonest

Youth Feedback:

____

____

____

7. Equivocating

Youth Feedback:

____

____

____

8. Exaggerating

Youth Feedback:

____

____

____

9. Excusing

Youth Feedback:

____

____

____

10. Falsifying

Youth Feedback:

____

____

____

11. Forked-tongue

Youth Feedback:

____

____

____

12. Full-of-trickery

Youth Feedback:

____

____

____

13. Hypocritical

Youth Feedback:

____

____

____

14. Inaccurate

Youth Feedback:

____

____

____

15. Insincere

Youth Feedback:

____

____

____

16. Loquacious

Youth Feedback:

____

____

____

17. Mendacious

Youth Feedback:

____

____

____

18. Plagiarizing

Youth Feedback:

____

____

____

19. Propagandizing

Youth Feedback:

____

____

____

20. Saying-white-lies

Youth Feedback:

____

____

____

21. Serving-'father-of-lies'

Youth Feedback:

____

____

____

22. Stating-whoppers

Youth Feedback:

____

____

____

23. Taking-unfair-advantage

Youth Feedback:

____

____

____

24. Untruthful

Youth Feedback:

____

____

____

(Some of the) Sources Consulted:

Wikipedia [researched not less than 145 references for this Section]

Books and Articles consulted (to include but a few) as listed below:

Barham, Patte B. & Brown, Peter Harry. *Marilyn: The Last Take*. Toronto: Dutton, 1992.

Brashler, William. *The Don: The Life and Death of Sam Giancana*. New York: Ballantine, 1977.

Capell, Frank A. *The Strange Death of Marilyn Monroe*. Indianapolis: Herald of Freedom, 1964.

Carroll, Ronald H. (Assistant District Attorney), and Alan B. Tomich (Investigator). "Reinvestigation of the Death of Marilyn Monroe," report of the L.A. County District Attorney's Task Force, December 1982. [See also: FBI File 66-1700-39]

Giancana, Antoinette, and Thomas C. Renner. *Mafia Princess: Growing Up in Sam Giancana's Family*, New York: Morrow, 1984.

Guiles, Fred Lawrence. *Legend: The Life and Death of Marilyn Monroe*. New York: Stein and Day, 1984.

Hoyt, Edwin P. *Marilyn: The Tragic Venus*. London: Robert Hale, 1967.

Hudson, James A. *The Mysterious Death of Marilyn Monroe*. New York: Volitant, 1968.

Mailer, Norman. *Marilyn: A Biography*. New York: Grosset & Dunlap, 1973. [See also, FBI report filed on 23 July 1973 that warned J. Edgar Hoover that Mailer was suggesting "that Bobby Kennedy might have been involved in Monroe's death]

Pepitone, Lena, and William Stadiem. *Marilyn Monroe Confidential*. New York: Pocket Books, 1980.

Sciacca, Tony. *Who Killed Marilyn Monroe?* New York: Manor, 1976. [See also, the Mafia bugging of Monroe's home in FBI File 67-B (1962)]

Slatzer, Robert. *The Strange Life and Curious Death of Marilyn Monroe.* New York: Pinnacle, 1974.

Spada, James. *Peter Lawford: The Man Who Kept The Secrets.* New York, Bantam, 1991.

Speriglio, Milo. *Marilyn Monroe: Murder Coverup.* Van Nuys, CA: Seville Publishing, 1982. [See also, L.A. Police Department document number 62-509-403]

Strasberg, Susan. *Bittersweet.* New York: Putnam's, 1980.

Summers, Anthony. *Goddess: The Secret Lives of Marilyn Monroe.* New York: Macmillan, 1985.

Tass Reports (5 in total). KGB Files: "The Kennedys and the Death of Marilyn Monroe". Full Disclosure of CIA Involvement in the Death of Marilyn Monroe, 1988.

Zolotow, Maurice. "Joe & Marilyn: The Ultimate L.A. Love Story." *Los Angeles Times*, February 1979, pp. 138,140, 238-247.

[**Nota Bene:** To the reader: It is the intention of this Author to expand upon the findings of this investigation (that **MM did not Murder MM**) into a book with that self-same title, sometime in the near future. Accordingly, the multitude of specifics detailing the exact references for this or that comment will be suspended until that date. It would be sheer folly, in the opinion of this Author, to disclose the 'trade secrets' or references (after gleaning hundreds of pages of notes on this intriguing topic) for someone else to steal the Author's thunder, as it were. Hence, the lack of meticulous notes as to the exact location where these claims originated. These points will all be disclosed in this upcoming future volume. Please be patient.]

DISCLAIMER: N.B. (*Nota Bene*)
All tunes/songs/video clips/links/quotes/etc. are herein provided to assist in Group Therapy Sessions, or privately, for individual study (to assist in learning) and for educational purposes *only*.

[#91: U-Tube Reference]
MM's Autopsy Report 2 (1962)
https://images.app.goo.gl/PQ75s8ZFPYiJjXvc6

[#92: U-Tube Reference]
MM's Autopsy Report 1 (1962)
https://images.app.goo.gl/vbHVCGqti6ZmwiyC8

[#93: U-Tube Reference]
MM's corpse covered in blue horse blanket
https://images.app.goo.gl/v1kmRpMZ8sHjT86aA

[#94: U-Tube Reference]
The Marilyn Monroe Files [MM did not commit suicide]
https://www.youtube.com/watch?v=biYs3hR4w_8

[#95: U-Tube Reference]
MM's black raven 1956 Thunderbird sold for $490,000
https://images.app.goo.gl/cFWFzXbyWRg5RuYdA

[#96: U-Tube Reference]
MM's funeral embalmer speaks out
https://www.youtube.com/watch?v=sQf0xd2fmBQ

[#97: U-Tube Reference]
MM's Happy Birthday dress sells for: $4.81 million Nov/2016
https://www.youtube.com/watch?v=ZaCGSGekmWg

[#98: U-Tube Reference]
MM's Happy birthday dress TBA at: Julien's Auctions 17 Nov/2016
https://www.youtube.com/watch?v=hD86L-V4V_o

[#99: U-Tube Reference]
MM's home for sale for $6.9 million (SOLD for $7.25 million!)
https://www.youtube.com/watch?v=Rh2nneczS_w

[#100: U-Tube Reference]
MM: EYEWITNESS August 1962: Why?
https://www.youtube.com/watch?v=MBNIRo09aAw

[#101: U-Tube Reference]
Who Killed Marilyn Monroe? (John Miner Marilyn Transcripts 1/4)
https://www.youtube.com/watch?v=NnAhE6lADts&t=69s

[#102: U-Tube Reference]
Who Killed Marilyn Monroe? (John Miner Marilyn Transcripts 2/4)
https://www.youtube.com/watch?v=svQs0lq6rvl&t=18s

[#103: U-Tube Reference]
Who Killed Marilyn Monroe? (John Miner Transcripts 3/4)
https://www.youtube.com/watch?v=0nF1ZN67VKY&t=6s

[#104: U-Tube Reference]
Who Killed Marilyn Monroe? (John Miner Transcripts 4/4)
https://www.youtube.com/watch?v=uQIqbzzofgM

[#105: U-Tube Reference]
Marilyn Monroe Auction - Christie's 1999 - Part 1/9
https://www.youtube.com/watch?v=YOAsqw-1scU

[#106: U-Tube Reference]
Marilyn Monroe Auction - Christie's 1999 - Part 4/9
https://www.youtube.com/watch?v=YbWD2Lt_-_4

[#107: U-Tube Reference]
Marilyn Monroe Auction - Christie's 1999 - Part 5/9

https://www.youtube.com/watch?v=4PoYbhiSKlM

[#108: U-Tube Reference]
Marilyn Monroe Auction - Christie's 1999 - Part 6/9
https://www.youtube.com/watch?v=C8uy47Hiy2A

[#109: U-Tube Reference]
MM murdered by Sam Giancana's henchmen [17 Feb/1992:
Entertainment Tonight expose]
https://www.youtube.com/watch?v=3JgKIMR0PvE

[#110: U-Tube Reference]
Maf: Last dog MM had
https://images.app.goo.gl/bTenr2jozYbA8bQs8

[#111: U-Tube Reference]
Maf Honey: MM's dog
https://images.app.goo.gl/xEwA8oJjv93H8ucP9

[#112: U-Tube Reference]
Douglas Kirkland (LOOK Magazine): MM
https://www.youtube.com/watch?v=qJ44Lepus9A

[#113: U-Tube Reference]
Look Magazine with MM: Douglas Kirkland
https://www.youtube.com/watch?v=UR_eHHtv1rs

[#114: U-Tube Reference]
MM's dress for sale: Julien Auction Nov/2016 [Inside Edition]
https://www.youtube.com/watch?v=zhfQGSLoEQ0

[#115: U-Tube Reference]
MM: 10 years later RARE (1972 Documentary)
https://www.youtube.com/watch?v=BbvmGUH3yLY

[#116: U-Tube Reference]
MM's Something's Got To Give! [8th April to 8th June 1962)]
https://www.youtube.com/watch?v=I-sLSxaaUxQ

[#117: U-Tube Reference]
MM's death: Current Affair (1 of 2)
https://www.youtube.com/watch?v=OVMzvvDHull

[#118: U-Tube Reference]
MM's Death: Current Affair (2 of 2)
https://www.youtube.com/watch?v=-I5BBkxuTpE

[#119: U-Tube Reference]
Marilyn's Suicide: Fact or Fiction? (1 of 2)
https://www.youtube.com/watch?v=YEokmJJKHpc

[#120: U-Tube Reference]
Marilyn's Suicide: Fact or Fiction? (2 of 2)
https://www.youtube.com/watch?v=AMbKIqghDYU

[#121: U-Tube Reference]
Marilyn Monroe: Suicide - Fact or Fiction? Part 1/2
https://www.youtube.com/watch?v=YEokmJJKHpc&t=20s

[#122: U-Tube Reference]
Marilyn Monroe: Suicide - Fact or Fiction? Part 2/2
https://www.youtube.com/watch?v=AMbKIqghDYU

[#123: U-Tube Reference]
Marilyn Monroe - Life After Death (1994)
https://www.youtube.com/watch?v=P-g8vUzmgNc

[#124: U-Tube Reference]
MM - Ultimate Investigation into a Suspicious Death
https://www.youtube.com/watch?v=LVyOmjWeYP0&t=155s

[#125: U-Tube Reference]
Rivals: MM vs. Jackie Kennedy (1 of 2)
https://www.youtube.com/watch?v=nQQ0X9ABXqM

[#126: U-Tube Reference]
Rivals: MM vs. Jackie Kennedy (2 of 2)
https://www.youtube.com/watch?v=X76t0SIC284

[#127: U-Tube Reference]
Jeanne Carmen & Johnny Rosselli RE: MM's death
Jeanne Carmen on Channel 9 News
https://www.youtube.com/watch?v=Rdep_Xunl_k

[#128: U-Tube Reference]

MM exhibit with Susan Strasberg: MM's 2 self-portraits
https://www.youtube.com/watch?v=Q_1qknmMaZA

[#129: U-Tube Reference]
Susan Strasberg: MM spent $5,000 on JFK b-day dress
https://www.youtube.com/watch?v=aqpDFZyUHlg

[#130: U-Tube Reference]
Susan Strasberg, Julie Miller 1988 Interview on MM
https://www.youtube.com/watch?v=MpWzOHqXp3g

[#131: U-Tube Reference]
MM: murder? Accident? Suicide?
https://www.youtube.com/watch?v=9ZeWij5QYCg

[#132: U-Tube Reference]
MM's best friend Jeanne Carmen says: MM was murdered!
https://www.youtube.com/watch?v=pt3ug9Pbg2E

[#133: U-Tube Reference]
MM's Childhood years in her own voice
https://www.youtube.com/watch?v=p34nlBUTyFM

[#134: U-Tube Reference]
MM's Teenage years in her own voice
https://www.youtube.com/watch?v=zbhS1HFwyMg

[#135: U-Tube Reference]
"After you get what you want, you don't want it!"[MM sings]
https://www.youtube.com/watch?v=pxro_JPV4sQ

[#136: U-Tube Reference]
MM's home in Brentwood SOLD 31 May 2017 for: $7.25 Million
USD!
https://www.youtube.com/watch?v=LjdvqqtMNpg

[#137: U-Tube Reference]
RFK was at MM's the day she died: Dominic Dunne
https://www.youtube.com/watch?v=K-xHnBwx9nc

[#138: U-Tube Reference]
MM Christie's Auction 1999 [part one]

Total sale: $13 Million dollars to Anna Strasberg
(who never in life ever met MM!]
https://www.youtube.com/watch?v=YOAsqw-1scU

[#139: U-Tube Reference]
MM Christie's Auction 1999 [part two]
https://www.youtube.com/watch?v=UmJvpjMRpm4

[#140: U-Tube Reference]
MM Times: Theories on her death
https://www.youtube.com/watch?v=YZDsY5ltPvg

[#141: U-Tube Reference]
MM Christie's Auction 1999 [Part Eight]
https://www.youtube.com/watch?v=t9nobULLf6o

[#142: U-Tube Reference]
MM Christie's Auction 1999 [Part Nine]
https://www.youtube.com/watch?v=Qgl4crL-Sec

[#143: U-Tube Reference]
MM's Man [documentary on James Dougherty]
https://www.youtube.com/watch?v=RaCgidLF-4I

[#144: U-Tube Reference]
MM: artifacts in Ripley's Believe It or Not! museum in Hollywood
https://www.youtube.com/watch?v=Wyqtz9kmvwU

[#145: U-Tube Reference]
MM: Sussan & John Strasberg, Jane Russell, etc.
https://www.youtube.com/watch?v=oh8itsg-QPo

[#146: U-Tube Reference]
MM: Larry King Live 1997 with those who met MM
https://www.youtube.com/watch?v=TweqbfFqueA

[#147: U-Tube Reference]
MM Remembered!: Larry King Live [1st June 2001]
https://www.youtube.com/watch?v=xp0Sis5Ya5g

[#148: U-Tube Reference]
The REAL MM: John Huston, Eli Wallach, etc.

https://www.youtube.com/watch?v=NIayZImEdjM&t=605s

[#149: U-Tube Reference]
Jeanne Carmen: MM, Frank Sinatra, JFK, RFK [start at: 20 min. mark]
https://www.youtube.com/watch?v=2QDfofFXPJg&t=1186s

[#150: U-Tube Reference]
Cal Neva Hotel history [MM there before her murder]
https://www.youtube.com/watch?v=G9xOTIei3Uc

[#151: U-Tube Reference]
Ralph Roberts, MM's Masseur: believes in foul play!
https://www.youtube.com/watch?v=xaO3vT7RIjo

[#152: U-Tube Reference]
MM and The Actor's Studio
https://www.youtube.com/watch?v=am_PvmskFnA

[#153: U-Tube Reference]
James Haspiel MM's photographer believes RFK had MM killed
https://www.youtube.com/watch?v=n5Uwrdw7mrg

[#154: U-Tube Reference]
MM's Happy Bday JFK dress SOLD: $4.81 million at Julien's Auction
https://www.youtube.com/watch?v=ZaCGSGekmWg

[#155: U-Tube Reference]
Why MM is still so closely followed in her personal effects
https://www.youtube.com/watch?v=ErVrFzjuGRw

[#156: U-Tube Reference]
MM Largest collection of memorabilia on Hotel Queen Mary
https://www.youtube.com/watch?v=yayvV_nSBWo

[#157: U-Tube Reference]
MM personal effects collected by Greg Schreiner
https://www.youtube.com/watch?v=kRmcwMhXaHg

[#158: U-Tube Reference]
MM did not commit suicide! [MM's assistant Betty Robin in 1962]

https://www.youtube.com/watch?v=wKHHv54fK_o

[#159: U-Tube Reference]
MARILYN: The Last Word [HARDCOPY (30 April to 7th May 1992) into murder of MM/ 1 of 4]
https://www.youtube.com/watch?v=MXN4mMpiWyc
[#160: U-Tube Reference]
MARILYN: THE LAST WORD [HARDCOPY Investigation into the murder of MM /2 of 4]
https://www.youtube.com/watch?v=Se97xRJkLY4

[#161: U-Tube Reference]
MARILYN: The Last Word [HARDCOPY Investigation into the murder of MM /3 of 4]
https://www.youtube.com/watch?v=Se97xRJkLY4

[#162: U-Tube Reference]
MARILYN: The Last Word [HARDCOPY Investigation into the murder of MM /4 of 4]
Timeline of her last day on earth hour by hour
https://www.youtube.com/watch?v=5xuxgiGrkPQ

[#163: U-Tube Reference]
MM Eulogy by Lee Strasberg 8th August 1962 (at 5 min. mark)
https://www.youtube.com/watch?v=iip1w8rAz6o

[#164: U-Tube Reference]
Marilyn Monroe Auction - Christie's 1999 - Part 3/6
https://www.youtube.com/watch?v=3MQC2j9C9ls&t=33s

[#165: U-Tube Reference]
Joan Collins on Marilyn Monroe [1997]
https://www.youtube.com/watch?v=NC0t088gHgU

[#166: U-Tube Reference]
Jane Fonda on MM
https://www.youtube.com/watch?v=JMwP0hJCl4s

[#167: U-Tube Reference]
Unsolved Mysteries: MM's death
https://www.youtube.com/watch?v=9BWgjBTxwHE

[#168: U-Tube Reference]
MM's birthday dress sold for $4.81 million in 2017
https://www.youtube.com/watch?v=ZaCGSGekmWg

[#169: U-Tube Reference]
Jeanne Carmen: Second Explosive interview [Frank Sinatra, MM, JFK, RFK]
Interview at: 7 to 11-minute mark & 20-22 minute mark RE: MM murder
https://www.youtube.com/watch?v=tmTDs_0EjmQ

[#170: U-Tube Reference]
Eunice Murray, Housekeeper to MM has conflicting stories
https://www.youtube.com/watch?v=nTY-R0mZ23M

[#171: U-Tube Reference]
Robert Mitchum on MM
https://www.youtube.com/watch?v=oZKUtW-aDHM

[#172: U-Tube Reference]
Joan Collins on MM: Beware the wolves in Hollywood
https://www.youtube.com/watch?v=NC0t088gHgU

[#173: U-Tube Reference]
Shelley Winters on MM
https://www.youtube.com/watch?v=cRvwjm3eq3g

[#174: U-Tube Reference]
Laurence Olivier on MM
https://www.youtube.com/watch?v=3q995YniCsQ

[#175: U-Tube Reference]
MM's home sold for $7.25 million in 2017
https://www.youtube.com/watch?v=LjdvqqtMNpg
[#176: U-Tube Reference]
Proof Positive that MM was murdered, that RFK was there!
https://www.youtube.com/watch?v=WNVhMilngbc

[#177: U-Tube Reference]
Secret Life Story of MM
https://www.youtube.com/watch?v=u9icRUDNHHM

[#178: U-Tube Reference]
MM & Joe DiMaggio
https://www.youtube.com/watch?v=fzguiNhVd1Q

[#179: U-Tube Reference]
What Joe DiMaggio took from MM's house after her death
https://www.youtube.com/watch?v=vjoMQdPeWJU

[#180: U-Tube Reference]
The home MM died in 4th August 1962 [then & now]
https://www.youtube.com/watch?v=0PR1qR81QvA&pbjreload=10

[#181: U-Tube Reference]
MM's memorabilia SOLD and collected
https://www.youtube.com/watch?v=kRmcwMhXaHg

[#182: U-Tube Reference]
MM's home SOLD in 10 days on 31 May 2017 for $7.25 million
https://www.youtube.com/watch?v=LjdvqqtMNpg&pbjreload=10

[#183: U-Tube Reference]
"Marilyn" song sung for MM in 1952 [starts at 8-minute mark]
https://www.youtube.com/watch?v=hOGVkWRUfWI

[#184: U-Tube Reference]
Details as to why MAFIA, CIA & FBI (w/LBJ) killed: MM, JFK, &
RFK
https://www.youtube.com/watch?v=0vHOcTO3rmc

[#185: U-Tube Reference]
Details of MM's embalming [so sad, so loveless]
https://www.youtube.com/watch?v=sQf0xd2fmBQ

[#186: U-Tube Reference]
Kelli Garner plays MM in "Secret Life of MM" [interview]
https://www.youtube.com/watch?v=T47RuHZIedM

[#187: U-Tube Reference]
Proof that MM's doctors think they killed her [but not the whole
story!]
https://www.youtube.com/watch?v=LVyOmjWeYP0

[#188: U-Tube Reference]
Anthony Summers who wrote MM biography: Goddess [1985 interview]
https://www.youtube.com/watch?v=RnxDzRxJqGc

[#189: U-Tube Reference]
How MM was murdered [see: 20-21,25-32,41-47 minute segments]
https://www.youtube.com/watch?v=TcoAEI08ms4
[#190: U-Tube Reference]
Jeanne Carmen knew that RFK was involved in MM's murder [1992 Interview]
https://www.youtube.com/watch?v=2QDfofFXPJg

[#191: U-Tube Reference]
Marilyn Monroe Party thrown at Ray Anthony's Home 1952
https://www.youtube.com/watch?v=hOGVkWRUfWI&list=RDhOG VkWRUfWI&start_radio=1

[#192: U-Tube Reference]
Ray Anthony - Marilyn
https://www.youtube.com/watch?v=cghX9sYcE9w&list=RDhOGVk WRUfWI&index=2

[#193: U-Tube Reference]
Marilyn Monroe - at the Big Band Ray Anthony Party 1952
https://www.youtube.com/watch?v=v6LO0GXCc_w&list=RDhOGV kWRUfWI&index=11

Sacrilegious:

Blasphemous

Cursed-(of God)

Heathen

Idolatrous

Impious

Mocking-the-Divine

Pagan

Profane

Sanctimonious

Ungodly

Wandering-stars

FOOD FOR THOUGHT:

For the Natural Man Striving to Become Spiritual

Meditation: (To Chew over one's Thoughts!):
Listen to what your child is trying to tell you *not* to do!:

Don't make me feel that my mistakes are sins. I have to learn to make mistakes without feeling that I am no good.

Rule #12: For Raising Delinquent Children:

"We read in the paper and hear on the air; Of killing and stealing and crime everywhere! We sigh and say as we notice the trend: 'This young generation, where will it end?'!"

Youth Feedback:

____

____

____

Rule #12: For Repentance (to turn your life around):

Reciprocate by forgiving others.

Youth Feedback:

____

____

____

Sacrilegious

When one thinks of an animal that might have the human quality of being 'sacrilegious', the magpie comes directly to mind. In my years of observing this rather noisy and messy bird, I can still hear its mocking shrill as if to deride whatever it comes across, and wheresoever it might be. The opposite to a sweet melodious sound, it disrupts the harmony and serenity of whatsoever neighborhood it invades.

As an anonymous writer once said: "To argue with Liberal Democrats is like playing chess with a pigeon: no matter how good I am at chess, the pigeon is just going to knock over the pieces, crap on the board, and strut around like it's victorious". So it is with the sacrilegious overly pious sanctimonious bigot. The one who always has a 'chip on his shoulder' against anyone who appears (to him) to be a 'goody-two-shoes' or someone trying hard to do what is right.

The classic example of the sacrilegious man is the thief on the cross (traditionally, on 'the left side' of our Lord), who derided Jesus crucified next to him, mocking Him and saying: "If thou be Christ, save thyself and us?!" (Luke 23:39) (See also Mark 15:15-20) The point in mocking religion whether that of one's own countrymen or that of another country is to promote oneself as a heathen or an atheist, to say that one is but an animal and fears neither God nor men (as if such an act invoked great intelligence?).

Agnostics (who are filled with doubts) say that there may or may not be a God, they really don't know. They think they are being rationalists and fair-minded in the view of scientific facts, but then these 'doubting Thomases' do not believe anything except what they can see, hear, feel, or taste. (See John 20:24-25) They are woefully inadequate to believe or to come to 'know' anything of any value, it seems, as they question and bring to uncertainty their entire world around themselves as if living in an epistemological earthquake: there are no markers, no landmarks, that specify anything for a surety, or a solid reference point.

To be sacrilegious (to mock God and the Divine) is also to pretend to believe in God (for ulterior purposes, such as to belong to a

Society of Friends, or to a Church, a Mosque, or Synagogue, or to a Kingdom Hall) but not to truly believe God really exists. The prime example is well-portrayed in the movie, *Elmer Gantry* (1960, played by Burt Lancaster) in which Gantry goes along with the Christian revivalist meetings but does not believe or appear to have faith that God is for real, that miracles can truly occur if one but believes.

As the Scriptures say: "The fool has said in his heart, There is no God"! (Psalms 14:1). Or, as JFK had intended to say in a speech in Dallas on 22nd November 1962 (before his life was cut short): 'Where there is no vision, the people perish!" (Proverbs 29:18).

Perhaps Otto von Bismarck puts it best: "There is only one greater folly than that of the fool who says in his heart there is no God, and that is the folly of the people that says with its head that it does not know whether there is a God or not."

12L.   Sacrilegious:

Youth Feedback:

1.   Blasphemous

Youth Feedback:

2.   Cursed-(of God)

Youth Feedback:

3.   Heathen

Youth Feedback:

4.   Idolatrous

Youth Feedback:

5.   Impious

Youth Feedback:

6. Mocking-the-Divine

Youth Feedback:

____

____

____

7. Pagan

Youth Feedback:

____

____

____

8. Profane

Youth Feedback:

____

____

____

9. Sanctimonious

Youth Feedback:

____

____

____

10. Ungodly

Youth Feedback:

____

____

____

11. Wandering-stars

Youth Feedback:

____

____

____

Self-destructive:

Abusive	Murderous [annihilating]
Alienated	Negligent
Being-effeminate	Non-ambitious
Content-to-be-average	Non-observant
Conforming-socially	Non-performing
Defective	Perplexing-to-
Deficient	understand
Depraved	Reprobative
Discouraged	Self-abusive
Dissipated	Self-hating
Failing	Squandering
Feeling-abandoned	Suicidal
Feeling-inadequate	Unregenerate
Feeling-inferior	Wanton
Feeling-like-a-loser	Wasteful
Having-a-meltdown	Weak
Lonely	
Mediocre	

FOOD FOR THOUGHT:

For the Natural Man Striving to Become Spiritual

Meditation: (To Chew over one's Thoughts!):
Listen to what your child is trying to tell you *not* to do!:

Don't demand explanations for my wrong behaviour. I really don't know why I did it. Don't tax my honesty too much. I am easily frightened into telling lies.

Rule #13: For Raising Delinquent Children:

"But can we be sure that it's their fault alone? That maybe a part of it isn't our own? Are we less guilty who place in their way: Too many things that can lead them astray?"

Youth Feedback:
____

____

____

Rule #13: For Repentance (to turn your life around):

Retain a remission by giving generously to those in need.

Youth Feedback:
____

____

____

Self-destructive

One might say that bees are self-destructive in that when they stick their stinger into someone, they die: much like the Kamakaze Japanese war pilots of WWII who flew directly into an enemy battleship to ensure their mutual self-destruction. Of suicidal behaviour, one thinks of the Malaysian Airlines Pilot of Flight MH370 (on 8th March 2014) who (it is widely believed!) flew an entire planeload of 227 passengers and twelve crew into the southern Indian Ocean until it ran out of fuel taking the lives of all on board with himself. Or, of Emperor Nero in Ancient Rome who fiddled while the City of Rome (he reportedly set on fire) burned.

One also thinks of the classic Old Testament story of Samson who in his final day of life pulled the pillars of a pagan temple together, so causing the walls and ceiling of the temple to fall upon his enemies, killing himself as well. The account states the dead which Samson slew at his death "were more than they which he slew in his life". (Judges 16:25-30)

Terrorists today use the same logic: they strap themselves with hi-explosive devices to ensure a long radius of destruction, killing their target as well as themselves. Behind this self-destructive behaviour, there can be a code of honor as in the old Rome and Japanese traditions of hari-kari: to fall upon one's sword when in defeat, that one's enemy may not gloat. One of the most famous examples of 'refusing to surrender to one's victorious enemy' occurred in 73-74 A.D. Masada (in Israel) became famous for mass suicides (estimated 960 of 967 non-combatants) of the Sicarii rebels and Jewish families of the Masada fortress who chose to die so that the troops of the (ancient) Roman Empire 'may not gloat'!

In an attempt to understand this self-destructive behaviour in early childhood, at its roots (as it were), I'm reminded of Ted Bundy's own explanation, as he puts it:

"What I was dealing with were very strong inhibitions against violent behaviour that were being conditioned into me, bred into me: in my environment, in my neighbourhood, in my church, in my school; things which said: 'NO! This is wrong! Even to think of it is wrong! But certainly, to do it is wrong!'. While I'm on that edge, and the last vestiges of restraint, the barriers to actually doing something are being tested constantly."

Al Wilson portrays this dark side of the 'reprobate mind' in his poem, "The Snake": A poem that portrays how illegal immigration can be like a snake that can turn on you without warning. [The Apostle Paul refers to reprobate minds, in Romans 1:21-22,28-32. But the Apostle Peter goes even further to state that those 'reprobates' are "natural brute beasts, made to be taken and destroyed", II Peter 2:12.]

One is reminded of the senseless death (some say, 'murder') of thirty-two-year-old Kate Steinle (on 1st July 2015). And how it is possible for an illegal immigrant (her killer) to take an innocent life and to be completely acquitted. [Similarly, if the woman in the Snake Poem did not pity the snake, this woman (in the poem) would have lived. But, instead, she died because she held the snake that was freezing and cold next to her bosom, and it bit her with its deadly venom.] If the US Immigration system in San Francisco (it is argued) had not offered 'sanctuary' to this repeat offender (who was an illegal immigrant), Kate Steinle would not have died.

Furthermore, the case can be made that if Germany had not opened its arms to illegal immigrants (and other refugees) in 2015, most probably the 1,250 German women who were sexually assaulted and/or raped on New Year's Eve (of that year 2015-2016) would not have been molested at all. [See, *Wikipedia*: "2015-2016 New Year's Eve Sexual Assault in Germany".]

The Bible states that there is a way that seems to a man to be 'right in his own eyes' (Proverbs 12:15) "but the end thereof are the ways of death" (Proverbs 16:25). And so it is with the spiritual or moral compass we use to guide our actions into the paths of righteousness. If we are not vigilant at all times, we can easily take a detour down the garden path to hit that proverbial 'wall' at supersonic speed. Hence, the oft-quoted truth: "Enter you in at the strait [narrow] gate: for wide is the gate, and broad is the way that leads to destruction, and many there be which go in thereat: Because strait is the gate, and narrow is the way, which leads unto life, and few there be that find it". (Matthew 7:13-14)

Wise words, comforting counsel, especially when we may seem to stand all alone in this world in doing what is right and letting the consequences follow. To go against the grain of popular opinion can alienate one from his peers as well as the rest of society. For as General Douglas MacArthur observed: "It's the age-old struggle: The roar of the crowd on one side, and the voice of your conscience on the other".

13M.   Self-destructive:

Youth Feedback:
____

____

____

1. Abusive

Youth Feedback:
____

____

____

2. Alienated

Youth Feedback:
____

____

____

3. Being-effeminate

Youth Feedback:
____

____

____

4. Content-to-be-average

Youth Feedback:
____

____

____

5. Conforming-socially

Youth Feedback:
____

____

____

6. Defective

Youth Feedback:

____

____

____

7. Deficient

Youth Feedback:

____

____

____

8. Depraved

Youth Feedback:

____

____

____

9. Discouraged

Youth Feedback:

____

____

____

10. Dissipated

Youth Feedback:

____

____

____

11. Failing

Youth Feedback:

____

____

____

12. Feeling-abandoned

Youth Feedback:

____

____

____

13. Feeling-inadequate

Youth Feedback:

____

____

____

14. Feeling-inferior

Youth Feedback:

____

____

____

15. Feeling-like-a-loser

Youth Feedback:

____

____

____

16. Having-a-meltdown

Youth Feedback:

____

____

____

17. Lonely

Youth Feedback:

____

____

____

18. Mediocre

Youth Feedback:

____

____

____

19. Murderous [annihilating]

Youth Feedback:

____

____

____

20. Negligent

Youth Feedback:

____

____

____

21. Non-ambitious

Youth Feedback:

____

____

____

22. Non-observant

Youth Feedback:

____

____

____

23. Non-performing

Youth Feedback:

____

____

____

24. Perplexing-to-understand

Youth Feedback:

____

____

____

25. Reprobative

Youth Feedback:

____

____

____

26. Self-abusive

Youth Feedback:

____

____

____

27. Self-hating

Youth Feedback:

____

____

____

28. Squandering

Youth Feedback:

____

____

____

29. Suicidal

Youth Feedback:

____

____

____

30. Unregenerate

Youth Feedback:

____

____

31. Wanton

Youth Feedback:

____

____

32. Wasteful

Youth Feedback:

____

____

33. Weak

Youth Feedback:

____

____

Thieving:

Embezzling

Extorting

Plundering

Purloining

Robbing

Stealing

Violating

FOOD FOR THOUGHT:

For the Natural Man Striving to Become Spiritual

Meditation: (To Chew over one's Thoughts!):
Listen to what your child is trying to tell you *not* to do!:

Don't protect me from the consequences. I need to learn from experience.

Rule #14: For Raising Delinquent Children:

"Too much money to spend: too much idle time; too many movies of passion and crime! Too many books not fit to be read; Too much evil in what they hear said!"

Youth Feedback:

____

____

____

Rule #14: For Repentance (to turn your life around):

Reinstatement in the household of faith by making new commitments!

Youth Feedback:

____

____

____

Thieving

When I think of an animal that looks like a robber, a thief, I think of the racoon, with its black mask around its eyes. As a nocturnal creature, it spends its time going through trash cans and farmer's chicken coops, trying to steal as many eggs as it can.

But when it comes to people, I think of political dictators who try to steal (or conquer) other people's lands and properties. Adolf Hitler is a classic example: He eyed the wealthy properties of the Jewish People in Nazi Germany, declared them unfit citizens ('enemies of the people') of his Third Reich. And he sent his SS (Secret Service) Gestapo henchmen to come calling on their doors in the wee hours of the morning, to arrest them, and to send them to 'Concentration Camps' (designed for political dissidents). Then he would confiscate all their lucrative properties and divvy them up for his inner circle of comrades, common thieves like himself.

Today, we have the conquest of Russia in Ukraine, the illegal annexation of the Ukrainian Crimea, and the Russian attempt to militarily overthrow the rest of Ukraine through the Ukrainian Donbas. These 'Slavic brothers' betrayed the mutual trust of Ukraine, for a mess of pottage. Like Hitler's take-over of Austria (claiming that Austria was German-speaking and hence, 'German'), so Vladimir Putin (President of Russia), the Ukrainian people argue, has taken over Crimea, claiming likewise, that it was 'Russian-speaking'; hence, part of Russia!

But perhaps an even greater 'thief' (similar to Judas who kept the money bag among our Lord's disciples, see: John 12:4-6) is the exiled Ukrainian President Viktor Yanukovych: who had a long history of theft (since he was a known juvenile delinquent, as a 'lady's purse thief' in his early youth). When he was finally ousted from the Ukrainian presidency on 22nd February 2014 (which he obtained through allegedly dishonest means: voter fraud and the like), he apparently accumulated the entire Ukrainian *public purse* (in the four short years he remained in Office, 2010-2014) allegedly totalling $70 billion.

Ukraine is a poor country with over 35% of the population in poverty, not able to make ends meet. Yet Yanukovych apparently (it is openly reported through Ukrainian secret service investigations) didn't care a whit about their starvation and hardships. Those few honest Ukrainian news reporters who tried to raise the alarm bell (while Yanukovych was President) mysteriously disappeared and/or met gruesome deaths.

Over $3 billion (as is now documented) went to the political cronies of Yanukovych, and a lot more money was spread throughout the world banking system [notably, the Swiss banks]. As money transfers were made in the names of various relatives (including Yanukovych's own son Olexander), it has been very difficult for current leaders in Ukraine to legally prosecute these account holders because they all have varied *'excuses'* how they came to receive billions of US dollars. The money trail was deliberately allowed to turn 'cold'. But the fact remains when Viktor Yanukovych fled for his life to Vladimir Putin (in Rostov-on-Don, Russia) the Ukranian Treasury was totally empty. (The question remains: How could all this money disappear into thin air?)

Viktor Yanukovych when he saw that the jig was up, that he was to be forcibly removed from power as a defunct Ukrainian President, through a People's Revolution, fled on the night of 21st February 2014 from Kyiv to Kharkiv, and then to Rostov-on-Don to meet with his political buddy, Vladimir Putin (also a man held in high suspicion of having fleeced the oil oligarchs of Russia). Two birds of a feather meet together, to count all their loot, it would appear.

Upon arriving to meet Putin, who magically supplies Yanukovych with total political protection from prosecution (to this very day), Viktor Yanukovych purchases a $150 million house (a modest sum for someone so filthy rich now) next to Putin's much more expensive villa. Of course, both men will swear on a stack of bibles that they only earn a maximum of $10,000 per month as their 'full salary' as President of their respective countries. Go figure, huh! If you believe that bunk, you will believe anything dictators tell you, even the outlandish lies of Adolf Hitler!

The Bible clearly states that no thief will enter into the Kingdom of God (unless they repent, as did one of the thieves on the cross next to the Crucified Christ, see Luke 23:39-43; Matthew 27:38). As Paul the Apostle declared: "Nay, you do wrong, and defraud and that your brethren. Know you not that the unrighteous shall not inherit the kingdom of God? Be not deceived: neither fornicators nor idolaters, nor adulterers, nor effeminate, nor abusers of themselves with mankind, **nor thieves,** nor covetous, nor drunkards, nor revilers, nor extortioners, shall inherit the Kingdom of God." (I Corinthians 6:8-10)

14N.   Thief-Like/Thieving:

Youth Feedback:

1.   Embezzling

Youth Feedback:

2.   Extorting

Youth Feedback:

3.   Plundering

Youth Feedback:

4.   Purloining

Youth Feedback:

5.   Robbing

Youth Feedback:

6. Stealing

Youth Feedback:

____

____

____

7. Violating

Youth Feedback:

____

____

____

(Some of the) Sources Consulted:

Wikipedia [under the various names cited in this section]
TheGuardian.com
Britannica.com

DISCLAIMER: N.B. (*Nota Bene*)
All tunes/songs/video clips/links/quotes/etc. are herein provided to assist in Group Therapy Sessions, or privately, for individual study (to assist in learning) and for educational purposes *only*.

[#194: U-Tube Reference]
Viktor Yanukovych sentenced 13 years in prison for treason
https://www.youtube.com/watch?v=OS05GrJVZgw

[#195: U-Tube Reference]
Proof positive that Putin is corrupt! [19 January 2021]
Putin's Palace: History of the world's largest bribe!
https://www.youtube.com/watch?v=ipAnwilMncl

[#196: U-Tube Reference]
Yanukovych's Palace in Kiev (2015)
https://www.youtube.com/watch?v=IfDeWAOkDjs

[#197: U-Tube Reference]
Yanukovych Estate in Kiev (2014) BBC
https://www.youtube.com/watch?v=BWlYGnXz5vA

[#198: U-Tube Reference]
Yanukovych Estate still in limbo (2017)
https://www.youtube.com/watch?v=fzM5yXkRiEY

[#199: U-Tube Reference]
How Yanukovych escaped from Ukraine (Feb/2014)
https://www.youtube.com/watch?v=vPpHdQxA0-w

[#200: U-Tube Reference]
Yanukovych the Thief's mansion he built with money from Ukrainian Treasury (2017)
https://www.youtube.com/watch?v=6eX2qce3W5l

[#201: U-Tube Reference]
Yanukovych spends $2.5 billion USD of taxpayer's money to build opulent Palace in Ukraine
https://www.youtube.com/watch?v=wwKyt7L1ets

[#202: U-Tube Reference]
Putin grants Yanukovych Russian citizenship (Oct/2014)
https://www.youtube.com/watch?v=mT0C5HFD_XQ

[#203: U-Tube Reference]
Yanukovych corruption involved $250 billion USD (2015)
https://www.youtube.com/watch?v=VgeAnyTFXJI

[#204: U-Tube Reference]
Ukrainian RADA ousts Yanukovych as President (22 Feb/2014)
https://www.youtube.com/watch?v=S5FLxHpKzOQ

[#205: U-Tube Reference]
Ukraine's 2004 Orange Revolution against Yanukovych
https://www.youtube.com/watch?v=0nYAM-Jbfh4

[#206: U-Tube Reference]
Yanukovych's political betrayal of Ukraine (2014)
https://www.youtube.com/watch?v=yZkqFRByOM0

[#207: U-Tube Reference]
Yanukovych leaks documentary (June 2014)
https://www.youtube.com/watch?v=tO556APIlik

[#208: U-Tube Reference]
Yanukovych to be tried for murder [28 Feb/2014]
https://www.youtube.com/watch?v=tJT5pZ6-2uY

[#209: U-Tube Reference]
Yanukovych Impeached [22 Feb/2014]
https://www.youtube.com/watch?v=Ndf_L-Owpi4

[#210: U-Tube Reference]
Yanukovych allegedly gave over $32 billion USD of Ukrainian funds to Putin [April 2014]
https://www.youtube.com/watch?v=mjelgXn0j9o

[#211: U-Tube Reference]
$120 Billion USD went missing while Yanukovych was President of Ukraine [April 2014]
https://www.youtube.com/watch?v=uj52avKzFsw

Treacherous:

Betraying

Being-a-traitor

Cheating

Counterfeiting

Designing

Disgraceful

Dodgy

Double-crossing

Drunken

Duplicitous

Evasive [like an eel]

False

Feigned

Filthy

Fraudulent

Idle

Indecent

Judas-like [quisling]

Lazy

Misleading

Pretending

Sloppy

Slothful

Snake-like

Unclean

Under-handed

Unseemly [in behaviour]

Wily

For the Natural Man Striving to Become Spiritual

Meditation: (To Chew over one's Thoughts!):
Listen to what your child is trying to tell you *not* to do!:

Don't put off when I ask honest questions. If you do, you will find that I stop asking them and will seek my information elsewhere. Also, Don't answer silly or meaningless questions: I just want you to keep busy with me.

Rule #15: For Raising Delinquent Children:

 "Too many children encouraged to roam, by too many parents who just won't stay at home!"

Youth Feedback:

____

____

____

Rule #15: For Repentance (to turn your life around):

Repeat the Resolve, especially when attending Church and partaking the Sacrament (Holy Communion or Lord's Supper).

Youth Feedback:

____

____

____

Treacherous

The most common symbol of treachery in the animal kingdom is the snake: in particular, the rattler (or rattlesnake) in the Western hemisphere, and the viper in the Eastern. The boa constrictor is a uniquely treacherous snake as it pretends to hug one's victim in its deadly coils until it finally crushes its prey to death, making its victim more palpable to be swallowed and digested by its internal gastric juices.

In the human world, through the annals of history, we think of Judas Iscariot who betrayed our Lord to His enemies with a kiss (as a sign of affection; see Luke 22:47-48) for thirty pieces of silver (Matthew 26:14-16; 27:3-5). The name 'Judas' became so hated even in the First Century of the Christian Era, that Jesus' own brother, Judas ('not Iscariot', John 14:22) had his name later changed to *'Jude'* (a letter he wrote in the New Testament by that name).

Today, we could compare the name of 'Adolf Hitler' likewise: Not too many people I know bear the name 'Hitler' today. Of more recent note, we can recall that the traitors, Julius and Ethel Rosenberg were executed as spies to Russia on 20 June 1953 by the electric chair in the United States. They had sold secrets of nuclear weaponry to the Russians, and they paid for it with their lives.

Oddly enough, this sort of treachery we can find emotionally acceptable; but the betrayals currently allegedly committed by Lyndon Baines Johnson and Edgar J. Hoover, under the auspices of rogue elements in both the FBI and the CIA, in cahoots with Chicago crime boss, Sam Giancana, in the deaths of Marilyn Monroe, John F. Kennedy, and Robert F. Kennedy, are still unresolved until this day. [see some of the YouTube videos posted below for more information on this *'treachery'*]

Even the more current treachery claims against Viktor Yanukovych (ousted Ukrainian President on 23rd of February 2014) warrants further investigation. As well as the still-unresolved murder (on 27 February 2015) of Boris Nemtsov (the Opposition Leader to Vladimir Putin in the Russian Kremlin). Time will eventually reveal all these hidden details, as the Truth will one day prevail.

Youth Feedback:

____

____

____

(Some of the) Sources Consulted:

Wikipedia [under the various names cited in this section]

DISCLAIMER: N.B. (*Nota Bene*)
All tunes/songs/video clips/links/quotes/etc. are herein provided to assist in Group Therapy Sessions, or privately, for individual study (to assist in learning) and for educational purposes *only*.

[#212: U-Tube Reference]
US: Who Killed Robert Kennedy? | Al Jazeera World
Sirhan Sirhan was not alone in killing RFK
https://www.youtube.com/watch?v=SVScM_9Tn-s&t=133s

[#213: U-Tube Reference]
LBJ questions JFK Warren Report-CBS
LBJ questions JFK Warren Report [Sept/1969]
https://www.youtube.com/watch?v=FeSug5GVCg8

[#214: U-Tube Reference]
Kennedy: A Legacy In Blood - Final Chapter -"Johnson- (The Head Of The Snake)"
LBJ & J.Edgar Hoover in cahoots to kill JFK
https://www.youtube.com/watch?v=xdZEP84SLS8&t=28s

[#215: U-Tube Reference]
Kennedy Assassination - Lyndon Johnson Killed JFK - The Men Who Killed Kennedy
LBJ Killed JFK (& RFK) [Documentary]
https://www.youtube.com/watch?v=NZKjm9ezTXQ

[#216: U-Tube Reference]
MAFIA MURDER OF MARILYN MONROE
Details as to why MAFIA, CIA & FBI (w/LBJ) killed: MM, JFK, & RFK
The Mafia Murder of Marilyn Monroe: Bill Truels, M.D.
https://www.youtube.com/watch?v=0vHOcTO3rmc

[#217: U-Tube Reference]
The Zapruder Film - JFK (6/7) Movie CLIP (1991) HD
The 6 shots that killed JFK [from the Movie: JFK]
https://www.youtube.com/watch?v=2nmGS8rVuIM

15.O. Treacherous:

Youth Feedback:

1. Betraying

Youth Feedback:

2. Being-a-traitor

Youth Feedback:

3. Cheating

Youth Feedback:

4. Counterfeiting

Youth Feedback:

5. Designing

Youth Feedback:

6. Disgraceful

Youth Feedback:

____

____

____

7. Dodgy

Youth Feedback:

____

____

____

8. Double-crossing

Youth Feedback:

____

____

____

9. Drunken

Youth Feedback:

____

____

____

10. Duplicitous

Youth Feedback:

____

____

____

11. Evasive [like an eel]

Youth Feedback:

____

____

____

12. False

Youth Feedback:

____

____

13. Feigned

Youth Feedback:

____

____

14. Filthy

Youth Feedback:

____

____

15. Fraudulent

Youth Feedback:

____

____

16. Idle

Youth Feedback:

____

____

17. Indecent

Youth Feedback:

____

____

18. Judas-like [quisling]

Youth Feedback:

____

____

____

19. Lazy

Youth Feedback:

____

____

____

20. Misleading

Youth Feedback:

____

____

____

21. Pretending

Youth Feedback:

____

____

____

22. Sloppy

Youth Feedback:

____

____

____

23. Slothful

Youth Feedback:

____

____

____

24. Snake-like

Youth Feedback:

____

____

____

25. Unclean

Youth Feedback:

____

____

____

26. Under-handed

Youth Feedback:

____

____

____

27. Unseemly [in behaviour]

Youth Feedback:

____

____

____

28. Wily

Youth Feedback:

____

____

____

Vulgar:

Being-a-busybody

Blundering

Contemptuous

Delinquent

Despising

Disdaining

Evil-speaking

Falsely-accusing

Foolish

Meddling

Miscalculating

Misdoing

Misjudging

Misreading [deliberately]

Misunderstanding-issues [deliberately]

Offensive

Slandering

Tattling

Transgressing

Trespassing

[Wishing for] wrong-doing

FOOD FOR THOUGHT:

For the Natural Man Striving to Become Spiritual

Meditation: (To Chew over one's Thoughts!):
Listen to what your child is trying to tell you *not* to do!:

Don't ever think that it is beneath your dignity to apologize to me! An honest apology makes me feel surprisingly warm toward you! Don't ever suggest that you are perfect or infallible. It gives me too much to live up to.

Rule #16: For Raising Delinquent Children:

"Kids don't make the movies; they don't write the books, That paint the bright pictures of gangsters and crooks. They don't make the liquor, they don't run the bars; They don't make the laws, and they don't buy the cars. They don't peddle the drugs that addle the brain; That's all done by older folks greedy for gain!"

Youth Feedback:
____

____

____

Rule #16: For Repentance (to turn your life around):

Rejoice: Expressing your thanks to God, and your Testimony to others!

Youth Feedback:
____

____

____

Vulgar

I think that all readers will agree that of all the animals in the world probably the best representative of what could be called 'vulgar' is the skunk. With such a potent stench, Nature well-endowed the skunk that even in death, it leaves its mark for a long time, as any roadkill can attest.

But among humans, we may think of Sir John Falstaff (in Shakespeare's plays, as in *Merry Wives of Windsor*, and *Henry IV, Parts I and II*) portrayed as a buffoonish and vulgar character, as this brief excerpt reveals: "Come, sing me a bawdy song; make me merry. I was as virtuously given as a gentleman need be, virtuous enough: swore little, diced not above seven times a week, went to a bawdy house not above once in a quarter of an hour, paid money, that I borrowed three or four times, lived well, and in good compass; and now I live out of all order, out of all compass." (*First Part of Henry IV*, III, iii).

There is hope, albeit 'faint hope', for the sordid social misfit (the guttersnipe, or truly vulgar person) as the movie, *My Fair Lady* (1964, with Audrey Hepburn) presents: With some attention, re-education, and a lot of corrections made, Audrey Hepburn, a Cockney-working girl, converts from a hopelessly bawdy-sounding street woman into a truly *Fair Lady!* Perhaps the same can be said of other 'conversion stories'.

Indeed, consider what Jesus said to the self-righteous religious leaders of His day: "The publicans and the harlots go into the kingdom of God before you" (Matthew 21:31; Luke 14:16-24; Matthew 22:1-10).

16P.   Vulgar:

Youth Feedback:

1. Being-a-busybody

Youth Feedback:

2. Blundering

Youth Feedback:

3. Contemptuous

Youth Feedback:

4. Delinquent

Youth Feedback:

5. Despising

Youth Feedback:

6. Disdaining

Youth Feedback:

____

____

____

7. Evil-speaking

Youth Feedback:

____

____

____

8. Falsely-accusing

Youth Feedback:

____

____

____

9. Foolish

Youth Feedback:

____

____

____

10. Meddling

Youth Feedback:

____

____

____

11. Miscalculating

Youth Feedback:

____

____

____

12. Misdoing

Youth Feedback:

____

____

13. Misjudging

Youth Feedback:

____

____

14. Misreading [deliberately]

Youth Feedback:

____

____

15. Misunderstanding-issues [deliberately]

Youth Feedback:

____

____

16. Offensive

Youth Feedback:

____

____

17. Slandering

Youth Feedback:

____

____

18. Tattling

Youth Feedback:
____

____

____

19. Transgressing

Youth Feedback:
____

____

____

20. Trespassing

Youth Feedback:
____

____

____

21. [Wishing for] wrong-doing

Youth Feedback:
____

____

____

Wicked:

Abominable	Infamous
Atrocious	Injurious
Corrupt	Lawless
Cruel	Malicious
Denying	Mischievous
Depraved	Naughty
Depressed	Nefarious
Diabolic	Noxious
Enjoying-to-kill	Pernicious
Following-bad-habits	Rebellious
Gangster-like	Satanic
Godless	Sinful
Guilty	Spotted
Hateful	Torture-loving
Heinous	Vicious
Horrid	Unholy
Hurtful	Wanting-to-assassinate
Immoral	
Incorrigible	

FOOD FOR THOUGHT:

For the Natural Man Striving to Become Spiritual

**Meditation: (To Chew over one's Thoughts!):
Listen to what your child is trying to tell you *not* to do!:**

Don't worry about the little amount of time we spend together. It is how we spend it that counts. Don't forget that I can't thrive without lots of understanding and encouragement; but I don't need to tell you that, do I?

Rule #17: For Raising Delinquent Children:

"Delinquent teenagers: Oh! How we condemn! The sins of the Nation and blame it on them! For in so many cases, it's sad, but it's true! The title *Delinquent!* fits older folks too!"

Youth Feedback:

____

____

____

Rule #17: For Repentance (to turn your life around):

Remember: Regardless of the offences, repentance ('to turn your life around') is the only way to obtain Forgiveness!

Youth Feedback:

____

____

____

Wicked

The animal-correlate to 'something wicked this way comes' would be the laugh of the hyena. The hyena seems to grin and laugh out loud in the most disturbing way as it circles around its prey seeking a vulnerable spot to attack and bite. With its ironclad jawbone, it can snap a leg (or foot) of its victim in one crushing blow, laughing all the time it kills its prey.

As to wicked personalities, there is, of course, the classic case of Ted Bundy, a serial killer of above-average intelligence, who murdered at least thirty-two women (and children) by his own confession, as the 'very definition of heartless evil' states his own viewpoint:

"Each time I harm someone, *each time I kill someone*, there'd be an enormous amount of (especially at first), an enormous amount of horror, of guilt, of remorse afterward. But then that impulse to do it again would come back even stronger... I still felt in my regular life, the full range of guilt, and remorse... regret... [I still had] this compartmentalized, very well-focused, area: it was like a black hole; it was like a crack, and everything that fell into that crack, just disappeared."

Now before the Ted Bundy of the 1970s, there was an equally horrific psychopath, Sam (Momo) Giancana, a dictionary definition of a psychopath, if ever there was one. Before he was fourteen years old, he allegedly murdered in cold blood, but his lawyer got him off the hook on a technicality. By age twenty, Momo was suspected of five additional murders but due to the fear and reluctance of witnesses to testify against him (and therefore a lack of hard evidence), he was simply remanded to a correctional institute for five years (but served only four).

Once released from Reformatory, Momo became the Chicago Crime boss (in 1957) and began to kill off all his rivals. He was implicated in the murders of Marilyn Monroe, John F. Kennedy, and Robert F. Kennedy (as related by Marilyn Monroe's close friend and confidant, Jeanne Carmen, and Momo's own right-hand man, the 'Silver Fox', Handsome Johnny Rosselli). So many theories have evolved over the past decades but the recent documentary on Momo's life may prove quite enlightening (see the

U-Tube reference below), as told by Momo's own relatives (who felt it was time to disclose to the world what really happened to these world-famous victims).

Youth Feedback:
____

____

____

DISCLAIMER: N.B. (*Nota Bene*)
All tunes/songs/video clips/links/quotes/etc. are herein provided to assist in Group Therapy Sessions, or privately, for individual study (to assist in learning) and for educational purposes *only*.

[#218: U-Tube Reference]
Momo: The Sam Giancana Story | JFK, Sinatra and the Mob | BEST OF MAFIA MOVIES
https://www.youtube.com/watch?v=obn1Y-bMk34&t=4s

17Q. Wicked:

Youth Feedback:
____

____

____

1. Abominable

Youth Feedback:
____

____

____

2. Atrocious

Youth Feedback:
____

____

____

3. Corrupt

Youth Feedback:
____

____

____

4. Cruel

Youth Feedback:
____

____

____

5. Denying

Youth Feedback:
____

____

____

6. Depraved

Youth Feedback:

____

____

____

7. Depressed

Youth Feedback:

____

____

____

8. Diabolic

Youth Feedback:

____

____

____

9. Enjoying-to-kill

Youth Feedback:

____

____

____

10. Following-bad-habits

Youth Feedback:

____

____

____

11. Gangster-like

Youth Feedback:

____

____

____

12. Godless

Youth Feedback:

____

____

____

13. Guilty

Youth Feedback:

____

____

____

14. Hateful

Youth Feedback:

____

____

____

15. Heinous

Youth Feedback:

____

____

____

16. Horrid

Youth Feedback:

____

____

____

17. Hurtful

Youth Feedback:

____

____

____

18. Immoral

Youth Feedback:

____

____

19. Incorrigible

Youth Feedback:

____

____

20. Infamous

Youth Feedback:

____

____

21. Injurious

Youth Feedback:

____

____

22. Lawless

Youth Feedback:

____

____

23. Malicious

Youth Feedback:

____

____

24. Mischievous

Youth Feedback:

____

____

25. Naughty

Youth Feedback:

____

____

26. Nefarious

Youth Feedback:

____

____

27. Noxious

Youth Feedback:

____

____

28. Pernicious

Youth Feedback:

____

____

29. Rebellious

Youth Feedback:

____

____

30. Satanic

Youth Feedback:

____

____

____

31. Sinful

Youth Feedback:

____

____

____

32. Spotted

Youth Feedback:

____

____

____

33. Torture-loving

Youth Feedback:

____

____

____

34. Vicious

Youth Feedback:

____

____

____

35. Unholy

Youth Feedback:

____

____

____

36. Wanting-to-assassinate

Youth Feedback:

____

____

____

Scene iii:
Reflections upon Negative character Traits

Consider the following thought-provoking quotes:

(1) Vice is a monster of so frightful mien,
As to be hated, needs but to be seen;
Yet seen too oft, familiar with her face,
We first endure, then pity, then embrace.
(Alexander Pope)

(2) Those of us who are or who have been so much influenced by violence in the media, in particular, pornographic violence, are not some kind of inherent monsters: **we are your sons, and we are your husbands. And we grew up in regular families**. And pornography can reach out and snatch a kid out of any house today. It snatched me out of my home.
(Ted Bundy)

(3) [On his pending death by electric chair:]
I can't say that being in the valley of the Shadow of Death is something I've become all that accustomed to, and that I'm strong, and that there's nothing bothering me. **Listen, it's no fun: It gets kind of lonely.** And yet I have to remind myself that everyone of us will go through *this* someday, one way or another, as countless millions who have walked this earth before us have. So, *this* is just an experience which we all will share.
(Ted Bundy)

(4) Faith is knowing what you want will eventually come to fruition as long as you believe it. And **if you feed your faith, you'll find that oftentimes your fears will starve to death**. Because if you believe in yourself, everyone else in the world will believe in you.
(Daniel Ally)

(5) There is a raging tiger inside every man whom God put on this earth. Every man worthy of the respect of his children spends his life building inside himself a cage to pen that tiger in.
(Murray Kempton)

(6) Listen, I'm no social scientist, and I haven't done a survey, and I don't pretend that I know what John Q citizen thinks about this, but I lived in prison for a long time [ten years] now, and I met a lot of men who were motivated to commit violence just like me. And without exception, everyone of them was deeply involved in pornography, without question, without exception: deeply influenced and consumed by the addiction to pornography.
(Ted Bundy)

(7) In the Book of Proverbs (in the Bible), it is promised of child-rearing: "Train up a child in the way he should go: and when he is old, he will not depart from it."
(Proverbs 22:6)

What this pithy saying captures is the notion that prayer and complete child-rearing in God-fearing principles will ensure that the individual will grow up into God-like personality traits. Put another way, if the wood becomes 'crooked' at an early age, it is rather difficult to make it 'straight'. It is much easier to prevent a child from falling into bad company, then to re-direct the child once these extremely critical 'formative' years are completed.

I'm reminded of the children's fable of Pinocchio in which the fox and the alley-cat trick Pinocchio into thinking that life outside School Days is much better, much more rewarding and exciting. But when *Pinocchio* finds that playing hooky can lead one to literally change into a 'jackass' (or donkey), he realizes none too late that listening to his conscience (personified by 'Jimminy Cricket') was (and still is) the best course of action. So, the story has a happy ending.

The entire argument for the desire to become a gangster or to adopt negative traits can be compared to the habit of becoming a chain smoker. Easy to start, easy to adopt, but difficult to free oneself once one is committed to that negative lifestyle. The smoker always tells himself: "It's up to me! I can quit whenever I like".

The difficulty is that a bad habit (like smoking) just isn't that easy to give up. Mark Twain, the humorist, once said: "To quit smoking is the easiest thing to do in the world. Why, I've done it at least a thousand times!" We smile at the humour of it, but the grim reality is that negative addiction can be life-threatening, and like the (boa constrictor, or) python snake that wraps itself around its victim, the more we exhale, the tighter the grip the snake makes until we can no longer breathe easily, and then the snake finishes its prey.

Negative character traits once developed into routine behaviour, and solidified into regular habits, prove quite formidable to break, like the seemingly soft cords that may be wrapped around one's arms: Once reinforced many times over, make it almost impossible to free oneself.

"The Twelve Steps" at AA's (Alcoholics Anonymous) have helped countless people off the road of permanent addiction: Their main or key step to full recovery is to fully acknowledge one's addiction (to admit, for example, that one is an Alcoholic), that one is addicted and in need of help. And then to look upward to a Higher Power for relief, restitution, and restoration of one's potential destiny in life.

Youth Feedback:

____

____

____

DISCLAIMER: N.B. (*Nota Bene*)
All tunes/songs/video clips/links/quotes/etc. are herein provided to assist in Group Therapy Sessions, or privately, for individual study (to assist in learning) and for educational purposes *only*.

[#219: U-Tube Reference]
Zager And Evans - In The Year 2525
https://www.youtube.com/watch?v=izQB2-Kmiic

[#220: U-Tube Reference]
In the year 2525 - a FanMade - music clip in 2020
https://www.youtube.com/watch?v=JNbUUSuiEho

In The Year 2525

In the year 7510
If God's a coming, He oughta make it by then
Maybe He'll look around Himself and say
Guess it's time for the judgment day

In the year 8510
God is gonna shake His mighty head
He'll either say I'm pleased where man has been
Or tear it down, and start again

Writer/s: Richard Lee Evans

[#221: U-Tube Reference]
I Am a Rock
https://www.youtube.com/watch?v=My9I8q-iJCI

I Am A Rock

I have no need of friendship; friendship causes pain.
It's laughter and it's loving I disdain.

Don't talk of love,
But I've heard the words before;

If I never loved I never would have cried.

I am shielded in my armor,
Hiding in my room, safe within my womb.
I touch no one and no one touches me.

Writer: Paul Simon

[#222: U-Tube Reference]
Lee Marvin- Born Under a Wand'rin' Star (HD-Stereo-Lyrics)
https://www.youtube.com/watch?v=2L8n_tQPNIQ

[#223: U-Tube Reference]
Lee Marvin I was born under a Wandering Star remastered
https://www.youtube.com/watch?v=NTymtAbaG08
Wand'rin' Star

Wheels are made for rolling, mules are made to pack
I've never seen a sight that didn't look better looking back

Mud can make you prisoner, and the plains can bake you dry
Snow can burn your eyes, but only people make you cry
Home is made for coming from, for dreams of going to
Which with any luck will never come true

Do I know where hell is? Hell is in "hello"
Heaven is goodbye forever, it's time for me to go

[#224: U-Tube Reference]
Yesterday when I was young (by Dusty Springfield w/lyrics)
https://www.youtube.com/watch?v=pSHI-NPC3Kg

Yesterday When I Was Young

Yesterday, when I was young,
So many happy songs were waiting to be sung,
So many wayward pleasures lay in store for me
And so much pain my dazzled eyes refused to see,

The game of love I played with arrogance and pride
and every flame I lit too quickly, quickly died;
The friends I made all seemed somehow to drift away
And only I am left on stage to end the play.

Writers: Aznaourian Charles, Kretzmer Herbert

[#225: U-Tube Reference]
Stone Poneys - Different Drum (Live)
A Different Drum [newer version by Linda Ronstadt]
https://www.youtube.com/watch?v=TGZznJXY1Xc&pbjreload=10

Different Drum

Yes, and I ain't saying you ain't pretty
All I'm saying is I'm not ready
For any person place or thing
To try and pull the reins in on me
So "Good-bye!" I'll be leaving
I see no sense in this crying and grieving
We'll both live a lot longer
If you live without me.

Writer: Michael Nesmith

[#226: U-Tube Reference]
Linda Ronstadt - When Will I Be Loved
https://www.youtube.com/watch?v=wYGK3Gvgall

When Will I Be Loved
(originally by The Everly Brothers)

I've been cheated
Been mistreated

When I find a new man
That I want for mine
He always breaks my heart in two
It happens every time

I've been made blue
I've been lied to

Writer: Phil Everly

The Lion of Righteousness
(Proverbs 28:1)

ACT III:
Seventeen Positive Character Traits: To Emulate

Scene i:
The Snow-white Tiger (or Lion): Symbol of (spiritual) Strength and (moral) courage

The tag 'Casper' to the white Tiger (or Lion) fits the friendliness of the 'New man', the disposition to want to do good, to do good to all mankind, to have 'Good Will to all men!' (as is commonly stated at Christmas time, along with: "Peace on Earth!") For it is epitomized in this very theme, the theme of a 'White Christmas,' as in a promise of better things to come, a sense of purity, to be (as the Scriptures say): purified and made 'white as snow' (see, Daniel 12:10; Isaiah 1:18; Daniel 11:35; Revelation 3:4;7:14).

It is a sense of cleansing, of a new birth to follow (as Spring follows Winter). But even more pervasive is the sense of serenity, the feeling that freedom is real. For to be truly free, one must 'know' the Truth and even come to know Him who is the God of Truth (John 8:32;14:6). Well has it been stated that: 'Wise men still seek Him".

As the (spiritual) symbol of moral courage, the snow-white (stripe-less) Tiger, a striking bright image that sticks in one's mind, is an overpowering force to be reckoned with. When the snow-white Tiger morphs into the 'White Lion' (as the reigning king of light), one is reminded that even the Son of Man (our Saviour) has been called: the Lion of Judah (Revelation 5:5), and what a bright light that 'White Lion' emulates (II Thessalonians 2:8; Hebrews 1:2-3).

Darkness melts into nothingness at the brightness of His Coming: (I Thessalonians 5:5; II Peter 3:12; Revelation 1:14-16).

Youth Feedback:
____

____

____

[#227: U-Tube Reference]
Elvis Presley - My Way (Aloha From Hawaii, Live in Honolulu, 1973)
https://www.youtube.com/watch?v=ixbcvKCl4Jc

My Way

I've lived a life that's full
I've traveled each and every byway

Yes, there were times, I'm sure you knew
When I bit off more than I could chew
But through it all when there was doubt
I ate it up and spit it out
I faced it all and I stood tall
And did it my way

Writer: Paul Anka

[#228: U-Tube Reference]
Devoted To You - Carly Simon & James Taylor - 1977
https://www.youtube.com/watch?v=fpK0kv3Cual

Devoted to You

Darlin' you can count on me
Till the sun dries up the sea
I'll be yours till endless time
I'll adore your charms sublime
I'll never give you reason to cry
I'd be unhappy if you were blue
Through the years our love will grow
Like a river it will flow

Scene ii:
Seventeen Positive Character Traits to Emulate

As with the seventeen negative character traits (ACT II, Scene ii), blank spaces have been created (as in a 'workbook') so that the reader (or participant in Group Therapy) can fill in their own personal thoughts, comments, or feelings, etc. as they wish. The aim of this endeavour is to assist the participant to recognize the good qualities that they do have. In so doing, improvements can be made, resulting in a better overall understanding and analysis of one's own disposition to do good.

Naturally, not all the entries will be entirely positive, but the realization that here (or there) there is a shortfall may energize the participant to stretch his ambition to do well, to the point that he may succeed and even excel in his self-improvement attempts. For unless there is a commitment on paper, it is quite difficult (or challenging) to actually see the 'big picture', to know what is what, and what still needs to be improved upon.

Youth Feedback:
____

____

____

DISCLAIMER N.B. (*Nota Bene*)
All tunes/songs/video clips/links/quotes/etc. are herein provided to assist in Group Therapy Sessions, or privately, for individual study (to assist in learning) and for educational purposes *only*.

[#229: U-Tube Reference]
The Monkees - I'm a Believer [official music video].flv
https://www.youtube.com/watch?v=rcnsao7Y0gk

I'm A Believer

I thought love was only true in fairy tales
Meant for someone else but not for me.
Love was out to get me

I thought love was more or less a givin' thing,
Seems the more I gave the less I got.
What's the use in tryin'?
All you get is pain.
When I needed sunshine I got rain.

Writer: Neil Diamond

Confident:

Assertive

Assured

Bold

Being-unmovable

Courageous

Dependable

Enduring

Faithful

Having-fidelity

Hopeful

Orderly

Persevering

Standing-fast

Striving [for the best]

Strong [in faith]

Trusting-in-God

Trustworthy

Zealous [in a good cause]

FOOD FOR THOUGHT:

For the Spiritual Man Striving to Become Saint-like

Uplifting Insight(s):

"Go placidly amid the noise and haste, and remember what peace there may be in Silence."

RULE #1: For Raising a Happy Home:

Be parents who try to understand their children; and who find the time to cultivate their friendship and love.

How to Obtain Guidance [From On High]:

'[A]nything a person can be reasoned into, he can be reasoned out of. An intellectual testimony is no stronger than the intellect that possesses it. Another person with a greater intellect can come along and by his superior reasoning power he can rob that person of his testimony. When, however, a testimony is obtained by the power of the Spirit and testified by the Holy Ghost, that testimony burns into the person's heart and is not easily destroyed." (Theodore M. Burton)

What Was the Original Church Like?

Christ organized His Church:

"And He gave some, Apostles: and some, Prophets; and some, Evangelists; and some, Pastors, and Teachers; For the perfecting of the Saints, for the work of the Ministry, for the edifying of the Body of Christ: Till we all come in the Unity of the Faith, and of the knowledge of the Son of God, unto a perfect man, unto the measure of the stature of the fulness of Christ: That we henceforth be no more children, tossed to and fro, and carried about with every wind of doctrine, by the sleight of men, and the cunning craftiness, whereby they lie in wait to deceive!" (Ephesians 4:11-14)

Confident

Perhaps in the animal kingdom, there is no more confidence-inspiring creature than the African male lion, as Ntwadumela ('he who greets with fire'), the King of the Jungle.

Among humans, Richard-The-Lionheart is a name attributed to Richard I, King of England, who crafted a Coat of Arms consisting of three lions. Other men of Hollywood fame that reflected confidence in their persona would include: Yul Brunner (especially in the film *The Brothers Karamazov* (1958); as well as in *The Magnificent Seven* western series (1960-1972); as well as Kirk Douglas, Sr. in *Spartacus* (1960); and of course 'the King of Hollywood', Clark Gable in *Gone With the Wind* (1939).

As to scriptural references, one need simply to consider the martyrdom of Stephen (Acts 6:5-15; 7). Picture yourself about to be stoned to death by overwrought fanatical Jewish bigots, and then consider Stephen's last words, knowing that soon he would meet his Maker: "Lord, lay not this sin to their charge" (Acts 7:59-60): A man, a martyr of extreme confidence, having complete faith in our Lord.

18A.   Confident:

Youth Feedback:

____

____

____

1. Assertive

Youth Feedback:

____

____

____

2. Assured

Youth Feedback:

____

____

____

3. Bold

Youth Feedback:

____

____

____

4. Being-unmovable

Youth Feedback:

____

____

____

5. Courageous

Youth Feedback:

____

____

____

6. Dependable

Youth Feedback:

____

____

____

7. Enduring

Youth Feedback:

____

____

____

8. Faithful

Youth Feedback:

____

____

____

9. Having-fidelity

Youth Feedback:

____

____

____

10. Hopeful

Youth Feedback:

____

____

____

11. Orderly

Youth Feedback:

____

____

____

12. Persevering

Youth Feedback:

____

____

____

13. Standing-fast

Youth Feedback:

____

____

____

14. Striving [for the best]

Youth Feedback:

____

____

____

15. Strong [in faith]

Youth Feedback:

____

____

____

16. Trusting-in-God

Youth Feedback:

____

____

____

17. Trustworthy

Youth Feedback:

____

____

____

18. Zealous [in a good cause]

Youth Feedback:

____

____

____

Exhibiting-an-excellent-spirit:

Being-symmetrical

Captivating

Charming

Critically-aware

Elegant

Enthralling

Exquisite

Fascinating

Graceful

Handsome

High-principled

Insightful

Listening [still small voice]

Lovely

Prayerful

Radiant

Resplendent

Self-conscious

Spiritual

Teachable

Transfiguring

Transforming [people]

Understanding

Visionary

Willing-to-convert

Wise

FOOD FOR THOUGHT:

For the Spiritual Man Striving to Become Saint-like

Uplifting Insight(s):

"As far as possible without surrender, Be on good terms with *all* persons."

RULE #2: For Raising a Happy Home:

Be parents of integrity who face facts and who live by the truth.

How to Obtain Guidance [From on High]:

"The first great revelation that anyone receives is called a testimony of the Gospel. A testimony presupposes revelation... Reason is not to be downgraded. We should use all the reason and judgment and sense and wisdom that we can get. But it is just preparatory; it just opens the door and the final testimony comes only from the Holy Ghost. And when the Holy Spirit speaks, then we know with absolute certainty. We say we have a testimony." (Bruce R. McConkie)

What Was the Original Church Like?

The Church must bear the name of Jesus Christ:

"For the husband is the head of the wife, even as Christ is the Head of the Church: and He is the Saviour of the body!" (Ephesians 5:23)

Exhibiting-an-excellent-spirit

Among creatures of the wild that exhibit an excellent spirit, I think of the white stripe-less Siberian Snow Tiger and the jet-black Jaguar, both members of the cat family. They seem to have a certain sheen or sleekness that makes them so fascinating to watch as they move within their natural habitat.

In the human world, I think of Daniel the Prophet of the Old Testament, of whom Scripture says he had "an excellent spirit" (Daniel 5:12; 6:3). The name 'Daniel' has accordingly been extolled throughout the centuries since as in *Daniel* Webster (who began the Webster dictionary series), and of course *Daniel* Boone, American frontiersman par excellence!

19B.   Exhibiting-an-excellent-spirit:

Youth Feedback:

____

____

____

1. Being-symmetrical

Youth Feedback:

____

____

____

2. Captivating

Youth Feedback:

____

____

____

3. Charming

Youth Feedback:

____

____

____

4. Critically-aware

Youth Feedback:

____

____

____

5. Elegant

Youth Feedback:

____

____

____

6. Enthralling

Youth Feedback:

____

____

____

7. Exquisite

Youth Feedback:

____

____

____

8. Fascinating

Youth Feedback:

____

____

____

9. Graceful

Youth Feedback:

____

____

____

10. Handsome

Youth Feedback:

____

____

____

11. High-principled

Youth Feedback:

____

____

____

12. Insightful

Youth Feedback:

____

____

____

13. Listening [still small voice]

Youth Feedback:

____

____

____

14. Lovely

Youth Feedback:

____

____

____

15. Prayerful

Youth Feedback:

____

____

____

16. Radiant

Youth Feedback:

____

____

____

17. Resplendent

Youth Feedback:

____

____

____

18. Self-conscious

Youth Feedback:

____

____

____

19. Spiritual

Youth Feedback:

____

____

____

20. Teachable

Youth Feedback:

____

____

____

21. Transfiguring

Youth Feedback:

____

____

____

22. Transforming [people]

Youth Feedback:

____

____

____

23. Understanding

Youth Feedback:

____

____

____

24. Visionary

Youth Feedback:

____

____

____

25. Willing-to-convert

Youth Feedback:

____

____

____

26. Wise

Youth Feedback:

____

____

____

Fair-minded:

Balanced

Believing-in-Karma

Believing-in-poetic-justice

Equitable

Even-handed

Fair [in judgments]

Keeping-unity [in the Faith]

Legitimate

Merit-based

Righteous

Straight

FOOD FOR THOUGHT:

For the Spiritual Man Striving to Become Saint-like

Uplifting Insight(s):

"Speak your Truth quietly and clearly; and listen to others, even the dull and ignorant: they too have their story."

RULE #3: For Raising a Happy Home:

Be parents who live within their means and who give their children examples of thrift, security, and stability.

How to Obtain Guidance [From On High]:

"Some young people may be discouraged, and they may compare their knowledge and testimony with that of others but let me plead with the young people never to become discouraged. Always remember that the full-bloom rose was once an unopened bud and that the ripened fruit was once just a blossom and that all great things come from small beginnings... Oh, a testimony does not all come at once, but if continually developed and cultivated, it is a power and a strength that will be felt forever." (Thorpe B. Isaacson)

What Was the Original Church Like?

The Church must have a foundation of Apostles and Prophets:

"Now therefore ye are no more strangers and foreigners, but fellow citizens with the Saints, and of the Household of God. And are built upon the Foundation of the Apostles and Prophets, Jesus Christ Himself being the Chief Cornerstone!" (Ephesians 2:19- 20)

Fair-minded

Among creatures that may be deemed 'fair-minded', or well-balanced, one may well consider the Australian duck-billed platypus, a creature of multi-talents, as well as one multi-faceted.

As to persons fair-minded, I think of Sir Thomas More in that classic movie *A Man for All Seasons* (1966, with Paul Scofield). The title says it all: just as the evergreen tree is ever-green throughout all the seasons, never changing, so a fair-minded man (one of high integrity) such as Sir Thomas More was (as depicted in this movie) is ever-honest through foul-and-fair weather alike.

I am also reminded of the character role of Mr. Spock (played by Leonard Nimoy) in the original *Star Trek* series who (akin to Sherlock Holmes before him) relied upon reason and logic to conclude the 'elementary deductions' necessary to solve each unknown mystery. Where honesty and the Truth are the desired outcomes, a fair-minded man is as transparent as can be hoped for in all his ways.

20C. Fair-minded:

Youth Feedback:

____

____

____

1. Balanced

Youth Feedback:

____

____

____

2. Believing-in-Karma

Youth Feedback:

____

____

____

3. Believing-in-poetic-justice

Youth Feedback:

____

____

____

4. Equitable

Youth Feedback:

____

____

____

5. Even-handed

Youth Feedback:

____

____

____

6. Fair [in judgments]

Youth Feedback:
____
____

____

7. Keeping-unity [in the Faith]

Youth Feedback:
____
____

____

8. Legitimate

Youth Feedback:
____
____

____

9. Merit-based

Youth Feedback:
____
____

____

10. Righteous

Youth Feedback:
____
____

____

11. Straight

Youth Feedback:
____
____

____

Friendly [as an '*ideal friend*']:

Affable

Amiable

Always-an-ally

Approachable

Being-a-buddy

Being-an-advocate

Being-an-associate

Being-a-benefactor

Being-a-sport

Being-a-confidante

Cordial

Courteous

Crony-like

Defending-one's-rights

Deferential

Dependable

Empathetic

Encouraging

Esteeming-the-best

Familiar

Having-fond-feelings

Honourable

Hospitable

Intimate

Keeping-one's-promises

Like-minded

Looking-for-the-best

Loyal

Out-going

Philia-loving

Preferring-others-to-self

Reliable

Sociable

Speaking-kindly

Speaking-uprightly

Supportive

Sympathetic

Wishing-one-well

Yearning-for-a-soulmate

FOOD FOR THOUGHT:

For the Spiritual Man Striving to Become Saint-like

Uplifting Insight(s):

"Avoid loud and aggressive persons: they are vexatious to the Spirit."

RULE #4: For Raising a Happy Home:

Be parents who are industrious, and who teach their children that most of life's good things come only from hard work.

How to Obtain Guidance [From on High]:

"[T]he testimony of believing without seeing... is the testimony of the Spirit... We should all seek for it. If the Lord wishes to add the testimony of the senses, we should be grateful; but the testimony when it comes will be in us a burning testimony, a testimony that will be a fire, if we so live that we keep it. We should see to it that it is fed by righteous works, proper living. We should see to it that it never becomes smothered by the ashes of transgression." (J. Reuben Clark, Jr.)

What Was the Original Church Like?

The true Church today must have the same Organization as Christ's original Church:

"Remember them which have the rule over you, who have spoken unto you The Word of God: whose faith follow, considering the end of their conversation. Jesus Christ the *same* yesterday, and today, and for ever." (Hebrews 13:7-8; cf. Ephesians 4:11-14) [see, Rule #1]

Friendly [as an *'ideal friend'*]

A man's best friend, it's said, is his dog. And for many a good reason: for starters, dogs tend to be by and large rather friendly companions. They are used as guide dogs or seeing-eye dogs for the sightless; for epileptics, whereby the dog sets off an alarm prior to the epileptic seizure (through a scent or odor the epileptic releases apparently prior to the seizure); as well as guard dogs; for comfort for the dying, and for a host of other very good reasons.

The anecdote is told (by Pepper Rodgers regarding his 'best friend'): "I had only one friend, my dog. My wife was mad at me, and I told her a man ought to have at least two friends. She agreed: and bought me another dog!"

For some people due to life's circumstances, it is nigh impossible to have a friend. I think of Anne Frank (a young thirteen-year-old Jewish girl in hiding until her capture and death in a Nazi extermination camp at age fifteen), as she relates in her own Diary:

'Paper has more patience than people,' I thought of this saying on one of those days when I was feeling a little depressed and was sitting at home with my chin in my hands, bored and listless... brooding. Yes, paper does have more patience, and since I'm not planning to let anyone else read this... 'diary' (unless I should ever find a real friend?!), it probably won't make a difference. Now, I'm back to the point that prompted me to keep a diary in the first place: *I don't have a friend!"*

As we can note, Anne Frank's real 'friend' was her Diary (which she named 'Kitty'). For many people, this diary (or Journal) is their means of going through life without a true friend. But what qualities make up those of a genuine friend? Immanuel Kant, the great rationalist, gives us his following insight:

"Everyone seeks to deserve friendship. Uprightness of disposition, sincerity, trustworthiness, conduct devoid of all falsehood and spite, and a sweet, cheerful, and happy temper, these are the elements which make up the character of a perfect friend. And once we have made ourselves fit objects of friendship, we may be sure that we shall find someone who will take a liking to us and choose us for a friend, and that on closer contact our friendship will grow and become more and more intimate."

But not all persons are sincere. Indeed, some people who complain that they have no friends, are themselves rather selfish, and seek only to use people, to turn friendship to suit their own self-centred purposes. Dale Carnegie lists six ways in which we may enhance our relations with others, 'to win friends and influence people,' as follows:

"In a nutshell: Six Ways to Make People Like You:

1: Become genuinely interested in other people.
2: Smile.
3: Remember that a person's name is to that person the sweetest and most important sound in any language.
4: Be a good listener. Encourage others to talk about themselves.
5: Talk in terms of the other person's interests.
6: Make the other person feel important and do it sincerely."

Your best friend is then the one who brings out the best in you. He who cares will share. For to have sympathy for another is to have his pain in your heart. In my view, the true friend is one who helps to bring you closer to God, for if God is your best friend, He will keep you as the 'apple of His eye'! (Deuteronomy 32:10) A faithful friend is the medicine of life (Ecclesiasticus 6:16). It is someone with whom we may dare to be ourselves, someone with whom we can grow separately without growing apart.

I personally do not believe that sexuality is the basis of all friendship. I believe that the feelings of the heart far surpass the mechanical physics of the flesh, that we tend to open up to those who open up to us, that the way to speak to another heart is from our own heart. As Samuel Taylor Coleridge puts it: "What comes from the heart, goes to the heart". Friendship cannot be forced. As with love, it comes when it comes.

As Sydney Smith puts it so pointedly: "True, it is most painful not to meet the kindness and affection you feel you have deserved and have a right to expect from others; but it is a mistake to complain of it, for it is of no use. You cannot extort friendship with a cocked pistol."

Even Jesus, our Lord, wanted his three closest disciples, Peter, James, and John, to stay awake with Him as he prayed his final prayer in the Garden of Gethsemane (just before his arrest), but they fell asleep (Mark 14:32-41; Matthew 26:36-45). Billy Graham puts this poignant moment into perspective: "How we need friends in time of testing! Jesus demonstrated His humanity when He asked His disciples to stay with Him. He wanted and needed them in His time of greatest trial. 'My soul is overwhelmed with sorrow to the point of death. Stay here and keep watch with me' (Matthew 26:38)".

As we can see, the best way to have a friend is to be one. Few there are, and fortunate they be, who can find a true soul mate: "A soul friend is someone with whom we can share our greatest joys and deepest fears, confess our worst sins and most persistent faults, clarify our highest hopes and perhaps most unarticulated dreams'. (Edward C. Sellner)

21D.   Friendly [as an *'Ideal Friend'*]

Youth Feedback:
____

____

____

1. Affable

Youth Feedback:
____

____

____

2. Amiable

Youth Feedback:
____

____

____

3. Always-an-ally

Youth Feedback:
____

____

____

4. Approachable

Youth Feedback:
____

____

____

5. Being-a-buddy

Youth Feedback:
____

____

____

6. Being-a-advocate

Youth Feedback:

____

____

____

7. Being-an-associate

Youth Feedback:

____

____

____

8. Being-a-benefactor

Youth Feedback:

____

____

____

9. Being-a-sport

Youth Feedback:

____

____

____

10. Being-a-confidante

Youth Feedback:

____

____

____

11. Cordial

Youth Feedback:

____

____

____

12. Courteous

Youth Feedback:

____

____

____

13. Crony-like

Youth Feedback:

____

____

____

14. Defending-one's-rights

Youth Feedback:

____

____

____

15. Deferential

Youth Feedback:

____

____

____

16. Dependable

Youth Feedback:

____

____

____

17. Empathetic

Youth Feedback:

____

____

____

18. Encouraging

Youth Feedback:

____

____

____

19. Esteeming-the-best

Youth Feedback:

____

____

____

20. Familiar

Youth Feedback:

____

____

____

21. Having-fond-feelings

Youth Feedback:

____

____

____

22. Honourable

Youth Feedback:

____

____

____

23. Hospitable

Youth Feedback:

____

____

____

24. Intimate

Youth Feedback:

____

____

____

25. Keeping-one's-promises

Youth Feedback:

____

____

____

26. Like-minded

Youth Feedback:

____

____

____

27. Looking-for-the-best

Youth Feedback:

____

____

____

28. Loyal

Youth Feedback:

____

____

____

29. Out-going

Youth Feedback:

____

____

____

30. *Philia*-loving

Youth Feedback:

____

____

____

31. Preferring-others-to-self

Youth Feedback:

____

____

____

32. Reliable

Youth Feedback:

____

____

____

33. Sociable

Youth Feedback:

____

____

____

34. Speaking-kindly

Youth Feedback:

____

____

____

35. Speaking-uprightly

Youth Feedback:

____

____

____

36. Supportive

Youth Feedback:

____

____

____

37. Sympathetic

Youth Feedback:

____

____

____

38. Wishing-one-well

Youth Feedback:

____

____

____

39. Yearning-for-a-soulmate

Youth Feedback:

____

____

____

Harmless:

Abhorring-evil

Abstaining-from-evil

Avoiding-what-is-unclean

Benign

Blameless

Child-like

Following-the-good

Humble

Incorruptible

Innocent

Innocuous

Inoffensive

Lowly

Meek

Moderate

Naive

Recompensing-*no*-evil

Resisting-the-Devil

Sound-in-mind-and-body

FOOD FOR THOUGHT:

For the Spiritual Man Striving to Become Saint-like

Uplifting Insight(s):

"If you compare yourself with others, you may become vain and bitter: for always there will be greater and lesser persons than yourself."

RULE #5: For Raising a Happy Home:

Be parents who have worthwhile goals in life, and who seek to have their children join them in their attainment.

How to Obtain Guidance [From on High]:

"The testimony of the still small voice whispering to our innermost beings is of more worth than outward signs or manifestations." (Henry D. Taylor)

What Was the Original Church Like?

The Church must claim divine authority:

"So also Christ glorified not Himself to be made an High Priest; but He that said unto Him, Thou art my Son, today have I begotten Thee. As He saith also in another place, Thou art a Priest forever after the Order of Melchisedec. Who in the days of his flesh, when he had offered up prayers and supplications with strong crying and tears unto Him that was able to save him from death, and was heard in that He feared;

Though He were a Son, yet learned He obedience by the things which He suffered; And being made perfect, He became the Author of Eternal Salvation unto all them that obey Him; *Called of God* an High Priest after the Order of Melchisedec." (Hebrews 5:4-10)

Harmless

Perhaps the best symbol of a harmless animal, I can think of, is the dove. Jesus said to all His disciples to "be wise as serpents, but harmless as doves". (Matthew 10:16)

To appear harmless, we can think of the personality of *Bambi* in the Walt Disney movie by that name, as well as our Savior's comment to Nathaniel, that in him there was no guile (John 1:47). Yet the deeper question remains: What can be said of the commandment, "Thou shalt not kill!" (Exodus 20:13). To appear 'harmless' the "Society of Friends" (or "Quakers", under William Penn in 1682) formed a new government and life in 'Pennsylvania' (known originally as "Penn's Woods") to hold as a tenet that we are to 'do violence to no man' (Luke 3:14). These scriptural interpretations have evolved into new religions.

It is worth having a closer look at the issue of 'being harmless' when faced with those evil persons (who may have 'their conscience seared with a hot iron,' as Paul vividly portrays it in: I Timothy 4:2) who would wish to do us harm, perhaps even to take our lives, if we let them.

I would reply that to submit oneself and one's loved ones to zero protection (either under the law or before one's assailant) is neither wise nor just.

Let me explain: To quote the entire verse: "And the soldiers likewise demanded of Him [Jesus], saying, And what shall we do? And He [Jesus] said unto them, "***Do violence to no man***, neither accuse any falsely and be content with your wages." (Luke 3:14)

What I take away from our Lord's reply is that He did not say to the soldiers: "Oh, soldiers, Do not kill, for that is the commandment of your God!" No, Jesus knew that these were soldiers who were pressed into duty to defend their country against violent offenders. He did not gainsay (or speak against) their job description! Instead, He clearly approved and supported their call to duty (to defend their country even unto their own death, or the loss of their own lives).

Now we need to ask ourselves this question: If Jesus approved of the duty soldiers have to defend their own country with their very lives; surely, would He not expect husbands to have the self-same duty: to protect their own wives, and family, with their very lives?!

That is what Jesus really meant (I would attest) when he said: "Greater love hath no man than this, that a man lay down his own life for his friends" (John 15:13). Jesus could have intended this sentence to imply the love of the soldier who lays down his life for his 'friends' (his fellow countrymen and women). As well He could have intended to say: that one should defend his 'friends' (to include: his beloved wife, children, and other family members, of course) to the point of even laying down his life for them, to protect them from harm.

Jesus did not say: "Greater love hath no man... [to] lay down his life for his *enemies*!" That is, for those who would attack with intent to commit violence against one's loved ones, that one should simply lay down his life (not resist the assault) in order to show love for his 'enemies'?! No, I do not think that is what Jesus meant at all when He instructed all His followers in His Sermon on the Mount to: "Love your enemies". (Matthew 5:44)

In fact, most readers apparently do not realize that Jesus himself spelled out precisely what He meant by His injunction to all Christians to "love your enemies" in that self-same verse, as follows: "Bless them that curse you, do good to them that hate you, and pray for them that despitefully use you, and persecute you."

Hence, we can now better understand the meaning of Christ's own prayer to His Father, when He said (of those soldiers who crucified Him): "Father, forgive them, for they know not what they do". (Luke 23:34). We must remember that Jesus did not ask forgiveness for those religious leaders who wanted His crucifixion, nor of those who betrayed him (as did Judas).

Instead, He specifically prayed these words in (His famous 'intercessory prayer' in) the Garden of Gethsemane prior to his betrayal and mock trial and crucifixion: "I pray for them [His true disciples]: *I pray not for the world* [meaning: those who would do 'violence' against My disciples], but for them which Thou has given Me; for they are Thine"! (John 17:9).

Apostle Paul lays this matter to rest in his declaration of duty that we all have to our own families (those we love), in the following words: "But if any provide not for his own [which I would contend includes: defending the life, health, limb, and safety of 'one's own'], and especially for those of his own house, he hath denied the faith, and is worse than an infidel" (I Timothy 5:8).

Arguably, this concept of being 'harmless' is as Jesus commanded when He instructed us to be: 'harmless as doves' (which doves, by the way, will fight to the death to defend themselves, their nests or their loved ones).

22E. Harmless:

Youth Feedback:
____
____
____

1. Abhorring-evil
Youth Feedback:
____
____
____

2. Abstaining-from-evil
Youth Feedback:
____
____
____

3. Avoiding-what-is-unclean
Youth Feedback:
____
____
____

4. Benign
Youth Feedback:
____
____
____

5. Blameless
Youth Feedback:
____
____
____

6. Child-like

Youth Feedback:

____

____

____

7. Following-the-good

Youth Feedback:

____

____

____

8. Humble

Youth Feedback:

____

____

____

9. Incorruptible

Youth Feedback:

____

____

____

10. Innocent

Youth Feedback:

____

____

____

11. Innocuous

Youth Feedback:

____

____

____

12. Inoffensive

Youth Feedback:

____

____

13. Lowly

Youth Feedback:

____

____

14. Meek

Youth Feedback:

____

____

15. Moderate

Youth Feedback:

____

____

16. Naïve

Youth Feedback:

____

____

17. Recompensing-no-evil

Youth Feedback:

____

____

18. Resisting-the-Devil

Youth Feedback:

____

____

____

19. Sound-in-mind-and-body

Youth Feedback:

____

____

____

Helpful:

Abetting

Befriending

Being-benevolent

Being-creative

Being-instrumental

Benefiting

Fully-experiencing-life

Ministering-to-others

Obliging

Servicing-others

Sprightly

Succouring

Supporting-the-weak

Useful

Working-independently

Vivacious

FOOD FOR THOUGHT:

For the Spiritual Man Striving to Become Saint-like

Uplifting Insight(s):

"Enjoy your achievements as well as your plans."

RULE #6: For Raising a Happy Home:

Be parents who have common sense, a capacity for friendship, and a sense of humour.

How to Obtain Guidance [From on High]:

"The best way to get a testimony... may not come like a flash of light... more than likely it will be the reassurance and a feeling in your heart, a reaffirmation that will come in a rather calm, natural but real way from day to day until you come to a realization that you do know, and that you know in a way that nobody could really tell you, because it is not just something that comes to your mind. It involves the whole being." (Loren C. Dunn)

What Was the Original Church Like?

The Church must have ***no paid ministry***:

"I have raised him [Man] in righteousness, and I will direct all his ways: he shall build my city, and he shall let go my captives, ***not for price nor reward***, saith the Lord of hosts!" (Isaiah 45:13)

"Feed the flock of God, which is among you, taking the oversight thereof, *not by constraint*, but willingly; ***not for filthy lucre***, but of a ready mind". (I Peter 5:2)

Helpful

Among the animal kingdom, perhaps one of the most 'helpful' of species was the carrier pigeon (used since 3,000 B.C. and throughout the centuries including both World Wars). Referred to as 'Pigeon Post' (or 'messenger pigeons') these homing pigeons were able to fly hundreds of miles to deliver medicine and messages taped to their legs during times of need.

Among helpful critters or creatures in the animated movie world, "Jiminy Cricket" comes to mind in Walt Disney's *Pinocchio* (1940). [Perhaps the "JC" in Jiminy Cricket was a euphemism for our Lord Jesus as Jiminy Cricket appears to be Pinocchio's 'conscience': 'the light that lights all men who come into the world,' John 1:9]

I'm also reminded of the tale of Little Red Riding Hood who is thoughtful and wants to help her ailing grandmother who lives in the dark woods (infested with wolves). Although the story of *Little Red Riding Hood* has varied endings throughout the ages, Luke's account of the Good Samaritan remains consistent.

In this parable, our Lord points out that sometimes the one to come to our aid, is not one whom we may expect, but it could even be a 'Samaritan' a race despised by the Jews (John 4:9). Jesus' point in relating this incident was in response to the question: "And who is my neighbor?" As we follow Jesus' narrative, we see that 'our neighbor' may not always be the one whom we would typically think would come to help us. But the one who 'shows mercy to us' could well be of a different race or social standing (than we might expect). (Luke 10:29-37)

23F. Helpful:

Youth Feedback:

____

____

____

  1. Abetting

Youth Feedback:

____

____

____

  2. Befriending

Youth Feedback:

____

____

____

  3. Being-benevolent

Youth Feedback:

____

____

____

  4. Being-creative

Youth Feedback:

____

____

____

  5. Being-instrumental

Youth Feedback:

____

____

____

6. Benefiting

Youth Feedback:

____

____

____

7. Fully-experiencing-life

Youth Feedback:

____

____

____

8. Ministering-to-others

Youth Feedback:

____

____

____

9. Obliging

Youth Feedback:

____

____

____

10. Servicing-others

Youth Feedback:

____

____

____

11. Sprightly

Youth Feedback:

____

____

____

12. Succouring

Youth Feedback:

____

____

____

13. Supporting-the-weak

Youth Feedback:

____

____

____

14. Useful

Youth Feedback:

____

____

____

15. Working-independently

Youth Feedback:

____

____

____

16. Vivacious

Youth Feedback:

____

____

____

Honest:

Chaste

Genuine

Gentle

Having-good-will

Having-moral-excellence

Having-strength-through-Grace

Impartial

In-earnest

Keeping-one's-word

Modest

Open-hearted

Pious

Plain-speaking

Pure [in heart]

Simplistic

Sincere

Straightforward

Truthful

Unreserved

Upright

Virtuous

Without-guile

FOOD FOR THOUGHT:

For the Spiritual Man Striving to Become Saint-like

Uplifting Insight(s):

"Keep interested in your own career, however humble: it is a real possession in the changing fortunes of time!'

RULE #7: For Raising a Happy Home:

Be parents who live in harmony with each other, and who do not quarrel in the presence of their children.

How to Obtain Guidance [From on High]:

"[A] testimony is not an automatic process; it comes only after you have 'hungered and thirsted' for it. This means you must have a desire much more intense than just a passive wanting." (John H. Vandenberg)

What Was the Original Church Like?

The Church must baptize *by immersion:*

"Then cometh Jesus from Galilee to Jordan unto John, to be baptized of him. But John forbad him, saying, I have need to be baptized of Thee, and comest Thou to me? And Jesus answering said unto him, Suffer it to be so now: for thus it becometh us to fulfil all righteousness. Then he suffered Him. ***And Jesus, when He was baptized, went up straightway out of the water:*** and, lo, the heavens were opened unto Him, and He saw the Spirit of God descending like a dove, and lighting upon Him: And lo a voice from heaven, saying, This is my Beloved Son, in whom I am well pleased." (Matthew 3:13-17)

Consider: "And John also was baptizing in Aeon near to Salim, because *there was much water there.*" (John 3:23) [The question needs to be asked: Unless John was baptizing by immersion, why would he feel compelled to go to a place where there was "much water"?]

Honest

The key element to integrity is consistency, to be just as honest on the outside as in the inside of one's being, one's persona. The animal with perhaps the longest memory (and therefore 'consistent' in it's behaviour), it is said, is the elephant: As it is trained in its youth, it remains true and faithful ('honest') throughout the remainder of its life.

The story is told that when a baby elephant is tied to a small tree (that it cannot break), it recalls that experience throughout its adult life. For even when it is fully grown (and can easily rip that small tree out from its roots with its massive giant trunk), it remains tethered (in its place) because it learned (or was conditioned) from a small elephant not to resist.

Perhaps the same can be said of 'honest folk' that they remain 'true to form,' true to their nature, as they were trained in their formative years. The saying: 'Train up a child in the way he should go: and when he is old, he will not depart from it" (Proverbs 22:6) applies quite aptly to the morally upright, truly honest, child.

Our Lord when He was calling His Apostles to 'come follow Him', said of Nathaniel (when Nathaniel first approached Him): "Behold an Israelite indeed, in whom is no guile!" (John 1:47) The concept of guile is the opposite to being honest. To be guileless, as Nathaniel was, was to be in fact an honest man. To be so praised by our Lord is indeed an honor without equal. It is a similar thing to having our Lord say to you: "Well, done! Thou good and faithful servant". (Matthew 25:21,23)

We think of Abraham Lincoln ('Honest Abe') as the epitome of an honest man, whose image is found not only on Mount Rushmore (in South Dakota) but on every 'Lincoln' penny in the United States. Many Christians (followers of the teachings of our Lord Jesus Christ) seek to avoid the dishonesty mentioned in Acts 5:1-11, of the married couple Ananias and Sapphira (apparently new converts to the early Christian Church) who proved to be 'fake converts', disingenuous Christians (nominal Christians, or Christians in name only) who thought they could lie not only to men but to the Holy Ghost. Their fate proved fatal: it was sealed when they imagined to themselves that dishonesty and the

Christian way of life were compatible.

The rewards of honesty, of honest living, to live consistent to one's known truths, the true principles of the Christian way of life can be seen in Jesus' own words: "He that is faithful in that which is least is faithful also in much". (Luke 16:10) For if we have been faithful over a few things, our Lord will make us ruler(s) over many things (Matthew 25:21,23).

This is a true principle that will never change, as Jesus Himself explains: "Give, and it shall be given unto you: good measure, pressed down, and shaken together, and running over, shall men give into your bosom. For with the same measure that ye mete withal it shall be measured to you again." (Luke 6:38)

24G.   Honest:

Youth Feedback:

____

____

____

1.   Chaste

Youth Feedback:

____

____

____

2.   Genuine

Youth Feedback:

____

____

____

3.   Gentle

Youth Feedback:

____

____

____

4.   Having-good-will

Youth Feedback:

____

____

____

5.   Having-moral-excellence

Youth Feedback:

____

____

____

6. Having-strength-through-Grace

Youth Feedback:

____

____

____

7. Impartial

Youth Feedback:

____

____

____

8. In-earnest

Youth Feedback:

____

____

____

9. Keeping-one's-word

Youth Feedback:

____

____

____

10. Modest

Youth Feedback:

____

____

____

11. Open-hearted

Youth Feedback:

____

____

____

12. Pious

Youth Feedback:

____

____

____

13. Plain-speaking

Youth Feedback:

____

____

____

14. Pure [in heart]

Youth Feedback:

____

____

____

15. Simplistic

Youth Feedback:

____

____

____

16. Sincere

Youth Feedback:

____

____

____

17. Straightforward

Youth Feedback:

____

____

____

18. Truthful

Youth Feedback:

____

____

____

19. Unreserved

Youth Feedback:

____

____

____

20. Upright

Youth Feedback:

____

____

____

21. Virtuous

Youth Feedback:

____

____

____

22. Without-guile

Youth Feedback:

____

____

____

Kind:

Abounding-in-good-works

Altruistic

Amiable

Approving-excellence

Beneficial

Charitable

Cheerful

Considerate

Diligent

Edifying

Favourable

Fervent-in-spirit

Forbearing

Generous

Good-natured

Having-Clemency

Hospitable

Humane

Lenient

Merciful

Philanthropic

Responsive

Tolerant

Upright

Warm-hearted

Wishing-to-please-others

FOOD FOR THOUGHT:

For the Spiritual Man Striving to Become Saint-like

Uplifting Insight(s):

"Exercise caution in your business affairs: for the world is full of trickery!"

RULE #8: For Raising a Happy Home:

Be parents who have ideals, and a compelling urge to serve rather than be served.

How to Obtain Guidance [From on High]:

"[T]he Holy Ghost may be constantly sending out messages like a broadcasting station. If you put yourself in tune, that is, knock or ask or seek, you may receive the message. It may be as if you were to open an imaginary window or door between your spirit mind and your physical mind and permit the message to come through. Spirit can talk to spirit, and you are part spirit -- just open that imaginary door and let the mortal mind receive. To open it requires study, prayer, action or works; or knock, and it shall be opened unto you." (Eldred G. Smith)

What Was the Original Church Like?

The Church must bestow the gift of the Holy Ghost by the laying on of hands:

"Now when the Apostles which were in Jerusalem heard that Samaria had received the Word of God, they sent unto them Peter and John: (For as yet He was fallen upon none of them: only they were baptized in the name of the Lord Jesus.) *Then laid they their hands on them,* and they received the Holy Ghost." (Acts 8:14-17)

Kind

Often kindness is connected with a deer, a doe, or an old milk cow (called: Betsy, or Gertrude, or Hazel?). It is this gentleness of the creature that we tend to refer to as: 'kindness'.

Among examples of the 'milk of human kindness', we can think of Melanie Hamilton (Ashley Wilkes' wife) in *Gone With the Wind* (1939, played by Olivia de Haviland), who epitomizes kindness to a superhuman degree. Mother Teresa once said: "Being unwanted, unloved, uncared for, forgotten by everybody, I think that is a much greater hunger, a much greater poverty than the person who has nothing to eat". Or, as Albert Schweitzer puts it: "Constant kindness can accomplish much. As the sun makes ice melt, kindness causes misunderstanding, mistrust, and hostility to evaporate."

The best part of a good man's life, said William Wordsworth, is "his little, nameless, unremembered acts of kindness and love." Mohammed the Prophet remarked that: "Kindness is the work of faith: and whoever has not kindness has not faith". It appears, as Robert Louis Stevenson notes: "The essence of love is kindness". For a 'kind word is like a Spring Day'. Even though wise sayings can fall on barren ground, 'a kind word is never thrown away'. (Arthur Helps). Kind words in effect can become like medicine to the sad and depressed, the forlorn and broken-hearted.

Indeed, William Penn sets the example of 'kindness', for all to follow: "I shall pass through this world but once. Any good therefore that I can do or *any kindness that I can show* to any human being, let me do it now. Let me not defer or neglect it, for I shall not pass this way again".

25H. Kind:

Youth Feedback:

____

____

1. Abounding-in-good-works

Youth Feedback:

____

____

2. Altruistic

Youth Feedback:

____

____

3. Amiable

Youth Feedback:

____

____

4. Approving-excellence

Youth Feedback:

____

____

5. Beneficial

Youth Feedback:

____

____

6. Charitable

Youth Feedback:

____

____

____

7. Cheerful

Youth Feedback:

____

____

____

8. Considerate

Youth Feedback:

____

____

____

9. Diligent

Youth Feedback:

____

____

____

10. Edifying

Youth Feedback:

____

____

____

11. Favourable

Youth Feedback:

____

____

____

12. Fervent-in-spirit

Youth Feedback:

____

____

____

13. Forbearing

Youth Feedback:

____

____

____

14. Generous

Youth Feedback:

____

____

____

15. Good-natured

Youth Feedback:

____

____

____

16. Having-clemency

Youth Feedback:

____

____

____

17. Hospitable

Youth Feedback:

____

____

____

18. Humane

Youth Feedback:

____

____

____

19. Lenient

Youth Feedback:

____

____

____

20. Merciful

Youth Feedback:

____

____

____

21. Philanthropic

Youth Feedback:

____

____

____

22. Responsive

Youth Feedback:

____

____

____

23. Tolerant

Youth Feedback:

____

____

____

24. Upright

Youth Feedback:

____

____

____

25. Warm-hearted

Youth Feedback:

____

____

____

26. Wishing-to-please-others

Youth Feedback:

____

____

____

Loving:

Adoring

Affectionate

Believing-in-pure-Christ-like-[*agapé*]-love

Blessing-those-who-hurt-you [your enemies]

Desiring-divine-love

Emotionally-intimate

Enthusiastic

Fearing-[revering]-God

Godly [seeks Godliness]

Having-strength-in-the-Lord

Hoping-for-all-good-things

Open-to-the-promptings-of-the-Spirit

Pious

Tolerant-of-others

Warm-hearted [warmth of spirit]

Wishing-to-be-holistic [well-rounded]

Wishing-to-be-one-with-God-[and with others]

FOOD FOR THOUGHT:

For the Spiritual Man Striving to Become Saint-like

Uplifting Insight(s):

"But let this not blind you to what virtue there is: Many persons strive for high ideals; and everywhere life is full of heroism!"

RULE #9: For Raising a Happy Home:

Be parents who are unswervingly loyal to their children, but who can express righteous indignation, and chastise them when it is necessary.

How to Obtain Guidance [From on High]:

"If you will read the word of the Lord, if you will serve in His cause, if in prayer you will talk with Him, your doubts will leave; and shining through all of the confusion of philosophy, so-called higher criticism, and negative theology will come the witness of the Holy Spirit that Jesus is in very deed the Son of God, born in the flesh, the Redeemer of the world resurrected from the grave, the Lord who shall come to reign as King of kings. It is your opportunity so to know. It is your obligation so to find out." (Gordon B. Hinckley)

What Was the Original Church Like?

The Church must practice divine healing:

"And He ordained twelve, that they should be with Him, and that He might send them forth to preach, And *to have power to heal sicknesses,* and to cast out devils!" (Mark 3:14-15)

Loving

The expression of 'love-birds' (so typical of humans in love) comes from the animal kingdom, of birds who preen each other, who appear to sing love songs to each other; hence, truly 'love birds' in both instances of the word.

As a very loving (forgiving) person, I think of Esther in the movie, *Ben-Hur* (1959). She is in love with her master, Judah Ben-Hur (Charlton Heston) but also enamored, enchanted, and wholly captivated by the message of *love* by a certain new Rabbi, Jesus of Nazareth. Her performance is very moving and completely credible.

In Scriptures, we think of the love of the father for his wayward 'prodigal' son, always on the lookout for his return, always ready to embrace him and to accept him back into the family circle (Luke 15:11-32). Such vigilance in love is also reflective of the Savior's love for each one of us: Always standing by the door of our hearts, and knocking, to await our voluntary response, to say: "Master, please enter!" (Revelation 3:20)

It is interesting to note that "life minus love generally equals zero" (Erwin W. Lutzer), or as Jean-Paul Sartre says: "In love, one and one are one". For the paradox occurs that in love 'two beings become one and yet remain two' (Erich Fromm). In the 'arithmetic of love', it seems, 'one plus one equals everything, and two minus one equals nothing' (Mignon McLaughlin). We can be two and have "but one heart between us" (Francois Villon). For love is that miracle "that can take two lives and weld them into one, take two souls, and bind them for life; take two hearts and fill them with enough passion and tenderness to last a lifetime". (Michele Weber)

Yet today, so many people find that prophecy of our Lord to be true, as He said (that in the Latter-Days) "the love of many shall [become] cold'! (Matthew 24:12) But what is the fall-out of this great loss of love? This coldness one towards another throughout the planet (like the 'social leprosy' we currently experience: of the Covid-19 pandemic)? Karl Menninger starkly states: "To cease to be loved is for the child practically synonymous with ceasing to live".

For if love is to be based on trust, it appears that we live in a time of a 'moral earthquake', wherein few people trust few people. Now if we learn to love only by actually loving, as we learn to swim only by entering the water, we realize, not only that we are shaped and fashioned by those who love us, but we are also the product of those who refuse to love us.

Yes, to be loved we need to be loveable. But to be told our love is inadequate and that we need to 'feel love' first for ourselves leads us to a quandary: In order to love ourselves, we need to become our own best friend, we need to be able to trust ourselves, to find solace in ourselves, to find comfort and joy and fulfilment in ourselves. At the risk of seeming narcissistic, we need to know that we are at peace within so that we can reach out and duplicate that similar friendship without, for in a certain sense, love can be seen as "friendship set on fire!" (Jeremy Taylor)

But to the point: What is Love? Is it merely 'an irresistible desire to be irresistibly desired' (as Robert Frost once said)? Or is it something more? Perhaps much more?

In general (as expounded by C.S. Lewis), we can see the concept of love in four parts: (1) Familial or *storge* love (as between a mother and her child); (2) Brotherly (sisterly) love as friendship or *phila*-love; (3) physical (sexual) love as *eros*, or erotic love; and (4) spiritual (or divine love) as *agapé* (in the Greek), or *caritas* (in the Latin).

Storge Love

For this first type of love, I'm reminded of our Lord's concern for His own mother, Mary, while He was crucified on the cross and was dying. (John 19:25-27) Henry Wadsworth Longfellow commented on this moving scene, as follows: "Even He that died for us upon the cross, in the last hour, in the unutterable agony of death, was mindful of his mother, as if to teach us that this holy love should be our last worldly thought, the last point of earth from which the soul should take its flight for heaven."

Philia Love

The second form of love, Philia (or brotherly) love, can be seen in 'learning how you aren't letting yourself feel loved and how you aren't letting others love you' (Barbara de Angelis). For "too many times we insist on loving people the way we want to love them instead of the way they need to be loved" (Joan Chittister). As Henry Ward Beecher says: "Love cannot endure indifference. It needs to be wanted. Like a lamp, it needs to be fed out of the oil of another's heart, or its flame burns low."

Everyone needs to know that they can make a difference (in loving our fellow-being). It will take patience and one's own precious time to discern all the beauty that love can reward us with. It is a learning curve and will take a lot out of us, but even though there is a risk that we will be hurt, or that our love will not be returned, the rewards (of transformation) offer more joy than we can find in simply natural things. I'm reminded of the 'wonderful love' between Jonathan and David which surpassed the love of women (I Samuel 1:26; I Samuel 20:41-42).

Yes, when love goes wrong, nothing seems to go right; but when it does happen, it can be more beautiful than anything else in your life, than anything you have ever known. As Augustine (of Hippo) clarifies this type of love: "What does love look like? It has the hands to help others. It has the feet to hasten to the poor and needy. It has the eyes to see misery and want. It has the ears to hear the sighs and sorrows of men. That is what love looks like."

Eros Love

The third type of love, the physical (sexual), eros (erotic) love can yield instant gratification. As one writer puts it so powerfully: "There is a love that begins in the head, and goes down to the heart, and grows slowly, but it lasts till death, and asks less than it gives. There is another love, that blots out wisdom, that is sweet with the sweetness of life and bitter with the bitterness of death, lasting for an hour; but it is worth having lived a whole life for that hour". (Ralph Iron) Carl Jung adds: 'Before Freud, nothing was allowed to be sexual; now everything is nothing but sexual".

Yet it is not all a bed of roses, even erotic love. Yes, everyone wants love (to love and be loved) we can agree, but to really love someone can ask for more than one thinks. It's not enough to have a loving physical relationship: people generally refuse to be treated merely as toys, as an object, or sexual playthings. If one dares to call the sexual aspect of love as 'true love,' it will demand a careful use of one's precious time, even reflection and (some) emotional intimacy.

Sex without love is not love: it is a sex act. And as a good bowel movement can be pleasant (and reduce 'tension in the belly'), so can this act. If viewed as *strictly* physical, it is not the 'real thing'. To achieve genuine satisfaction requires respect and dignity. Sexual intimacy can be (and I would argue 'should be') a special, and sacred, even a holy act of communion between two loving persons. 'Making love' (as it's commonly referred to) should involve a genuine element of *love*, complete love, not a mere grunting and release of bodily desires.

Fruit flies and gorillas can multiply and reproduce their own kind, but among the human family, there should be a bit of romance, courting, even 'sparking' (to use the old term) before we engage in actual foreplay and 'making love' or consummating the love-act (preferably in a committed relationship, such as marriage) to begin the lifelong love affair of 'pleasuring' each other.

As this work focuses on the youth around the world, and the *youth* perspective, I would like to conclude this brief narrative on *physical* love [although not my own point of view] with the words of the fourteen-year-old Anne Frank (from her Diary, 'Kitty'):

"Love, what is love? I don't think you can really put it into words! Love is understanding someone, caring for him, sharing his joys and sorrows. This eventually includes physical love. You've shared something, given away and received something in return, whether or not you're married, whether or not you have a baby. Losing your virtue doesn't matter, as long as you know that for as long as you live, you'll have someone at your side who understands you! (And who doesn't have to be shared with anyone else!)".

Agapé (Caritas) Love

The fourth (and final) general aspect of 'love' is the spiritual (to include emotional intimacy of the highest order), also known as *agapé (caritas)* love. It has been said that "there are no Ten Commandments when it comes to love. There is only one: to love unconditionally" (Marlene Dietrich). But I beg to differ. On the one hand, it can be beautiful to know that one is loved and to feel that love (like the sun shining on both sides) both intimately, emotionally, psychologically, and spiritually. But on the other hand, if there is no real direction or inner meaning to one's union with another, to be a sort of 'Bonnie & Clyde' type of love, misses the mark of what 'true love' (*agapé*) love is all about. There is a fork in the road that divides genuine 'unconditional' love from the ersatz version, the type of love that (as libertarians famously portray) is defined as: "a free spirit, to do whatever you like, as long as it feels good!".

Immanuel Kant expounds upon this invisible 'red line' that separates these two types of 'unconditional loves': "There are two kinds of love: the love of good-will, and the love of good-pleasure. The love of good-will consists of the wish and inclination to promote the happiness of others; the love of good-pleasure, the satisfaction which we ourselves derive from appreciating the perfections of another."

Perhaps the best (greatest) instance of *agapé* love is the love of our Savior for us, His sometimes-disobedient children. Through Heavenly Father's 'Plan of Happiness' for each one of us, a 'Way' has been prepared for us (John 14:6) to return to His grace (I Peter 5:10; Jeremiah 1:4-5).

In John 3:16, it is clearly stated that because of His divine *agapé* love for all His children, God has provided for us a Lamb, even the 'Lamb of God' (John 1:29,36; Revelation 7:9-14) to be sacrificed for our sins, that through His atonement (Romans 5:8-11) we can be saved (from our sins) and return with honor and humility to our Heavenly Home (Ecclesiastes 12:7; 5:15).

Our Lord has given unto us a 'new commandment' that we should "love one another, as I have loved you, that you also love one another. By this shall all men know that you are my disciples if you have love one to another" (John 13:34-35). For this love of God is "shed abroad in our hearts by the Holy Ghost" which Heavenly Father gives to us. (Romans 5:5; John 15:26).

John the Beloved Apostle speaks in his first Epistle of a "manner of love the Father has bestowed upon us" (I John 3:1) stating: "Hereby perceive we the love of God, because He laid down His life for us: and we ought to lay down our lives for the brethren" (I John 3:16).

John then expounds further concerning this *agape* love as follows:

"In this was manifested the love of God toward us, because that God sent His only begotten Son into the world, that we might live through Him. Herein is love, not that we loved God, but that He loved us, and sent His Son to be the propitiation for our sins...

If we love one another, God dwells in us, and His love is perfected in us. Hereby know we that we dwell in Him, and He in us, because He has given us of His Spirit. And we have seen and do testify that the Father sent the Son to be the Savior of the world. **Whosoever shall confess that Jesus is the Son of God, God dwells in him, and he in God.** And we have known and believed the love that God has to us. God is love, and he that dwells in love dwells in God, and God in him. Herein is our love made perfect"! (I John 4:9-10, 12b-17)

To conclude, as Martin Luther King, Jr. so aptly puts it: "*Agapé* does not begin by discriminating between worthy and unworthy people, or any qualities people possess. It begins by loving others for their sakes."

261.   Loving:

Youth Feedback:
____

____

____

1.   Adoring

Youth Feedback:
____

____

____

2.   Affectionate

Youth Feedback:
____

____

____

3.   Believing-in-pure-Christ-like-[agapé]-love

Youth Feedback:
____

____

____

4.   Blessing-those-who-hurt-you [your enemies]

Youth Feedback:
____

____

____

5.   Desiring-divine-love

Youth Feedback:
____

____

____

6. Emotionally-intimate

Youth Feedback:

____

____

____

7. Enthusiastic

Youth Feedback:

____

____

____

8. Fearing-[revering]-God

Youth Feedback:

____

____

____

9. Godly [seeks Godliness]

Youth Feedback:

____

____

____

10. Having-strength-in-the-Lord

Youth Feedback:

____

____

____

11. Hoping-for-all-good-things

Youth Feedback:

____

____

____

12. Open-to-the-promptings-of-the-Spirit

Youth Feedback:

____

____

____

13. Pious

Youth Feedback:

____

____

____

14. Tolerant-of-others

Youth Feedback:

____

____

____

15. Warm-hearted [warmth of spirit]

Youth Feedback:

____

____

____

16. Wishing-to-be-holistic [well-rounded]

Youth Feedback:

____

____

____

17. Wishing-to-be-*one*-with-God-[and with others]

Youth Feedback:

____

____

____

Obedient:

Acquiescent

Amenable

Biddable

Compliant

Group-thinking

Deferential

Docile

Obliging

Resigned

Socially-conditioned [in thinking]

Socially-conforming [in behaviour]

Subdued

Submissive

Tame

FOOD FOR THOUGHT:

For the Spiritual Man Striving to Become Saint-like

Uplifting Insight(s):

"Be yourself. Especially, do not feign affection! Neither be cynical about love: for in the face of all aridity and disenchantment, it is perennial as the grass!"

RULE #10: For Raising a Happy Home:

Be parents whose decisions are controlled, not by what their children desire, but by what they need.

How to Obtain Guidance [From on High]:

"The first essential, therefore, in gaining a testimony, is to make certain that one's personal spiritual 'house-keeping' is in proper order. His mind and body must be clean if he would enjoy the indwelling of the Holy Ghost by which he could know the certainty of spiritual things." (Harold B. Lee)

What Was the Original Church Like?

The Church must teach that God and Jesus Christ are separate and distinct individuals:

"And now I [Christ] am no more in the world, but these are in the world, and I come to Thee. Holy Father, keep through Thine own name those whom Thou hast given Me, that they may be one, as We are!" (John 17:11)

"Jesus saith unto her [Mary Magdalene], Touch Me not; For I am not yet ascended to My Father: but go to My brethren, and say unto them, *I ascend unto My Father,* and your Father; and to My God, and your God." (John 20:17)

Obedient

Within the animal kingdom perhaps no animal appears to exemplify 'obedience' more than the well-trained military Guard Dog. Their fierce attack mode is so disturbing and devastating (even upon their own bodies) that these dogs have an average 'work-life' span of only two to four years (after training). The German Shepherd is the favourite choice for this highly aggressive trade, as evidenced during the Nazi regime in World War II. These obedient (often robot-like) creatures would throw themselves onto minefields, or into battle (even to their deaths) without any hesitation if ordered to do so. Horses in battle were known to be just as obedient.

In the human sphere of events, we can cite similar examples of total (heroic) obedience, as demonstrated by the Japanese Kamikaze World War II pilots who would dive their aircraft into an enemy destroyer or battleship, without regard to their own personal safety or life, as an act of suicide.

One of the best examples of obedience can be found in the words of the great Native (Apache) Chief, Geronimo, as he relates in his own words:

"While living I want to live well. I know I have to die sometime, but even if the heavens were to fall on me, I want to do what is right. There is one God looking down on us all. We are all children of the one God. God is listening to me. The sun, the darkness, the winds, are listening to what we now say."

But is that all there is to 'obedience': to yield one's will to live, one's sense of self-preservation, for a higher cause (so perceived)? We're reminded of the Savior's parable of the two sons: when asked to do what his father wished, the one son said: 'Yes, father!" but did not do it. The other son, who initially said, "No!" repented and then did what his father wanted him to do. Jesus asked the listeners gathered around him: "Which of these two did the will of his father?". Everyone, of course, said it was the one who said 'No!" but relented and later did what his father asked of him. (Matthew 21:28-31)

Likewise, the story is told of a Roman Centurion (a Captain in the

Roman Legion who had authority over 100 soldiers): He related to Jesus: "I am a man under authority, having soldiers under me: and I say to this man, Go, and he goes; and to another, Come, and he comes; and to my servant, Do this, and he does it"! Jesus marvelled at this soldier's strict code of obedience, for the Centurion had said to Jesus, that it was not necessary for Him to come to heal his sick servant: He simply need but 'say the word' and the Centurion believed his servant would be well! (Matthew 8:5-13) Jesus praised the faith of this Centurion, for obedience is the first principle of Heaven.

Yet the deeper concern rests with the spirit of the law, not simply the 'letter' (that is, to do merely what is the minimal expected). As one writer aptly puts it: 'There are two kinds of men who never amount to much: those who cannot do what they are told, and those who can do nothing else."

In the Old Testament (I Samuel 15), this principle is emphasized: 'To obey is better than to sacrifice'! We can see how King Saul of Israel (in fearing the voice of the people over the voice of God) chose to be selective in his obedience to the Lord's command to destroy Israel's enemy completely. He saved the finest part of the spoils of war, thinking that if he gave some of the captured animals as a sacrifice to the Lord, it would be acceptable for King Saul to keep the rest for himself! He had the audacity to say to (the Lord's duly appointed Prophet) Samuel: "I have performed the commandment of the Lord" (I Samuel 15:13).

But he did not perform (or keep) the Lord's commandment to him: In holding back part of the proceeds, the spoils of war, for himself, Saul greatly displeased the Lord, and so he was told: "To obey is better than sacrifice... Because you have rejected the word of the Lord, He has rejected you from being King" (I Samuel 15:22-23). The Spirit of the Lord left Saul never to return to him as he became corrupted by lust for material gain, in defiance of God's explicit command: Total war against Israel's enemy.

We can see in the New Testament, as well, that a married couple, Ananias and Sapphira, acted similarly to King Saul. This couple thought they could disobey the injunction given to the Lord to the early Saints: to hold *all things* in common; that is, to sell what they have and to give **the entire proceeds** to the Lord's cause, His

Church.

They thought they were clever. They reasoned: Who would know (except themselves) if they kept a part of their proceeds for themselves? So, they held back part of the proceeds, lying to (the Lord's Prophet) Peter that they had surrendered everything to the Lord's cause. For their dishonesty as well as their disobedience (like King Saul) in keeping back part of what they were to disengage from, to be only partially obedient to the Lord's commandment, they were put to death. (Acts 5:1-11)

As Immanuel Kant clarifies our Christian duty to obey God: "We must do what is in our power; we must do what we ought; the rest we should leave to God. That is true submission to the divine will." For as delayed obedience is disobedience, so too is partial obedience.

Or put another way: "There are no amendments to the Ten Commandments". For, as Augustine points out: "Obedience is in a way the mother of all virtues". To be truly obedient, not only to the letter but to the Spirit of our Heavenly Father's will (Romans 7:6), we need to exercise and apply personal self-discipline. As it says in Proverbs: "He that has no rule over his own spirit is like a city that is broken down and without walls." (Proverbs 25:28)

27J.   Obedient:

Youth Feedback:

____

____

____

1. Acquiescent

Youth Feedback:

____

____

____

2. Amenable

Youth Feedback:

____

____

____

3. Biddable

Youth Feedback:

____

____

____

4. Compliant

Youth Feedback:

____

____

____

5. Group-thinking

Youth Feedback:

____

____

____

6. Deferential

Youth Feedback:

____

____

____

7. Docile

Youth Feedback:

____

____

____

8. Obliging

Youth Feedback:

____

____

____

9. Resigned

Youth Feedback:

____

____

____

10. Socially-conditioned [in thinking]

Youth Feedback:

____

____

____

11. Socially-conforming [in behaviour]

Youth Feedback:

____

____

____

12. Subdued

Youth Feedback:

____

____

____

13. Submissive

Youth Feedback:

____

____

____

14. Tame

Youth Feedback:

____

____

____

Peaceful:

Being-agreeable

Being-still

Calm

Contented

Enjoying-heavenliness

Happy

Having-a-grave-demeanor

Humble

Joyful

Minding-one's-own-business

Noiseless

Patient

Placid

Quiet

Rejoicing

Restful

Serene

Silent

Sober-minded

Solemn [in attitude]

Worry-free

FOOD FOR THOUGHT:

For the Spiritual Man Striving to Become Saint-like

Uplifting Insight(s):

"Take kindly the counsel of the years, gracefully surrendering the things of youth."

RULE #11: For Raising a Happy Home:

Be parents who make their children feel that their home is the happiest place in the world.

How to Obtain Guidance [From on High]:

"The time will come when no man or woman will be able to stand on borrowed light. Each of you will have to be guided with the light within himself. If you do not have it, how can it stand?"
(Heber C. Kimball)

What Was the Original Church Like?

The Church must teach that God and Jesus Christ have bodies of flesh and bone:

"And as they thus spake, Jesus Himself stood in the midst of them, and saith unto them, Peace be unto you! But they were terrified and affrighted, and supposed that they had seen a spirit. And He said unto them, Why are ye troubled? and why do thoughts arise in your hearts? Behold my hands and my feet, that it is I Myself: handle Me, and see: **For a spirit hath not *flesh and bones*, as ye see Me have!**

And when He had thus spoken, He shewed them His hands and His feet. And while they yet believed not for joy, and wondered, He said unto them, Have ye here any meat? And they gave Him a piece of a broiled fish, and of an honeycomb. And He took it, and did eat before them." (Luke 24:36-43; see also, Acts 1:9-11)

Peaceful

One of the most serene, calm, peaceful creatures I know of is the elegant swan, as it glides effortlessly across the water giving a relaxed sense of beauty to all around. I still recall those moments traveling in East Ukraine and watching the many swans in the giant extensive streams flowing throughout their magnificent parks.

Together with the large lakes, and bridges, ponds, trees, and vast arrays of shrubs along the riverbank, I can still picture in my mind the perfect stillness of these sleek creatures adding the final touch of grace, and peace throughout nature's home. Doves as well appear to be peace-loving creatures.

For this reason, I suppose, our Lord when he blessed the 'peace-makers' of the world, added: "for they shall be called the children of God". (Matthew 5:9) To some extent I see a similar sense of peacefulness in the classic movie: *The Yearling* (1946, with Gregory Peck) in which a farm boy yearns to have a yearling (a young baby fawn) as his pet. The story and its setting is a throwback to an era in which society as a whole appeared a lot more *peaceful* than it is today. As J. Reuben Clark, Jr. put it: "We must learn and practice, as a nation and as a world, the divine principles of the Sermon on the Mount. There is no other way to Peace!".

It is true that inner peace creates outer peace, for it is the 'peace of God that surpasses all understanding' (Philippians 4:7). As John F. Kennedy noted: "Peace does not rest in charters and covenants alone: It lies in the hearts and minds of the people." After all, "Peace is not the absence of conflict, but the presence of God no matter what the conflict" (Anon).

In the words of Mother Teresa: "If we have no peace, it is because we have forgotten that we belong to each other.' Or, to put it simply (as a slogan): "No God, no Peace; Know God, know Peace!".

28K.   Peaceful:

Youth Feedback:

____

____

____

1.   Being-agreeable

Youth Feedback:

____

____

____

2.   Being-still

Youth Feedback:

____

____

____

3.   Calm

Youth Feedback:

____

____

____

4.   Contented

Youth Feedback:

____

____

____

5.   Enjoying-heavenliness

Youth Feedback:

____

____

____

6. Happy

Youth Feedback:

____

____

7. Having-a-grave-demeanor

Youth Feedback:

____

____

8. Humble

Youth Feedback:

____

____

9. Joyful

Youth Feedback:

____

____

10. Minding-one's-own-business

Youth Feedback:

____

____

11. Noiseless

Youth Feedback:

____

____

12. Patient

Youth Feedback:

____

____

____

13. Placid

Youth Feedback:

____

____

____

14.   Quiet

Youth Feedback:

____

____

____

15. Rejoicing

Youth Feedback:

____

____

____

16. Restful

Youth Feedback:

____

____

____

17. Serene

Youth Feedback:

____

____

____

18. Silent

Youth Feedback:

____

____

____

19. Sober-minded

Youth Feedback:

____

____

____

20. Solemn [in attitude]

Youth Feedback:

____

____

____

21. Worry-free

Youth Feedback:

____

____

____

Self-Reliant:

Authentic

Cogent

Dependable

Distinctive

Individualistic [like Robinson Crusoe]

Infallible

Pioneer-stock

Safe

Secure

Sound

Staunch

Tried-(and found true)

Trusty

Unerring

Valid

FOOD FOR THOUGHT:

For the Spiritual Man Striving to Become Saint-like

Uplifting Insight(s):

"Nurture strength of spirit to shield you in sudden misfortune."

RULE #12: For Raising a Happy Home:

Be parents of true intimacy, for (emotional) intimacy is what makes a marriage, not a ceremony, not a piece of paper from the State.

How to Obtain Guidance [From on High]:

"[K]nowing and doing lead to the revelation from God which we call a testimony. Neither can do it alone. This was the great message of James the Apostle, 'Faith, if it hath not works, is dead, being alone.' (James 2:17)" (John A. Widtsoe)

What Was the Original Church Like?

The Church Officers must be called of God:

"And no man taketh this honour unto himself, but he that is **called of God**, as was Aaron!" (Hebrews 5:4)

"And take thou [Moses] unto thee Aaron thy brother, and his sons with him, from among the children of Israel, that he may minister unto Me in the priest's office, even Aaron, Nadab and Abihu, Eleazar and Ithamar, Aaron's sons." (Exodus 28:1)

"And thou [Moses] shalt put upon Aaron the holy garments, and anoint him, and sanctify him; that he may minister unto Me in the Priest's Office. And thou shalt bring his sons, and clothe them with coats: And thou shalt anoint them, as you didst anoint their father, that they may minister unto Me in the Priest's Office: For their anointing shall surely be an everlasting Priesthood throughout their generations. Thus did Moses: according to all that the Lord commanded him, so did he!" (Exodus 40:13-16)

Self-Reliant

Among animals that are 'self-reliant', I think of the turtle, who carries his house with him. It's like traveling in an RV (Recreational Vehicle). Whenever he wishes, the turtle can hunker down and slip into his own private lodge, to rest or to sleep. Its tough outer shell would keep away wanna-be predators. So it's 'Home Sweet Home' wherever he roams!

The camel likewise is self-reliant when it travels into the extremely hot blistering heat of the desert: It carries two 'humps' (which form its back) which when filled with water can last several days or weeks at a time until he can arrive at the next watering hole.

In the movie, *Naked Jungle* (1954, with Charlton Heston and Eleanor Parker), there is the Robinson-Crusoe theme of a man who leaves civilization to carve his own mini-kingdom in the Jungles of Africa. The story emphasizes self-reliance to an extreme until the plot thickens and the mail-order bride, the stunning beautiful Eleanor Parker, teaches Heston a lesson in intimacy and trust beyond material security.

Behind self-reliance is the quality of a sound and resilient work ethic. As Thomas S. Monson put it so practically: 'Work will win when wishy-washy wishing won't!'. In building self-reliance, I'm reminded of something Richard M. Nixon once stated: "We are faced with a choice between the work ethic that built this nation's character; and, the new welfare ethic that could cause the American character to weaken."

"For nothing is so intolerable to a man," said Blaise Pascal, "as being fully at rest, without passion, without business, without entertainment, without care. It is then that he recognizes that he is empty, insufficient, dependent, ineffectual. From the depths of his soul now comes at once boredom, gloom, sorrow, chagrin, resentment, and despair."

I am intrigued by Adolf Hitler's own reasons for not becoming an ordinary clerk (as was his father): "I did not want to become a civil servant. All attempts on my father's part to inspire with love or pleasure in this profession by stories from his own life accomplished the exact opposite. I yawned and grew sick to my stomach at the thought of sitting in an office, deprived of my liberty; ceasing to be master of my own time and being compelled to force the content of a whole life into blanks that had to be filled out." *(Mein Kampf)*

It appears that: "Men may suffer terribly from the death of a loved one, the breakup of a marriage, or some other personal tragedy. But what brings them to the point of immobilization most often is the loss of their job." (Myron Brenton)

Yes, we should turn to God to help us to become as self-reliant as possible (Matthew 11:29-30), for He cares even for the sparrows of the air (Luke 12:6-7; Matthew 10:29-31). But also recall that though God gives every sparrow its food, "He does not throw it into their nest" (Josiah Holland).

29L.   Self-Reliant:

Youth Feedback:
____

____

____

1. Authentic

Youth Feedback:
____

____

____

2. Cogent

Youth Feedback:
____

____

____

3. Dependable

Youth Feedback:
____

____

____

4. Distinctive

Youth Feedback:
____

____

____

5. Individualistic [like Robinson Crusoe]

Youth Feedback:
____

____

____

6. Infallible

Youth Feedback:

____

____

____

7. Pioneer-stock

Youth Feedback:

____

____

____

8. Safe

Youth Feedback:

____

____

____

9. Secure

Youth Feedback:

____

____

____

10. Sound

Youth Feedback:

____

____

____

11. Staunch

Youth Feedback:

____

____

____

12. Tried-(and found true)

Youth Feedback:

____

____

____

13. Trusty

Youth Feedback:

____

____

____

14. Unerring

Youth Feedback:

____

____

____

15. Valid

Youth Feedback:

____

____

____

Temperate:

Abstaining

Abstinent

Being-checked

Being-curbed

Constant

Dispassionate

Economical

Even

Equable

Forgoing

Frugal

Having-continence

Having-integrity

Having-scruples

Having-self-control

Having-self-restraint

Having-a-sound-mind

Moderate

Prudent

Sacrificing

Sparing

Steady

Thoughtful

Thrifty

FOOD FOR THOUGHT:

For the Spiritual Man Striving to Become Saint-like

Uplifting Insight(s):

"But do not distress yourself with imaginings. Many fears are born of fatigue and loneliness. Beyond a wholesome discipline: Be gentle with yourself!"

RULE #13: For Raising a Happy Home:

Be parents who have discovered the secret of a happy marriage: To love to be with each other all of the time.

How to Obtain Guidance [From on High]:

"Any accountable person can gain a testimony if he will obey the laws upon which the receipt of such knowledge is predicated... 1. The seeker must desire to know the truth of the Gospel... 2. He must study and learn everything possible with relation to the matter involved... 3. The applicant must practice the principles and truths which he learns and bring his life into harmony with them... 4. He must constantly pray to the Father and exercise faith that the truth will be manifested by revelation through the Holy Ghost." (Hugh B. Brown)

What Was the Original Church Like?

The Church must claim revelation from God:

"Surely the Lord God will do nothing, but **He revealeth His secret** unto His servants the Prophets!" (Amos 3:7)

Temperate

Possibly the best example of a 'temperate' animal would be the porcupine. If anyone gives it trouble, it simply rolls into a ball with all its prickly quills set off as a defense. Many a farm pup has tried to create an argument with a porcupine, only to discover the excruciating pain of several needle-sharp pins stuck into its nose. If the porcupine does not bother you, why bother with it?

In the film industry, my favourite example of the 'temperate man' is the US Marshall in *High Noon* (played by Gary Cooper,1952) together with his Quaker wife (Grace Kelly). But even a 'temperate' man can lose 'his cool' as witnessed in the ending of that movie (when he throws his tin star into the dust in front of the townspeople he was sworn to protect). Another example of a 'temperate' man is John Wayne in *The Quiet Man* (1952), who likewise reaches the limits of his 'temperance'.

So, what does it mean to have a 'temperate' temper? Of course, it is to seek to achieve Aristotle's concept of 'The Golden Mean' in which we seek 'the sweet spot' between both opposing extremes. Virginia Woolf describes this character trait quite emphatically: "The man who is aware of himself is henceforward independent: and he is never bored, and life is only too short, and he is steeped through and through with a profound yet temperate happiness. He alone lives, while other people, slaves of ceremony, let life slip past them in a kind of dream."

One of the best instances of the temperate personality in recorded history is the demeanor of our Lord during His 'mock trial': The Trial that made a mockery of Justice for all mankind to review for all time. He always remained at an even keep, never once losing His temper.

How can one become so temperate? So self-controlled? So well-disciplined? According to Immanuel Kant (another example of the temperate personality), one needs only to follow one's conscience, as the moral guide: "The Judge within us is just. He takes the action for what it is and makes no allowance for human defectiveness if only we have the will to listen to his voice and do not stifle it." As Kant makes even more clear: "Without discipling his inclinations, man can attain to nothing. Therefore, in self-mastery, there resides an immediate worth, for to be lord of oneself is to be independent of all things."

The Scriptures speak of being 'temperate' as being of a sound mind (Titus 2:2), as well as being sober-minded (I Thessalonians 5:6; Titus 2:6; I Peter 1:13), to be self-governing (I Corinthians 9;25). We are not to serve our 'belly' (Philippians 3:19), but to curb our gluttonous desires for food, to avoid all sensual appetites (Acts 24:25; Galatians 5:23; II Peter 1:6).

30M. Temperate:

Youth Feedback:

____

____

____

1. Abstaining

Youth Feedback:

____

____

____

2. Abstinent

Youth Feedback:

____

____

____

3. Being-checked

Youth Feedback:

____

____

____

4. Being-curbed

Youth Feedback:

____

____

____

5. Constant

Youth Feedback:

____

____

____

6. Dispassionate

Youth Feedback:

____

____

____

7. Economical

Youth Feedback:

____

____

____

8. Even

Youth Feedback:

____

____

____

9. Equable

Youth Feedback:

____

____

____

10. Forgoing

Youth Feedback:

____

____

____

11. Frugal

Youth Feedback:

____

____

____

12. Having-continence

Youth Feedback:

____

____

____

13. Having-integrity

Youth Feedback:

____

____

____

14. Having-scruples

Youth Feedback:

____

____

____

15. Having-self-control

Youth Feedback:

____

____

____

16. Having-self-restraint

Youth Feedback:

____

____

____

17. Having-a-sound-mind

Youth Feedback:

____

____

____

18. Moderate
Youth Feedback:

____

____

____

19. Prudent
Youth Feedback:

____

____

____

20. Sacrificing
Youth Feedback:

____

____

____

21. Sparing
Youth Feedback:

____

____

____

22. Steady
Youth Feedback:

____

____

____

23. Thoughtful
Youth Feedback:

____

____

____

24. Thrifty

Youth Feedback:

____

____

____

Tender-Hearted:

Being-alive-to-one's-feelings

Being-reconciled-to-God

Being-renewed-to-life

Charitable

Compassionate

Empathetic

Forgiving

Forbearing

Having-pity [on others]

Long-suffering

Meek-and-lowly

Merciful

Mild

Passionate

Repentant

Soft

Sympathetic

Warm-hearted

FOOD FOR THOUGHT:

For the Spiritual Man Striving to Become Saint-like

Uplifting Insight(s):

"You are a child of the Universe, no less than the trees and the stars: you have a right to be here!"

RULE #14: For Raising a Happy Home:

Be parents who establish their marriage on the principles of: Faith, Prayer, Repentance, Forgiveness, Respect, Love, Compassion, Work, and Wholesome Recreational Activities.

How to Obtain Guidance [From on High]:

"A testimony of Jesus is the key to successful living. It was so in the spirit world, for those who overcame Satan there did so 'by the blood of the Lamb, and by the word of their testimony.' (Revelation 12:11) It is so here in this life, and it will be so in the life to come, for there is no other name given, in heaven or in earth, whereby we must be saved. In one's testimony that Jesus is the Christ, so far as he can do anything about it, resides the power of God unto salvation." (Marion G. Romney)

What Was the Original Church Like?

The Church must be a Missionary Church:

"Go ye therefore, and **teach all nations**, baptizing them in the name of the Father, and of the Son, and of the Holy Ghost: *Teaching them to observe all things whatsoever I have commanded you:* and, lo, I am with you always, even unto the end of the world. Amen." (Matthew 28:19-20)

Tender-hearted

Of the tender-hearted animals, perhaps the gentle doe (female deer) comes across as the most innocent and harmless of nature's own. One thinks of the movie, *Bambi:* How endearing and tender-hearted this young little deer appears to be. Turtledoves, of course, appear to be tender and non-intrusive as well.

In cinema art, I'm reminded of *Snow White and the Seven Dwarfs* (1937, animated) who (as her name suggests) is pure, innocent, and tender-hearted. Marlene Dietrich put it well when she said: "Tenderness is greater proof of love than the most passionate of vows". Indeed, to be loved, as Ovid says, "one needs to be loveable". And what better proof of love can there be than to love sweetly and tenderly (as Elvis implies in his song: "Love Me Tender")?

I am referring to all forms of love and not simply the 'mere physical'. For to love is to 'receive a glimpse of heaven' (Karen Sunde). This power to love, after all, can make us appear even God-like, especially as we learn to forgive one another. The redeeming quality (the acid test as it were) is the quality of our mercy within our love. As Shakespeare so eloquently puts it:

> **"The quality of mercy is not strained;**
> It droppeth as the gentle rain from heaven
> Upon the place beneath. It is twice blest:
> It blesseth him that gives and him that takes.
> **... It is an attribute to God himself,**
> And earthly power doth then show likest God's
> When mercy season justice."
> *(The Merchant of Venice)*

In the Scriptures, we are taught: "Be ye therefore merciful, as your Father also is merciful. Judge not, and ye shall not be judged: condemn not, and ye shall not be condemned; forgive, and ye shall be forgiven: Give, and it shall be given unto you; good measure, pressed down, and shaken together, and running over, shall men give into your bosom. For with the same measure that ye mete withal it shall be measured to you again." (Luke 6:36-38)

Our Lord is very specific with regard to His commandment that we should forgive those who ask for forgiveness: "For if you forgive men their trespasses, your heavenly Father will also forgive you: But if ye forgive not men their trespasses, neither will your Father forgive your trespasses"! (Matthew 6:14-15)

A surprise to some (believers included) there appears to be a condition added to whether or not we may choose to forgive another who has wronged us, as the Lord exemplifies: "Take heed to yourselves: If thy brother trespass against thee, rebuke him; and *if he repent*, forgive him". (Luke 17:3) If a brother then refuses to repent and refuses to acknowledge what wrong he has done against you (and even 'gaslights you', to make you imagine that these were only 'imaginary wrongs, that cannot be substantiated), then it appears clear that we may choose not to forgive such a wrong-doer.

Let me delve a bit deeper into this oft-misunderstood Christian doctrine: One writer has claimed: "If I can't love Hitler, I can't love at all"! (A.J. Muste). In view of our Lord's injunction to us all (as Christian believers) to love (even) our enemies (Matthew 5:44), we might think that it behooves us to love Adolf Hitler (the Fuehrer of the Third Reich). And as a proof of that love, to forgive him of all his past crimes, to have a forgiving loving heart towards him?! But this 'love' entails a 'forgiveness' that may not be wholly endorsed (as warranted by Luke 17:3, previously cited).

Consider, for instance, the true account of one of Ted Bundy's last child murders: Imagine that this twenty-year-old girl was your own flesh-and-blood daughter, one who was mutilated and murdered for the sexual gratification of a psychopath, upon whom Ted Bundy left his teeth marks on her left buttock. And it was this very last evidence (as based upon Bundy's own dental impression) that finally convicted him and led him to the electric chair. (Can you find it in your heart to forgive Bundy his heinous murder of your child?!)

In his last taped interview shortly before his electrocution, Ted Bundy says:

"I'm aware that I can't begin to understand the pain that the parents of these children, and these young women, that I've harmed feel. And I can't restore really much to them if anything, and I won't pretend to. **And I won't expect them to forgive me, and I'm not asking for it.** That kind of forgiveness is of God. And if they have it, they have it; and if they don't maybe they'll find it someday?".

As we can see from Bundy's own 'confession', he does not appear to have repented: nowhere does he state that he is genuinely sorry for what he did; nor does he even attempt to ask forgiveness?! According to Luke 17:3, it can be interpreted to mean that the heart-broken mothers and fathers, and loving family members and friends of these tortured and murdered victims need not feel a Christian obligation to forgive the heinous acts that a Ted Bundy committed on their darling loved ones.

Yet Ted Bundy does plead for his own life indirectly as he appeals to reason, oddly enough:

"What I`m talking about is going beyond retribution: What people want with me is going beyond retribution and punishment. Because there is no way in the world, that killing me is going to restore those beautiful children to their parents, and correct, and soothe the pain."

He goes further (in some detail) to attempt to explain (perhaps, even to justify) his murderous acts, as follows:

"I can only hope, those whom I have harmed, those whom I have caused so much grief (even if they don't believe my expression of sorry and remorse) will believe what I'm saying now: And what scares me ... what scares and appals me ... when I see what's on cable TV, ... graphic violence on screen, particularly as it gets into homes, to children, that they may be a Ted Bundy, who has that vulnerability, that predisposition to be influenced by that kind of ... violence."

Indeed, Shakespeare (as if to plead for the Ted Bundys of the world) asks this haunting question (in *Hamlet)*:

"What if this cursed hand
Were thicker than itself with brother's blood,
Is there not rain enough in the sweet heavens
To wash it white as snow?"

In short, I think we need to rely upon the words of the Apostle Paul who clarifies the parameters of what it means to be 'tender-hearted': "Let all bitterness, and wrath, and anger, and clamor, and evil speaking, be put away from you, with all malice: And be ye kind one to another, **tenderhearted**, forgiving one another, even as God for Christ's sake has forgiven you" (Ephesians 4:31-32).

31N.   Tender-Hearted:

Youth Feedback:
____

____

____

1.   Being-alive-to-one's-feelings

Youth Feedback:
____

____

____

2.   Being-reconciled-to-God

Youth Feedback:
____

____

____

3.   Being-renewed-to-life

Youth Feedback:
____

____

____

4.   Charitable

Youth Feedback:
____

____

____

5.   Compassionate

Youth Feedback:
____

____

____

6. Empathetic

Youth Feedback:

____

____

____

7. Forgiving

Youth Feedback:

____

____

____

8. Forbearing

Youth Feedback:

____

____

____

9. Having-pity [on others]

Youth Feedback:

____

____

____

10. Long-suffering

Youth Feedback:

____

____

____

11. Meek-and-lowly

Youth Feedback:

____

____

____

12. Merciful

Youth Feedback:

____

____

____

13. Mild

Youth Feedback:

____

____

____

14. Passionate

Youth Feedback:

____

____

____

15. Repentant

Youth Feedback:

____

____

____

16. Soft

Youth Feedback:

____

____

____

17. Sympathetic

Youth Feedback:

____

____

____

18. Warm-hearted

Youth Feedback:

____

____

____

Thankful:

Acknowledging-higher-powers

Appreciative

Aware-of-details

Being Grateful

Cherishing

Comforting

Consoling

Deserving-praise

Gratifying

Having-propriety

Pleasing

Prizing

Praising-holiness

Refreshing

Rejuvenating

Seeing-worth-in-the-smallest-things

Sharing-newness-of-life

Solacing

Treasuring

Valuing

Welcoming

Worshipful

FOOD FOR THOUGHT:

For the Spiritual Man Striving to Become Saint-like

Uplifting Insight(s):

"And whether or not it is clear to you, no doubt the Universe is unfolding as it should!"

RULE #15: For Raising a Happy Home:

Be parents who have the ability to talk things over, who can tell it to each other as it is; for 'incompatibility' is usually another way of saying: "We couldn't talk".

How to Obtain Guidance [From on High]:

"This power, known as testimony of the Gospel, is one of the most dynamic forces in the world when it comes into a person's heart. It is that divine power which lights up men's souls and gives them deep feelings, indescribable inward peace, unbounded joy, and great understanding. Yes, it endows them even with hidden treasures of knowledge. It guides them back to God."
(Milton R. Hunter)

What Was the Original Church Like?

The Church needs to be *restored* to the original Truths of the Gospel:

"And He [God] shall send Jesus Christ, which before was preached unto you: Whom the heavens must receive **until the times of Restitution of All Things,** which God hath spoken by the mouth of all His holy Prophets since the world began!" (Acts 3:20-21)

Thankful

When I feed the birds with leftover breadcrumbs, I notice how truly thankful they are: The sound of their cooing sounds like the most pleasant symphony, especially when they are very hungry. Parrots, well-trained, can even tell you "Thank you!" in the language of your choice, whenever you feed them.

In the movie repertoire, I think of that classic Western, *The Hanging Tree* (1959) in which young beautiful Maria Schell plays the role of Elizabeth, a girl psychologically blinded by the trauma of her father's death in a stagecoach holdup. Thanks to the medical attention of a (physician) gunslinger, Doctor Joseph Frail (played by Gary Cooper), she is able to see again. She is deeply grateful to Dr. Frail, which complicates the plot.

Helen Keller (in the dramatized movie, *The Miracle Worker*, 1962) is ever grateful to her teacher Anne Sullivan, who helps her to learn the magic of language, that thereby she could overcome the communication barrier caused by her blindness and deafness (when she was nineteen months old). The details of the movie were based on Keller's own autobiography *(The Story of My Life)*.

We are reminded of the ten lepers whom Jesus healed of their leprosy, but only one leper returned to Him to give Him thanks. (Luke 17:12-18) Incredible, but true! Hence, ingratitude can be utterly stunning. It is a great evil to be an unthankful ingrate for everything Heavenly Father has given us.

Recall that historical incident at the end of World War II in which it was suggested to Joseph Stalin (dictator of Soviet Russia) that he state a few words of thanks to the American Allies for all the war equipment they gave to the Soviets (gratis), without which it can easily be debated that Stalin would not have been able to defeat the Nazi hordes who invaded his country in 1941. His famous reply was: "Why should I thank America for their [material] support? They have stopped giving it, haven't they?".

Paul states that we as Christians need to give thanks "for all things unto God and the Father in the name of our Lord Jesus Christ" (Ephesians 5:20). He adds: "Now thanks be unto God which always causes us to triumph in Christ" (II Corinthians 2:14).

320. Thankful:

Youth Feedback:

____

____

____

1. Acknowledging-higher-powers

Youth Feedback:

____

____

____

2. Appreciative

Youth Feedback:

____

____

____

3. Aware-of-details

Youth Feedback:

____

____

____

4. Being-grateful

Youth Feedback:

____

____

____

5. Cherishing

Youth Feedback:

____

____

____

6. Comforting

Youth Feedback:

____

____

____

7. Consoling

Youth Feedback:

____

____

____

8. Deserving-praise

Youth Feedback:

____

____

____

9. Gratifying

Youth Feedback:

____

____

____

10. Having-propriety

Youth Feedback:

____

____

____

11. Pleasing

Youth Feedback:

____

____

____

12. Prizing

Youth Feedback:

____

____

____

13. Praising-holiness

Youth Feedback:

____

____

____

14. Refreshing

Youth Feedback:

____

____

____

15. Rejuvenating

Youth Feedback:

____

____

____

16. Seeing-worth-in-the-smallest-things

Youth Feedback:

____

____

____

17. Sharing-newness-of-Life

Youth Feedback:

____

____

____

18. Solacing
Youth Feedback:

____

____

____

19. Treasuring
Youth Feedback:

____

____

____

20. Valuing
Youth Feedback:

____

____

____

21. Welcoming
Youth Feedback:

____

____

____

22. Worshipful
Youth Feedback:

____

____

____

Upstanding:

Above-board

Aware-of-wrong-doing

Conscientious

Dedicated [to the Truth]

Ethical

Frank

Having-good-manners

Having-integrity

Honest

Honorable

Just

Moral

Non-pretentious

Respectful

Righteous

Saintly

Scrupulous

Suave

Upright

Valiant

Virtuous

FOOD FOR THOUGHT:

For the Spiritual Man Striving to Become Saint-like

Uplifting Insight(s):

"Therefore, be at Peace with God, whatever you conceive Him to be, and whatever your labors and aspirations in the noisy confusion of life, keep Peace with your soul!"

RULE #16: For Raising a Happy Home:

Be parents who ensure children are entitled to birth within the bonds of matrimony; and that their children are reared by a father and a mother who honour marital vows with complete fidelity.

How to Obtain Guidance [From on High]:

"Everyone of you who has a testimony and bears it is telling about a personal revelation from God. It is nothing less, or it isn't a testimony, because the Holy Ghost revealed it to you. If you have a testimony, it is a revelation." (Spencer W. Kimball)

What Was the Original Church Like?

The Church must practice Sacred Ordinances, such as Baptisms for the Dead:

"For if the dead rise not, then is not Christ raised!"
(I Corinthians 15:16)

"Else what shall they do which are **baptized for the dead**, if the dead rise not at all? Why are they then baptized for the dead?"
(I Corinthians 15:29)

"Behold, I [God] will send you Elijah the Prophet before the Coming of the Great and Dreadful Day of the Lord: And he shall turn the heart of the fathers to the children, and the heart of the children to their fathers, lest I come and smite the earth with a curse."
(Malachi 3:5-6)

Upstanding

Among animals, we may think of the Giraffe, in its tall stature as imitating something (someone) 'upstanding'; or the Llama, with its stiff long neck, as a very erect, honourable and sociable creature.

Job in the Old Testament was noted as an upstanding believer in God: as a man that was "perfect and upright and one that served God, and [shunned] evil" (Job 1:1).

To be upstanding is to be saintly, upright, and conscientiously dedicated to the Faith: one who is just. One such disciple was Jude (in the New Testament) the blood brother to our Lord, who forewarns us that in the Latter Days there will arise 'mockers' who "should walk after their own ungodly lusts", who should be "sensual, having not the Spirit" (Jude 17-19).

We are taught to build up our faith (by contrast to these mockers), to pray in the Holy Ghost, and to keep ourselves in the love of God "looking for the mercy of our Lord Jesus Christ unto eternal life" (Jude 20-21).

33P. Upstanding:

Youth Feedback:

____

____

____

   1. Above-board

Youth Feedback:

____

____

____

   2. Aware-of-wrong-doing

Youth Feedback:

____

____

____

   3. Conscientious

Youth Feedback:

____

____

____

   4. Dedicated [to the Truth]

Youth Feedback:

____

____

____

   5. Ethical

Youth Feedback:

____

____

____

6. Frank

Youth Feedback:

____

____

____

7. Having-good-manners

Youth Feedback:

____

____

____

8. Having Integrity

Youth Feedback:

____

____

____

9. Honest

Youth Feedback:

____

____

____

10. Honourable

Youth Feedback:

____

____

____

11. Just

Youth Feedback:

____

____

____

12. Moral

Youth Feedback:

____

____

____

13. Non-pretentious

Youth Feedback:

____

____

____

14. Respectful

Youth Feedback:

____

____

____

15. Righteous

Youth Feedback:

____

____

____

16. Saintly

Youth Feedback:

____

____

____

17. Scrupulous

Youth Feedback:

____

____

____

18. Suave

Youth Feedback:

____

____

19. Upright

Youth Feedback:

____

____

20. Valiant

Youth Feedback:

____

____

21. Virtuous

Youth Feedback:

____

____

Vigilant:

Acute

Alert

Anxious

Avid

Bearing-all-things

Beyond-rebuke

Cautious

Complete

Examining-all-things

Holistic

Instant-in-Prayer

Keen

Mindful

Praying-without-ceasing

Prompt

Quick

Ready

Seeking-perfection

Sharp

Striving [for The Good]

Wary

Watchful

Wholesome

Wide-awake

FOOD FOR THOUGHT:

For the Spiritual Man Striving to Become Saint-like

Uplifting Insight(s):

"With all it's sham, drudgery, and broken dreams, it is still a beautiful world! Be careful! Strive to be Happy!"

RULE #17: For Raising a Happy Home:

Remember always that: In family relationships there must be mutual sacrifices among the husband, wife, and children, else true love is not there!

How to Obtain Guidance [From on High]:

"You can seek the Almighty in your closets. He is not a God that is afar off; not one whose ears are closed, or whose arm is withdrawn from His children; but He is a God whose eye is upon the humblest creature that lives, of every race and color, and whose love is extended to the whole human family. It is to Him that you should appeal for a testimony of the truth of this work ... And if you will do this, in humility and faith, we have no fear as to the results of your prayers: For God will hear and answer every soul."
(Abraham H. Cannon)

What Was the Original Church Like?

The Church will be known by its fruits, its good deeds:

"Even so every good tree bringeth forth good fruit; but a corrupt tree bringeth forth evil fruit. A good tree cannot bring forth evil fruit, neither can a corrupt tree bring forth good fruit. Every tree that bringeth not forth good fruit is hewn down, and cast into the fire! Wherefore **by their fruits ye shall know them!**" (Matthew 7:17-21)

Vigilant

The classic instance of a *vigilant* creature is, of course, the owl, that appears to be ever watchful, keeping wide-open eyes as he monitors or surveys his immediate surroundings.

In the *Book of Esther*, we see that Queen Esther is ever vigilant for her people, who were all-too-often persecuted by the anti-Semites of her day. Because of Queen Esther's raw courage and her vigilance in seeing to the protection and safety of her people, the Jews, she was able to ward off a great evil to be done against them, turning the tables (as it were) on her enemy, Haman, and saving her people from certain death (Esther 7:1-10).

Peter in the New Testament speaks of this need to be ever vigilant: "Be sober, **be vigilant**; because your adversary the devil, as a roaring lion, walks about seeking whom he may devour" (I Peter 5:8). Peter thus admonishes the Saints to resist the devil, to remain 'steadfast in the faith', that our Lord (after that we may have 'suffered a while' in this life) will make us *perfect* (I Peter 5:9-10).

We see that as an example of *being vigilant* in the faith, Paul praises the saints at Berea who followed our Lord's injunction to 'search the Scriptures' (John 5:39): Who also sought to see if these things spoken of by teachers of the Gospel were actually true (Acts 17:10-12).

Indeed, for vigilance is a virtue that (as the name suggests) entails continually verifying both the sources and content of our Lord's teachings: to see whether those things are true. (Acts 17:11)

34Q. Vigilant:

Youth Feedback:

____

____

____

1. Acute

Youth Feedback:

____

____

____

2. Alert

Youth Feedback:

____

____

____

3. Anxious

Youth Feedback:

____

____

____

4. Avid

Youth Feedback:

____

____

____

5. Bearing-all-things

Youth Feedback:

____

____

____

6. Beyond-rebuke

Youth Feedback:

____

____

____

7. Cautious

Youth Feedback:

____

____

____

8. Complete

Youth Feedback:

____

____

____

9. Examining-all-things

Youth Feedback:

____

____

____

10. Holistic

Youth Feedback:

____

____

____

11. Instant-in-Prayer

Youth Feedback:

____

____

____

12. Keen

Youth Feedback:

____

____

____

13. Mindful

Youth Feedback:

____

____

____

14. Praying-without-ceasing

Youth Feedback:

____

____

____

15. Prompt

Youth Feedback:

____

____

____

16. Quick

Youth Feedback:

____

____

____

17. Ready

Youth Feedback:

____

____

____

18. Seeking-perfection

Youth Feedback:

____

____

____

19. Sharp

Youth Feedback:

____

____

____

20. Striving [for The Good]

Youth Feedback:

____

____

____

21. Wary

Youth Feedback:

____

____

____

22. Watchful

Youth Feedback:

____

____

____

23. Wholesome

Youth Feedback:

____

____

____

24. Wide-awake

Youth Feedback:

____

____

____

Scene iii:
Reflections upon Positive character traits

Reflections Upon (God-fearing) Positive Character Traits

To be 'good' (God-fearing) is a good thing. Something that logicians would call: a tautology (A=A).

Yet in the real world, it is amazing to discern that so many persons shrink from the prospect of doing 'good,' or of being 'good,' although admittedly many persons wish to be well-thought-of, to be considered 'of good report,' praise-worthy, or even godly! (Philippians 4:8)

But the concept of 'God-fearing' is quite something else, something unique in and of itself. When one fears (truly trembles and fears) to disobey God, he holds utmost reverence and love towards his God. Or, to put it in another way: He wishes to do and to say *only* those things that are pleasing in His sight.

And that is all that can be expected of His children: To be obedient, to seek to please 'Heavenly Father,' and to be worshipful and loyal to the bitter end, to the last breath in this mortal probation. It is said of Job, that despite his sufferings and tests, and trials, it never did enter his mind or lips to curse God (Job 2:9-10). On the contrary, Job stated the ultimate creed of all true Christians: "Though He [should] slay me, yet will I trust in Him" (Job 13:15). Would to God that we all could achieve that high level of self-mastery as His Disciples.

In assisting one to become converted to Christ, the words of Don Marquis, come vividly (even forcibly) to mind: "It is very insulting to attempt to reform people. When you behead a person, you leave him his soul as it is. But when you reform him, you change his soul, and it is a dangerous thing to tamper with human souls."

One can especially see the perils of fake (or false) pretexts to a wolfish or demonic 'tampering of a human soul' in our Lord's own words: "Woe unto you, scribes and Pharisees, hypocrites! For ye compass sea and land to make one proselyte, and when he is made, ye make him twofold more the child of hell than yourselves". (Matthew 23:15)

We see then that only the Holy Ghost (Holy Spirit) should (and must) convert the new soul onto Christ, not our own actions. We are to be at best but the instruments of this Godly influence, nothing more.

Youth Feedback:
____

____

____

DISCLAIMER: N.B. (*Nota Bene*)
All tunes/songs/video clips/links/quotes/etc. are herein provided to assist in Group Therapy Sessions, or privately, for individual study (to assist in learning) and for educational purposes *only*.

[#230: U-Tube Reference]
Elvis Presley - Peace In The Valley (With Lyrics) View 1080 HD
https://www.youtube.com/watch?v=1VQS7e27pDw&list=RD8H9T7427Ebl&index=22

(There'll Be) Peace In The Valley
[See, Isaiah 11:6-9; 26:3; 55:12; 65:25; Psalms 4:8; 122:7-8; Revelations 21:4; I Corinthians 15:51-52]

There will be peace in the valley for me, some day
There will be peace in the valley for me, oh Lord I pray
There'll be no sadness, no sorrow

Well the bear will be gentle And the wolves will be tame
And the lion shall lay down by the lamb, oh yes
And the beasts from the wild
Shall be led by a child
And I'll be changed, changed from this creature that I am, oh yes!

Writer: Thomas A. Dorsey

[#231: U-Tube Reference]
The Sounds of Silence (w/explanation by Art Garfunkel & Paul Simon)
https://www.youtube.com/watch?v=y6cR5furQac

[#232: U-Tube Reference]
Simon & Garfunkel - The Sound of Silence (from The Concert in Central Park)
Sounds of Silence [color: Simon & Garfunkel]
https://www.youtube.com/watch?v=NAEppFUWLfc

The Sound Of Silence

"Fools," said I, "You do not know
Silence like a cancer grows
And the people bowed and prayed
To the neon god they made
And the sign flashed out its warning
In the words that it was forming
And the sign said, "The words of the prophets
Are written on the subway walls"

Writer: Simon Paul

[#233: U-Tube Reference]
JUDY COLLINS - Turn Turn Turn (1966).mp4
Turn, turn, Turn [See, Ecclesiastes 3:1-8; 8:5-8]
https://www.youtube.com/watch?v=K3kKqfTjsj0

[#234: U-Tube Reference]
Turn Turn Turn Byrds STEREO HiQ Hybrid JARichardsFilm 720p
https://www.youtube.com/watch?v=bCcFyR0MITQ

Turn! Turn! Turn!

To everything - turn, turn, turn
There is a season - turn, turn, turn
And a time to every purpose under heaven

A time to be born, a time to die
A time to plant, a time to reap
A time to kill, a time to heal

A time for love, a time for hate
A time for peace, I swear it's not too late!

Writer: Seeger Peter

Section Two: The Problem Solved

The Good Wolf Becomes the Good Tiger

Isaiah 1:25, 27; 11:6
Psalms 51:6-7, 10-13
Psalms 19:8-9

Introduction to Section Two

As has been duly noted, the proposed Solutions to the extreme violence problem of the Métis youth (and of youth in general) in our society, is to be found internally. A Great Teacher once said: "For from *within*, out of the heart of men, proceed: evil thoughts, adulteries, fornications, murders, thefts, covetousness, wickedness, deceit, lasciviousness, an evil eye, blasphemy, pride, foolishness: All these evil things come from *within*, and defile the man". (Mark 7:21-23; Matthew 15:16-20). He further adds that to think otherwise, is to "lack understanding" (Mt. 15:16).

Modern moralists often cite the age-old truth: "As a man thinks, so is he!" (Proverbs 23:7). Upon further reflection, we can see that the emotions do indeed affect us: either negatively, or positively. Emotions can kill. [See as well, *Emotional Intelligence,* Daniel Goleman.]

But they can also uplift (and with the use of adrenaline), actually save lives. Accounts are rampant that claim and affirm that in a tragedy, such as in a car accident, mothers were able to overturn cars in order to save a loved one pinned down. Martial Arts (in its mysterious secrets) can accomplish mind-boggling feats, such as a Karate expert being able to shatter several bricks with the naked hand. The evidence is simply overwhelming and need not be argued or demonstrated here.

So, what is the point? Simply this: (Even as Socrates said:) The answer to our own questions are *within* us! The solutions to our many seemingly insoluble issues, and perplexing problems, can be found from *within*. Immanuel Kant, the Great Rationalist, once said (as is now written on his tombstone): "Two things never cease to amaze me: The starry skies without, and the moral law *within*". [See also, *The Brain's Way of Healing* (2015), Norman Doidge.]

Of course, the key indicator to change (or convert) from negative character traits to positive ones is to have the burning desire to do so! The story is told of Archimedes who used to dunk the heads of his wanna-be disciples into a barrel of water until they kicked and waved their hands to be let up. "When you had your head submerged in water," Archimedes would say: "What was the thing you desired the most?!". The student would shout emphatically: "Air!". "Well then," Archimedes would add: "When you desire to study mathematics as much as you desired to breathe air, come and see me!".

So, to desire, truly heartily desire, to become a God-fearing person, one needs to truly believe, to hunger and to thirst after righteousness (Matthew 5:6), to have faith in oneself, as well as in a higher power, faith in God! Without faith, it is impossible to please God (Hebrews 11:6). If one does not desire to please God, then he is a reprobate, a *wandering star* "to whom is reserved that blackness of darkness for ever" (Jude 13).

But more to the point: we have basically two types of personalities: those who seek to have a genuinely active conscience void of offense to God and to their fellow man; and then the other: those who speak lies in hypocrisy "having their conscience seared with a hot iron" (I Timothy 4:2).

Jesus said: "He who is not with me is against me" (Matthew 12:30). What did He mean? Did He mean that there are those who are outside the mercy of God, those who will be cast out, never to enter the Kingdom of God? Let's see what the Scriptures say.

Jesus says in His great intercessory prayer given in Gethsemane: "I pray not for the world, but for them which Thou hast given me"! (John 17:9). What is Jesus saying? Are not all to be saved, to be forgiven, to be blessed, to find Heavenly rest when they die? Apparently not. Read the Word of God! For God does not lie. Neither will He be mocked. What one sows, so shall he reap!

But then how can one become saved? How can one become an acceptable "good and faithful servant", to "enter into the joy of His Lord"? (Matthew 25:21, 23) How can the leopard lose his spots, as the Prophet Jeremiah asks? (Jeremiah 13:23). Can a tiger lose his stripes, and become stripe-less, white as snow? Indeed, can we lose our 'stripes' and be forgiven of all our faults, to become as white as snow?

Isaiah the Prophet clarifies: When he speaks of the future Messiah (who is Christ), he says "But by his (Christ's) stripes we are healed". (Isaiah 53:5) For as the Lord promises through Isaiah the

Prophet: "Though your sins be as scarlet, they shall be as white as snow". (Isaiah 1:18).

The answer to this conversion process is found throughout the prophetic 53rd chapter of Isaiah: Speaking of our Lord, Isaiah states emphatically that God (our Heavenly Father) shall "make His (Christ's) soul an offering for sin" (verse 10).

But there are conditions: This gift of total forgiveness came with a price. Apostle Paul says: "What? Know ye not that .... ye are not your own? For ye are bought with a price"! (I Corinthians 6:19-20).

The price God requires of us is to convert our stony heart into a heart of flesh. (Ezekiel 11:19): That we may accept Jesus as the Christ, the Son of the Living God, to have faith in Him, to the point that one wishes to become like Him, to become Christ-like, to become a Christian.

How is this conversion possible? Consider King Agrippa who is moved to near-conversion as he listens to the Apostle Paul bear his testimony, his conversion story, as follows: When he was first known as 'Saul of Tarsus', he was on his way to Damascus to imprison, persecute, and even to kill Christian believers (having the legal authority from the Jewish leaders in Jerusalem to do so).

En route he had a religious revelation: Christ Himself appeared to Saul and blinded him with the glory of His presence. Saul then realized the error of his ways, and turned himself around ('repented'), which means that Saul now wished to become 'Paul', the negative hateful Saul desired to become the loving understanding 'Paul, the Apostle of our Lord'.

Perhaps this one conversion impressed the teachings and influence of Christianity the world over more than any other conversion story?! But when Paul bore this witness to King Agrippa, the King (although convinced by the veracity of Paul's statements) could at best declare: "Almost you persuade me to become a Christian!" (Acts 26:28).

But *almost* does not cut it. It is not enough! So, after Paul leaves King Agrippa's presence, we never again hear of King Agrippa: It's as if he died or ceased to exist thereafter! It's Paul's story that still remains and resurfaces again and again even to this very day! (Acts 9:1-9; Acts 22:1-16; Acts 26:9-19)

The Final (Proposed) Solution to Youth Crime

What can be said of the Second Part of this Book? The proposed solution is a spiritual solution, an innermost cleansing, conversion of the self, the inner man, the soul, the character of this individual into a new creature (in Christ), into a completely changed, greatly improved 'child of God.! No longer a B.B.-type personality, desiring to inflict violence, or harm on innocent bystanders, and even upon those seeking to help him, to improve and to better his welfare.

But a spiritual self seeks to offer succor, and to secure the trust of those around him, to do the *will* of our Heavenly Father, which is to help one another: Not to look for 'filthy lucre' (to be a mercenary) but to seek the happiness and well-being of one's own kindred, one's own humankind, the purpose for which humanity is on this planet today: To help, not hinder; to become better, not more bitter, with the test and trials life offers each one of us.

Granted that this book offers a positive improvement on the human condition, that it offers hope (in lieu of: despair), let us "put our shoulder to the wheel to push along, to do our duty with a heart full of song" (as one Christian hymn so aptly implores us to do). Yet this happy 'sunshine in the soul' (alas) cannot be for everyone.

There are those, the social misfits (the 'un-popped popcorn') who for whatsoever reason cannot develop even the smallest blade of faith, nor can they find their way, no matter how bright the light shines before them. They can be helped for only a short period of time for as the damaged car battery that cannot 'hold (or maintain) it's charge', once that charger is taken away, they turn stone-cold dead in their feelings for others.

The Judas Iscariots of the world can spend three and a half years watching miracles and good works of our Lord, listening to his countless Sermons, and excellent advice, but at the end of it all, nothing appears to sink into their consciousness, into their understanding, as they fall victim to doubt, and betray the Lord, even with a kiss (Luke 22:47-48).

They purport that their 'conscience' is telling them, forcing them, to do this betrayal, but the truth is: They are *wandering stars*, (Jude 23) 'to whom the mist of darkness is reserved for ever' (2 Peter 2:17). They have no light in themselves, for there is no hope for such reprobates. [Romans 1:28-32; II Peter 2:12]

But not everyone who has poor or negative habits is doomed to fail. On the contrary, there is a second chance given to all those who deep within themselves find this tiny spark (this 'candle in the wind'), a budding desire willing to eventually bloom like a tiny seed, the smallest mustard seed, that sprouts into a great mustard tree! (Matthew 13:31)

With little, seemingly insignificant beginnings, great things can be brought to pass. Consider (for example) the Lord's words that if your faith be as tiny as the smallest grain of a mustard seed, yet if you have even that much faith (or that 'little' faith), you can say to yonder mountain: "Be you removed form hence and it shall be removed!" (Matthew 17:20; Luke 17:6).

So is the magnificent power of even the smallest atomic particle of faith: just like an atomic bomb (when that littlest atom is split) great power (almost beyond belief) can be released! If only you have that iota of true genuine faith in our Lord, in the Powers that Be, in the God of this Universe!

To recap: If B.B. (or anyone else) truly desires to put his (imperfect) past behind him, the way is open and clear, like a path cut into the wild untamed jungle of life, to take hold upon life, to live to the intended extent of his potential: To become a mature well-adjusted adult, to contribute to Society (instead of to contaminate the Golden Moments, the choice opportunities currently offered to him).

Much good can be said of new beginnings: Barabbas, a convicted murderer, condemned to death by the Roman Courts (as recounted in the Bible) was given a second chance at life, (Matthew 27:15-17,21,26; Luke 23:17-19,24-25). As well, Fyodor Dostoevsky who was to be executed in front of a firing squad but (mere moments before his death) a stay of execution arrived!

Dostoevsky saw this merciful pardon as a sign of divine Providence, and later converted to Christianity, whole-heartedly accepting Jesus as the Christ, the Son of the living God!

Also, Lazarus (someone whom Jesus loved dearly; see, John 11:30-36) literally received a new life, a new beginning, as Jesus raised him from the dead, having been dead for four days (John 11:14-17, 38-45). One wonders what did Lazarus do with the extension to his mortal life? No one knows. But I would assume that he was thrilled beyond belief to see his loved ones again, as they were too!

Likewise (in a much smaller way perhaps), I too enjoyed the liberty of a Second Chance at life. For EPS (The Police who watched my attack video) said that it was truly a miracle that my life was spared: That Angels from on High were present fighting to protect me that I should live, to deflect about half of the lethal knife stabs in my direction.

For those twenty-two knife wounds that pierced my body did not end my life, because I was able to successfully survive the blood infections. For those blood infections could easily lead to blood poisoning as the possible threat was there for many weeks thereafter.

Yes, some credit can be given to modern medicine, to our technological advances. But in my own mind, I see that it is by God's *grace* I was saved, after all that I (or the best skilled surgeons) could do. Nothing less!

Youth Feedback:

____

____

____

DISCLAIMER: N.B. (*Nota Bene*)
All tunes/songs/video clips/links/quotes/etc. are herein provided to assist in Group Therapy Sessions, or privately, for individual study (to assist in learning) and for educational purposes *only*.

[#235: U-Tube Reference]
Elvis Presley, "Who Am I" with lyrics, Beautiful Gospel song
https://www.youtube.com/watch?v=0bxPJJ7vhK0

Who Am I?

When I think of how He came so far from glory
Came to dwell among the lowly such as I
To suffer shame and such disgrace
On Mount Calvary take my place
Then I ask myself this question
Who am I?

Who am I that The King would bleed and die for?
Who am I that He would pray not my will, Thy Lord?

Writer: Charles F. Goodman

Section Two:
The Problem Solved (Proposed Solutions)

ACT IV:

Scene i:
The Concept of Conversion:
From Negative to Positive Habits

Our birth is but a sleep and a forgetting;
The Soul that rises with us, our life's Star,
Hath had elsewhere its setting,
And cometh from afar:
Not in entire forgetfulness,
And not in utter nakedness,
But trailing clouds of glory do we come
From God, who is our home:
Heaven lies about us in our infancy!
    William Wordsworth, 1770-1850 (Italics added)

Concept of Conversion: The Metamorphosis of Nature, Both Physical and Spiritual

Yes, I've been granted a second chance at life: It is the goodness, Grace, and merciful bounty of an ever-loving Providence to grant me this Second Lease on Life. Others before me, as even historic figures, such as Lazarus (whom Jesus raised from the dead); and Barabbas (for whom Jesus was substituted that Barabbas might live), all felt as I feel now: A new man, a newborn baby! When I now think of life, I think of each day (as a newborn babe) as a new creation, as John Wayne so aptly describes it:

"Tomorrow (the time that gives a man or a country just one more chance) is just one of many things that I feel are wonderful in life. ... Or Church bells sending out their Invitations. A mother meeting her firstborn. The sound of a kid calling you 'Dad' for the first time. There's a lot of things great about life. But I think tomorrow is the most important thing. Comes in to us at midnight very clean, ya know. It's perfect when it arrives, and it puts itself in our hands. It hopes we've learned something from Yesterday!"

The value of Time can never be underestimated. It is said that *love* is a four-letter word that is spelled: T-I-M-E! There is a lot of powerful truth impacted in that simple phrase, isn't there?! No matter what we may like to do in life, we have only so much *time* allotted to each one of us: Not one minute more!

The story is told (perhaps mythical) that when Queen Elizabeth I was dying, she offered her physician up to one-half of her Kingdom to extend her life for only one year. He replied that he could not extend it for one more month, or one more week, nor even one more day, for all the money in the world!

Of course, the Queen already knew this fact to be true (we may suppose), but the point remains a poignant one: When it is our time to die, no one can take our place: we must face our own death; so likewise: should we all live our own life, as surely as we will die our own death. That is, we should not let someone (or something) else determine what (kind of) life we are to live. We should dare to live, as we will one fine day surely dare to die! That is the cycle of life.

No mystery here: we are born, we live, and then the curtain falls, the music fades, the lights go out, and the play is over. For our life is like a play if we think about it: We come unto the stage (as an observer) when the play has already begun; we stay for a while; and then we must leave before the play ends.

So, while we are here on this earth: we note that, if possible, we would like to help others (all we can) just as 'they' helped us while we were in our formative years. In some cases of abuse and neglect in this critical early phase of life, we keenly feel the lack of love in our lives. As is commonly understood, we are the product (either) of those who love us, or of those who refuse to love us. What we make of the hand of cards Fate deals to us is our choice. Sometimes it is not so much the cards in our hand that determines our outcome, but how (well) we play these cards dealt to us!

The Conversion Process

Now, above and beyond this magic or beauty of nature's metamorphosis (the changing of a slow crawling perhaps even ugly caterpillar into a stunning lovely butterfly that can fly) is the miracle of spiritual conversion! Similar to the birth of new life, life reproducing itself, is the truly amazing new birth of a spiritual being: To change from a hostile natural man (who is self-centered, focused solely on his own personal self-preservation) into a spiritually sensitive caring individual (who sees himself as a part of the greater whole or body) of Society.

What to me is astounding is that life itself is dwarfed in comparison to the benevolence and far-reaching (even eternal) progression of this *new creature* in Christ, this new spiritual creation. It has often been noted that some lovers (who are truly and deeply fond of each other) tend to slowly resemble each other.

I have often heard (in my nearly seven decades of life) that genuine lovers (true *soulmates*, as they are called) can actually predict each other's words, thoughts, and certain actions even before they are apparent or displayed. Something akin to the paradox common among sets of twins: as telepathy, or the meeting, or union of minds!

Of course, genuine lasting permanent conversion to a principle (or set of principles) connected to a religious (or political) platform of beliefs can appear desirable by those 'outsiders' who view that process from afar (or outside the 'web of belief'). Consider for instance the excitement noted by a German citizen during one of Hitler's Nazi rallies:

"Goose pimples rose all over me, my hair stood on end, my eyes filled with tears of love and gratitude for this greatest of all conquerors of human misery and shame, and my breath came in little gasps. If I had not known that the Leader would have scorned such adulation, I might have fallen to my knees in unashamed worship. But instead, I drew myself to attention (raised my arm in the eternal salute of the ancient Roman Legions) and repeated the holy words, "Heil Hitler!" (George Lincoln Rockwell)

As we can see in sports games, political speeches, religious services, sometimes the listener (or outside observer) finds himself overcome with the desire to belong (to attach himself) to this or that particular set of beliefs, or doctrines, but lacks the emotional or spiritual catalyst to do so.

The Spiritual Conversion

What I have found from my own personal direct experience is that in spiritual matters (in particular) there can be an accessibility of contact (or communication) with higher powers if we pay the price, if we allow our spirit (and personality) to be carved, or created, or molded by a divine yet real presence of the Holy Ghost (typically referred to as: The Holy Spirit of God).

In this particular work, I have addressed the most rudimentary (or basic) understanding of the Christian believer, as one who is Spirit-filled and follows doctrine (through personal revelation) for his walk with God. As Moses talked with God, "face to face, as a man speaks with his friend" [Exodus 33:11], so I believe can the truly humble converted follower (disciple) of our Lord do likewise.

We see this form of communication in part through Francis D'Assisi, the Joan of Arcs, Joseph Smiths, and other impressionable souls who sought to learn (and hence to do) the straightforward will of God.

In the follow-up Edition (the so-called 'Second Edition'), to this work, it is my intention *Deo Volente* ('God Willing') to present a finished product (one that will hopefully glean the many insights and ideas presented or to be presented in the current e-book version of this First Edition). For those followers who have begun to walk the path towards 'perfecting the Saints', a more detailed analysis (both psychologically and philosophically) will be presented: To begin the walk on the pathway to Holiness, and Sanctification.

But we cannot run before we can walk! It is imperative to 'catch the vision' (which is actually not that difficult if we work at it: "precept upon precept; line upon line; here a little, and there a little"; see, Isaiah 28:10,13). James, the blood brother to our Lord (Matthew 13:55) states in his brief but piercing and powerful Epistle that we ought not to presume upon ourselves that we would be able to do this or that (thing) in the future. We need instead to be always mindful of the *will* of our Lord in each of our lives.

As James succinctly put it in his own words: "Go to now, ye that say, Today or tomorrow we will go into such a city, and continue there a year, and buy and sell, and get gain: Whereas ye know not what shall be on the morrow. For what is your life? It is even a vapour, that appears for a little time, and then vanishes away! For that ye ought to say, If the Lord will, we shall live, and do this or that." (James 4:13-15)

So, it is with this strict adherence to the *will* of the Lord that I likewise comment regarding this (much) anticipated up-and-coming Second Edition as a confirmation (and perhaps even a conclusion) of this new project, a new view (even a vision) of how we may progress spiritually, morally, and even divinely, into the Presence of our Lord.

God's grace and goodness are needed now perhaps more than ever before, as we enter into the last leg of civilization before His Beloved Son returns to save us from ourselves (see, Revelation 11:17-18; II Thessalonians 2:8; Matthew 24:3, 21-22, 36-39; Luke 21:7, 25-28; cf. Genesis 6:5-7,11-13; Luke 17:26-30).

My advice and admonition to all my readers (those who can see the merit in this marvellous work) is to work at their individual self-improvement one day at a time, to master one principle at a time: for with the reinforced habit of regular self-introspection, miracles can indeed happen.

And this reality should not confound, nor contradict, one's own inner sense of well-being, as it is the most natural and plainest of all expressions this life can afford. When it comes right down to it, when we analyze the molecular structure of life itself, and come to the atomic component parts, and sub-atomic particles, we will see (as if in a new revelation, or flash of perfect insight) that life itself is a miracle. No wonder then, that all life has to offer at its core, at it's innermost centre, is itself: the miracle of miracles!

Conversion (especially religious conversion) has at times appeared to occur in an instant, as the conversion of Saul of Tarsus en route to Damascus. But when we more carefully unravel and examine the events leading up to that metamorphosis, we see that (as with the example of the cocoon which the caterpillar spins around itself) many other factors (some unseen and unknown) are at play, to orchestrate the final product.

When a woman gives birth, her time comes when it comes: so likewise, the conversion one experiences can melt one into submission (not through fear or fright or force but) as cold butter melts in the presence of (and exposure to) the hot sun in a sweltering Summer's Day.

It is all perfectly normal, natural, and in no way disruptive of one's own self-esteem, or feelings of self-worth. The lesser submits to the greater, the willing servant to the merciful Master; the child to his father; and the disciple to his Lord: All is as it should be. All is in perfect order. All is well in the end!

Scene ii:
To Convert from Caligula to Casper

Perhaps the most challenging of all conversions is to convert from someone as dreaded and dead spiritually as Caligula, oft acclaimed as the most perverse, and evil of all the Roman Emperors (as the Roman Empire dipped and descended into the darkest history known to man, prior to the Dark Ages).

[BBC (British Broadcasting Corporation) has produced an MTV (Made-for-TV) version of the Caligula Saga.] His story is frightful: The depraved mindset of a virtually totally unhinged Emperor coupled with virtually unlimited power to do as he pleased with whomsoever he willed. [Caligula in this work is represented (or thought of) as a dark (midnight) character living in the shadows of lower existence (the underground, as Dostoevsky would describe it).]

Caligula is best seen as a 'black wolf' or 'black fox' just as the documentary on the personality of Adolf Hitler is entitled: "The Black Fox" (1962) or The Grey Wolf: The Escape of Adolf Hitler (2014). The word, *black*, is not intended in the least as a racist statement (or slur). It is merely to use 'night and day' as terms suited to evil or good persons: The way that the old Western movies used to portray the bad guy as the one wearing the black hat, and the good guy as the one wearing the white hat. (A bit stereotypical, I admit, but it serves the purpose of simplicity in this work).

In contrast to Caligula, at the opposite end of the spectrum is: 'Casper' (originally, taken from the animated cartoons, "Casper, the Friendly Ghost"; and later the movie series of *Casper*, from 1995-2006). Casper *in this work* is portrayed as a friendly white tiger (or lion) which represents the mammoth-like power of good over evil, just as the light at daybreak overwhelms the darkness of the night. The night instantly yields to the bright early morning sun and is immediately dispelled or dissipated thereby. The darkness cannot in any way resist the light.

The Caligula-persona seeks to hurt people, whereas the Casper-persona seeks to help people. I think of two conversion stories (both true) along this line:

(1) The one, entitled: *The Cross and The Switchblade*, is the conversion of Nicky Cruz, a New York Gang-leader. This true story (made into a movie, *The Cross and the Switchblade,* 1970) depicts an idealistic (perhaps naive) New York City minister, David Wilkerson, who attempts to convert a rather violent hot-tempered street gangster, Nicky Cruz. The hoodlum gangster listens to the Preacher preach while he, Nicky Cruz the gangster, is bound and determined that this will be David Wilkerson's last sermon.

But something unusual happens, not at all what Nicky Cruz expected: The Holy Spirit enters into Nicky Cruz giving him an overwhelmingly compassionate feeling that brings him to tears while he is listening to this Preacher preach his 'last sermon'. This hardened criminal turns to Christ and becomes a part of the Billy Graham Crusades.

(2) The second conversion is the classic conversion story of Saul of Tarsus (referred to earlier). Saul of Tarsus as a fanatical persecutor of the Christian sect (following the death of our Lord) is en route to Damascus with legal papers authorizing him to persecute, imprison, and even to put to death any Christians hiding in that region. (Acts 7:58-60; 8:1-3; 9:1-5; 22:3-5, 19-20; 26:9-11)

But on his way there, he has a most startling revelation! From seeking to hurt the Christian people, Saul comes head-on to a burning vision (akin to the vision Moses had with the burning bush, see Exodus 3:2-5; Acts 7:30-33). A loud voice speaks through the brightness of the light saying: "Saul, Saul, why do you persecute me?". Saul falls to his knees at this overpowering vision, asking: "Who are you, Lord?". The Lord answers Paul: "I am Jesus, whom you persecute!" [Acts 26:9-15]

After this blinding vision, Saul of Tarsus becomes converted to the Christian *way* (Acts 9:2; 22:4), much to the chagrin of his Jewish masters in Jerusalem. And the rest, as they say, is history: Saul becomes Paul the Apostle, perhaps the greatest single influence for Christianity in those early years of the Pristine Church until this day?! (cf. Acts 22:14-15, 21; 26:15-18).

Religious Conversion

But what exactly is involved in the Conversion process? William James, in his book *Varieties of Religious Experience*, offers this insight:

"How real, definite, and memorable an event, a sudden conversion may be to him who has the experience. ... Theology, combining this fact with the doctrines of election and grace, has concluded that the Spirit of God is with us at these dramatic moments in a peculiarly miraculous way, unlike what happens at any other juncture of our lives. At that moment, ... an absolutely new nature is breathed into us, and we become partakers of the very substance of the Deity."

It appears that the determining factor, the catalyst, as it were, in this conversion process from Caligula to Casper is of a spiritual dimension, and not simply an emotional or psychological experience. Communication from our physical dimensional reality to that of the 'other side' is present in this conversion.

For without a divine experiential interaction between these two world views (these two apparent realities) there cannot be genuine credibility. For example, Paul the Apostle testified of what he knew to be true but was nevertheless labeled 'mad' by Governor Festus (Acts 26:24) who refused to acknowledge a spiritual reality.

The Apostle Peter, also aware of disbelief among the populace, points out that what he (and the other Apostles with him) experienced on the Mount of Transfiguration was no 'cunningly devised fable', but the truth spoken by "holy men of God... as they were moved by the Holy Ghost" (II Peter 1:16-21).

In this book, 'Caligula' is represented by the big bad wolf, whereas 'Casper' (originally, the *white* friendly ghost) is represented by the *white* wolf morphed into a *white* tiger (without any black stripes) and ultimately into a giant *white* lion, the lion of righteousness (Proverbs 28:1).

The Old Testament prophet Jeremiah once asked: "Can the Ethiopian change his skin [colour], or the leopard his spots?" He then answers his own questions: "Then may ye also do good, that are accustomed to do evil"! (Jeremiah 13:23).

But the startling truth is that even as we can find today a purely white tiger (without 'spots' or stripes), or a purely white lion, so likewise (in a deeper spiritual way) can a Caligula convert into a Casper (Isaiah 11:6). For, as Jesus said: "With God, all things are possible"! (Matthew 19:26; Mark 10:27)

   Youth Feedback:
____

____

____

DISCLAIMER: N.B. (*Nota Bene*)
All tunes/songs/video clips/links/quotes/etc. are herein provided to assist in Group Therapy Sessions, or privately, for individual study (to assist in learning) and for educational purposes *only*.

[#236: U-Tube Reference]
David Wilkerson -- The Vision 1973
https://www.youtube.com/watch?v=c2gBTY70-mY

[#237: U-Tube Reference]
Nicky Cruz story & Testimony
https://www.youtube.com/watch?v=cc6KgYiaB60

The New (or Second) Birth

The need for a new (or second) birth has been with mankind throughout the Ages of Time. It may be referred to as a reawakening or a rediscovering of oneself or of one's relationship with another: William James once described this revolution or, rebirth in a married relationship, as follows: "Two different persons, both of whose wedded lives had been beautiful from the beginning, relate that not until a year or more after marriage did, they awake to the full blessedness of married life. So, it is with the religious experience."

But the philosopher-psychologist William James also describes the opposite: How it is possible for some persons never to experience this 'new or second birth', as follows:

"Some persons, ... never are, and possibly never under any circumstances could be, converted. Religious ideas cannot become the center of their spiritual energy: They may be excellent persons, servants of God in practical ways, but they are not children of His kingdom. ... They are life-long subjects of *barrenness and dryness.* To the end of their days, they refuse to believe, their personal energy never gets to its religious center, and the latter remains inactive in perpetuity."

Even Albert Einstein has something to say about this 'mystical' feeling of the *new birth*:

> "The most beautiful emotion we can experience is the mystical. ... He to whom this emotion is a stranger, who can no longer wonder and stand rapt in awe, is as good as dead. To know *that what is impenetrable to us* really exists, manifesting itself as the highest wisdom and the most radiant beauty, ... This knowledge, this feeling, is at the centre of *true* religiousness. In this sense, and in this sense only, I belong to the rank of devoutly religious men."

This 'mystical feeling' is further expounded, as "the bedrock of religious faith. In it the soul, acting as a unity with all its faculties, rises above itself and becomes Spirit; it asserts its claim to be a citizen of Heaven"! (Dean William Ralph Inge)

How are we to inwardly develop this *mystical experience* is explained by Herman Hesse: "We must become so alone, so utterly alone, that we withdraw into our innermost self. It is a way of bitter suffering. But then our solitude is overcome, we are no longer alone, for we find that our innermost self is the Spirit, that it is God, the Indivisible. And suddenly we find ourselves in the midst of the world, yet undisturbed by its multiplicity, for in our innermost soul we know ourselves to be one with all Being."

In summary, Don Marquis captures this self-same sentiment: "All religion, all life, all art, all expression come down to this: to the effort of the human soul to break through its barrier of loneliness, of intolerable loneliness, and to make some contact with another seeking soul, or with what all souls seek, which is (by any name): God"!

To better understand what it is to experience this *mystical feeling*, I like Milton R. Hunter's description the best: "One feels the power of the Holy Ghost enter his body as if it were a wave of electricity. While he is under that spiritual influence, he experiences an indescribable joy throughout his whole being. Yes, he feels a love for everybody, and everything far surpassing his natural ability to feel love and joy on other occasions. ... Such a dynamic experience leaves a lasting impression on the recipient that times does not dim and that he can never deny."

Youth Feedback:

____

____

____

DISCLAIMER: N.B. (*Nota Bene*)
All tunes/songs/video clips/links/quotes/etc. are herein provided to assist in Group Therapy Sessions, or privately, for individual study (to assist in learning) and for educational purposes *only*.

[#238: U-Tube Reference]
Donovan & Crystal Gayle - Catch The Wind
https://www.youtube.com/watch?v=TMknrmuDD0o&pbjreload=10

Catch The Wind

In the warm hold of your love and mine

To feel you all around me
And to take your hand along the sand

For me to love you now
Would be the sweetest thing 'twould make me sing

For standin' in your heart
Is where I want to be and long to be
Ah, but I may as well try and catch the wind.

Writer(s): Donovan Leitch

A. To be Born Again:

1. Let us be clear on one point here: there are those who saw the miracles of our Lord (as did Judas Iscariot and the Jewish religious leaders of Christ's Day, The Scribes and Pharisees) who still refused to believe in Him, as the Son of God, who refused to allow the Spirit of God to convert them that they may become 'born again'.

Jesus makes this point with regard to the 5,000 persons He fed through the miracle of multiplying five barley loaves of bread and two small fish (John 6:5-13):

"When the people, therefore, saw that Jesus was not there, neither His disciples, they also took shipping, and came to Capernaum, seeking for Jesus. And when they had found Him on the other side of the sea, they said unto Him, Rabbi, when camest Thou hither? Jesus answered them and said, Verily, verily, I say unto you, Ye seek Me, not because ye saw the miracles, but because ye did eat of the loaves, and were filled.

Labour not for the meat which perishes, but for that meat which endures unto everlasting life, which the Son of Man shall give unto you: Then said they unto Him, What shall we do, that we might work the works of God? Jesus answered and said unto them, This is the work of God, that ye believe on Him whom He has sent... *It is the Spirit that quickens; the flesh profits nothing:* the words that I speak unto you, they are Spirit, and they are life.

But there are some of you that believe not. For Jesus knew from the beginning who they were that believed not, and who should betray Him... From that time many of His disciples went back, and walked no more with Him." (John 6:24-29,63-64,66)

Jesus makes it crystal clear that "Except a man be born again, he cannot see the Kingdom of God" (John 3:3). Nicodemus (a Jewish leader in the Sanhedrin, the Jewish Assembly in Jerusalem) asks Jesus: 'How can a man be 'born again' when he is old? Can he enter the second time into his mother's womb and be born?" (v.4). But Jesus answers him that: "Except a man be born of water [by baptism] and of the Spirit [by the Holy Ghost], he cannot enter the Kingdom of God" (v.5).

Jesus then explains: "That which is born of the flesh is flesh; and that which is born of the Spirit is spirit. Marvel not that I said unto you, Ye must be born again. The wind blows where it lists [wants], and you hear the sound thereof, but cannot tell whence it comes, and whither it goes: so is every one that is born of the Spirit." (vv.6-8)

We can see that the Spirit of God (like a fire) is burning in the hearts of all true believers. But then again there are others, the deadwood, the driftwood, the unpopped popcorn, who no matter how much the Spirit of God is burning, feel nothing, react as if they were totally spiritually dead.

As Loren C. Dunn describes it: "We're told even the devils believe [James 2:19], but it hasn't make any difference in their lives. Then there are those who love the truth, and when that happens their lives change. When that happens, they live the principles of the Gospel of Jesus Christ even when they're on a desert island all by themselves, because they love the truth, and they are committed to that principle of testimony so much that it has changed their lives."

To go back to William James, we see that: "The real witness of the Spirit to the *second birth* is to be found only in the disposition of the genuine child of God, the permanently patient heart, the love of self eradicated."

2. There are of course other ways to be 're-born' in the sense of altering one's personal identity other than through the monastic approach of life in a monastery or in a nunnery, such as: military training, Police Academy training, or Security or Law Enforcement special training, through Martial Arts, or even belonging to a gang to develop a hoodlum identity, or by joining a big business, or Corporation, to join a law firm, or public transit company, or any number of a host of specialized training centers, to be dedicated to an art form (such as painting, sketching, music, or writing). But the bottom line remains that nothing really changes a person internally (or psychologically) as much as the *religious conversion*.

As R.M. Burke describes his own religious conversion:
"I was ... letting ideas, images, and emotions flow of themselves, as it were, through my mind. All at once, without warning of any

kind, I found myself wrapped in a flame-coloured cloud. ...
The next [thing] I knew the fire was within myself. Directly afterward there came upon me a sense of exultation, of immense joyousness accompanied or immediately followed by an intellectual illumination impossible to describe. ... I became conscious in myself of eternal life."

Youth Feedback:
____

____

____

Points to Ponder:

1. John 3:5-6

"Jesus answered, Verily, verily, I say unto thee, Except a man be born of water and of the Spirit, he cannot enter into the Kingdom of God. That which is born of the flesh is flesh; and that which is born of the Spirit is spirit."

2. Romans 8:5-8

"For they that are after the flesh do mind the things of the flesh; but they that are after the Spirit the things of the Spirit. For to be carnally minded is death; but to be spiritually minded is life and peace. Because the carnal mind is enmity against God: for it is not subject to the law of God, neither indeed can be. So then they that are in the flesh cannot please God."

3. John 3:3

"Jesus answered and said unto him [Nicodemus], Verily, verily, I say unto thee, Except a man be born again, he cannot see the Kingdom of God.

4. John 1:12-13

"But as many as received Him, to them gave He power to become the Sons of God, even to them that believe on His name:

Which were born, not of blood, nor of the will of the flesh, nor of the will of man, but of God."

5. I John 2:29

"If ye know that He is righteous, ye know that every one that doeth righteousness if born of Him."

6. Titus 3:4-7

"But after the kindness and love of God our Saviour toward man appeared, Not by works of righteousness which we have done, but according to His mercy He saved us, by the washing of the regeneration, and the renewing of the Holy Ghost; Which He shed on us abundantly through Jesus Christ our Saviour; That being justified by His grace, we should be made heirs according to the hope of Eternal Life.

7. James 1:18

"Of His own will begat He us with the Word of Truth, that we should be a kind of first-fruits of His creatures."

8. I Peter 1:3

"Blessed be the God and Father of the our Lord Jesus Christ, which according to His abundant mercy hath begotten us again unto a lively hope by the resurrection of Jesus Christ from the dead."

9. Isaiah 43:7

"Even every one that is called by My name: for I have created him for My glory, I have formed him: Yea, I have made him."

10. II Corinthians 5:17

"Therefore if any man be in Christ, he is a new creature: old things are passed away; behold, all things are become New."

11. Romans 6:4

"Therefore we are buried with Him by baptism into death: that like as Christ was raised up from the dead by the Glory of the Father, even so we also should walk in newness of life."

12. Ephesians 2:13-18

"But now in Christ Jesus ye who sometimes were far off are made nigh by the blood of Christ. For He is our Peace, who hath made both one, and hath broken down the middle wall of partition between us; Having abolished in His flesh the enmity, even the law of commandments contained in the ordinances; for to make in Himself of twain one New man, so making peace;

And that He might reconcile both unto God in one body by the cross, having slain the enmity thereby; And came and preached Peace to you which were afar off, and to them that were nigh. That through Him we both have access by one Spirit unto the Father."

13. Ezekiel 36:26-27

"A New heart also will I give unto you, and a New Spirit will I put within you: and I will take away the stony heart out of your flesh, and I will give you an heart of flesh. And I will put My Spirit within you, and cause you to walk in My statutes, and ye shall keep My judgments, and do them."

14. Romans 7:22

"For I delight in the Law of God after the inward man."

15. II Peter 1:2,4

"Grace and Peace be multiplied unto you through the knowledge of God, and of Jesus our Lord... Whereby are given unto us exceeding great and precious promises: that by these ye might be partakers of the divine nature, having escaped the corruption that is in the world through lust."

16. Ephesians 4:22-24

"That ye put off concerning the former conversation the old man, which is corrupt according to the deceitful lusts; And be renewed in the Spirit of your mind; And that ye put of the New man, which after God is created in righteousness and true holiness."

17. Romans 8:29

"For whom He did foreknow, He also did predestinate to be conformed to the image of His Son, that He might be the Firstborn among many brethren."

18. I John 3:9

"Whosoever is born of God doth not commit sin; for his seed remaineth in him: and he cannot sin, because he is born of God."

19. I John 5:1-2

"Whosoever believeth that Jesus is the Christ is born of God: and everyone that loveth Him that begat loveth Him that is begotten of Him. By this we know that we love the children of God, when we love God, and keep His commandments."

20. I John 2:29

"If ye know that He is righteous, ye know that everyone that doeth righteousness if born of Him."

21. I John 4:7

"Beloved, let us love one another: for love is of God; and everyone that loveth is born of God, and knoweth God."

B. To Recognize the New Birth: The Second Blessing

William James in his masterpiece, *The Varieties of Religious Experience*, describes how we might recognize the 'new birth', as follows:

"It is natural that those who personally have traversed such an experience [the second birth] should carry away a feeling of its being a miracle rather than a natural process. Voices often heard, lights seen, or visions witnessed; ... and it always seems, after the surrender of the personal will, as if an extraneous higher power had flooded in and taken possession. ... The sincere Christian is quite a new fabric, from the foundation to the top-stone. He is a new man, a new creature."

1. To recognize the validity of the second birth does not come to all Christians. Paul says that we need to rightly divide the word of truth, to study the Scriptures, to show ourselves "approved unto God" (II Timothy 2:15). He goes on to say that we should not be 'double-tongued' but to hold 'the mystery of the faith in a pure conscience' (I Timothy 3:8-9). We do not know the things which God has prepared for us, for those whom He loves, except that He reveals those things to us "by His Spirit: for the Spirit searches all things, yea, the things of God" (I Corinthians 2:9-10).

Paul goes on to explain: "For what man knows the things of a man, save the spirit of man which is in him? Even so the things of God knows no man, but the Spirit of God. Now we have received, not the spirit of the world, but the spirit of God; that we might know the things that are freely given to us of God. Which things also we speak, not in the words which man's wisdom teaches, but which the Holy Ghost teaches; comparing spiritual things with spiritual. But the natural man receives not the things of the Spirit of God: for they are foolishness unto him: neither can he know them, because they are spiritually discerned." (I Corinthians 2:11-14).

There are persons pretending to be teachers of the truth, Paul says, who speak lies in hypocrisy: "having their conscience seared with a hot iron" (I Timothy 4:1-2). Paul admits that of sinners, he was chief (before his conversion, his second birth) but he points out that we need to avoid 'vain jangling' of those who 'desire to be teachers of the law' but who understand neither what they say, nor whereof they affirm (I Timothy 1:12-15, 6-7).

These are they who are not aware of true Christian principles, that are necessary for a full and faithful fellowship with the Saints. The Apostle Peter gives graphic detail as to the falling away in the faith of these hapless souls, saying that "it had been better for them [the apostates] not to have known the way of righteousness, than, after they have known it, to turn from the holy Commandment delivered unto them"! (II Peter 2:21).

He then adds: "But it is happened unto them according to the true proverb [Proverbs 26:11], The dog is turned to his own vomit again; and the sow that was washed to her wallowing in the mire [Jeremiah 48:26]" (II Peter 2:2). I'm reminded of the Russian proverb that says: "No matter how many times you feed a wolf, he will still return to the forest"! Some people never can change or convert even to their betterment (Acts 26:28).

2. But for those who recognize the eternal value and worth of the second chance at life, the second birth, life begins anew. It is a glorious dream, there is no end to the sweet fruits of the Holy Spirit (Philippians 4:6-9; Galatians 5:22-25; II Corinthians 9:8-11). One feels (perhaps for some previously lost souls: See, I Corinthians 6:9-11; 14:38) that life is truly worth living: that no matter what happens to one for the remainder of his days, whether for good or ill, it really doesn't matter anymore! (cf. I Peter 1:13-14, 23; 2:1-3; 3:13-17)

As Martin Luther King, Jr. puts it: "We've been to the mountain: we have seen the vision! God is with us!" For this realization, this transformation of spirit, when it comes down to it: It is all that matters! Nothing else really matters anymore, now does it?

The full comprehension that you have put your hand to the plow (figuratively speaking, see, Luke 9:62), knowing that there is no looking back (Luke 17:31-32), this coming to the knowledge of the goodness of our Lord God fills me with Heavenly joy, a joy that cannot be gainsaid or lightly diminished. It is one of the sweetest fruits of the Spirit and one which will buoy you up, come what may. You may be fed to the lions, or sawn in half, or suffer any of the cruelties the early Saints and Prophets did before you, and throughout it all: the Lord your God will be with you to the bitter end. He will never leave you, nor abandon you! You are one with Him! Whether in life or in death, it is all the same: you will experience perfect peace, as one eternal round.

As Martin Luther King, Jr. describes this feeling of conversion (not long before his martyrdom): "At that moment I experienced the presence of the Divine as I had never before experienced Him. It seemed as though I could hear the quiet assurance of an inner voice, saying, 'Stand up for righteousness, stand up for Truth. God will be at your side forever.' Almost at once, my fears began to pass from me. My uncertainty disappeared. I was ready to face anything... God had given me inner calm."

Youth Feedback:
____

____

____

1. Experiencing Converted Feelings of Fellowship and Satisfaction:

Youth Feedback:

____

____

____

Points to Ponder:

(a) II Corinthians 7:1,11

"Having therefore these promises, dearly beloved, let us cleanse ourselves from all filthiness of the flesh and spirit, perfecting holiness in the fear of God... For behold this selfsame thing, that ye sorrowed after a godly sort, what carefulness it wrought in you, yea, what clearing of yourselves, yea, what indignation, yea, what fear, yea, what vehement desire, yea, what zeal, yea, what revenge! In all things ye have approved yourselves to be clear in this matter."

(b) Ephesians 3:14-19

"For this cause, I bow my knees unto the Father of our Lord Jesus Christ, Of Whom the whole family in heaven and earth is named, That He would grant you, according to the riches of His glory, to be strengthened with might by His Spirit in the inner man; That Christ may dwell in your hearts by faith; that ye, being rooted and grounded in love, May be able to comprehend with all Saints what is the breath, and length, and depth, and height; And to know the love of Christ, which passeth knowledge, that ye might be filled with all the fullness of God."

(c) Colossians 3:2-3,9-10,15-17

"Set your affections on things above, not on things on the earth. For ye are dead, and your life is hid with Christ in God... Lie not one to another, seeing that ye have put off the old man with his deeds; And have put on the New man, which is renewed in knowledge after the image of Him that created him... And let the Peace of God rule in your hearts, to the which also ye are called in one body; and be ye thankful. Let the Word of Christ dwell in you richly in all wisdom; teaching and admonishing one another in psalms and hymns and spiritual songs, singing with Grace in your hearts to the Lord. And whatsoever ye do in Word or Deed, do all in the name of the Lord Jesus, giving thanks to God and the Father by Him."

(d) I Thessalonians 5:9,15,18,22-23

"For God hath not appointed us to wrath, but to obtain salvation by our Lord Jesus Christ... See that none render evil for evil unto any man; but ever follow that which is good, both among yourselves, and to all men... In everything give thanks: for this is the Will of God in Christ Jesus concerning you... Abstain from all appearance of evil. And the very God of Peace sanctify you wholly; and I pray God your whole Spirit and soul and body be preserved blameless unto the Coming of our Lord Jesus Christ."

(e) Hebrews 10:4,9,10,12-20,22-24

"For it is not possible that the blood of bulls and of goats should take away sins!... Then said He, Lo, I come to do Thy will, O God... By the which Will we are sanctified through the offering of the body of Jesus Christ once for all... But this Man, after He had offered one sacrifice for sins for ever, sat down on the right hand of God; henceforth expecting till His enemies be made His footstool.

For by one offering He hath perfected for ever them that are sanctified. Whereof the Holy Ghost also is a witness to us: for after that He had said before, This is the Covenant that I will make with them after those days, saith the Lord, *I will put My laws into their hearts, and in their minds will I write them;* And their sins and iniquities will I remember no more.

Now where remission of these is, there is no more offering for sin. Having therefore, brethren, boldness to **enter into the holiest by the blood of Jesus, By a New and Living way,** which he hath consecrated for us, through the veil, that is to say, His flesh...

Let us draw near with a true heart in full assurance of faith, having our hearts sprinkled from an evil conscience, and our bodies washed with pure water. Let us hold fast the profession of our faith without wavering; (for He is faithful that promised;) And let us consider one another to provoke unto love and to good works."

(f) Hebrews 13:20-21

"Now the God of Peace, that brought again from the dead our Lord Jesus, that Good Shepherd of the sheep, through the blood of the Everlasting Covenant, Make you perfect in every good work to do His will, working in His sight, through Jesus Christ; to Whom be glory for ever and ever. Amen!"

2. Rich Promises of God to Become Fellow-citizens with the Saints, to Become Heirs of His Glory:

Youth Feedback:

____

____

____

Points to Ponder:

(a) Galatians 3:7,13-14,16,22-29

"Know ye therefore that they which are of faith, the same are the children of Abraham... Christ hath redeemed us from the curse of the Law, being made a curse for us: for it is written, Cursed is everyone that hangeth on a tree: That the blessing of Abraham might come on the Gentiles through Jesus Christ; that we might receive the promise of the Spirit through faith... Now to Abraham and his seed were the promises made. He saith not, And to seeds, as of many; but as of one, And to thy seed, which is Christ!...

But the Scripture hath concluded all under sin, that the promise by faith of Jesus Christ might be given to them that believe. But before faith came, we were kept under the law, shut up unto the faith which should afterwards be revealed. Wherefore the Law was our schoolmaster to bring us unto Christ that we might be justified by faith. But after that faith is come, we are no longer under a schoolmaster.

For ye are all the children of God by faith in Christ Jesus. For as many of you as have been baptized into Christ have put on Christ. There is neither Jew nor Greek, there is neither bond nor free, there is neither male nor female: for ye are all one in Christ Jesus. And if ye be Christ's, then are ye Abraham's seed, and heirs according to the promise."

(b) Hebrews 3:7-14,18-19

"Wherefore (as the Holy Ghost saith, Today if ye will hear His voice, Harden not your hearts, as in the provocation, in the day of temptation in the wilderness: when your fathers tempted me, proved me, and saw my works forty years. Wherefore I was grieved with that generation, and said, They do always err in their heart; and they have not known My ways. So I sware in My wrath, They shall not enter into My rest).

 Take heed, Brethren, lest there be in any of you an evil heart of unbelief, in departing from the living God. But exhort one another daily, while it is called Today; lest any of you be hardened through the deceitfulness of sin, For we are made partakers of Christ, if we hold the beginning of our confidence stedfast unto the end!...

And to whom sware He that they should not enter into His rest, but to them that believed not? So we see that they could not enter in because of unbelief."

(c) Hebrews 4:1-3,6,11

"Let us therefore fear, lest, a promise being left us of entering into His rest, any of you should seem to come short of it. For unto us was the Gospel preached, as well as unto them: but the Word preached did not profit them, not being mixed with faith in them that heard it. For we which have believed do enter into rest...

Seeing therefore it remaineth that some must enter therein, and they to whom it was first preached entered not in because of unbelief... Let us labor therefore to enter into that rest, lest any man fall after the same example of unbelief!"

C. To Have Faith: What is Faith?

To recognize the New Birth is to have *faith* in Christ:

Faith in Christ brings us to believe in God (I Peter 1:21); yet in order to develop this belief, it begins as a tiny (mustard-like) seed, the mere desire *to have the desire* to believe in Christ. As is oft said: We may believe, but we need help for our unbelief. Or, as one writer puts it: "The best way to develop faith is to starve your doubts".

In keeping with the two-wolf analogy, we can see it all depends on which wolf you may choose to feed, after all! Or, in the case of the budding seed, whether we choose to water it and care for it, to allow it to grow into a mighty tree. Eventually, when this seed inside us (to mix metaphors here) begins to grow, our initial mere desire to believe grows (or evolves) into a firm conviction which in turn becomes a staunch faith in our Lord.

To believe in God means: to believe in His existence, His living presence, in our lives. So then, we need to examine ourselves, to see whether we are in the faith or not (II Corinthians 13:5): Firstly, to define what is this faith we purport to believe in? Peter asks every Christian believer to always be ready "to give an answer to every man that asks you *a reason of the hope* that is in you" (I Peter 3:15).

And, secondly, to do so, we need to have a testimony based on an inner conviction, a deep faith that eliminates fear and doubt. We can believe in the sun, even if it isn't shining; and in love, even when we are alone; so can we believe in God even when He is silent. As Johnny Cash puts it: "When you stand with Him, you must renew the stand daily; you must daily be on guard: the hounds of hell are not going to stop snapping at your heels. The devil and his demons aren't going to give up on you as long as they can find a vulnerable spot once in a while."

Youth Feedback:
____

____

____

[#239: U-Tube Reference]
Simon & Garfunkel - Bridge over Troubled Water (from The Concert in Central Park)
https://www.youtube.com/watch?v=WrcwRt6J32o

Bridge Over Troubled Water

When you're weary, feeling small,
When tears are in your eyes
I will dry them all
I'm on your side
Oh when times get rough
And friends just can't be found

I will comfort you
I'll take your part

Writer: Paul Simon

1. The Definition of Faith: How Is it Understood?

Youth Feedback:

____

____

____

Points to Ponder:

(a) Hebrews 11:1

"Now faith is the substance of things hoped for, the evidence of things not seen."

(b) Mark 11:12

"And Jesus answering saith unto them, Have faith in God."

(c) John 14:1

"Let not your heart be troubled: ye believe in God, believe also in me."

(d) John 6:29

"Jesus answered and said unto them, This is the work of God, that ye believe on Him whom He hath sent."

(e) Acts 20:21

"Testifying both to the Jews, and also to the Greeks, repentance toward God, and faith toward our Lord Jesus Christ."

(f) John 5:46-47

"For had ye believed Moses, ye would have believed Me: for he wrote of Me. But if ye believe not his writings, how shall ye believe My words?!"

"Believe in the Lord your God, so shall ye be established; believe his prophets, so shall ye prosper."

2. God's Promises:

Youth Feedback:

____

____

____

Points to Ponder

(a) Romans 4:13, 20-21

"For the promise, that he should be heir of the world, was not to Abraham, or to his seed, through the law, but through the righteousness of faith."

"He [Father Abraham] staggered not at the promise of God through unbelief; but was strong in faith, giving glory to God; And being fully persuaded that, what He had promised, He was able also to perform."

(b) James 1:12

"Blessed is the man that endureth temptation: for when he is tried, he shall receive the crown of life, which the Lord hath promised to them that love him."

(c) James 2:5

"Harken, my beloved brethren, Hath not God chosen the poor of this world rich in faith, and heirs of the kingdom which he hath promised to them that love him?"

(d) Hebrews 10:23, 36

"Let us hold fast the profession of our faith without wavering; (for he is faithful that promised.)"

"For ye have need of patience, that, after ye have done the will of God, ye might receive the promise."

(e) I John 2:25

"And this is the promise that he hath promised us, *even* eternal life."

(f) Acts 1:1-5

"The former treatise have I made, O Theophilus, of all that Jesus began both to do and teach, Until the day in which he was taken up, after that he through the Holy Ghost had given commandments unto the apostles whom he had chosen: To whom also he shewed himself alive after his passion by many infallible proofs, being seen of them forty days, and speaking of the things pertaining to the kingdom of God.

And, being assembled together with them, commanded them that they should not depart from Jerusalem, but wait for *the promise of the Father*, which, saith he, ye have heard of me. For John truly baptized with water; but ye shall be baptized with the Holy Ghost not many days hence."

(g) Acts 2:32-33, 39

"This Jesus hath God raised up, whereof we all are witnesses. Therefore being by the right hand of God exalted, and having received of the Father *the promise of the Holy Ghost*, he has shed forth this, which ye now see and hear."

"For the promise is unto you, and to your children, and to all that are afar off, *even* as many as the Lord our God shall call."

(h) Acts 13:22-23, 32-33

"And when he had removed him, he raised up unto them David to be their king; to whom also he gave testimony, and said, I have found David the *son* of Jesse, a man after mine own heart, which shall fulfil all my will. Of this man's seed hath God according to *his* promise raised unto Israel a Saviour, Jesus:"

"And we declare unto you glad tidings, how that the promise which was made unto the fathers, God hath fulfilled the same unto us their children, in that he hath raised up Jesus again; as it is also written in the second psalm, Thou are my Son, this day have I begotten thee."

(i) Galatians 3:6-9, 14, 29

"Even as Abraham believed God, and it was accounted to him for righteousness. Know ye therefore that they which are of faith, the same are the children of Abraham. And the scripture, foreseeing that God would justify the heathen through faith, preached before the gospel unto Abraham, saying, In thee shall all nations be blessed. So then they which be of faith are blessed with faithful Abraham."

"That the blessing of Abraham might come on the Gentiles through Jesus Christ; that we might receive the promise of the Spirit through faith."

"And ye *be* Christ's, then are ye Abraham's seed, and heirs according to the promise."

(j) Ephesians 1:3, 5, 13

"Blessed *be* the God and Father of our Lord Jesus Christ, who hath blessed us with all spiritual blessings in heavenly *places* in Christ:"

"Having predestinated us unto the adoption of children by Jesus Christ to himself, according to the good pleasure of his will,"

"In whom ye also trusted, after that ye heard the word of truth, the gospel of your salvation: in whom also after that ye believed, ye were sealed with that *holy Spirit of promise.*"

(k) Ephesians 3:6

"That the Gentiles should be fellow heirs, and of the same body, and partakers of his promise in Christ by the gospel."

(l) I Timothy 4:8

"Henceforth there is laid up for me a crown of righteousness, which the Lord, the righteous judge, shall give me at that day: and not to me only, but unto all them also that love his appearing."

(m)   II Timothy 1:1

"Paul, an apostle of Jesus Christ by the will of God, according to the promise of life which is in Christ Jesus,"

(n) Hebrews 4:1

"Let us therefore fear, lest, a promise being left us of entering into his rest, any of you should seem to come short of it."

(o) Hebrews 6:13, 17-20

"For when God made promise to Abraham, because he could swear by no greater, he sware by himself,"

"Wherein God, willing more abundantly to shew unto the heirs of promise the immutability of his counsel, confirmed it by an oath: That by two immutable things, in which it was impossible for God to lie, we might have a strong consolation, who have fled for refuge to lay hold upon the hope set before us: Which hope we have as an anchor of the soul, both sure and steadfast, and which entereth into that with the veil; Whither the forerunner is for us entered, even Jesus, made an high priest for ever after the order of Melchisedec."

(p) Hebrews 9:14-15

"How much more shall the blood of Christ, who through the eternal Spirit offered himself without spot to God, purge your conscience from dead works to serve the living God? And for this cause he is the mediator of the New Testament, that by means of death, for the redemption of the transgressions that were under the first testament, they which are called might receive the promise of eternal inheritance."

(q) Luke 24:49

"And, behold, I send the *promise of my Father* upon you: but tarry ye in the city of Jerusalem, until ye be endued with power from on high."

(r) I Kings 8:56

"Blessed be the Lord, that hath given rest unto his people Israel, according to all that he promised: there hath not failed one word of all his good promise, which he promised by the hand of Moses his servant."

(s) Psalms 105:42-45

"For he remembered his holy promise, and Abraham his servant. And he brought forth his people with joy, and his chosen with gladness: And gave them the lands of the heathen: and they inherited the labour of the people; That they might observe his statutes, and keep his laws. Praise ye the Lord."

3. Conversion Through the Holy Ghost:

Youth Feedback:

____

____

____

Points to Ponder:

(a) Romans 12:3

"For I [the Apostle Paul] say, through the Grace given unto me, to every man that is among you, not to think of himself more highly than he ought to think; but to think soberly, according as God hath dealt to every man the measure of faith."

(b) Acts 11:21

"And the hand of the Lord was with them: and a great number believed, and turned unto the Lord."

(c) Peter 1:1

"Simon Peter, a servant and an Apostle of Jesus Christ, to them that have obtained like precious faith with us through the righteousness of God and our Saviour Jesus Christ."

(d) Jude 20-21

"But ye, beloved, building up yourselves on your most holy faith, praying in the Holy Ghost, Keep yourselves in the love of God, looking for the mercy of our Lord Jesus Christ unto eternal life."

(e) I Thessalonians 1:2-3

"We give thanks to God always for you all, making mention of you in our prayers; Remembering without ceasing your work of faith, and labour of love, and patience of hope in our Lord Jesus Christ, in the sight of God and our Father."

(f) Mark 1:14-15

"now after that John was put in prison, Jesus came into Galilee, preaching the Gospel of the Kingdom of God, And saying, The time is fulfilled, and the Kingdom of God is at hand: repent ye, and believe the Gospel!"

(g) I Corinthians 12:4-7,9

"Now there are diversities of gifts, but the same Spirit. And there are differences of administrations, but the same Lord. And there are diversities of operations, but it is the same God which worketh all in all. But the manifestation of the Spirit is given to every man to profit withal... To another faith by the same Spirit; to another the gifts of healing by the same Spirit."

(h) John 20:30-31

"And many other signs truly did Jesus in the presence of His disciples, which are not written in this book: But these are written, that ye might believe that Jesus is the Christ, the Son of God; and that believing ye might have life through His name."

(i) John 17:20-21

"Neither pray I for these alone, but for them also which shall believe on me through their word; That they may be one; as Thou, Father, art in me, and I in Thee, that the world may believe that Thou hast sent Me."

4. Through Faith and Conversion into the Gospel Light, We Receive Access to God and His Truth:

Youth Feedback: _______________________________

____

____

Points to Ponder:

(a) Acts 10:36,42-43

"The Word which God sent unto the children of Israel, preaching Peace by Jesus Christ: (He is Lord of All:)... And He commanded us to preach unto the people, and to testify that it is He which was ordained of God to be Judge of quick and dead. To Him give all the Prophets witness, that through His name whosoever believeth in Him shall receive remission of sins."

(b) Acts 13:38-39

"Be it known unto you therefore, men and brethren, that through this Man [Jesus the Christ] is preached unto you the forgiveness of sins: And by Him all that believe are justified from all things, from which ye could not be justified by the Law of Moses."

(c) Mark 16:14-16

"Afterward He [Jesus] appeared unto the Eleven as they sat at meat, and upbraided them with their unbelief and hardness of heart, because they believed not them which had seen Him after He was risen. And He said unto them, Go ye into all the world, and preach the Gospel to every creature. He that believeth and is baptized shall be saved; but he that believeth not shall be damned."

(d) Acts 15:7-9

"And when there had been much disputing, Peter rose up, and

said unto them, Men and brethren, ye know how that a good while ago God made choice among us, that the Gentiles by my mouth should hear the Word of the Gospel, and believe. And God, which knoweth the hearts, bare them witness, giving them the Holy Ghost, even as He did unto us; And put no difference between us and them, purifying their hearts by faith."

(e) *John 12:35-36*

"Then Jesus said unto them, Yet a little while is the Light with you. Walk while ye have the Light, lest darkness come upon you: for he that walketh in darkness knoweth not wither he goeth. While ye have Light, believe in the Light, that ye may be the children of Light."

(f) *Numbers 21:8-9*

"And the Lord said unto Moses, Make thee a fiery serpent, and set it upon a pole: and it shall come to pass, that everyone that is bitten, when he looketh upon it, shall live. And Moses made a serpent of brass, and put it upon a pole, and it came to pass, that if a serpent had bitten any man, when he beheld the serpent of brass, he lived."

(g) *John 3:15*

"And as Moses lifted up the serpent in the wilderness, even so must the Son of Man be lifted up: That whosoever believeth in Him should not perish, but have eternal life."

(h) *I Timothy 1:4*

"Neither give heed to fables and endless genealogies, which minister questions, rather than godly edifying which is in faith: so do!"

(i) *I Peter 1:3,5*

"Blessed be the God and Father of our Lord Jesus Christ, which according to His abundant mercy hath begotten us again unto a lively hope by the resurrection of Jesus Christ from the dead... Who are kept by the power of God through faith unto salvation ready to be revealed in the last time."

(j) John 1:12

"But as many as received Him, to them gave He power to become the Sons of God, even to them that believe on His name."

(k) Romans 5:1-2

"Therefore being justified by faith, we have peace with God through our Lord Jesus Christ: By Whom also we have access by faith into this grace wherein we stand, and rejoice in hope of the glory of God!"

5. Without Faith, We Cannot Please God:

Youth Feedback:

____

____

____

Points to Ponder:

(a) Hebrews 11:6

"But without faith it is impossible to please Him [God]: for he that cometh to God must believe that He is, and that He is a rewarder of them that diligently seek Him."

(b) Romans 4:16

"Therefore it is of faith, that it might be of Grace; to the end the promise might be sure to all the seed; not to that only which is of the faith of Abraham; who is the father of us all."

(c) Matthew 13:57-58

"And they were offended in him. But Jesus said unto them, A prophet is not without honour, save in his own country, and in his own house. And he did not many mighty works there because of their unbelief."

(d) Matthew 17:19-21

"Then came the disciples to Jesus apart, and said, Why could not we cast him out? And Jesus said unto them, Because of your unbelief: for verily I say unto you, If ye have faith as a grain of mustard seed, ye shall say unto this mountain, Remove hence to yonder place; and it shall remove; and nothing shall be impossible unto you. Howbeit this kind goeth not out but by prayer and fasting."

(e) Mark 16:9-14

"Now when *Jesus* was risen early the first *day* of the week, he appeared first to Mary Magdalene, out of whom he had cast seven devils. And she went and told them that had been with him, as they mourned and wept. And they, when they had heard that he was alive, and had been seen of her, believed not.

After that he appeared in another form unto two of them, as they walked, and went into the country. And they went and told it unto the residue: neither believed they them. Afterward he appeared unto the eleven as they sat at meat, and upbraided them with their unbelief and hardness of heart, because they believed not them which had seen him after he was risen."

(f) Romans 11:22-23

"Behold therefore the goodness and severity of God: on them which fell, severity; but toward thee, goodness, if thou continue in *his* goodness: otherwise thou also shall be cut off. And they also, if they abide not still in unbelief, shall be graffed in: for God is able to graff them in again."

(g) Hebrews 3:12

"Take heed, brethren, lest there be in any of you an evil heart of unbelief, in departing from the living God."

(h) Titus 1:15-16

"Unto the pure all things *are* pure: but unto them that are defiled and unbelieving *is* nothing pure; but even their mind and conscience is defiled."

(i) Revelations 21:8

"But the fearful, and unbelieving, and the abominable, and murderers, and whoremongers, and sorcerers, and idolaters, and all liars, shall have their part in the lake which burneth with fire and brimstone: which is the second death."

6. With Faith, Christ Can Dwell in Our Hearts:

Youth Feedback:

____

____

____

Points to Ponder:

(a) Acts 16:27-34

"And the keeper of the prison awaking out of his sleep, and seeing the prison doors open, he drew out his sword, and would have killed himself, supposing that the prisoners had been fled. But Paul cried with a loud voice, saying, Do thyself no harm: for we are all here. Then he called for a light, and sprang in, and came trembling, and fell down before Paul and Silas, And brought them out, and said, Sirs, what must I do to be saved?

And they said, Believe on the Lord Jesus Christ, and thou shalt be saved, and thy house. And they spake unto him the Word of the Lord, and to all that were in his house. And he took them the same hour of the night, and washed their stripes; and was baptized, he and all his, straightway. And when he had brought them into his house, he set meat before them, and rejoiced, believing in God with all his house."

(b) Romans 15:13

"Now the God of hope fill you with all joy and peace in believing, that ye may abound in hope, through the power of the Holy Ghost."

(c) Isaiah 28:16

"Therefore thus saith the Lord God, Behold, I lay in Zion for a foundation a stone, a tried stone, a precious corner stone, a sure foundation: he that believeth shall not make haste."

(d) I Peter 2:5-7

"Ye also, as lively stones, are built up a spiritual house, an holy priesthood, to offer up spiritual sacrifices, acceptable to God by Jesus Christ. Wherefore also it is contained in the Scripture, Behold, I lay in Sion a chief corner stone, elect, precious: and he that believeth on Him shall not be confounded. Unto you therefore which believe He is precious."

(e) Ephesians 3:16-19

"That He would grant you, according to the riches of His glory, to be strengthened with might by His Spirit in the inner man; That Christ may dwell in your hearts by faith; that ye, being rooted and grounded in love, May be able to comprehend with all Saints what is the breadth, and length, and depth, and height; And to know the love of Christ, which passeth knowlege, that ye might be filled with all the fullness of God."

7. By Faith, We Resist the Devil and Become Strong in Christ:

Youth Feedback:

____

____

____

Points to Ponder:

(a) Galatians 2:20

"I am crucified with Christ: nevertheless I live; yet not I, but Christ liveth in me: and the life which I now live in the flesh I live by the faith of the Son of God, who loved me, and gave himself for me."

(b) Romans 11:19-22

"Thou wilt say then, The branches were broken off, that I might be graffed in. Well; because of unbelief they were broken off, and thou standest by faith. Be not high-minded, but fear: For if God spared not the natural branches, take heed lest He also spare not thee. Behold therefore the goodness and severity of God: on them which fell, severity; but toward thee, goodness, if thou continue in His goodness: otherwise thou also shalt be cut off."

(c) I John 5:4-5

"For whatsoever is born of God overcometh the world: and this is the Victory that overcometh the world, even our faith. Who is he that overcometh the world, but he that believeth that Jesus is the Son of God?

(d) I Peter 5:8-10

"Be sober, be vigilant; because your adversary the devil, as a roaring lion, walketh about, seeking whom he may devour: Whom resist stedfast in the faith, knowing that the same afflictions are accomplished in your brethren that are in the world. But the God of all grace who hath called us unto His eternal glory by Christ Jesus, after that ye have suffered a while, make you perfect, establish, strengthen, settle you."

(e) *Ephesians 6:15-16*

"For in Christ Jesus neither circumcision availeth anything, nor uncircumcision, but a new creature. And as many as walk according to this rule, Peace be on them, and mercy, and upon the Israel of God."

(f) *Psalms 27:13-14*

"I had fainted, unless I had believed to see the goodness of the Lord in the land of the living. Wait on the Lord: be of good courage, and He shall strengthen thine heart: wait, I say, on the Lord."

(g) *I Timothy 1 :5*

"Now the end of the commandment is charity out of a pure heart, and of a good conscience, and of faith unfeigned."

(h) *Acts 14:22*

"Confirming the souls of the disciples, and exhorting them to continue in the faith, and that we must through much tribulation enter into the Kingdom of God."

(i) *I Corinthians 16:13-14*

"Watch ye, stand fast in the faith, quit you like men, be strong. Let all your things be done with charity."

(j) *I Timothy 1:19*

"Holding faith, and a good conscience; which some having put away concerning faith have made shipwreck."

8. True Faith Is Known by It's Fruit: A Shield Against All Danger:

Youth Feedback:

____

____

____

Points to Ponder:

(a) James 2: 20-24,26

"But wilt thou know, O vain man, that faith without works is dead? Was not Abraham our Father justified by works, when he had offered Isaac his son upon the altar? Seest thou that faith wrought with his works, and by his works was faith made perfect? And the Scripture was fulfilled which saith, Abraham believed God, and it was imputed unto him for righteousness: and he was called the Friend of God. Ye see then how that by works a man is justified, and not by faith only... For as the body without the spirit is dead, so faith without works is dead also."

(b) Matthew 17:20

"And Jesus said unto them [His disciples] ... If ye have faith as a grain of mustard seed, ye shall say unto this mountain, Remove hence to yonder place; and it shall remove; and nothing shall be impossible unto you."

(c) Ephesians 6:13-18

"Wherefore take unto you the whole armour of God, that ye may be able to withstand in the evil day, and having done all, to stand. Stand therefore, having your loins girt about with Truth, and having on the breastplate of Righteousness; And your feet shod with the preparation of the Gospel of Peace; Above all, taking the shield of Faith, wherewith ye shall be able to quench all the fiery darts of the wicked. And take the helmet of Salvation, and the sword of the Spirit, which is the Word of God: Praying always with all prayer and supplication in the Spirit, and watching thereunto with all perseverance and supplication for all Saints."

(d) I Thessalonians 5:5-9

"Ye are all the children of Light, and the children of the day: we are not of the night, nor of darkness. Therefore let us not sleep, as do others; but let us watch and be sober. For they that sleep sleep in the night; and they that be drunken are drunken in the night. But let us, who are of the day, be sober, putting on the breastplate of faith and love; and for an helmet, the hope of Salvation. For God hath not appointed us to wrath, but to obtain Salvation by our Lord Jesus Christ."

D. To be Justified: What is Justification?

To have hope in Christ, allows us to be justified before God (see, I Peter 1:17-23)

It is this justification (Romans 3:20-26), through our *Propitiation* (our 'Price Paid' through our Lord) whereby our Heavenly Father through our faith in His Son, can accept us into His presence, "being **justified** through faith" (we "rejoice in hope of the Glory of God") (Romans 5:1-2). For we are "**justified** in the name of the Lord Jesus, and by the Spirit of our God"! (I Corinthians 6:11).

As Paul further clarifies: "being now **justified** by His blood, we shall be saved from wrath through Him... reconciled to God [the Father] by the death of His Son... by Whom we have now received the Atonement" (Romans 5:9-11). Paul expounds the definition of this Atonement (or, At-one-ment), as 'GRACE' (or, 'God's Riches At Christ's Expense'), a free gift, this 'gift by grace', which leads to "Justification". (Romans 5:11-18)

Paul concludes that: "even so by the righteousness of One [Christ] the free gift [the Atonement of Christ] came upon all men unto Justification of life" (Romans 5:18). So then we see that this is our 'hope in Christ' (that): Grace may "reign through righteousness unto eternal life by Jesus Christ our Lord' (Romans 5:21).

For it is by the faith of Abraham,' ("the father of us all") who "against hope believed in hope" and "staggered not at the promise of God through unbelief; but was strong In faith, giving glory to God" that righteousness was imputed to him. And so to us, as Abraham's children (spiritually speaking), can we receive this 'justification' from God through our belief, our faith, on Him who raised Jesus our Lord from the dead (to pay for our offenses). (Romans 4:16-25)

To better understand the concept of 'hope' (towards 'justification in Christ'), we can see that 'hope is the parent of faith' (C.A. Bartol). 'Hope never abandons you, you abandon hope' (George Weinberg). For as John Ray says: "If it were not for hope, the heart would break."

If faith is 'believing what we cannot prove' (Alfred, Lord Tennyson), then "Hope is faith holding out its hand in the dark" (George Iles). Just as "Faith is the only known cure for fear" (Lena K. Sadler), so hope is the only known cure for despair.

But what in essence is 'hope'? Anthony Reading in *Hope & Despair*, labels 'hope as 'a vision that things can be better'. More specifically, he defines it as: "an anticipatory emotion, an expectant savoring in our mind of a desired future occurrence that we believe... would turn out better than would otherwise be expected" (pp.3-4).

What I hold to be lacking in this definition of 'hope' is the added insight that 'hope' involves patience. I think of Peter's reference to 'hope': as this 'hope in Christ that is in us', as something more than a mere philosophical construct. As James, the blood brother to our Lord, put it so aptly in his Epistle: "Knowing this, that the trying of your faith works patience. But let patience have her perfect work, that ye may be perfect and entire, wanting nothing'. (James 1:3-4)

Paul the Apostle also clearly delineates the essence of hope as 'patience' as follows: "For whatsoever things were written aforetime were written for our learning, that we through patience and comfort of the Scriptures might have hope. Now the God of patience and consolation grant you to be like-minded one toward another according to Christ Jesus: That ye may with one mind and one mouth glorify God, even the Father of our Lord Jesus Christ." (Romans 15:4-6)

Paul then concludes, as I do, with his blessing to all believers: "Now the God of hope fill you with all joy and peace in believing, that ye may abound in hope, through the power of the Holy Ghost". (Romans 15:13)

Youth Feedback:
____

____

____

[#240: U-Tube Reference]
Elvis - If That Isn't Love
https://www.youtube.com/watch?v=JfxgGg9awsM&list=RD8H9T7
427Ebl&index=6

If That Isn't Love

He left the splendor of heaven
Knowing His destiny
Was the lonely hill of Golgotha
There to lay down His life for me

Yeah if that isn't love
Then heaven's a myth
There's no feeling like this
If that isn't love

Songwriter: Dottie Rambo

1. Instances of Justification:

Youth Feedback:

____

____

____

Points to Ponder:

(a) Isaiah 45:25

"In the Lord shall all the seed of Israel be justified, and shall glory!"

(b) I Timothy 3:16

"And without controversy great is the mystery of godliness: God was manifest in the flesh, justified in the Spirit, seen of angels, preached unto the Gentiles, believed on in the world, received up into glory."

(c) James 2:24-25

"Ye see then how that by works a man is justified, and not by faith only. Likewise also was not Rahab the harlot justified by works, when she had received the messengers, and had sent them out another way?"

(d) Luke 16:15

"And he said unto them, Ye are they which justify yourselves before men; but God knoweth your hearts: for that which is highly esteemed among men is abomination in the sight of God."

(e) Job 13:18; 25:4

"Behold now, I have ordered my cause; I know that I shall be justified."

"How then can man be justified with God? or how can he be

clean that is born of a woman?"

(f) Matthew 12:37

"For by thy words thou shalt be justified, and by they words thou shalt be condemned."

(g) Romans 3:24, 28

"Being justified freely by is grace through the redemption that is in Christ Jesus:"

"Therefore we conclude that a man is justified by faith without the deeds of the law."

(h) Romans 4:2

"For if Abraham were justified by works, he hath whereof to glory; but not before God."

(i) Romans 5:1, 9

"Therefore being justified by faith, we have peace with God through our Lord Jesus Christ:"

"Much more then, being now justified by his blood, we shall be saved from wrath through him."

(j) Romans 8:30-33

"Moreover whom he did predestinate, them he also called: and whom he called, them he also justified: and whom he justified, them he also glorified. What shall we then say to these things? If God *be* for us, who can be against us? He that spared not his own Son, but delivered him up for us all, how shall he not with him also freely give us all things? Who shall lay any thing to the charge of God's elect? It is God that justifieth."

(k) I Corinthians 6:9-11

"Know ye not that the unrighteous shall not inherit the kingdom of God? Be not deceived: neither fornicators, nor idolaters, nor adulterers, nor effeminate, nor abusers of themselves with mankind, Nor thieves, nor covetous, nor drunkards, nor revilers, nor extortioners, shall inherit the kingdom of God. And such were some of you: but ye are washed, but ye are sanctified, but ye are justified in the name of the Lord Jesus, and by the Spirit of our God."

(l) Galatians 2:16-17

"Knowing that a man is not justified by the works of the law, but by the faith of Jesus Christ, even we have believed in Jesus Christ, that we might be justified by the faith of Christ, and not by the works of the law: for by the works of the law shall no flesh be justified. But if, while we seek to be justified by Christ, we ourselves also are found sinners, is therefore Christ the minister of sin? God forbid."

2. Man Could Not Fulfill the Requirement of Perfect Obedience:

Youth Feedback:

____

____

____

Points to Ponder:

(a) Leviticus 18:12

"Ye shall therefore keep my statutes, and my judgments: which if a man do, he shall live in them: I am The Lord!"

(b) Romans 10:5-6,8-9

"For Moses describeth the Righteousness which is of the Law, That the man which doeth those things shall live by them. But the Righteousness which is of faith speaketh on this wise...

The word is nigh thee, even in thy mouth, and in thy heart: that is, the Word of faith, which we preach; That if thou shalt confess with thy mouth the Lord Jesus, and shalt believe in thine heart that God hath raised Him from the dead, thou shalt be saved."

(c) Psalms 130:3-5,7-8

"If Thou, Lord, shouldest mark iniquities, O Lord, who shall stand? But there is forgiveness with Thee, that Thou mayest be feared. I wait for the Lord, my soul doth wait, and in His Word do I hope... Let Israel hope in the Lord: for with the Lord there is mercy, and with Him is plenteous Redemption. And He shall redeem Israel from all his iniquities."

(d) Galatians 2:16-17, 21

"Knowing that a man is not justified by the works of the law, but by the faith of Jesus Christ, even we have believed in Jesus Christ, that we might be justified by the faith of Christ, and not by the works of the law: for by the works of the law shall no flesh be justified. But if, while we seek to be justified by Christ, we ourselves also are found sinners, *is* therefore Christ the minister of sin? God forbid."

"I do not frustrate the grace of God: for if righteousness *come* by law, then Christ is dead in vain."

(e) *Galatians 3:11*

"But that no man is justified by the law in the sight of God, *it is* evident: for, The just shall live by faith."

(f) *Exodus 23:7*

"Keep thee far from a false matter; and the innocent and righteous slay thou not: for I will not justify the wicked."

(g) *Isaiah 5:20-24*

"Woe unto them that call evil good, and good evil; that put darkness for light, and light for darkness; that put bitter for sweet, and sweet for bitter! Woe unto them that are wise in their own eyes, and prudent in their own sight! Woe unto them that are mighty to drink wine, and men of strength to mingle strong drink: Which justify the wicked for reward and take away the righteousness of the righteous from him!

Therefore as the fire devoureth the stubble, and the flame consumeth the chaff, so their root shall be as rottenness, and their blossom shall go up as dust: because they have cast away the law of the Lord of hosts, and despised that word of the Holy One of Israel."

(h) *Micah 6:8*

"He hath shewed thee, O man, what is good; and what doth the Lord require of thee, but to do justly, and to love mercy, and to walk humbly with thy God?"

3. Justification by Faith:

Youth Feedback:
____

____

____

Points to Ponder:

(a) Acts 13:39

"And by Him [Jesus] all that believe are justified from all things, from which ye could not be justified by the Law of Moses."

(b) John 5:24

"Verily, Verily, I [Christ] say unto you, He that believeth My Word, and believeth on Him that sent Me, hath everlasting life, and shall not come into condemnation; but is passed from death unto life."

(c) Romans 3:21-26

"But now the Righteousness of God without the Law is manifested, being witnessed by the Law and the Prophets; Even the Righteousness of God which is by faith of Jesus Christ unto all and upon all them that believe: for there is no difference: For all have sinned, and come short of the glory of God;

Being justified freely by His Grace through the Redemption that is in Christ Jesus: Whom God hath set forth to be a propitiation through faith in His blood, to declare His Righteousness for the remission of sins that are past, through the forbearance of God; To declare, I say, at this time His Righteousness: that He might be just, and the Justifier of him which believeth in Jesus."

(d) I Corinthians 6:11

"And such were some of you: but ye are washed, but ye are sanctified, but ye are justified in the name of the Lord Jesus, by the Spirit of our God."

(e) Isaiah 61:10

"I will greatly rejoice in the Lord, my soul shall be joyful in my God; for He hath clothed me with the garments of Salvation, He hath covered me with the robe of Righteousness, as a bridegroom decketh himself with ornaments, and as a bride adorneth herself with her jewels."

(f) Romans 5:8-11,15-16,18

"But God commendeth His love toward us, in that, while we were yet sinners, Christ died for us. Much more then, being now justified by His blood, we shall be saved from wrath through Him. For if, when we were enemies, we were reconciled to God by the death of His Son, much more, being reconciled, we shall be saved by His life. And not only so, but we also joy in God through our Lord Jesus Christ, by Whom we have now received the Atonement!...

But not as the offence, so also is the free gift. For if through the offence of one many be dead, much more the Grace of God, and the gift of Grace, which is by one man, Jesus Christ, hath abounded unto many. And not as it was by one that sinned, so is the gift: for the judgment was by one to condemnation, but the free gift is of many offences unto justification!...

Therefore as by the offence of one judgment came upon all men to condemnation; even so by the Righteousness of One the free gift came upon all men unto Justification of Life."

(g) Romans 4:24-25

"Jesus our Lord... was delivered for our offences, and was raised again [from the dead] for our justification."

(h) Galatians 3:24-26

"Wherefore the law was our schoolmaster to bring us unto Christ, that we might be justified by faith. But after that faith is come, we are no longer under a schoolmaster. For ye are all the

children of God by faith in Christ Jesus."
(i)   Galatians 3:8-9

"And the scripture, foreseeing that God would justify the heathen through faith, preached before the gospel unto Abraham, saying, In thee shall all nations be blessed. So then they which be of faith are blessed with faithful Abraham."

(j)   Galatians 5:4-5

"Christ is become of no effect unto you, whosoever of you are justified by the law; ye are fallen from grace. For we through the Spirit wait for the hope of righteousness by faith."

4. Justification Entitles Us to Inheritance in God's Glory:

Youth Feedback:

____

____

____

Points to Ponder:

(a) Psalms 32:1-2

"Blessed is he whose transgression is forgiven, whose sin is covered. Blessed is the man unto whom the Lord imputeth not iniquity, and in whose Spirit there is no guile."

(b) Isaiah 50:7-9

"For the Lord God will help me; therefore shall I not be confounded: therefore have I set my face like a flint, and I know that I shall not be ashamed. He is near that justifieth me; who will contend with me? Let us stand together: who is mine adversary? let him come near to me. Behold, the Lord God will help me!"

(c) Titus 3:5-7

"Not by works of Righteousness which we have done, but according to His mercy He saved us, by the washing of Regeneration, and Renewing of the Holy Ghost; Which He shed on us abundantly through Jesus Christ our Saviour; That being justified by His Grace, we should be made heirs according to the hope of Eternal Life.'

(d) Romans 8:28-30

"And we know that all things work together for good to them that love God, to them who are the called according to His purpose... For whom He did foreknow, He also did predestinate... Moreover whom He did predestinate, them He also called: and whom He called, them he also justified: and whom He justified, them He also glorified."

"He shall see of the travail of his soul, and shall be satisfied: by his knowledge shall my righteous servant justify many; for he shall bear their iniquities."

- 561 -

E. To be Redeemed: What is Redemption?

To have love in Christ is 'charity', the pure love of Christ:

To have divine love, *agapé* love (charity, or the pure love of Christ) allows us to be redeemed before God (the "Holy Father": John 17:11). The common thread in understanding all three concepts that Paul the Apostle refers to as: Faith, hope, and charity (I Corinthians 13:13) is patience. As someone once said: "Patience with others is love; patience with self is hope; patience with God is faith" (Adel Bestavros).

1. Yet what is this concept of Redemption in Christ and how is it amplified through divine love? Paul the Apostle points out that even though we "all have sinned, and come short of the glory of God", it is possible that we may become "justified freely by His Grace through the Redemption that is in Christ Jesus" (Romans 3:23-24). John explains this concept of *Redemption* succinctly in his Gospel in one verse alone: "For God [the Father] so loved the world, that He gave His only begotten Son, that whosoever believes in Him should not perish, but have everlasting life." (John 3:16)

2. Now for many intellectuals of this world, imbued with the wisdom of the world, this call to arms, to become a soldier in Christ, to follow the cross of Christ, to bear His cross, to take upon us His name, His death for our sins, is deemed to be laughable, and totally absurd. They mock the love of God and the Plan of Happiness, the Lord's Plan of Salvation. They did in Christ's day, and in the times following His crucifixion, death, and resurrection, and they do still today. That is nothing new.

3. But what all too many faith-followers and faith-deniers have over-looked is that God knows all our hearts and minds, and thoughts, that in His wisdom, he has brought "to nought things that are", that *redemption* may prevail. Let me explain, from the words of the Apostle Paul: "The foolishness of God is wiser than men; and the weakness of God is stronger than men...

But God has chosen the foolish things of the world to confound the wise; and God has chosen the weak things of the world to confound the things which are mighty; And base things of the world, and things which are despised, has God chosen, yea, and things which are not, to bring to nought things that are: That no flesh should glory in His presence" (I Corinthians 1:25-29).

4. Paul then adds this clincher: "But of Him are ye in Christ Jesus, who of God is made unto us wisdom, and righteousness, and sanctification, and *redemption*". (v.30). Christ obtained this 'eternal redemption' for us through His own blood! (Hebrews 9:12)

5. As Paul explains in greater depth that our conscience is purged "to serve the living God" through the blood of Christ "who through the eternal Spirit offered Himself without spot to God": "And for this cause He is the Mediator of the New Testament, that by means of death, for the *redemption* of the transgressions that were under the First [Old] Testament, they which are called might receive the promise of eternal inheritance. (Hebrews 9:14-15)

6. And what does it mean to be *redeemed* from the Fall? to become sons and daughters of God? to be (as Paul just hinted): heirs of 'eternal inheritance? as the children or seed of Abraham, in the household of faith? Paul again clarifies that the Lord Himself via the Holy Ghost has promised each of His true believers as follows, in His own words: "I will put my laws into their hearts, and in their minds will I write them; And their sins and iniquities will I remember no more"! (Hebrews 10:15-17)

7. Hence, we can be *redeemed* and sanctified (purified from sin), as Paul emphasizes: "We are sanctified through the offering of the body of Jesus Christ once for all... For by one offering He has perfected forever them that are sanctified... by the blood of Jesus, By a new and living way, which He has consecrated to us, through... His flesh"! (Hebrews 10:10,14,19-20)

8. It is through His *redemption*, that Christ has predestinated us "unto the adoption of children" unto Himself, "according to the good pleasure of His will'. As Paul clarifies: "In Whom we have *redemption* through His blood, the forgiveness of sins, according to the riches of His grace... In whom also we have obtained an inheritance... in Whom also after that ye believed, ye were sealed with the Holy Spirit of promise, which is the earnest of our inheritance until the *redemption* of the purchased possession, unto the praise of His glory". (Ephesians 1:5,7,11-14)

9. It is in this 'hope of the Gospel", Paul explains, that we may become perfect in Christ, a hope 'that is laid up for you in heaven', that we may become "partakers of the inheritance of the saints in light', giving thanks unto the Father "who has delivered us from the power of darkness, and has translated us into the kingdom of His dear Son: In Whom we have *redemption* through His blood, even the forgiveness of sins"! (Colossians 1:5,12-14)

10. In a few short verses, Paul has encapsulated the entire concept of *redemption*, with its latent promise(s) to each of us as believers in Christ with the one proviso, of course: "That ye might walk worthy of the Lord unto all pleasing, being fruitful in every good work, and increasing in the knowledge of God" (v.10).

11. And herein is the labor of love that the servants of the Lord extoll, even "the mystery hid from ages and from generations, but now is made manifest to His saints", as Paul exults: "To whom God would make known what is the riches of the glory of this mystery (among the Gentiles); which is Christ in you, the hope of glory... that we may present every man perfect in Christ Jesus" (Colossians 1:26-29). All we need to do, Paul exclaims is to: "continue in the faith grounded and settled, and be not moved away from the hope of the Gospel" (v.23).

12. So then in order to be *redeemed* of Christ and by Christ and for Christ, what we need to do is to simply follow Paul's dictum, the personality, or persona of the True Believer converted to Christ, as follows: "Put on therefore, as the elect of God, holy and beloved, bowels of mercies, kindness, humbleness of mind, meekness, longsuffering; Forbearing one another, if any man have a quarrel against any: even as Christ forgave you, so also do ye. And Above all these things put on charity, which is the bond of perfectness.

Let the Peace of God rule in your hearts, to the which also ye are called in one body; and be ye thankful. Let the Word of Christ dwell in you richly in all wisdom; teaching and admonishing one another... And whatsoever ye do in word or deed, do all in the name of the Lord Jesus, giving thanks to God and the Father by Him." (Colossians 3:12-17)

13. Having read these in-depth instructions from our Lord's chosen Apostle, Paul, what can we take away from all of these deep spiritual truths and blessings?

One key and very simple, straightforward fact (that our planet refuses still to this day, I maintain, to acknowledge, to recognize, and especially: to try to fully comprehend that): God loves us, each one of us, no matter what we have done with our time, our talents, our bodies, or our lives.

That is the resounding conclusion I have come to at the end of the day, at the end of this long search into my soul to try to understand why or how it is that a fifteen-year-old Métis youth would wish to harm me, let alone kill me!

Let me explain just a little what I mean: The oft-quoted phrase: "It takes a village to raise a child" (Anon) makes me realize that: *Yes!* This child, this psycho-kid who tried to end my life for no other reason than 'to watch me die' brings me to the conversion of Johnny Cash.

14. In his conversion story, Johnny Cash created a spiritual movie called: *Gospel Road*, in which he sings these words: "I never thought I needed help before, I thought that I could do things by myself; But now I just can't take it anymore, And with a humble heart, on bended knee, I'm begging you please, for help!". Quite an admission by the former drug addict turned-around-for-Christ convert to confess!

15. Elvis Presley also shared a similar sentiment in his introduction to his song: "You'll Never Walk Alone!" in which he says: "You've never stood in that man's shoes, or saw things through his eyes, or stood and watched with helpless hands while the heart inside you dies; so, help your brother along the way, no matter where he starts, For the same God who made you, made him too!"

16. It's this very sentiment that inspired Johnny Cash to write the song: "Man In Black" (1971) in which he explains: "I wear the black for those who never read, Or listened to the words that Jesus said: About the Road to Happiness through love and charity; Why you'd think He's talking straight to you and me!".

17. In scriptural lingo, John the Beloved stated the self-same message, as he states: "He that says he is in the light, and hates his brother, is in darkness even until now. He that loves his brother abides in the light... But he that hates his brother is in darkness, and walks in darkness, and knows not where he goes, because that darkness has blinded his eyes". (I John 2:9-11)

John is very clear to define this 'light', as follows: "God is light, and in Him is no darkness at all. If we say that we have fellowship with Him, and walk in darkness, we lie, and do not the truth. But if we walk in the light, as He is in the light, we have fellowship one with another, and the blood of Jesus Christ His Son cleanses us from all sin." (I John 1:5-7)

18. Now if we do sin, as John says, there is a hope in Christ: "He that commits sin is of the devil; for the devil sins from the beginning. For this purpose the Son of God was manifested, that he might destroy the works of the devil". (I John 3:8) But, John adds, "And if any man sin, we have an Advocate with the Father, Jesus Christ the righteous: And He is the propitiation [price-paid] for our sins: and not for ours only, but also for the sins of the whole world". (I John 2:1-2)

19. So we see that there are two sets of humanity (two wolves fighting inside each one of us): As the Apostle John so aptly describes these two 'wolves': "They [the bad wolves] are of the world: therefore speak they of the world, and the world hears them. We [the good wolves] are of God: he that knows God hears us; he that is not of God hears us not. Hereby know we the Spirit of truth, and the spirit of error." (I John 4:5-6)

20. John becomes more specific: "In this the children of God are manifest, and the children of the devil: whosoever does not righteousness is not of God, neither he that loves not his brother... Whosoever hates his brother is a murderer: and ye know that no murderer has eternal life abiding in him". (I John 3:10,15)

21. We now have arrived at a conundrum, a fork in the road: Which wolf shall win? Well, the simple answer is: "The One You Feed!", as this book attempts to demonstrate. But the innermost center-most truth remains: How to feed this wolf? The one that we

know to be 'good', the one we wish to 'win'?! John again has the answer to our quest: "Beloved, let us love one another: for love is of God; and everyone that loves is born of God, and knows God. He that loves not knows not God; for God is love'! (I John 4:7-8)

22. But John qualifies this love, as it is not a random gift without conditions, as follows: "Herein is love, not that we loved God, but that He loved us, and sent His Son to be the propitiation for our sins... Hereby know we that we dwell in Him, and He in us, because He has given us of His Spirit. And we have seen and do testify that the Father sent the Son to be the Saviour of the world. Whosoever shall confess that Jesus is the Son of God, God dwells in him, and he in God. And we have known and believed the love that God has to us. God is love; and he that dwells in love dwells in God, and God in him." (I John 4:10,13-16)

23. Then John asks us this question (the one that determines which wolf we will feed!): "We love Him, because He first loved us. If a man say, I love God, and hates his brother, he is a liar: for he that loves not his brother whom he has seen, How can he love God whom he has not seen?" (I John 4:19-20)

24. Now to be precise, John the Apostle (aka: the Revelator) reveals to us what we must do to qualify for this love of God in our lives: "By this we know that we love the children of God, when we love God, and keep His commandments. For this is the love of God, that we keep His commandments: and His commandments are not grievous.

25. For whatsoever is born of God overcomes the world: and this is the Victory that overcomes the world, even our faith. Who is He that overcomes the world, but he that believes that Jesus is the Son of God?...

He that believes on the Son of God has the witness in himself: he that believes not God has made him a liar; because he believes not the record that God gave of His Son. And this is the record, that God has given to us eternal life, and that life is in His Son. He that has the Son has life; and he that has not the Son of God has not life". (I John 5:2-5,10-12)

26. Once again, John asks that piercing question, to separate the goats from the lambs, the bad wolves from the good ones: "Hereby perceive we the love of God, because He laid down His life for us: and we ought to lay down our lives for the brethren. But whoso has this world's good[s], and sees his brother have need, and shuts up his bowels of compassion from him, How dwells the love of God in him?" (I John 3:16-17) Indeed, at the end of the day, that is how we can come to know which wolf we are feeding, and which path we are choosing, whether it leads to life (even life eternal), or to certain death.

27. As John states in his Gospel: "He that believes on Him [Christ] is not condemned: but he that believes not is condemned already, because he has not believed in the name of the only begotten Son of God. And this is the condemnation, that light is come into the world, and men loved darkness rather than light, because their deeds were evil. For everyone that does evil hates the light, neither comes to the light, lest his deeds should be reproved. But he that does truth comes to the light, that his deeds may be manifest, that they are wrought in God". (John 3:18-21)

The question still remains: "Which One Will You (choose to) Feed?!"

  Youth Feedback:
____

____

____

DISCLAIMER: N.B. (*Nota Bene*)
All tunes/songs/video clips/links/quotes/etc. are herein provided to assist in Group Therapy Sessions, or privately, for individual study (to assist in learning) and for educational purposes *only*.

[#241: U-Tube Reference]
Johnny Cash - Redemption
https://www.youtube.com/watch?v=W08MS3ndUX0

[#242: U-Tube Reference]
Johnny Cash - Redemption/Lyrics
https://www.youtube.com/watch?v=q4quYBKS6Po

Redemption

And the blood was the price
That set the captives free
And the numbers that came
Through the fire and the flood Clung to the tree

And a small inner voice Said
"You do have a choice."
The vine engrafted me
And I clung to the tree.

Writer: Bob Marley

1. Our Freedom Is Bought with a Price in Christ:

Youth Feedback: _______________________________

____

____

Points to Ponder:

(a) I Corinthians 6:19-20

"What? know ye not that your body is the Temple of the Holy Ghost which is in you, which ye have of God, and ye are not your own? For ye are bought with a price: therefore glorify God in your body, and in your spirit, which are God's."

(b) I Corinthians 7:22-23

"For he that is called in the Lord, being a servant, is the Lord's freeman: likewise also he that is called, being free, is Christ's servant. Ye are bought with a price; be not ye the servants of men."

(c) John 8:32; 14:6

"And ye shall know the truth, and the truth shall make you free."

"Jesus said unto him, I am the way, the truth, and the life: no man cometh unto the Father, but by me."

(d) Romans 3:22-25

"Even the righteousness of God which is by faith of Jesus Christ unto all and upon all them that believe: for there is no difference: For all have sinned, and come short of the glory of God; Being justified freely by his grace through the redemption that is in Christ Jesus: Who God hath set forth to be a propitiation through faith in his blood, to declare his righteousness for the remission of sins that are past, through the forbearance of God."

(e) Romans 8:31-32

"What then shall we say to these things? If God be for us, who can be against us? He that spared not his own Son, but delivered him up for us all, how shall he not with him also freely give us all things?"

(f) I John 2:1-2

"My little children, these things write I unto you, that ye sin not. And if any man sin, we have an advocate with the Father, Jesus Christ the righteous: And he is the propitiation for our sins: and not for our's only, but also for the sins of the whole world."

(g) I John 4:9-10

"In this was manifested the love of God toward us, because that God sent his only begotten So into the world, that we might live through him. Herein is love, not that we loved God, but that he loved us, and sent his Son to be the propitiation for our sins."

(h) I Peter 1:3, 15-19

"Blessed *be* the God and Father of our Lord Jesus Christ, which according to his abundant mercy hath begotten us again unto a lively hope by the resurrection of Jesus Christ from the dead."

But as he which hath called you is holy, so be ye holy in all manner of conversation; Because it is written, **Be ye holy; for I am holy.** And if ye call on the Father, who without respect of persons judgeth according to every man's work, pass the time of your sojourning here in fear: Forasmuch as ye know that ye were not redeemed with corruptible things, *as* silver and gold, from your vain conversation received by tradition from your fathers; But with the precious blood of Christ, as of a lamb without blemish and without spot."

2. We Are (Can Be) Redeemed from the Bondage of Sin in the Blood of Christ:

Youth Feedback:

____

____

____

Points to Ponder:

(a) Isaiah 44:21-22

"Remember these, O Jacob and Israel: for thou art My servant: I have formed thee; thou art My servant: O Israel, thou shalt not be forgotten of Me! I have blotted out, as a thick cloud, thy transgressions, and, as a cloud, thy sins: return unto Me; for I have Redeemed thee!"

(b) Matthew 20:27-28

"And whosoever will be chief among you, let him be your servant: Even as the Son of Man came not to be ministered unto, but to minister, and to give his life a ransom for many."

(c) Acts 20:28

"Take heed therefore unto yourselves, and to all the flock, over the which the Holy Ghost hath made you overseers, to feed the Church of God, which He hath purchased with His own blood."

(d) Hebrews 9:11-12

"But Christ being come an High Priest of good things to come, by a greater and more perfect tabernacle, not made with hands, that is to say, not of this building. Neither by the blood of goats and calves, but by His own blood He entered in once into the holy place, having obtained eternal Redemption for us."

(e) I Peter 1:18-19

"Forasmuch as ye know that ye were not redeemed with corruptible things, as silver and gold, from your vain conversation received by tradition from your fathers; But with the precious blood of Christ, as of a lamb without blemish and without spot!"

3. We Are Redeemed by Christ from the Law (and its Curse):

Youth Feedback:

____

____

____

Points to Ponder:

(a) Galatians 4:4-5

"But when the fulness of the time was come, God sent forth His Son, made of a woman, made under the Law, To redeem them that were under the Law, that we might receive the adoption of sons."

(b) Romans 8:15, 23

"For ye have not received the spirit of bondage again to fear; but ye have received the Spirit of adoption, whereby we cry, Abba, Father."

"And not only *they*, but ourselves also, which have the firstfruits of the Spirit, even we ourselves groan within ourselves, waiting for the adoption, *to wit*, the redemption of our body."

(c) Romans 9:4

"Who are Israelites; to whom *pertaineth* the adoption, and the glory, and the covenants, and the giving of the law, and the service *of God*, and the promises."

(d) Ephesians 1:4-5, 7

"According as he hath chosen us in him before the foundation of the world, that we should be holy and without blame before him in love:
Having predestinated us unto the adoption of children by Jesus Christ to himself, according to the good pleasure of his will."

"In whom we have redemption through his blood, the forgiveness of sins, according to the riches of his grace."

(e) Galatians 3:13

"Christ hath redeemed us from the curse of the law, being made a curse for us: for it is written, Cursed is every one that hangeth on a tree."

(f) Romans 3:24

"Being justified freely by his grace through the redemption that is in Christ Jesus."

(g) Hebrews 9:12, 15

"Neither by the blood of goats and claves, but by his own blood he entered in once into the holy place, having obtained eternal redemption *for us.*"

"And for this cause he is the mediator of the new testament, that by means of death, for the redemption of the transgressions that were under the first testament, they which are called might receive the promise of eternal inheritance."

(h) Colossians 1:14

"In whom we have redemption through his blood, even the forgiveness of sins."

(i) Luke 21:25-28

"And there shall be signs in the sun, and in the moon, and in the stars; and upon the earth distress of nations, with perplexity; the sea and the waves roaring; Men's hearts failing them for fear, and for looking after those things which are coming on the earth: for the powers of heaven shall be shaken. And then shall they see the Son of man coming in a cloud with power and great glory. And when these things begin to come to pass, then look up, and lift up your heads; for your redemption draweth nigh."

Scene iii:
To Emulate *Agapé* (Christ-like) love

A. To Love as if you've never been hurt!

1. Many of us have been hurt at some time in our lives, by some person or other, whether intentionally or accidentally (through thoughtless comments, or insensitive situations). To love is to put oneself at risk. To risk the possibility (even the likelihood) to be hurt is what entails love in its finest moment, those challenging moments (to kiss and makeup), in which we can turn the lemons (of a sour relationship) into lemonade (a much sweeter connection), as we may tend to reflect upon with deep affection afterward. As Shakespeare once said: "The course of true love never did run smooth" (*A Midsummer Nights Dream*).

2. At the core of *agapé* love is the concept of forgiveness and mercy. Many people (including some Christian believers) have not quite grasped the concept of genuine forgiveness, the need to completely and sincerely apologize, to repent, and to make restitution for the harm one may have inadvertently caused another. Jesus said that our Heavenly Father will forgive us our trespasses *as we forgive others* their trespasses against us (Matthew 6:15).

The assumption is that we need (or are 'required') to forgive others who trespass against us whether or not they ask for that forgiveness, or even whether they desire to do so or not, or attempt to say (and do) anything more than utter a casual: "I'm sorry!". [See The Five Languages of Apology, by Chapman and Thomas, 2006.]

The Scriptures clearly state in the Gospel of Luke that Jesus said: "Take heed to yourselves: If thy brother trespass against thee, rebuke him; and *if he repent*, forgive him'! (Luke 17:3) This act of forgiveness appears to be conditional, just as our Heavenly Father forgives us only if we forgive each other, and only if we fully repent, ask for that forgiveness, and do not repeat that same offense.

3. Consider the parable of the wicked servant: As Jesus tells the story, there was a servant who owed 10,000 talents (an impossible sum of money to ever repay) to his master. Because he could not repay this debt, his Master was determined to throw him into debtor's prison, but the servant begged for forgiveness, and his master had compassion on him and forgave all that debt. But shortly thereafter another servant who owed a very small amount of money (only 100 pence, much less than a single talent) to this same servant (who had been just forgiven of a huge debt) pleaded with that servant for more time that he may repay this small pittance of only 100 pence.

    But the wicked servant had no compassion on him and threw him into prison until he could collect that debt. When the Master found out about this wicked act, he recalled his servant, and recalled that debt, and threw that wicked servant into prison so that he could learn his lesson: *Tto forgive those who ask for forgiveness.* Then Jesus added these chilling words: "So likewise shall My Heavenly Father do also unto you, if ye from your hearts forgive not every one his brother their trespasses"! (Matthew 18:23-35)

4. The Apostle Paul speaks of husbands to love their wives as Christ does the Church. Quite a tall order! But one that I do not think Paul thought to be impossible; otherwise, why would he so instruct the Saints? So, if we can emulate Christ-like love, how do we go about to do it? The answer may appear simple, but it is by no means, easy (to perform). For starters, we need to get past ourselves; that is, we need to see ourselves as Heavenly Father sees us: as His children, and as His children, as someone who can be 'perfect' (as Jesus says) even as your Heavenly Father is perfect (Matthew 5:48).

    So, to return to the question: "How is it to be done?" Everywhere on all sides we hear that: "No one is perfect!". So, once again: "What is to be done?" The answer is actually quite simple, as I see it: For the answer is within each one of us. As the wise Cherokee Chief so stated: "We have two wolves fighting each other inside each one of us: One good; and the other, the opposite, not at all good. Which one wins? The one we feed!" as the Chief rightly concludes.

5. As we focus on the positive attributes of a Godly (good) character, and as we feed upon the Word of God (as provided in revealed Scripture), we gradually replace our old ('inferior' or relatively speaking, 'negative') habits with good ones. And as this book specifically outlines in some great detail, there are numerous steps along the path to (ultimate) perfection. which if taken one by one, will eventually lead us to understand, realize, and embrace our new nature, our new life (with God as our Partner, and with the Holy Ghost as our constant Companion).

    As we follow this 'moral compass,' we find ourselves enjoying the fruits of this Spirit, the pure unadulterated joy of the Gospel, which cannot be even remotely compared to any physical or earthly or worldly pleasure by far.

    It is a journey of a lifetime, a destiny not only divine in its origin but one that will lead us to the fullness of abundant life, a sense of purpose that gives us the inner strength we need hour by hour, day by day, to overcome the depression and depravities of this earthly sojourn, to unite us, to join us to the Higher Powers that be, the life afterlife, even to life everlasting.

6. The Apostle Peter asked Jesus: "How oft shall my brother sin against me, and I forgive him? till seven times?" (Luke 18:21) Jesus said unto him: "I say not unto you, Until seven times: but, unto seventy times seven"! (v.22)

    Now that is a really tall order! Jesus asked his followers, those who would call themselves 'Christians' to not only love our enemies but to forgive them as well (should they ask us to) that we may be "the children" of our "Father which is in Heaven". (Matthew 5:43-45)

[#243: U-Tube Reference]
Jackie Evancho - The Lord's Prayer (from *Dream With Me* concert)
https://www.youtube.com/watch?v=Vg2AsS4CErM

The Lord's Prayer

Our Father which art in heaven Hallowed be Thy name. Thy kingdom come, thy will be done on earth as it is in heaven. Give us this day our daily bread and forgive us our debts as we forgive Our debtors. And lead us not into temptation but deliver us from evil. For Thine Is the kingdom and the power and the glory for ever. Amen

[#244: U-Tube Reference]
The Seekers I'll Never Find Another You (1967)
https://www.youtube.com/watch?v=hqMZePE7SQk

I'll Never Find Another You

There is always someone
For each of us, they say
I could search the whole world over
Until my life is through
But I know I'll never find another you
But if I should lose your love, dear
I don't know what I'd do
For I know I'll never find another you.

B. Seventy Points to Ponder

1. *No libertines, nor libertarianism: no extreme unrestrictive liberties:*

"As free, and not using your liberty for a cloak of maliciousness, but as the servants of God". *(1 Peter 2:16)*

2. *Fleshy lusts war against the soul, as two wolves inside us fighting each other: the lustful against the loving:*

"The Lord knoweth how to deliver the godly out of temptations, and to reserve the unjust unto the day of judgement to be punished:

But chiefly them that walk after the flesh in the lust of uncleanness and despise government. Presumptuous are they, self-willed, they are not afraid to speak evil of dignities...

But these, **as brute beasts, made to be taken and destroyed,** speak evil of the things that they understand not; and shall utterly perish in their own corruption; And shall receive the reward of unrighteousness, as they that count it pleasure to riot in the daytime. Spots they are and blemishes, sporting themselves with their own deceivings while they feast with you; Having eyes full of adultery, and that cannot cease from sin; beguiling unstable souls: an heart they have exercised with covetous practices; cursed children!...

These are wells without water, clouds that are carried with a tempest; to whom the mist of darkness is reserved for ever. For when they speak great swelling words of vanity, they allure through the lusts of the flesh, through much wantonness, those that were clean escaped from them who live in error. While they promise them Liberty, they themselves are the servants of corruption: for of whom a man is overcome, of the same is he brought in bondage". *(II Peter 2:9-10, 12-14, 17-19)*

3. *Turn our conscience towards God:*

"We have also a more sure word of prophecy; whereunto ye do well that ye take heed, as unto a light that shineth in a dark place, until the day dawn, and the day star arise in your hearts." *(II Peter 1:19)*

4. If you do well and suffer for it, take it patiently:

"For this is thank-worthy, if a man for conscience toward God endure grief, suffering wrongfully. For what glory is it , if when ye be buffeted for your faults, ye shall take it patiently? But if, when ye do well, and suffer for it, ye take it patiently, this is acceptable with God." *(I Peter: 2:19-20)*

5. With well-doing, put to silence foolish men:

"Having your conversation [behaviour] honest among the Gentiles: that, whereas they speak against you as evildoers, they may by your good works, which they shall behold, glorify God in the day of visitation. Submit yourselves to every ordinance of man for the Lord's sake: whether it be to the king, as supreme: Or unto governors, as unto them that are sent by him for the punishment of evildoers, and for the praise of them that do well." *(I Peter 2:12-14)*

6. Christ suffered for us leaving us an Example: that we should follow His steps:

"For even hereunto were ye called: because Christ also suffered for us, leaving us an example, that ye should follow his steps"! *(I Peter 2:21)*

7. As sheep gone astray are now returning to the Shepherd of our Souls:

"For ye were as sheep going astray; but are now returned unto the Shepherd and Bishop of your souls." *(I Peter 2:25)*

8. Christ when He suffered, He threatened not:

"Who, when he was reviled, reviled not again; when he suffered, he threatened not; but committed himself to him that judgeth righteously." *(I Peter 2:23)*

9. *By Christ's stripes, we are healed:*

"Who his own self bare our sins in his own body on the tree, that we, being dead to sins, should live unto righteousness: by whose stripes ye were healed." *(I Peter 2:24)*

10. *Christ: that 'living stone':*

"If so be ye have tasted that the Lord *is* gracious. To whom coming, *as* unto a living stone, disallowed indeed of men, but chosen of God, *and* precious." *(I Peter 2:3-4, 6-8)*

"Be it known unto you all, and to all the people of Israel, that by the name of Jesus Christ of Nazareth, whom ye crucified, whom God raised from the dead, even by him doth this man stand here before you whole. This is the stone which was set at nought of you builders, which is become the head of the corner." *(I Acts 4:10-11)*

"Jesus saith unto them, Did ye never read in the scriptures, The stone which the builders rejected, the same is become the head of the corner: this is the Lord's doing, and it is marvellous in our eyes? Therefore say I unto you, The kingdom of God shall be taken from you, and given to a nation bringing forth the fruits thereof. And whosoever shall fall on this stone shall be broken: but on whomsoever it shall fall, it will grind him to powder." *(Matthew 21:42-44)*

"And have ye not read this scripture; The stone which the builders rejected is become the head of the corner: This was the Lord's doing, and it is marvellous in our eyes?" *(Mark 12:10-11)*

"The stone which the builders refused is become the head stone of the corner. This is the Lord's doing; it *is* marvellous in our eyes." *(Psalms 118:22-23)*

11. *We too become as 'living stones':*

"Ye also, as lively stones, are build up a spiritual house, an holy priesthood, to offer up spiritual sacrifices, acceptable to God by Jesus Christ." *(I Peter 2:5)*

"And in the days of these kings shall the God of heaven set up a kingdom, which shall never be destroyed: and the kingdom shall not be left to other people, but it shall break in pieces and consume all these kingdoms, and it shall stand for ever." *(Daniel 2:44)*

12. *Ye are a chosen generation... a peculiar people:*

"But ye *are* a chosen generation, a royal priesthood, an holy nation, a peculiar people; that ye should shew forth the praises of him who hath called you out of darkness into his marvellous light:" *(I Peter 2:9)*

13. *Submit yourselves to every ordinance of men 'for the Lord's sake' (Police, Sheriffs, Law Enforcement Officers, etc.):*

"Submit yourselves to every ordinance of man for the Lord's sake: whether it be to the king, as supreme; Or unto governors, as unto them that are sent by him for the punishment of evildoers, and for the praise of them that do well." *(I Peter 2:13-14)*

14. *Be subject to Masters, not only to 'the good and gentle' but also to 'the froward':*

"Servants, *be* subject to *your* master with all fear; not only to the good and gentle, but also to the froward." *(I Peter 2:18)*

15. *Christ committed Himself to "Him who judged righteously':*

"Who, when he was reviled, reviled not again; when he suffered, he threatened not; but committed himself to him that judgeth righteously." *(I Peter 2:23)*

16. *Our behaviour should be: 'the hidden man/woman of the heart'... 'a meek and quiet spirit':*

"But let it be the hidden man of the heart, in that which is not corruptible, even the ornament of a meek and quiet spirit, which is in the sight of God of great price." *(I Peter 3:4)*

17. Be ye of one mind, having compassion one of another, love as brethren, be courteous':

"Finally, *be ye* all of one mind, having compassion one of another, love as brethren, *be* pitiful, *be* courteous:" *(I Peter 3:8)*

18. Not rendering evil for evil, but contrariwise: blessings:

"Not rendering evil for evil, or railing for railing: but contrariwise blessing; knowing that ye are there unto called, that ye should inherit a blessing." *(I Peter 3:9)*

"But I say unto you, Love your enemies, bless them that curse you, do good to them that hate you, and pray for them which despitefully use you, and persecute you." *(Matthew 6:44)*

19. He who will love life, and see good days, let him refrain his tongue from evil:

"For he that will love life, and see good days, let him refrain his tongue from evil, and his lips that they speak no guile." *(I Peter 3:10)*

20. Let him avoid evil and do good:

"Let him eschew evil, and do good; let him seek peace, and ensue it." *(I Peter 3:11)*

21. Eyes of the Lord are over the righteous, and His ears are open unto their prayers:

"For the eyes of the Lord *are* over the righteous, and his ears are open unto their prayers: but the face of the Lord is against them that do evil." *(I Peter 3:12)*

22. The face of the Lord is against them that do evil:

"For the eyes of the Lord *are* over the righteous, and his ears are open unto their prayers: but the face of the Lord is against them that do evil." *(I Peter 3:12)*

23. If ye suffer for righteousness' sake, happy are ye, be not afraid of their terror, neither be troubled:

"But and if ye suffer for righteousness' sake, happy are ye: and be not afraid of their terror, neither be troubled." *(I Peter 3:14)*

24. It is better if the will of God be so, that ye suffer for well-doing:

"For it is better, if the will of God be so, that ye suffer for well doing, than for evil doing." *(I Peter 3:17)*

25. We should live to the will of God, not to the lusts of men:

"That he no longer should live the rest of his time in the flesh to the lusts of men, but to the will of God." *(I Peter 4:2)*

26. Arm yourselves likewise (like Christ) 'with the same mind to cease from sin':

"Forasmuch then as Christ hath suffered for us in the flesh, arm yourselves likewise with the same mind: for he that hath suffered in the flesh hath ceased from sin." *(I Peter 4:1)*

27. Avoid the will of the Gentiles (described):

"For the time past of our life may suffice us to have wrought the will of the Gentiles, when we walked in lasciviousness, lusts, excess of wine, revellings, banquetings, and abominable idolatries: Wherein they think it strange that ye run not with them to the same excess of riot, speaking evil of *you*." *(I Peter 4:3-4)*

28. Be sober, and watch unto prayer:

"But the end of all things is at hand: be ye therefore sober, and watch unto prayer." *(I Peter 4:7)*

29. Have 'fervent charity' among yourselves:

"And above all things have fervent charity among yourselves: for charity shall cover the multitude of sins. Use hospitality one to another without grudging. As every man hath received the gift, even so minister the same one to another, as good stewards of the manifold grace of God." *(I Peter 4:8-10)*

30. *Minister (to one another) 'as of the ability which God giveth':*

"If any man speak, let him *speak* as the oracles of God; if any man minister, let him do it as of the ability which God giveth: that God in all things may be glorified through Jesus Christ, to whom be praise and dominion for ever and ever. Amen." *(I Peter 4:11)*

31. *Be partakers of Christ's suffering: Rejoice:*

"Beloved, think it not strange concerning the fiery trial which is to try you, as though some strange thing happened unto you: But rejoice, inasmuch as ye are partakers of Christ's sufferings; that, when his glory shall be revealed, ye may be glad also with exceeding joy. If ye be reproached for the name of Christ, happy *are ye*; for the spirit of glory and of God resteth upon you: on their part he is evil spoken of, but on your part he is glorified." *(I Peter 4:12-14)*

"Yet if any man suffer as a Christian, let him not be ashamed; but let him glorify God on this behalf." *(I Peter 4:16)*

32. *Be not a murderer, or a thief, or evil doer or even a busybody:*

"But let none of you suffer as a murderer, or *as* a thief, or *as* an evildoer, or as a busybody in other men's matters." *(I Peter 4:15)*

"Whosoever hateth his brother is a murderer: and ye know that **no murderer hath eternal life abiding in him**." *(I John 3:15)*

33. *If we suffer 'according to the will of God,' commit to keeping your soul to God 'in well-doing':*

"Wherefore let them that suffer according to the will of God commit the keeping of their souls *to Him* in well doing, as unto a faithful Creator." *(I Peter 4:19)*

34. Feed the flock of God which is among you:

"Feed the flock of God which is among you, taking the oversight thereof, not by constraint, but willingly; not for filthy lucre, but of a ready mind; Neither as being lords over God's heritage, but being ensamples to the flock. And when the chief Shepherd shall appear, ye shall receive a crown of glory that fadeth not away. *(1 Peter 5:2-4)*

35. Be subject one to another: for God giveth Grace to the humble:

"Likewise, ye younger, submit yourselves unto the elder. Yea, all of you be subject one to another, and be clothed with humility: for God resisteth the proud, and giveth grace to the humble. Humble yourselves therefore under the mighty hand of God, that he may exalt you in due time." *(I Peter 5:5-6)*

36. Cast all care upon God 'for He careth for you':

"Casting all your care upon him; for he careth for you. *(I Peter 5:7)*

37. The devil 'as a roaring lion, walketh about, seeking whom he may devour':

"Be sober, be vigilant; because our adversary the devil, as a roaring lion, walketh about, seeking whom he may devour." *(I Peter 5:8)*

38. Resist the Devil, being 'steadfast in the faith":

"Whom resist stedfast in the faith, knowing that the same afflictions are accomplished in your brethren that are in the world." *(I Peter 5:9)*

39. After we have suffered 'a while', the God of all Grace will make us perfect:

"But the God of all grace, who hath called us unto his eternal glory by Christ Jesus, after that ye have suffered a while, make you perfect, stablish, strengthen, settle *you.*" *(I Peter 5:10)*

40. Be ye perfect, even as your Father in Heaven is perfect:

"Be ye therefore perfect, even as your Father which is in heaven is perfect." *(Matthew 5:48)*

41. 'Exceeding great and precious promises': to be 'partakers of the Divine nature':

"Whereby are given unto us exceeding great and precious promises: that by these ye might be partakers of the divine nature, having escaped the corruption that is in the world through lust." *(II Peter 1:4)*

42. To become the children, (literal) Sons and daughters of God:

"Behold, what manner of love the Father hath bestowed upon us, that we should be called the sons of God: therefore the world knoweth us not, because it knew him not. Beloved, now are we the sons of God, and it doth not yet appear what we shall be: but we know that, when he shall appear, we shall be like him; for we shall see Him as he is. And every man that hath this hope in him purifieth himself, even as he is pure." *(I John 3:1-3)*

"The Jews answered him, saying, For a good work we stone thee not; but for blasphemy; and because that thou, being a man, makest thyself God. **Jesus answered them, Is it not written in your law, I said, Ye are gods?** If he called them gods, unto whom the word of God came, and the scripture cannot be broken; Say ye of Him, whom the Father hath sanctified, and sent into the world, Thou blasphemest; because I said, I am the Son of God?" *(John 10:33-36)*

"For in him we live, and move, and have our being; as certain also of your own poets have said, For **we are also His offspring**." *(Acts 17:28)*

"For as many as are led by the Spirit of God, they are the sons of God. For ye have not received the spirit of bondage again to fear; but ye have received the Spirit of adoption, whereby we cry, Abba,

Father. The Spirit itself beareth witness with our spirit, that we are the children of God: And if children, then heirs; heirs of God, and joint-heirs with Christ; if so be that we suffer with Him, that we may be also glorified together." *(Romans 8:14-17)*

43. With all diligence, add to your faith all the following:

"But the wisdom that is from above is first pure, then peaceable, gentle, *and* easy to be intreated, full of mercy and good fruits, without partiality, and without hypocrisy. And the fruit of righteousness is sown in peace of them that make peace." *(James 3:17-18)*

"And beside this, giving all diligence, add to your faith virtue; and to virtue knowledge; And to knowledge temperance; and to temperance patience; and to patience godliness; And to godliness brotherly kindness; and to brotherly kindness charity. For if these things be in you, and abound, they make *you* that ye shall neither *be* barren nor unfruitful in the knowledge of our Lord Jesus Christ." *(II Peter 1:5-8)*

44. Make your calling and election sure: for in doing all of these things, ye shall not fail:

"But he that lacketh these things is blind, and cannot see afar off, and hath forgotten that he was purged from his old sins. Wherefore the rather, brethren, give diligence to make your calling and election sure: for if ye do these things, ye shall never fall." *(II Peter 1:9-10)*

45. To do these things shall enter the 'everlasting kingdom of our Lord' : as 'heirs of the Kingdom':

"For so an entrance shall be ministered unto you abundantly into the everlasting kingdom of our Lord and Saviour Jesus Christ." *(II Peter 1:11)*

"According as his divine power hath given unto us all things that pertain unto life and godliness, through the knowledge of him that hath called us to glory and virtue:" *(II Peter 1:3)*

"And when the chief Shepherd shall appear, ye shall receive a crown of glory that fadeth not away." *(I Peter 5:4)*

"But the God of grace, who hath called us unto his eternal glory by Christ Jesus, after that ye have suffered a while, make you perfect, stablish, strengthen, settle you. *(I Peter 5:10)*

"But rejoice, inasmuch as ye are partakers of Christ's sufferings; that, when his glory shall be revealed, ye may be glad also with exceeding joy." *(I Peter 4:13)*

"Let that therefore abide in you, which ye have heard from the beginning. If that which ye have heard from the beginning shall remain in you, ye also shall continue in the Son, and in the Father. And this is the promise that he hath promised us, even eternal life." *(I John 2:24-25)*

"Hearken, my beloved brethren, Hath not God chosen the poor of this world rich in faith, and heirs of the kingdom which he hath promised to them that love him?" *(James 2:5)*

46. *Who will harm you, if you be followers of that which is good?*

"And who *is* he that will harm you, if ye be followers of that which is good?" *(I Peter 3:13)*

47. *Have a good conscience!* (What is conscience?)

"Having a good conscience; that, whereas they speak evil of you, as of evildoers, they may be ashamed that falsely accuse your good conversation in Christ." *(I Peter 3:16)*

48. *Holy men of God spoke as they were moved by the Holy Ghost ! (Who is the "Holy Ghost"?)*

"For the prophecy came not in old time by the will of man: but holy men of God spake *as* they *were* moved by the Holy Ghost." *(II Peter 1:21)*

49. In the Lord's prayer, we pray that God may 'deliver us from evil'! (How might this deliverance occur?)

"And lead us not into temptation, but deliver us from evil: For thine is the kingdom, and the power, and the glory, for ever. Amen'." *(Matthew 6:13)*

"And the Lord shall deliver me from every evil work, and will preserve me unto his heavenly kingdom: to whom *be* glory for ever and ever. Amen'." (*2 Timothy 4:18*)

50. Lord knows how to deliver the Godly out of temptation" (Give examples in your own life):

"The Lord knoweth how to deliver the godly out of temptations, and to reserve the unjust unto the day of judgment to be punished." *(II Peter 2:9)*

"We know that we have passed from death unto life, because we love the brethren. He that loveth not his brother abideth in death. **Whosoever hateth his brother is a murderer: and ye know that no murderer hath eternal life abiding in him.** Hereby perceive we the love *of God*, because he laid down his life for us; and we ought to lay down our lives for the brethren. *(I John 3:14-16)*

51. The way of the evil tiger! (Once mounted, can we safely dismount from this 'tiger'?):

"But there were false prophets also among the people, even as there shall be false teachers among you, who privily shall bring in damnable heresies, even denying the Lord that bought them, and bring upon themselves swift destruction. And many shall follow their pernicious ways; by reason of whom the way of truth shall be evil spoken of. And through covetousness shall they with feigned words make merchandise of you: whose judgment now of a long time lingereth not, and their damnation slumbereth not." *(II Peter 2:1-3)*

"But if ye have bitter envying and strife in your hearts, glory not, and lie not against the truth. This wisdom descendeth not from above, but is earthly, sensual, devilish. For where envying and strife is, there is confusion and every evil work." *(James 3:14-16)*

52. People who are "unlearned and unstable" wrest (twist) the Scriptures to their own destruction:

"And account that the longsuffering of our Lord is salvation; even as our beloved brother Paul also according to the wisdom given unto him hath written unto you; As also in all his epistles, speaking in them of these things in which are some things hard to be understood, which they that are unlearned and unstable wrest, as *they do* also the other scriptures, unto their own destruction." *(II Peter 3:15-16)*

53. The Lord is not slack concerning His promise (to return one fine day with a fiery host of Angels, to set the world on fire):

"Knowing this first, that there shall come in the last days scoffers, walking after their own lusts, And saying, Where is the promise of his coming? for since the fathers fell asleep, all things continue as *they were* from the beginning of the creation. For this they willingly are ignorant of, that by the word of God the heavens were of old, and the earth standing out of the water and in the water:" *(II Peter 3:3-5)*

"But the heavens and the earth, which are now, by the same word are kept in store, reserved unto fire against the day of judgment and perdition of ungodly men. But, beloved, be not ignorant of this one thing, that one day is with the Lord as a thousand years and a thousand years as one day." *(II Peter 3:7-8)*

54. Lord is waiting for all to repent (as many as are to become the children of God), so He patiently waits:

"The Lord is not slack concerning his promise, as some men count slackness; but is longsuffering to us-ward, not willing that any should perish, but that all should come to repentance." *(II Peter 3:9)*

55. A New Heaven and a New earth to be formed:

"Nevertheless we, according to his promise, look for new heavens and a new earth, wherein dwelleth righteousness." *(II Peter 3:13)*

"And I saw a new heaven and a new earth: for the first heaven and the first earth were passed away; and there was no more sea. *(Revelation 21:1)*

56. This old polluted earth shall be dissolved and from the molten material, a New birth:

"But the heavens and the earth, which are now, by the same word are kept in store, reserved unto fire against the day of judgment and perdition of ungodly men." *(II Peter 3:7)*

"But the day of the Lord will come as a thief in the night; in the which the heavens shall pass away with a great noise, and the elements shall melt with fervent heat, the earth also and the works that are therein shall be burned up. Seeing then that all these things shall be dissolved, what manner of persons ought ye to be in all holy conversation and godliness. Looking for and hasting unto the coming of the day of God, wherein the heavens being on fire shall be dissolved, and th elements shall melt with fervent heat?" *(II Peter 3:10-12)*

57. New earth shall be formed only for the righteous:

"Seeing then that all these things shall be dissolved, what manner of persons ought ye to be in all holy conversation and godliness." *(II Peter 3:11)*

"Nevertheless we, according to his promise, look for new heavens and a new earth, wherein dwelleth righteousness. Wherefore, beloved, seeing that ye look for such things, be diligent that ye may be found of him in peace, without spot, and blameless." *(II Peter 3:13-14)*

"Ye therefore, beloved, seeing ye know these things before, beware lest ye also, being led away with the error of the wicked, fall from your own stedfastness." *(II Peter 3:17)*

58. Our fellowship is with the Father, and the Son:

"That which we have seen and heard declare we unto you, that ye also may have fellowship with us: and truly our fellowship is with the Father, and with his Son Jesus Christ." *(I John 1:3)*

"Little children, let no man deceive you: he that doeth righteousness is righteous, even as he is righteous." *(I John 3:7)*

"Whosoever is born of God doth not commit sin; for his seed remaineth in him: and he cannot sin, because he is born of God." *(I John 3:9)*

59. What is the Nature of God? (He is light, John says):

"If we say that we have fellowship with him, and walk in darkness, we lie, and do not the truth." *(I John 1:6)*

60. Blood of Jesus Christ cleanses us from 'all sin':

"But if we walk in the light, as he is in the light, we have fellowship on with another, and the blood of Jesus Christ his Son cleanseth us from all sin." *(I John 1:7)*

"If we confess our sins, he is faithful and just to forgive us our sins, and to cleanse us from all unrightousness." *(I John 1:9)*

61. To know Jesus is to keep His commandments:

"That which we have seen and heard declare we unto you, that ye also may have fellowship with us: and truly our fellowship *is* with the Father, and with his Son Jesus Christ. And these things write we unto you, that your joy may be full. This then is the message which we have hard of him, and declare unto you, that God is light, and in him is no darkness at all. If we say that we have fellowship with him, and walk in darkness, we lie, and do not the truth:" *(I John 1:3-6)*

62. He that saith he is in the light, but hateth his brother, is in darkness still (unconverted!):

"He that saith he is in the light, and hateth his brother, is in darkness even until now. He that loveth his brother abideth in the light, and there is none occasion of stumbling in him. But he that hateth his brother is in darkness, and walketh in darkness, and knoweth not whither he goeth, because that darkness hath blinded his eyes." *(I John 2:9-11)*

63. Love not the world:

"Love not the world, neither the things that are in the world. If any man love the world, the love of the Father is not in him. For all that is in the world, the lust of the flesh, and the lust of the eyes, and the pride of life, is not of the Father, but is of the world. And the world passeth away, and lust therefore: but he that doeth the will of God abideth for ever." *(I John 2:15-17)*

"For all flesh is as grass, and all the glory of man as the flower of grass. The grass withereth, and the flower thereof falleth away." *(I Peter 1:24)*

64. No lie is of the Truth:

"I have not written unto you because ye know not the truth, but because ye know it, and that no lie is of the truth. Who is a liar but he that denieth that Jesus is the Christ? He is anti-christ, that denieth the Father and the Son. Whosoever denieth the Son, the same hath not the Father: [but] he that acknowledgeth the Son hath the Father also." *(I John 2:21-23)*

"For without *are* dogs, and sorcerers, and whoremongers, and murderers, and idolaters, and whosoever loveth and maketh a lie." *(Revelation 22:15)*

65. Who are: The Anti-Christs?

"Little children, it is the last time: and as ye have heard that anti-christ shall come, even now are there many anti-christs; whereby we know that it is the last time. They went out from us, but they were not of us; for if they had been of us, they would no doubt have continued with us: but they went out, that they might be made manifest that they were not all of us." *(I John 2:18-19)*

"For if after they have escaped the pollutions of the world through the knowledge of the Lord and Savour Jesus Christ, they are again entangled therein, and overcome, the latter end is worse with them than the beginning. For it had been better for them not to have known the way of righteousness, than, after they have known it, to turn from the holy commandment delivered unto them. But it is happened unto them according to the true proverb, The dog *is* turned to his own vomit again; and the sow that was washed to her wallowing in the mire." *(II Peter 2:20-22)*

66. *The same anointing of the Holy Ghost 'teaches you of all things' (and is 'no lie'):*

"But the anointing which ye have received of him abideth in you, and ye need not that any man teach you: but as the same anointing teacheth you of all things, and is truth, and is no lie, and even as it hath taught you, ye shall abide in him." *(I John 2:27)*

67. *Love not in word only, but in 'deed'! ('works vs. faith' argument, not mere words):*

"But whoso hath this world's good, and seeth his brother have need, and shutteth up his bowels *of* compassion from him, how dwelleth the love of God in him? My little children, let us not love in word, neither in tongue; but in deed and in truth. And hereby we know that we are of the truth, and shall assure our hearts before him." *(I John 3:17-19)*

"What doth it profit, my brethren, though a man say he hath faith, and have not works? can faith save him? If a brother or sister be naked, and destitute of daily food, And one of you say unto them, Depart in peace, be ye warmed and filled; notwithstanding ye give them not those things which are needful to the body; what doth it profit? Even so faith, if it hath not works, is dead, being alone.

Yea, a man may say, Thou hast faith, and I have works: shew me thy faith without thy works, and I will show thee my faith by my works. **Thou believest that there is one God; thou doest well: the devils also believe**, and tremble. But wilt thou know, O vain man, that faith without works is dead?" *(James 2:14-20)*

"For as the body without the spirit is dead, so faith without works is dead also." *(James 2:26)*

68. Those that die in God, shall not taste of death, for it shall be sweet unto them:

"Peter seeing him saith to Jesus, Lord, and what shall this man do? Jesus saith unto him, If I will that he tarry till I come, what is that to thee? follow thou me. Then went this saying abroad among the brethren, that that disciple should not die: yet Jesus said not unto him, He shall not die; but, If I will that he tarry till I come, what is that to thee? This is the disciple which testifeth of these things and wrote these things: and we know that his testimony is true." *(John 21:21-24)*

"I protest by your rejoicing which I have in Christ Jesus our Lord, I die daily." *(I Corinthians 15:31)*

"And I, if I be lifted up from the earth, will draw all men unto me. This he said, signifying what death he should die." *(John 12:32-33)*

69. Beware the Fake Conversions:

"Woe unto you, scribes and Pharisees, hypocrites! for ye compass sea and land to make one proselyte, and when he is made, ye make him twofold more the child of hell than yourselves." *(Matthew 23:15)*

"When the unclean spirit is gone out of a man, he walketh through places, seeking rest and findeth none. Then he saieth, I will return into my house from whence I came out; and when he is come, he findeth it empty, swept, and garnished. Then goeth he, and taketh with himself seven other spirits more wicked than himself, and they enter in and dwell there: And the last state of that man is worse than the first. Even so shall it be also unto this wicked generation." *(Matthew 12:43-45)*

70. How oft shall I forgive my brother/sister who offends me?:

"Take heed to yourselves: If thy brother trespass against thee, rebuke him; **and if he repent**, forgive him. And if he trespass against thee seven times in a day, and seven times in a day turn again to thee, saying, **I repent**; thou shalt forgive him." *(Luke 17:3,4)*

"Then came Peter to him, and said, Lord, How oft shall my brother sin against me, and I forgive him? till seven times? Jesus saith unto him, I say not unto thee, Until seven times: but, Until seventy times seven." *(Matthew 18:21-22)*

Youth Feedback:

____

____

____

Scene iv:
Reflections Upon the Conversion Process

The Apostle Paul two thousand years ago explained the typical confusion that besets the newly converted ('babes in Christ' as he described them) who still feed upon but 'the milk' of the Gospel! (See, I Corinthians 3:1-2; I Peter 2:2).

1. In delineating the difference between the Spiritual and the Natural (or physical) state of man, Paul stated that in order to understand the Spirit, you need to speak it's language, for spiritual things are interpreted or best understood through The Spirit of God, (that is, through 'spiritual things'!). Let the Spirit interpret the Spirit, just as Scripture is used to help us to interpret or better understand 'Scripture'. (I Corinthians 2:9-14) In Paul's words: "The natural man receives not the things of the Spirit of God: for they are foolishness unto him: neither can he know them, because they are spiritually discerned" (I Corinthians 2:14).

2. This view (that knowledge exists in entirely two separate realms: the spiritual vs. the natural) is not an original concept with Paul the Apostle. Several centuries prior to Paul, Plato argued in a similar vein in his famous 'cave analogy' (at the end of Book IX of *The Republic*). Plato presented a hypothetical situation that certain cave dwellers were tied into a fixed position in a cave with a fire behind their backs. They had inanimate objects projected onto the wall of the cave to make them think that these 'shadows' were the real thing, when in fact they were only 'shadows'.

3. One day, one of their comrades escaped from the cave, discovered the 'real world' and returned eventually to share his 'Good News' with his former friends, the cave people! But owing to his difficulty in re-adjusting to the darkness of the cave, he could not even clearly and properly identify the shadows on the cave wall to verify that he was indeed capable of an even 'greater truth'! To his amazement, the cave-dwellers rejected his claim of a better, 'real' world outside of their familiar comfort zone! So he was ridiculed, persecuted, as someone not fit for their company, a social leper, an outcast, who is no doubt 'mad'.

4. We can instantly see the similarity in this reaction socially to those who propose that God spoke to them, or that they have had

Holy Communion with extraterrestrial Beings from another world, the 'real world'! Plato is arguing for the simple Concept of (perfect) Goodness, to show (later in his book) that there is a perfect world, a word of Forms, of which our world is but a draft copy or an imperfect facsimile.

5. If one were to draw what he would think to be a 'straight line', for example, that line would not be 'perfectly straight' but the thought or concept of 'perfect straightness' exists elsewhere (in Plato's World of Ideals or Perfect Forms). For this reason (among others), historically famous philosophers, such as Immanuel Kant, Aristotle, and even more recently Karl Popper, have labelled (rightly or wrongly) Plato's other-worldly Theory of Forms, as 'empty formalism'.

6. But to return to the argument presented at hand, Paul himself presented his vision, his direct experience, of this 'other world' before a royal audience: King Agrippa, his wife Bernice, and Governor Festus. Paul was imprisoned because of his 'beliefs', his adamant adherence to the (spiritual) facts of his case! As a result of his declarations, Paul was deemed to be 'mad' by Governor Festus (see, Acts 26:24).

7. Of course, to this list of persecuted Saints, extending from Ancient Prophets to the Apostles and disciples of the early Pristine Church of Christ, could be added the names of Modern-day soothsayers, poets, and gifted savants, such as: Francis D'Assisi, Joan of Arc, Joseph Smith, Jr., and others, all of whom claimed divine communication(s).

8. The philosopher William James comments on his 'reflections of spiritual communications', as follows:

"The great field for this sense of being the instrument of a higher power is of course 'inspiration.' It is easy to discriminate between the religious leaders who have been habitually subject to inspiration and those who have not. ... In the Hebrew prophets... in Mohammed, ... in Fox, in Joseph Smith, something like it appears to have been frequent, sometimes habitual. We have distinct professions of being under the direction of a foreign power, and serving as its mouthpiece."

9. As we can see, this introduction of 'new (higher) knowledge' to existing civilizations is naturally met with initial disbelief, even outright hostility at times. When the early Saints during Pentecost received this 'higher knowledge', they were deemed to be "full of new wine" (Acts 2:13). Later, they were forbidden to speak of 'these things', to the point of persecution, and death (Acts 3:18;4:13-21; 5:26-33).

10. Even to this day, the same attitude exists among the religious extremists who wish to maintain their hold and power over their populace, to reject any and every claim to 'higher revelations', as witnessed in the martyrdom of both Joseph Smith and his brother Hyrum at the hands of an enraged mob: Similar to the 'mob' (as "grievous wolves," Acts 20:29) that sought to put Paul the Apostle to death because of his preaching. (Acts 20:22-29; 21:13-14;30-36; 23:10-35).

11. In the full realization that no matter what occurs in certain people's lives, they will never change: (As they pride themselves in remaining steadfast to the status quo), I am moved to include as my concluding thought (upon the *Concept of Conversion*) the following insight from Billy Graham:

"In every phase of life we face this recurring question: 'What think ye of Christ?'. In youth, too happy to think: I've plenty of time. In manhood, too busy to think: I must make a living. In maturity, too anxious to think: I've more urgent problems. Declining years, too old to think: my pattern of life is set. As death approaches, too ill to think: the Spirit is flown, the day of opportunity is past, the harvest is gone, and now God's Judgment Day!"

Youth Feedback:

[#245: U-Tube Reference]
Peter and Gordon - A World Without Love (HD) 1964
https://www.youtube.com/watch?v=Tdx6lLvvRyg

A World Without Love

Birds sing out of tune
And rain clouds hide the moon

I don't care what they say
I won't stay in a world without love

So I wait and in a while
I will see my true love smile
She may come, I know not when
When she does, I'll know

Scene v:
Personal Revelation

A. Prelude to fully recognizing "Personal Revelation"
(or "Inspiration":

From the age of ten (when I received my first Gideon's New Testament bible in Grade 5), I began to read the Scriptures and to pray to God, (Our Heavenly Father) as Jesus taught us (through the Lord's Prayer, Matthew 6:9-13); and as I was encouraged to do so by the Polish Roman Catholic Church in my early childhood years.

I would implement my prayers (to see if God were truly listening) especially in seeking the location of our half dozen (or so) milk cows we had on the farm.

Dad had to work doing odd jobs to supplement the family income and to pay for the lease on the 1/4-section farm we rented. After school, my younger brother Robin and I had 'the calling' to call to the cows to try to locate them in the various possible bushes and groves of trees throughout this pastureland we called home. This task was especially difficult in the winter when it became so dark so fast.

1. If we did not locate these cows by the time dad returned home from his job (usually shovelling coal or grain), there would be High Heaven to pay (if you know what I mean!). Dad loved us, I am sure, but he seemed to love us all the more when we got the job done, and did it right.

2. So, on several occasions, I resorted to prayer, and to pray in earnest: To ask God to let us know where these cows were each night after school. It was usually quite dark by the time we began our 'adventures' accompanied by our three dogs: Rex (a male German Shepherd), Fuzzy (a very short female Scottish Terrier, and Butch (a stray red Lab dog that we adopted after he wandered to our farm badly beaten by a previous owner).

   With this motley collection of rag-tag dogs (usually running in all different directions), my younger brother and I would try to locate these stray elusive critters.

We both knew what would happen if the cows were not in their corral before dad returned home from a 'hard day's night'.

3. It was on one particular early evening in winter (as I still so vividly recall) that the night had no moon: it was stark dark, you could feel the darkness around you; so there was little hope we could easily find these cows [who insisted in playing 'hide and seek' finding the most difficult spots to hide in, or so it seemed].

There were tall thick snow drifts like sand dunes everywhere, several packs of coyotes were yelping in sporadic choruses from all sides: it became too difficult to discern that very quiet cow bell on the lead cow.

I sometimes thought that what was wanted was a really loud cow bell, like a ringing Church tower, on that supposed lead-cow, or even better yet: a loud foghorn, or a firetruck siren, as you had to be forty feet away from Betsy before you could hear her tiny bell softly go: 'dingle, dingle, dingle' — That wouldn't startle a field mouse?!

4. On this particularly dark and dreary night, we looked everywhere, that is: in all the usual places, and still no hide nor hair of these mysterious 'ghost-riders of the fields'.

Rather reluctantly, We decided to return to the farmyard (as it was bitterly cold and our little boots were full of snow): to face the music from 'good ol' Dad when I suddenly decided to pray as I never did before! or so it seemed.

And then it happened: that very faint tingle of a cow bell, or was it — but our imagination?

Instantly, the dogs and Robin and I rushed to where we thought the sound seemed to echo ever so faintly?! There they were, those brute beasts, still trying to chew tall grass growing above the snow in an opening in the forest.

Funny thing later, as I thought about it: we could never hear the cow bells from that far away spot before? I then knew deep in my heart that God had answered my boyish prayer.

B. After the death of dad (when I was eleven), mom gave up leasing the Farm and the family (all seven children!) moved into the Town of Two Hills to live as 'city slickers' (in a town of a thousand people or so).

1. By this time, I was deeply engrossed in Bible reading: I read the New Testament beginning from the last book first (a habit I had followed ever since, even until today: always wanting to know how the story ends before I would begin to read it).

For a young imaginative mind still imbued with playing "Cowboys & Indians" (with cap-guns) it was a fascinating read: All those creatures with several heads and so forth... I never mocked the Scriptures but always treated them with the deepest respect and utmost reverence. My uncles and aunts would visit us occasionally and always at the end of a long-heated argument resort to the words: "But the Bible says...", although I wondered if any of them ever read any of it?!

Notwithstanding, and initially in a superstitious sort of way, I had a healthy fear for the Word of God, especially as I had just recently seen *The Ten Commandments* (1956 with Charlton Heston) in our little town Lux Theatre. It left an indelible impression upon me that I haven't quite forgotten to this very day.

2. I did not attend Church in those years, however, as mom had all of us re-baptized into the Ukrainian Orthodox Church after dad's passing (in 1965), and I did not understand the Ukrainian language. So, what was the point of going?! The Old Priests didn't seem to like children anyway, because whenever I came to the Church to Pray (in private) around midnight, the Priest would lock the doors and threaten to call the Police. They didn't think it was possible for a kid, a youth, a young teenager, to just

want to pray where God supposedly was.
So, I left Churchgoing to the adults and became a sort of John the Baptist (or Robinson Crusoe) type of Christian: Always wanting to be alone, in my own little wilderness or private island.

3. But then it happened when I was about fourteen years of age, I decided to have a *dialogue* with Heavenly Father: No more *monologue*, I wished for sincere and genuine communion with God, to touch His face as it were. [To be continued in **Scene vii**.]

Scene vi:
How Can We Draw Nigh unto God?

To Receive Personal Revelation:
[A personal Interpretation]

1. The key reason for us to receive personal revelation is that we may become converted to the Gospel of our Lord and once truly converted (as Peter eventually was), we are to 'strengthen' (or, help to convert) our Brethren (Luke 22:32), to Preach the Word. (2 Timothy 4:2)

2. In order to overcome our natural man, we need to lean upon Christ and His ways. Let us overcome this 'natural man' who is an enmity with God (James 4:4) for to be carnally-minded, we cannot please God (Romans 8:5-8; Romans 7:15,19).

3. Only as we surrender in humility to the Spirit of God (to be spiritually-minded), to be led by continual personal revelation, can we know the will of God and therefore be able to do it. (James 8:14,16; Romans 7:18; Romans 8:10)

4. As we pray to know the will of the Lord, the Spirit of God will help us according to the will of God. (Romans 8:26-28)

5. But as we seek to obey our God and to say and do all things pleasing in His sight, we need to realize that the *true* purpose (or ultimate aim) to receive the Holy Ghost is that we may bear witness to others of the Truth). (Acts 1:8)

6. For to convert (through the Holy Ghost) a sinner from his ways, as James says, is to: "save a soul from death, and shall hide a multitude of sins". (James 5:20)

7. Now it is not we ourselves who 'convert' others to the Truth, but the Holy Ghost that dwells in us, insofar as we sanctify ourselves, as Peter says, to be worthy of that Holy Presence to: "give an answer to every man" who may ask us "a reason of the hope" that is in us! (I Peter 3:15)

8. As the Gospel writers tell us, we need not worry, nor premeditate beforehand what we shall say (much like bearing

our testimonies in Church) as the Spirit of Truth will inform us of all things and bring all things to our remembrance. (John 14:16-17,26; Luke 12:12; Mt. 10:16-22; Mark 13:9-13)

A. To bear witness of the Truth, is to suffer persecution:

1. Be not ashamed to suffer for Christ:

    Beloved, think it not strange concerning the fiery trial which is to try you, as though some strange thing happened unto you: But rejoice, inasmuch as ye are partakers of Christ's sufferings; that, when his glory shall be revealed, ye may be glad also with exceeding joy. If ye be reproached for the name of Christ, happy *are ye*; for the spirit of glory and of God resteth upon you: on their part he is evil spoken of, but on your part he is glorified. *(I Peter 4:12-14)*

    Yet if any man suffer as a Christian, let him not be ashamed; but let him glorify God on this behalf. *(I Peter 4:16)*

    Wherefore let them that suffer according to the will of God commit the keeping of their souls to Him in well doing, as unto a faithful Creator. *(I Peter 4:19)*

2. All who live godly in Christ Jesus shall suffer persecution:

    Yea, and all that will live godly in Christ Jesus shall suffer persecution. *(1 Timothy 3:12)*

3. They shall lay hands on you and persecute you... into prisons:

    But before all these, they shall lay their hands on you, and persecute you, delivering you up to the synagogues, and into prisons, being brought before kings and rulers for my name's sake. And it shall turn to you for a testimony. Settle it therefore in your hearts, not to meditate before what ye shall answer: For I will give you a mouth and wisdom, which all your adversaries shall not be able to gainsay nor resist.

And ye shall be betrayed both by parents, and brethren, and kinsfolks, and friends; and some of you shall they cause to be put to death. And ye shall be hated of all men for my name's sake. *(Luke 21:12-17)*

4. We are to speak "as the oracles of God" (as led by personal revelation). (I Peter 4:11)

5. We are to remember that our God is not the God of the Dead, but of the Living. (Luke 20:38)

6. That we need to be valiant for our Lord; otherwise, He will spew us out of His mouth as lukewarm. (Revelation 3:16)

7. To fall away, after we have received personal revelation from the Holy Ghost, may cause us to sin against the Holy Ghost, a sin that is arguably 'unpardonable'. (as the Apostle Peter describes it):

   "For if after these reprobates have "escaped the pollution of the world through the knowledge of the Lord and Savior Jesus Christ, they are again entangled therein, and overcome, the latter end is worse with them than the beginning.

   For it had been better not to have known the way of righteousness, than, to turn from the Holy commandment delivered unto them.

   But it is happened unto them according to the true proverb: The dog is turned to his own vomit again; and the sow that was washed to her wallowing in the mire." (2 Peter 2:20-22)

8. Therefore, my fellow Saints, my dear brothers & sisters: Let us remain faithful and true to our Lord, to His Gospel, to the Truths that have been already revealed to us.

   There is no turning back! We have put our shoulder to the wheel! As our Lord has said: "Remember Lot's wife!" (Luke 17:32) for no man who shall put his hand to the plow and looks back "is fit for the Kingdom of God." (Luke 9:62)

B. In Conclusion, let us be valiant in our Testimonies. Let us continually seek to obtain personal revelation for ourselves, each according to his faith, and the strength and trial of that faith.

As Peter the Apostle admonishes us: There shall come in the last days, scoffers who shall say: "Where is the Promise of His Coming? For since the fathers fell asleep, all things continue as they were from the beginning of Creation!" (II Peter 3:3-4)

1. Peter also provides the answer to this question:

   "The Lord is not slack concerning His promise... but is long-suffering to us-ward, not willing that any should perish, but that all should come to repentance!

   "But the Day of the Lord will come as a thief in the night; in the which the Heavens shall pass away with a great noise, and the elements shall melt with fervent heat, the earth also and the works that are therein shall be burned up"! (II Peter 3:9-10)

2. Peter continues: "Seeing then that all these things shall be dissolved, **what manner of persons ought ye to be** in all holy conversation and godliness, looking for and hasting unto the Coming of the Day of God, wherein the heavens being on fire shall be dissolved, and the elements shall melt with fervent heat?" (II Peter 3:11-12)

3. Peter concludes: "Nevertheless we, according to His promise, look for New Heavens and a New Earth, wherein dwelleth righteousness". (II Peter 3:13)

4. Peter makes it crystal clear that these are not 'cunningly devised fables' (II Peter 1:16-21).

5. As John the Beloved Apostle has profoundly declared:

   "We are of God: he that knoweth God, heareth us" (I John 4:1-6); for "he that keepeth His commandments dwelleth in him, and He in him. And thereby we know that He abideth in us, by the Spirit which He hath given us". (I

John 3:24)

6. I so testify that it is this Sacred Spirit "which He hath given us" (even the Holy Ghost) which will lead us via a 'still small voice', or through whisperings and gentle promptings to guide and direct us to do the will of our Holy Father.

(See, I Kings 19:11-12; Psalms 4:4-5; Psalms 46:10; John 14:16-18)

Scene vii:
My Testimony of my Conversion Story
(at Age Fourteen)

One day (when I was almost fourteen), during summer vacation (from school in 1967), I had begun to read the Old Testament (from beginning to end).

I came to the part in Judges 6:36-40, in which Gideon (who was preparing his soldiers to battle against tens of thousands of his enemies) wanted to know whether God was on his side, and would definitely give him the victory, to know whether God truly would answer his prayers. He prayed (as a sure sign of God's favor) that the Lord God would pour water (or make wet) a fleece that Gideon apparently had kept in secret.

The next day, the Lord did as Gideon requested. Then (perhaps thinking that someone may have poured water on his fleece?), Gideon asked the Lord not to be angry with him but that he would like to see the reverse happen: that God would 'make wet' (pour water) all along the outside of this fleece but to keep the fleece perfectly dry.

And, lo and behold, when Gideon went to check out the fleece, it was dry all throughout although surrounded by water! So then, Gideon knew that the Lord was on his side and that he would indeed win this battle against overwhelming odds.

1. I thought that this biblical story was simply amazing almost beyond belief, especially as I later read that Gideon had only 300 soldiers to go to battle for him. The way he won the battle was incredibly bold and clever! The Lord was truly on his side.

2. So, later that week, as I was deep in contemplation and wondering just how was it possible for Gideon to win such a big victory with only 300 men against tens of thousands of the enemy, I began to more precisely focus on my own testimony to determine whether it were possible for me to receive 'inspiration' (or 'personal revelation') for myself.

3. After all, I was praying 'religiously' at least once each day

('Before I lay me down to sleep!') and I always thought about God and the Bible keeping a prayer (as it were) in my heart at all times. I soon realized I needed to be alone to seek the Lord's Spirit in private in order to have an answer to my prayers (as was the case with Gideon).

A. So, one rather hot summer day, I retired to the open field not far from the Town of Two Hills where I grew up. I made certain I was alone: I had gone far into the field and found a slight slope or hill in which I could rest and look upwards into the sky. Not a cloud to be seen: a perfectly beautiful placid blue sky, with not even a bird to be heard or seen anywhere. Total peace and serenity.

For a long time now (especially since Dad was gone and I was the 'surrogate Father' for my six younger siblings), I felt a profound urge to reach out and touch the face of God!

1. For me, in my own child-like creative mind, I still maintained a child-like faith. I believed that if the Bible said it was *so*, then it was *so!* (No 'ands, ifs, or buts' about it!) I knew deep inside my being that God lived, but I felt I needed to have this one ultimate test, this final confirmation as if it were a life-and-death struggle (like Gideon had). Only then, I believed: I could rest with full assurance in the knowledge that 'my Redeemer liveth!" (Job 19:25)

   For if there truly was a God (as I was led to believe and never doubted), why would He not wish to show Himself to me? To connect with me in a truly personal way? If God is real, and if He is my Heavenly Father, then wouldn't He want me to know that He truly cares for me (as His child) and that I matter to Him in His own personal sort of way?

2. So then, while glancing deep into the heavens, and seeming to pierce my vision beyond my mortal view, I spoke out loud the following words (to the best of my recollection):

   "Oh, Lord my God, I know that Thou art God! And I know that Thou livest! and that Thou can hear and answer prayer, even my smallest prayers. But be Thou not angry with me, be not offended by this small request: I simply need to know, like Gideon of Old, for a surety that Thou art real, that Thou art alive and present next to me right now! That thou hearest my prayer! And I will serve Thee forever!"

I then searched in my heart and in my mind what exact request I should make to the Heavens that would satisfy my boyish wonder, my deepest need, my most powerful desire to be heard by my 'Father' (who is in Heaven).

3. I then asked God, if it were possible (and I know that with God all things are possible), that if He would not mind (and I thought that He might not mind as he answered Gideon's request) that I would at this very instant — hear the sound of a crow cawing. (For there were no birds anywhere in sight and I was alone in a wide-open field.)

4. No sooner did I speak the words, when at that very instant, I heard the loudest most distinct sound of a crow cawing as if it were perched on my very shoulder! I immediately jumped up startled at the very loud sound of the crow and looked all around in all directions: I could see no crow anywhere, no bird anywhere, no animal anywhere (except for the odd gopher popping in and out of it's hole).

5. I fell to my knees in humble adoration and prayed such a prayer as if all my heart would burst and all my body would melt into tears (like soft butter on a hot day), tears not of sorrow or sadness, but of utter joy, and a bursting forth of unstoppable gladness: I knew God loved me! He accepted me! I was His own son! I too had my very tiny little version of the 'burning bush'! I talked to God, the Creator of the Universe, and He heard me!

6. Such an experience pierced through me over and over again for all these decades ever since! For even to this very day, whenever I would hear the sound of a crow cawing, I would feel a refreshing rush (or wave) of emotion come over me as a soothing soft caress!

I wonder sometimes if this was the kind of experience Joan of Arc was purported to have?! Who knows?

But for me, this private channel to my Father (in Heaven) was a privilege beyond treasure: He became my guiding Star, my confidante, my personal friend.

B. Since that boyhood experience to this very day, I have had many instances of personal revelation throughout my life, as my testimony has grown in leaps and bounds even until the latest major event on 26th September 2018!

1. At 3:33 a.m. on that fateful day, my life was almost forfeited by a knife-stabbing fifteen-year old youth, an orphan Native boy born to a woman on crystal meth, abused every which way since a child, a crystal meth addict since he was twelve, and apparently unloved and unwanted by the Society that (or so it appears) refused both to love him, or to take proper care of him, as one of their own.

2. I could only reflect: What a different life I had when I was his age! I thought upon Psalms 41:1-2, 11, which says: "Blessed is he that considers the poor: the Lord will deliver him in time of trouble. *The Lord will preserve him and keep him alive:* and thou wilt not deliver him unto the will of his enemies. By this I know that thou favors me, because mine enemy does not triumph over me."

3. As it says in Psalms 103:13, "Like as a father pities his children, so the Lord pities them that fear him." Adam Clark in his Bible commentary *comments on this verse*, as follows:

"Nothing can place the tenderness and concern of God for his creatures in a stronger light than this, ... 'Father, I have sinned against Heaven and before thee, and am not worthy to be called thy son!' [Luke 15:21] The same in kind, but infinitely more exquisite, does God feel when the penitent falls at His feet, and implores His mercy through Christ crucified." (Vol. 3, p. 544)

4. As, we choose to draw nigh to God, He will draw nigh to us! [Psalms 145:18-20; James 4:8 (vv.5-10); Hebrews 7:19]

What is/was your own Spiritual life experience(s) at age fourteen (or, thereabouts)?

Youth Feedback:

____

____

____

What sense can be made of Child Crime Laws in Canada? What is the Answer to Child Crime? Will a soft do-nothing approach resolve Child Crime?

Youth Feedback:

____

____

____

DISCLAIMER: N.B. (*Nota Bene*)
All tunes/songs/video clips/links/quotes/etc. are herein provided to assist in Group Therapy Sessions, or privately, for individual study (to assist in learning) and for educational purposes *only*.

[#246: U-Tube Reference]
Kris Kristofferson & Rita Coolidge - Please don't tell me how the story ends (1978)
https://www.youtube.com/watch?v=KLeDe5yRi8s

Please Don't Tell Me How The Story Ends

This could be our last good night together
We may never pass this way again.

Just let me enjoy it 'til it's over, or forever
Someday these may be all we remember of each other

Never's just the echo of forever
Lonesome as a love that might have been.
Let me go on lovin' and believin' 'til it's over
Please don't tell me how the story ends.

Writer: K Kristofferson

The love of many shall become cold!
(Matthew 24:3-4, 12)

ACT V:
Final Reflections Upon Child Crime in Canada

Scene i:
The Negative Factor

The youth who attempted murder (on my life) had just turned fifteen years old (a month earlier). There are many other examples of fourteen to fifteen-year-old youths who reveal their lives to be all messed up. Here in Canada, Omar Kadr comes to mind who at age fifteen killed a US Marine and wounded (blinded in one eye) another US soldier (a sniper) with a home-made grenade Omar Kadr had made to kill 'the enemy'.

Our Canadian PM (Prime Minister) Justin Trudeau re-patriated this ex-patriated youth after he took the life of a US Marine. The PM then paid (a total of) $20 million to Omar Kadr: To cover his legal fees ($9.5 million) and to help him start a new life ($10.5 million). Today, Mr. Kadr (fully pardoned by the Canadian Justice System earlier in 2020) is a thriving businessman in Edmonton, Alberta Canada. He appears to have put his life back together again, and is a contributor to Society, as well. Ten million dollars can jumpstart certain individuals who arguably commit even 'murder' (or take a human life recklessly) as a child of fifteen years of age.

In the case of B.B., no amount of money was ever offered or provided by the Government (as an award) either to compensate me for my situation; or, to help B.B. to readjust to a better life. Perhaps when he is a legal adult (as was Omar Kadr when he received this generous payout), B.B. can look forward to a significant payment from the taxpayers of Canada (by August 2021 when he turns eighteen years of age)?

In 1939, there was a poem written in *The New Yorker* that depicts the mentality of these troubled youth: It depicts their attitude and mindset at a very young age, as follows:

"When they tell him to eat his dinner, he will just laugh at them,
And he will not take his nap, because he does not care to...
He will not speak to nobody because he doesn't have to.

And when they come to look for him they will not find him,
He will not go out in the fresh air or eat his vegetables,
Or make wee-wee for them, and he will get thin as a marble.
He will not do nothing at all.
He will just sit there in the noonday sun."

My point in reflecting upon these negative character traits is that there can be hope at the end of the tunnel, at times. Who knows but if large cash payouts were to be paid to wayward troubled youth, even these 'planks of crooked wood' can *one fine day* be made 'straight'?!

 Youth Feedback:
____

____

____

DISCLAIMER: N.B. (*Nota Bene*)
All tunes/songs/video clips/links/quotes/etc. are herein provided to assist in Group Therapy Sessions, or privately, for individual study (to assist in learning) and for educational purposes *only*.

[#247: U-Tube Reference]
Kris Kristofferson & Rita Collidge-It Sure Was (Love)
https://www.youtube.com/watch?v=0aUcSJqYRxA

It Sure Was (Love)

I'll be livin off of the good times
That you've given me to face
I have had my share of the sunshine
I can stand a little rain.

So we don't give a damn what they say
We've got something they can't take away
'Cause whatever comes tomorrow
It sure was love while it lasted.

Writer: Kris Kristofferson

[#248: U-Tube Reference]
season of heart by John Denver with lyrics.wmv
https://www.youtube.com/watch?v=NR3VlbH0LTo

Seasons Of the Heart

So I don't know how to tell you, it's difficult to say.
I never in my wildest dreams imagined it this way.
... There's a stranger in our home.
When I'm lying right beside you is when I'm most alone.

And I think my heart is broken, there's an emptiness inside.
So many things I've longed for have so often been denied.
Still I wouldn't try to change you, there's no one that's to blame.
... We just don't feel the same.

Writer: John Denver

Scene ii:
The Positive Factor

Of course, in life (as in nature) there must be an opposition in all things, a counterweight to every negative factor. In the realm of *Positive Mental Thinking*, positive character traits can be learned, developed, and passed on from father to son, to grandson, and so on down the line for generations to come.

1. I think of the fourteen-year-old girl, Anne Frank, who wrote so eloquently in her personal diary ('Kitty') about her life in hiding from Nazi Jew-hunters. Yes, she was eventually captured (when fifteen) for the crime of being Jewish and died in a Nazi concentration camp (along with her mother and older sister). But before her capture, she left a legacy that has been made into movies. She believed in people: that there was good in every human being if we would but look for it. Who can forget one of her last entries in 1943 as she said:

"Why do I always think and dream of the most awful things and want to scream in terror? Because, in spite of everything, I still don't have enough faith in God. He's given me so much, which I don't deserve, and yet each day I make so many mistakes! Thinking about the suffering of those you hold dear can reduce you to tears: in fact, you could spend the whole day crying. The most you can do is pray for God to perform a miracle and save at least some of them."

2. Likewise (to leave an indelible impression upon society for generations to come), the boy-prophet Joseph Smith, Jr. was found worthy at age fourteen to receive a heavenly visitation that marked the beginning of the Restoration of Christ's original Church on earth (in fulfilment of divine prophecy in Revelation 14:6-7). At this tender age of experiencing the First Vision, Joseph Smith was severely persecuted as he testifies:

"I have thought since, that I felt much like Paul, when he made his defence before King Agrippa, and related the account of the vision he had when he saw a light, and heard a voice; but still there were but few who believed him; some said he was mad; and he was ridiculed and reviled. But all this did not destroy the reality of his vision. He had seen a vision, he knew he had! [Acts 26] .... So it was with me. I had actually seen a light, and in the midst of that light I saw two Personages, and they did, in reality, speak *to me!"* *(For the full "Testimony", see, Pearl* of Great Price, The Church of Jesus Christ of Latter-Day Saints)

3. Indeed, Joan of Arc as well had visions (heard voices) as early as thirteen years of age and though an illiterate peasant girl, she influenced the world forever, and at such a tender age. Who can forget one of her last remarks as she reportedly said:

"Do you think you can frighten me by telling me that I am alone? France is alone; and God is alone; and what is my loneliness before the loneliness of my country and my God? I see now that the loneliness of God is His strength! What would He be if He listened to your jealous little counsels? Well, my loneliness shall be my strength too: it is better to be alone with God! His friendship will not fail me, nor His counsel, nor His love! In His strength, I will dare, and dare, and dare, until I die!"
(Revised by George Bernard Shaw, *Saint Joan*)

4. Other boys and girls at these tender ages became froward wayward delinquents forming gangs and committing evil deeds. *Bad Seed* they have been dubbed (as the movie titles in 1956, and again in the 2018 remake suggest).

5. But the good far outweighs the bad, as History makes clear. Yes, we have a lot to be grateful for even though these three youth I mentioned, eventually died for their beliefs, but their lives have not been lost in vain.

They have become the shining beacon to all ages to come to indicate that, despite their young and tender ages, there is a very positive outcome (for especially the youth of today) that can lead to a spiritual-faith-bound life, if one but believes. And that is the essence of a positive disposition: to but believe. For out of this healthy good seed, comes fruit that can benefit all mankind!

Youth Feedback:
____

____

____

[#249: U-Tube Reference]
Carly Simon - Nobody Does It Better - The Spy Who Loved Me
https://www.youtube.com/watch?v=SaV-6qerkql&pbjreload=10

Nobody Does It Better
(from "The Spy Who Loved Me" soundtrack)

I tried to hide from your love light
But like Heaven above me
The spy who loved me
Is keeping all my secrets safe tonight

Whenever you hold me
There's some kind of magic inside you
That keeps me from running
But just keep it coming

Writers: Carole Sager, Marvin Hamlisch

Scene iii:
Reflections Upon Child Crime in Canada

As I reflected upon what to say to address the issue of woeful child neglect in our education system, in Canada (and around the world), I could not say it better than this true story of Cliff Evans.

I am so grateful to Jean E. Mizer (beyond words to express) for the simple, direct, and very moving description of a problem all too common in our schools even until today.

In my opinion, I truly believe the failure in our educational system for all **ciphers in the snow** can lead to an increase of child despondency and despair which all too often results in criminal and suicidal behaviour.

Youth Feedback:

____

____

____

DISCLAIMER: N.B. (*Nota Bene*)
All tunes/songs/video clips/links/quotes/etc. are herein provided to assist in Group Therapy Sessions, or privately, for individual study (to assist in learning) and for educational purposes *only*.

Cipher in the Snow, written by Jean E. Mizer, was first published in *The NEA Journal,* 50:8-10, 1964.
(See *Wikipedia* for additional information.)

Cipher in the Snow [as summarized by Mike Kostelny]

In 1964, Jean E. Mizer tells the brief account (some say, 'True Story') of a certain Cliff Evans, a public-school teenager from The Milford Corners School District. On a cold February morning, this fifteen-year-old 9th Grader politely requests the yellow-school-bus driver to let him off the bus near a snowbank. The driver complies. Cliff Evans steps off the bus; but then immediately collapses dead into the snowbank, much to everyone's horror!

The School Authorities and Police Investigation determine that he died through no apparent physical illness but (oddly enough) from total neglect both at home (where he lived with his stepdad and mother), as well as in the school, where he was treated as a 'nothing', a cipher, a zero by his school mates.

In the words of the Author, Jean Mizer:

> "How do you go about making a boy into a zero? The grade-school records showed me... The 3rd Grade note [read]: 'Cliff won't talk. Uncooperative. Slow learner.' [Later Grade comments]: 'Dull, slow-witted, low I.Q.' They became correct! [Evans' 7th Grade IQ score] was 83. But his IQ in the 3rd Grade had been 196. The score didn't go under 100 until the 7th Grade. Even shy, timid, sweet children have resilience: It takes time to break them."

The closing remarks echo the teacher's resolve that no one from now on will be allowed to graduate thinking himself (or herself) into a zero, a cipher!

Nota Bene: As 'Cipher in the Snow (1973)' video clip is NOT AVAILABLE for viewing via U-Tube anymore due to copyright restrictions, I have replaced it with the following video clip (see, below): "Burning Bridges". This video clip graphically portrays the result of dysfunctional relationships: A compelling WARNING for 'ciphers' who grow up only to 'Burn their own Bridges'!

[#250: U-Tube Reference]
Burning Bridges (from Kelly's Heroes movie clip)
https://www.youtube.com/watch?v=HG7p3KHwS_E

Years have passed and I keep thinking what a fool I've been,
I look back into the past and think of way back then,
I knew that I lost everything I thought that I could win,
I guess I should have listened to my friends.

All the Burning Bridges that have fallen after me,
All the lonely feelings and the burning memories,
Everyone I left behind each time I closed the door,
Burning Bridges lost for everymore.

Put on the whole Armour of God
Ephesians 6:11-18

Epilogue:
"We who are about to die, salute you!"

In Ancient Rome, the Gladiators who were to fight to their death one against another, had a remarkable code of honour which they expressed to their cheering audience: "We who are about to die, salute you!" In like manner, we the aging generation express our dying words to our fledgling youth: "We who are about to die, salute *You*! May you prove yourselves honourable: To overcome despair with hope, and even the death (of our civilization) with a brighter faith in tomorrow!"

1. But when all is said and done, there is typically more 'said' than 'done'! How true these words ring when it comes to a conclusion on this matter! What can be done to rectify a seemingly hopeless situation? What options do we have?

2. One thing for certain, *love* (however trite it may sound) is the answer. Perhaps the only answer? But certainly the ultimate answer! For without love in one's world, one's sphere of influence, what can be said of these helpless, hapless waifs? Are they hopeless as well? Karl Menninger in his classic book, *Love Against Hate* (1970), argues that *love* 'cures all sorrow'. He claims: "Die we must, ultimately, but in the meantime we can live, if we can love" (p.5). He adds: "Love is stronger than hate, and therefore, stronger than death" (p.6).

3. Louis Pasteur spoke of two contrary laws fighting inside each one of us (as with the 'two wolves' analogy): "The one a law of blood and death ever imagining new means of destruction...The other, a law of peace, work, and health ever evolving new means of delivering man from the scourges which beset him" (p.5, *Love Against Hate*, as quoted by K. Menninger).

4. We have this 'deep persistent instinct', says Karl Menninger that wages the impulse to *live and love* against our innate self-destructiveness (p.5). In the vulnerable delicate formative years of the curious child, who is deprived of the extra supply of love to sweeten each step of his development, says Menninger: This frustrated child eventually reacts with bitterness and confusion. Some of these waifs give up altogether "the idea of attaining adulthood and become irresponsible weaklings" (p.24). "To know ourselves", concludes Menninger is: "to become aware of our destructiveness as well as of our constructiveness" (p.6).

5. We can see then that aggression is generally the result of extreme frustration, just as when love is denied (or suppressed) it tends to lead to hate. So, what is the answer? Again, at the risk of sounding quite trite, it is: *Hope!* As one (anonymous) writer put it: "Hope ... looks for the good in people instead of harping on the worst: ...it regards problems, large or small, as opportunities... it lights the candle instead of cursing the darkness". Perhaps, as John Ray puts it: "If it were not for hope, the heart would break"?!

6. In attempting to examine the root problem of social violence among the youth today, it almost immediately becomes apparent that the 'lifeboat' (to keep the lives of the very young from drowning in the deep waters of depression and despair), *the family unit,* is virtually non-existent, or exists as a phantom upon the seas of life.

Hence, the child in his early years may call out to his mommy or daddy while still afloat on these cold waters, but after a time, the light wanes and soon fades into the distance, as the little infant child surrenders to the powers of darkness, and sinks to the bottom of this cesspool, thereby ending a potentially healthy normal life of sunny dispositions.

7. He emerges from this 'sea of life' a new creature, a type of sea monster, transformed over time (over long periods of neglect) to become a terror to all who may try to come to know him, to befriend him. His 'friends' (so-called) are never close friends, only mere acquaintances, buddies who form a gang (or hang out in a group home), and who become nothing more than anti-social misfits, outcasts, the dregs of society, the unwanted, unloved undesirables, *Les Misérables*, in the worst sense of the term.

8. Such is the lot of those who choose to forsake the right way, who become lost in the seaweed, who drift as driftwood, or *'wandering stars'.* As the blood brother to our Lord put it so graphically: "Clouds they are without water, carried about of winds; trees whose fruit withers, without fruit, twice dead, plucked up by the roots; Raging waves of the sea, foaming out their own shame; *wandering stars,* to whom is reserved the blackness of darkness for ever". (Jude 12-13).

9. What remains is shocking to state: that after 2,000 years of human civilization (after the New Testament was disseminated to all the world), we still have this on-going problem with *'wandering stars',* a persistent growing problem that simply refuses to go away. Despite our amazing technological breakthroughs (almost in every field of knowledge), we still have failed in the home, to a large part because our priorities are apparently so skewed?! [See, William Gairdner's book, *The War Against the Family* (1992).]

10. A child's cry for sympathy, for support, for succor, continues unabated, but alas unheeded, unattended, as if there were actually something more important, more vital, more crucial to the survival of our species then to 'take care of our own'?! Even the US Marines hold to a high code of honor when they declare: "We leave *no man* behind!". Where is Society's 'code of honor'?!

11. The song, "Where have all the flowers gone?" is an anti-war song: it is poignant, it is haunting, it is thought-provoking, and of course: True! The answer for our youth may not be 'blowing in the wind'?! It may not be akin to 'trying to catch the wind' either! It may be as simple as returning to our roots, our spiritual roots, to seeking the Spirit. For as Jesus said: "The wind bloweth where it [wishes] and thou hearest the sound thereof, but canst not tell whence it cometh, and whither it goeth: So is everyone that is born of the Spirit." (John 3:8)

12. I believe in our youth. They are the future of Planet Earth. For now is the time (while we draw breath as the older Generation and as the current Society) to educate, instruct, assist, inform and advise the youth of today: That we are here on the earth to help one another. For soon (all too soon) will come the time for each of us to prepare to meet our Maker, our God, The Father of our Spirits, our Heavenly Father. And the youth of today (as adults of tomorrow) will be left to fend for themselves.

13. To recap, as was stated in the Ancient Roman Arena by the Gladiators then, still rings true today: "We who are about to die, salute *You!*". So likewise, I see that this torch from The Elders, the current older Generation, will one fine day be passed on to the able hands of today's Youth, the future leaders of this world we all live in!

14. I'm also reminded of that pro-freedom song, "In Flanders' Fields" (composed on 3rd May 1915). I used to recite it in my youth every Remembrance Day, the 11th Day of the 11th month, when the World War I Armistice was signed (at 11:00 a.m.) to end "The War to end *all* war". Sadly, that hope was not realized. Several wars followed, and it may be that several World Wars may still be forthcoming?!

15. Man's inhumanity to Man, never ceases to amaze me! Somehow deep down inside, I do believe, that the answer (to violence) resonates within each one of us.

These two wolves are still fighting: Which wolf will we as a Society choose to feed? The decision is, of course, an individual one: it starts as an *atom*, (the individual) 'the smallest unit' of Society, but then expands into a *molecule* (of persons, various groups, clubs, fraternities, Political Parties, and so forth), and finally comprises the whole body Politic.

What we choose to do will determine both the direction and destiny for our Society, and even our complete civilization. Will we carelessly steer into an iceberg and sink like the Titanic, or will we choose caution, and a caring disposition, to steer into calm waters, with smooth sailing and sunny skies?

16. For as a (very) Good Book says: "See, I [God] have set before you this day *life* and good, and death and evil... I [God] call heaven and earth to record this day against you, that I [God] have set before you life and death, blessing and cursing: therefore choose *life*, that both you and your seed may live!" (Deuteronomy 30:15,19).

17. In the closing lines of his poem, "In Flanders' Fields", the author, John McCrae, an Army physician (who later died in this War, WWI), warned the youth (the young future leaders of Tomorrow) in these grave (rather sobering words):

"We are the Dead! Short days ago,
We lived, felt dawn, saw sunset glow,

Loved and were loved: and now we lie
In Flanders' Fields!

Take up our quarrel with the foe
If ye break faith with us who die,
We shall not sleep, though poppies grow
In Flanders' Fields!"

Youth Feedback:

____

____

____

DISCLAIMER: N.B. (*Nota Bene*)
All tunes/songs/video clips/links/quotes/etc. are herein provided to assist in Group Therapy Sessions, or privately, for individual study (to assist in learning) and for educational purposes *only*.

[#252: U-Tube Reference]
In Flanders Fields by John McCrae (May 1915)
https://www.youtube.com/watch?v=K6BlOkpdkg8

***In Flanders Fields* Poem**
By Lieutenant Colonel John McCrae

In Flanders fields the poppies grow

We are the dead: Short days ago,
We lived, felt dawn, saw sunset glow,
Loved and were loved: and now we lie
In Flanders fields!

Take up our quarrel with the foe
To you, from failing hands, we throw
The torch: be yours to hold it high!

(Composed at the battlefront on May 3, 1915
during the second battle of Ypres, Belgium)

www.ingramcontent.com/pod-product-compliance
Lightning Source LLC
Chambersburg PA
CBHW021139160726
47994CB00001B/5